THE 100 BEST STOCKS YOU CAN BUY

2012

PETER SANDER
AND
SCOTT BOBO

Adamsmedia

AVON, MASSACHUSETTS

Published by
Adams Media, a division of F+W Media, Inc.
57 Littlefield Street, Avon, MA 02322. U.S.A.
www.adamsmedia.com

ISBN 10: 1-4405-0053-3
ISBN 13: 978-1-4405-0053-4
eISBN 10: 1-4405-2613-3
eISBN 13: 978-1-4405-2613-8

Printed in the United States of America.

10 9 8 7 6 5 4 3 2 1

Library of Congress Cataloging-in-Publication Data
is available from the publisher.

This publication is designed to provide accurate and authoritative information with regard to the subject matter covered. It is sold with the understanding that the publisher is not engaged in rendering legal, accounting, or other professional advice. If legal advice or other expert assistance is required, the services of a competent professional person should be sought.

—From a *Declaration of Principles* jointly adopted by a Committee of the American Bar Association and a Committee of Publishers and Associations

Many of the designations used by manufacturers and sellers to distinguish their product are claimed as trademarks. Where those designations appear in this book and Adams Media was aware of a trademark claim, the designations have been printed with initial capital letters.

This book is available at quantity discounts for bulk purchases.
For information, please call 1-800-289-0963.

Contents

Dedication

We continue to dedicate this book to all of you active investors who have the sense of purpose and independence of thought to make your own investing decisions, or at least, to ask the right questions. You continue to be wise enough—and inquisitive enough—to realize that not all the answers can be found in one place, and smart enough to seek the convenience of a good place to start.

Acknowledgments

Peter is thrilled to have research partner and life friend Scott Bobo on board as an official author of this book. He also recognizes the good work of Value Line Inc. and their Investment Survey, which does more than any other known source to turn piles of facts and figures into a simple readable page. Next, no book happens without the added value of exercise to keep a body in shape and a mind clear, and to that end he offers his thanks to his exercise companions. And of course his family—which has gone through a restructuring since the last edition—gets all the credit for the inspiration to engage in this enterprise.

Scott would like to dedicate this book to his lovely wife Lori, who, without actually saying it, reminds him every day that it's only money. May she remain patient and tolerant of a shaggy lawn. He'd also like to dedicate this work to his late father William Bobo, who worked every day of his life to provide for his family.

PART I

THE ART AND SCIENCE OF INVESTING IN STOCKS

By Peter Sander

The Art and Science of Investing in Stocks

Peter Sander

Congratulations (once again if you're a perennial reader) on your purchase of the 2012 edition of *The 100 Best Stocks You Can Buy*.

If you bought this book, you're probably an astute and experienced individual investor who invests in individual stocks in individual companies. Now, that might not seem so profound, but with some 10,000 mutual funds, 8,000 hedge funds, and countless exchange traded funds (ETFs) and index funds out there, it's not inconceivable that the individual stock investor is becoming an endangered species.

But that's just not so. For not only your own wealth but also for the efficient allocation of capital to businesses and ideas that work best, millions still engage in this sort of "pure" investing for all or part of their wealth. Yet, much of what we hear about in the financial media these days is still about mutual funds, hedge funds, ETFs, and other investment "products." Are the media catering to your needs or to the needs of the professional fund manager? One wonders sometimes—either way, we do exist, but we tend to exist rather quietly. Anyway, off the soapbox. Even if you buy just a few shares of one company, you're an individual investor. You're participating actively in the economy, and you're buying your share of the company with hopes of participating in its success. Like a homeowner choosing to take part in the work of owning a home as a "do-it-yourselfer" you're participating in the individual satisfaction, responsibility, and control that comes with doing it yourself.

If you succeed, you accept the benefits of increased wealth (and reduced fees) along with the satisfaction and sense of accomplishment of doing it yourself. If you fail, it's true you'll have no one to blame but yourself. But at least you won't be forced to drink the poison of having someone else lose your money for you. In the entrepreneurial spirit that so characterizes America and much of the Western world, you'll pick yourself up, dust yourself off, learn from the mistakes, and go out and try it again.

Every edition of *The 100 Best Stocks You Can Buy*—this 2012 edition included—is intended to be a core tool for the individual investor. Sure, it's hardly the only tool available. Today's explosion of Internet-based investing tools has made this book one of hundreds of choices for acquiring investing information. With the speed of cyberspace, our book will hardly be the most current source. In fact—we'll admit by way of a disclaimer—that because of the typical book publication cycle, we're at least six months out of date. If you check our research, you'll be able to come up with two to as many as four quarters of more current financial information, news releases, and so forth.

Does that make our book a poor information source? Not at all. Unless you're watching the news wires in real time, regardless of what information source you use, there will probably be some room for a current refresh or update. More to the point—the companies we choose are chosen in large measure because things don't change so much, and because they avoid the temptation to manage short-term, quarter-to-quarter performance. The companies we choose are chosen *because* they have sustainable performance, so who cares if the latest figures or news releases are in? In *100 Best Stocks You Can Buy 2012*, as with all of our previous editions, we focus on the *story*, not just the latest facts and figures.

As such, *100 Best Stocks* is intended as a handy guide and core reference for your investing; not as a be-all end-all investing source. Thus, as much as a source of facts and numbers itself, *100 Best Stocks* is intended to present the story for each company and to serve as a model for selecting the best companies and stocks to invest in.

To that same point, *100 Best Stocks* goes well beyond just being a stock screen or a "study" of stocks to invest in. Analysis forms the basis of *100 Best Stocks*, but it isn't the rigid, strictly numbers-based selection and analysis so often found in published "best stocks" list. Sure, we look at earnings, cash flow, balance sheet strength, and so forth, but we'll also look far beyond those things. We'll look at the intangible and often subtle factors that make truly great businesses—that is, companies—great. That, once again, is the *story.*

Great companies have good business fundamentals, but what makes them really great is the presence of intangibles and subtleties that will *keep* them great—or make them greater—in the future.

So the selection of the *100 Best Stocks* continues to go far beyond being a simple numbers-based stock screen. It's a selection and analysis of really good businesses you would want to buy and own, not just for past results but for future outcomes. Now, does "future" mean "forever"? No, not hardly, not anymore. Nothing is really forever these days—as those who invested in GM or Eastman Kodak or AIG or Bank of America can attest. So while the

100 Best Stocks list correlates well with the notion of "blue chip" stocks, the discussion proceeds with the harsh reality that "blue chip" no longer means "forever."

As the book title suggests, we feel that the 100 companies listed and analyzed in the pages that follow are the best companies to own for 2012. That said, the word "own" has become a more active concept these days. Gone are the days of "own forever," like the halcyon days when Peter's parents, Jerry and Betty Sander, bought their thirty-five shares of General Motors, lovingly placed the stock certificate in their safety deposit box, and henceforth bought nothing but GM cars. Today, there is no forever; the economy, technology, and consumer tastes simply change too fast, and the businesses that participate in the economy by necessity change with it. Ownership is a more active concept than it was even ten or twenty years ago.

So going forward, we offer the 100 best companies to own now and in 2012, and that have the best chances of not only surviving but evolving with—or even ahead of—the economy based on their current market position and approach to doing business. But as we all found out during the past two years, nothing is sacred in the business world and things can fall apart with astounding speed. What does that mean?

Simply this: You can't take anything you read in the following pages as "investment advice" or as hard, unwavering truths. The world simply changes too fast, and the analysis of a business (and especially the *value* of a business) is not a precise science, it is inherently a combination of science and art. True business value is subject to different interpretations and different opinions, and further, we must layer in the pace and effects of change.

What that means is simple and straightforward: You'll have to take the information presented, do your own assessment, reach your own conclusions, and take your own actions. Anything else would go beyond our intentions, and more importantly, stop short of the mark for you.

With that in mind, make the most of what follows, and good luck with your investing!

SO WHY BUY AN INVESTING BOOK THESE DAYS?

The Internet is great: anything you want at your fingertips, practically real-time, latest news, latest analysis, latest numbers. News and numbers are great, and they will inevitably help you take the latest facts into consideration and add points and counterpoints to your investment decision. But is the Internet enough?

Consider what a book like *The 100 Best Stocks You Can Buy* has to offer. It gives not just facts and figures, but also a collection of business stories and a stock selection mindset. A thought process you can browse through, one you can see applied repeatedly to different situations.

You might not align to the set of 100 stocks we offer here because they are too expensive or don't appeal to your tastes or just don't suit your needs or interests at the moment. That's okay. Even if you don't choose from the 100 stocks offered here, you can follow the thought processes, the choices and decisions made, as a model for your *own* choices.

Being an individual investor is rather like being an airplane pilot. You are ultimately in control of this aircraft; you are in control of your finances. And that means taking responsibility for your own decisions, regardless of the information sources—the gauges, charts, ground control folks you have helping you out. So you must develop your own mindset and set of investment knowledge and tools—that's where this book comes in.

Remember, in investing, like life, it's the thought that counts.

What's New for 2012

Three years ago, Peter was added to the *100 Best* team as a coauthor to bring a unique value-investing perspective and to update the approach to selecting stocks and investing in general. When he came on board, he also brought Scott Bobo as a researcher, and technology and marketing expert, to lift this book beyond financial analysis into the more intangible world of a company's complete story in the marketplace. This year, Scott joins the team as a full-fledged coauthor.

We have also added a sister book, as well: *100 Best Aggressive Stocks You Can Buy 2012.*

The 100 Best Aggressive Stocks You Can Buy

100 Best Stocks is designed to serve the needs of a broad market of investors. While there are common threads across all stocks, some, like Apple and Google, and last year, Chipotle and NetApp, are recognizably more rapidly evolving and aggressive than, say, Campbell Soup and Kraft Foods. We offered a range of risk profiles, and more aggressive investors could make use of the *100 Best* list and *100 Best* approach.

But we felt that many of the more interesting stories we looked at could be valued using our principles, but were simply too aggressive or risky to put on the main *100 Best* list. We saw a need to bring some of these more aggressive companies to light, particularly as we move to a more dividend-focused model for the *100 Best* list, and particularly as many investors seek more ambitious growth in a climate of reduced market returns as a whole. So this year, we are releasing *100 Best Aggressive Stocks You Can Buy 2012* in parallel to the "core" book.

That book places more emphasis on the story, the intangibles, and the future. We moved four stocks—Chipotle, NetApp, Panera, and Peet's—to the *100 Best Aggressive* list, and came up with ninety-six more entries, some of which we had considered for the *100 Best* list in the past, for this new book. There are eighteen stocks on *both* lists. More aggressive investors—or those looking for a few good plays for your "opportunistic" portfolio are encouraged to buy our new book.

About Your Authors

First, a bit about us.

Peter is an independent professional researcher, writer, and journalist specializing in personal finance, investing, and location reference, as well as other general business topics. He has written twenty-five books on these topics, has written numerous financial columns and done independent privately contracted research and studies. He comes from a background in the corporate world, having experienced a twenty-one-year career with a major West Coast technology firm.

He is most emphatically an individual investor, and has been since the age of twelve, when his curiosity at the family breakfast table got the better of him. He started reading the stock pages with his parents. He had an opportunity during a one-week "project week" in the seventh grade to read about, and learn about, the stock market. He read Louis Engel's *How to Buy Stocks*, then the pre-eminent—and one of the only—books about investing available at the time (it first appeared in 1953; he thinks he read a 1962 paperback edition). He read Engel, picked stocks, and made graphs of their performance by hand with colored pens on real graph paper. He put his hard-earned savings into buying five shares of each of three different companies. He watched those stocks like a hawk and salted away the meager dividends to reinvest. He's been investing ever since, and in combination with twenty-eight years of home ownership and a rigorous, almost sacrificial savings regimen, he accumulated quite a respectable net worth for someone in the corporate, and hence self-employed, ranks.

Yes, he has an MBA from a top-rated university (Indiana University, Bloomington), but it isn't an MBA in finance. He also took the coursework and certification exam to become a Certified Financial Planner (CFP). By design and choice, he has never worked in a financial profession. His goal has always been to share his knowledge and experience in an educational way, a way helpful for the individual as an investor and a personal financier to make their own decisions.

He has never made money giving investment advice or managing money for others, nor does he intend to.

An Eye for Value

A few years ago, it dawned on Peter that he has really made his living finding value, and helping or teaching others to find value. Not just in stocks, but other things in business and in life. And what does he mean by "value"? Simply, the current and potential *worth* of something (or someone) as compared to its price or cost. As it turns out, he's made a career out of assessing the value of people, places, and companies.

His last assignment at a high-tech firm was to find value in customers. *People.* His title: customer valuation manager. At the time, around the turn of the millennium, his team was building a "customer relationship management" platform, and his job was to segment millions of customers by value, and to assign values to each one to help target messaging and so-called "one-to-one" marketing campaigns. A tricky enterprise, no doubt, because no company can really know what a customer is truly worth, down to the penny, especially going forward. It became an exercise in looking at previous buying behavior, considering other known customer attributes internal and external to the business, assessing the customer's cost (marketing and support costs), making some assumptions, and testing results.

At the time, he did not really grasp that the same exact process really applied to investing, too. But a sharp editor at John Wiley & Sons' "Dummies" division put two and two together and hired him to write *Value Investing for Dummies.* The light went on. Whether it's people or stocks, the thought process is the same. Take what you know (fundamentals), add some intuition (intangibles), make some assumptions, proceed carefully, and evaluate the results.

The same publisher—different division—gave him another chance two years later, this time to write a complete reference guide to places to live. Hundreds of places to live appraised for value and ranked top to bottom, best to worst. Value is extremely important in deciding where you would want to live. Sure, the "best" places to live might include Greenwich, Connecticut; Jupiter, Florida; or Palo Alto, California. But most of us can't afford them. So the true "best places" for most of us are the places that deliver the most value for the money, now and in the future. The resulting book, *Cities Ranked & Rated: More Than 400 Metropolitan Areas Evaluated in the U.S. and Canada*, and its sister publication *Best Places to Raise Your Family*, finally went beyond the "study" and short list to truly answer the question most of us have—what's the best place to live *for my money*?

The same value approach works in the world of business and stock investing. It isn't just the biggest or the richest corporations that we should be putting our hard-earned money into. If that were the case, we'd simply buy GE or ExxonMobil and move on. But do these companies represent the best *value* for your investing dollar? Maybe, but maybe not.

Just like customers or places to live, we want companies that produce the greatest return, the highest value, *per dollar invested*. And *for the amount of risk taken*. The amount of risk taken translates into additional dollars that an investment might cost, analogous to living in a great place rampant with crime or with questionable schools that might cost you more in the long term. The companies we will identify as among the *100 Best* have, in our assessment, the greatest long-term *value*, and if you can buy these companies at a *reasonable price* (a factor which we leave out of this analysis because this is a book and prices can change considerably), then these investments deliver the best prospects.

Later we'll come back to describe some of the attributes of value that we look for.

Scott Joins the Team

Peter's long-time friend and colleague J. Scott Bobo has officially joined the author team. Scott has been huge not only in identifying the *100 Best Stocks* but also analyzing them and explaining their pros and cons crisply and in plain English so that you can make the best use of the list. Having Scott on the team allows you to get the combined wisdom and observations of two people, not just one, in an arena where one plus one almost always equals something greater than two.

Scott is relatively new to the professional writing game but has been an investor since age fourteen, when he made the switch from analyzing baseball box scores to looking at the numbers and charts in the business section. In his twenty-plus years in engineering and technology management, he's learned that a unique product value proposition is important to the success of any company. He has also learned (the hard way) that proper financial fundamentals are critical. From a development manager's perspective, comprehending a new product's risk/reward proposition is one of the keys to a company's success. From an investor's perspective, it's also one of the keys to successful value investing in a dynamic, innovation-driven market.

Scott adds a strong analytical touch. But he is most at home as an applications engineer, explaining how a company's products work and how they apply to a customer's needs. Consequently, and in addition to analytical legwork, Scott really adds an extraordinary and very real-world sense of how a company's products "fit" in the marketplace. Determining whether a company's products are relevant, best-in-class, and have a competitive advantage over others is an oft-overlooked core skill for a value investor. Scott brings this skill to the table in a big way.

Scott is not only "officially" part of this writing team, he is the co-creator and the driving force behind our *100 Best Aggressive Stocks You Can Buy 2012* mentioned earlier.

What's Changed for 2012

With our arrival on the scene in 2010 and the wild ride our markets gave us in 2008–2009, the *100 Best* book series went through some pretty major changes—not revolutionary, perhaps, but strongly evolutionary. In that first year, we struck some twenty-six companies from the prevailing 2009 list, as we felt that there were too many commodity producers, defense contractors, and others that weren't comfortably placed in an era of volatile markets and public sector cutbacks. That storm blew through in 2010; in 2011, we made more moderate changes, deleting fourteen stocks from the list as we became more focused on current returns—dividends. This year, for the 2012 list, we've made twelve changes, down slightly from last year's fourteen—in what we would call, like last year, more of an adjustment than a full restructuring of the list. Tables 3, 4, and 5 detail the twelve deletions and additions to the 2012 list.

The methodology used for analysis and selection of the *100 Best Stocks* remains largely unchanged. In 2010, we kept many of the basic tenets of previous editions, including a focus on fundamentals, a long-term horizon, and clearly defined reasons to buy and not to buy. In 2010, we placed more emphasis on "fundamentals that really count," including cash flow, profit margins, and balance sheet strength. We also placed a greater weight on "intangibles"—those hard-to-quantify factors like brand strength, customer loyalty, and market position that seem to over and over separate the winners from the losers. We also shifted toward higher value-add companies and away from low-margin commodity producers subject to the whims of the marketplace and business cycle.

We continue to place more focus on dividends. More and more, especially in today's volatile markets, we feel that investors should get paid something to commit their precious capital to a company; it's a sign of good faith to investors and provides at least some return while waiting for a larger return in the future or if things happen to go south later on. "A bird in the hand," as they say. So, as it turns out, some ninety-five of the 100 stocks picked pay at least some dividends—that's up from ninety-one on the 2011 *100 Best* list. Those that don't, like Apple and Google, are on the list because of other obvious factors of excellence; we can turn our heads the other way on the dividend. Additionally, for dividend-paying stocks, we started to place more emphasis on companies with a track record for regular dividend *increases*. Of the eighty-six dividend-paying stocks on both the 2011 and 2012 *100 Best Stocks* list, fifty-nine of them increased their dividends within the past year. As in the 2011 edition, we will give you a performance report on our 2011 picks, which again turned out to be a pretty good story. Finally, we will continue with our "stars" lists identifying the best stocks in five different categories:

1. Yield Stars (stocks with strong and growing dividends—Table 6)
2. Safety Stars (solid performers in any market—Table 7)
3. Growth Stars (companies positioned for above-average growth—Table 8)
4. Recovery Stars (companies that cut costs and are otherwise positioned well for an economic recovery—Table 9)
5. Moat Stars (companies with significant sustainable competitive advantage—Table 10)

So, if you're an investor partial to any of these factors, like Safety, these lists are for you.

A Downer, Then an Upper

When we put the finishing touches on *The 100 Best Stocks You Can Buy 2011*, the markets had just finished a remarkable roller-coaster ride. We had endured the 54 percent drop from October 2007 through the March 9, 2009, Dow Jones Industrial Average low of 6,547. Optimism from better (or at least less bad) employment reports, industrial production statistics, and consumer confidence led the markets to a recovery beginning in the last half of 2009 and continuing into April 2010. That rebound, some 68 percent from the March 2009 low, was enough to bring back confidence to many investors.

But the roller-coaster ride wasn't over. The BP Gulf of Mexico oil well disaster and the Greek debt crisis highlighted the vulnerability of the recovery, particularly to unsustainable levels of debt. Through April 2010, the markets had almost developed a sense of complacency—*anything* that happened would be better than the recession just endured, and most of the news really indicated more of an economic tailwind. That, of course, was augmented by the monetary tailwind provided by the Fed in the form of continued low interest rates and massive cash infusions primarily from bond and mortgage purchases. All seemed well.

But when all seems well, particularly in today's rapidly changing markets, be sure that we're just one bad event, or one bad story, from a reversal. In fact, the markets had been absorbing the bad news about BP and Greece (and Portugal and Spain and Ireland) and some bad housing numbers pretty well, but there was a growing sense of concern about a "double dip" recession. What if all this Fed "quantitative easing" didn't work? What if the debt burdens of sovereign nations and the banking system once again became too large to tolerate? Could we afford any more bailouts? What if the BP spill contributed to yet another spike in the price of oil? While earnings reports through the spring season were strong, doubts began to swirl.

Then it was a trading event—not a news event or a company or industry-driven business event—that roiled the markets. A large investment institution began selling an unusually large quantity of S&P 500 futures contracts. The markets took note, and so did the computer-driven algorithms of many big traders, now geared up for the computerized rapid-fire so-called "high frequency" trading. These algorithms saw the sales, and immediately took their owners out of the market. They took bids out of the market on key securities of all kinds, including stocks, ETFs, and other trading instruments. The result, on May 6, 2010, was the so-called "flash crash," in which the averages and most individual securities lost huge percentages in one day, only to gain most of it back in a few minutes (although for some it took a few hours).

Still, the markets were rattled, and many investors started to head for the exits. Not in droves; there was really no ensuing panic. But the markets entered an era of uncertainty that lasted about two months, with the major averages declining about 16 percent during that period.

That volatility lasted through most of the summer of 2010. At summer's end, employment and consumer spending seemed to pick up once again. The BP well was capped, and the European debt crisis had seemingly gone away (from the new headlines, anyway). We entered another period of steady and almost complacent growth, with the major averages regaining the 16 percent plus another 16 percent or so as a bonus, peaking in February 2011. Individual stocks, including many on our *100 Best* list, hit new highs not seen in three years or more. Then the news turned bad again—this time with the fall of the Mubarak government in Egypt, subsequent Middle Eastern unrest, and in particular, the conflict in Libya. Continued weakness in real estate markets didn't help. The markets turned downward again, although there was no "trading" catalyst this time, no "flash crash." The period of relative steady gains and complacency gave way once again to volatility and some pretty sharp declines, which lasted through most of March. By April, the markets seemed to get used to this latest news, and earnings reports—thanks to years of cost cutting, improved operational efficiencies, and pent up demand—were stellar. Regardless of the news, corporate America seemed on the right track.

Now mind you, this book isn't supposed to be about the past—it's supposed to be about the *future*, specifically the future of your investments. We know that. But we feel that it's important to set the climate and context for this and next year's performance, and would feel derelict in our duties if we didn't drive home the challenges—particularly the challenges of news-driven and trading-driven volatility. We think the markets will continue with large swings in sentiment, but relatively short cycles of upside and downside performance over the next few years. Probably the biggest fear, outside of some major news event like a political crisis, is that inflationary forces really take hold resulting from the flood of easy money encircling the globe— indeed there are already signs of that in the form of rising commodity prices, although we feel that at least some of that is a trading-driven cycle much like we saw in 2008. Nevertheless, investors, particularly in companies that buy a lot of commodity materials, need to stay alert. We are also concerned about the effects of the Fed finally withdrawing some of its quantitative easing and other monetary support mechanisms that have been propping up the market for the past two years.

Anyway, the point remains not to scare people off from investing, it is to say that now, more than ever, investors must stay focused on what they invest in. The kind of volatility we've seen recently can actually provide some buying opportunities, so even those really pricey stocks that *everyone* thinks are best to own can be had if the time is right.

Remember that investing in stocks is still about buying shares of a business, and just because there's a "flash crash" doesn't mean that IBM or Johnson & Johnson or Abbott Laboratories are any worse off as companies. It simply means that the market has taken a different approach, probably an irrational one, to evaluating them. It is imperative, as an investor, that you invest in good businesses. If you do, the price of the shares will come out okay in the long term. And if you want to sleep at night, businesses with steady results will tend to be less volatile. Finally, for further insulation against the ups and downs of the markets, we're favoring stocks that pay dividends, because no "flash crash" can take away money you've received and socked in the bank, right?

Now it's time to uphold a recently added tradition and see how we did with last year's picks.

Report Card: Recapping Our 2011 Picks

We continue to believe that it makes no sense to make stock recommendations, and especially to sell them to the public in book form, unless we step back at least for a second to appraise the collective performance of our recommendations. After all, if our list performs the same as the markets as a whole, you'd save a lot of money and time by simply buying a market index ETF or some similar instrument. And if, like many mutual funds, our picks performed worse, there's little reason to buy our book other than to discover what to avoid.

In that context, we once again examine the performance our *100 Best Stocks* list, this time the list prepared for 2011. However, this year we will simplify the analysis a bit. Because of the aforementioned volatility during the 2008–2010 period, we did a more detailed contextual analysis of the 2010 *100 Best* list to show not only overall performance of the list, but also how those stocks performed during the deep down cycles and up cycles of the 2009 bust and subsequent recovery. We wanted to show not only how well our stocks "played offense" during good markets, but also how well they played defense during bad ones.

With the markets returning to a dynamic but less wildly volatile pattern, we discontinue the down cycle and up cycle analysis in favor of a simple year-to-year performance comparison. The publishing schedule mandates that we evaluate performance from April 1, 2010, through April 1, 2011.

Evaluating the List

There are many ways to evaluate the performance of a group of stocks over time. Some are simplistic, such as simply averaging the percent gain in each share price. But such a method may not weight a portfolio very realistically, for it assumes you buy the same number of shares of Apple at $348 as you would Duke Energy at $18. We felt, as a result, that it was better to take the approach of an investor with $100,000 to invest who invested $1,000 in each of the *100 Stocks* across the board, regardless of share price. Sure, you end up with some weird quantities of shares in your portfolio, but the portfolio, and thus the performance metrics, isn't weighted in favor of more expensive stocks.

The Bottom Line

If you had invested $100,000 in our *100 Best Stocks 2011* list, $1,000 in each of the 100 stocks, on April 1, 2010, you would have had $119,953.22 on April 1, 2011, not including dividends paid during that period. The return is just short of 20 percent, 19.95 percent to be exact.

Now, didn't markets rise anyway through this period? What's the magic here? Why choose the stocks from this list and this book? Here's the answer: If you had invested in the S&P 500 average through an index fund or an ETF, you would have $113,098.21—a 13 percent gain for the period. The *100 Best Stocks 2011* list outperformed the markets by almost 7 percent—a 50 percent return bonus, if you want to look at it that way.

BETTER YET WITH DIVIDENDS

Last year, the performance analysis included dividends, not just the raw stock price. In a year where we place even greater focus on dividends, why did we omit them from the analysis? The answer is simplicity: We wanted to make the comparison more "apples to apples"—that is, centered on just the stock prices and how they compared with the market performance in total. But you're curious anyway, right? Well, if dividends had been included, you would have achieved about another $2,150 in annual return from the *100 Best Stocks* list, compared to about $1,850 for a comparable "basket" of S&P 500 stocks. More growth plus more income—not a bad combination.

Winners and Losers

The full list of the *100 Best Stocks 2011* and how they did through the comparison period can be found in Appendix A. At this point, we'll give a short overview of what really worked and what didn't within the list. First, the winners:

▼ **Table 1: Performance Analysis: Winners**

TOP WINNERS, ONE-YEAR GAIN/LOSS, APRIL 1, 2010–APRIL 1, 2011

Company	Symbol	Price 4/1/2010	Price 4/1/2011	% change	Dollar gain, $1,000 invested
Chipotle Mexican Grill	CMG	$114.48	$274.00	139.3%	$1,393.43
Tractor Supply	TSCO	$29.70	$61.06	105.6%	$1,055.89
Caterpillar	CAT	$63.99	$113.12	76.8%	$767.78
Panera	PNRA	$76.38	$127.87	67.4%	$674.13
Marathon Oil	MRO	$32.09	$53.55	66.9%	$668.74
Alexander & Baldwin	ALEX	$32.75	$54.47	66.3%	$663.21
Deere	DE	$59.74	$98.60	65.0%	$650.49
Starbucks	SBUX	$24.24	$37.25	53.7%	$536.72
Fluor	FLR	$47.60	$72.92	53.2%	$531.93
ConocoPhillips	COP	$52.02	$79.68	53.2%	$531.72
Apple	AAPL	$235.97	$348.45	47.7%	$476.67
DuPont	DD	$37.91	$55.19	45.6%	$455.82
Schlumberger	SLB	$64.57	$93.70	45.1%	$451.14
Lubrizol	LZ	$93.14	$133.80	43.7%	$436.55
Pall Corporation	PLL	$40.39	$57.98	43.6%	$435.50
Dover	DOV	$47.00	$67.24	43.1%	$430.64
Chevron	CVX	$76.69	$108.32	41.2%	$412.44
FMC	FMC	$61.16	$86.12	40.8%	$408.11
NetApp	NTAP	$34.26	$48.20	40.7%	$406.89
United Healthcare	UNH	$32.99	$45.61	38.3%	$382.54

The "winners" list is interesting on closer review. It shows a rather eclectic mix of businesses, from relatively high-flying consumer-driven growth issues like Chipotle, Panera, Starbucks, Tractor Supply, and Apple to heavy industry-driven Caterpillar and Deere, mixed in with some more classic energy picks like Marathon and ConocoPhillips. Reward usually follows risk, and Chipotle and Panera may be a bit risky for most of you now, especially at these prices—so we've conveniently removed them from the 2012 *100 Best* list and included them instead in *100 Most Aggressive Stocks You Can Buy 2012*. But that risk-reward thing breaks down a bit—who woulda thunk a bunch of money could be made on the likes of DuPont, Alexander & Baldwin, and Pall Corporation? These are great companies and of course, we think they belong on the *100 Best* list, but it goes to show that great businesses can plod along for years before finally being discovered. These companies dominated their niches and worked on operational efficiencies while the chips were down, blooming vibrantly when the ice and snow of economic winter finally melted away. Long story short: Excellence can come from anywhere on the list.

Now, for the losers:

▼ Table 2: Performance Analysis: Losers

TOP LOSERS, ONE-YEAR GAIN/LOSS, APRIL 1, 2010–APRIL 1, 2011

Company	Symbol	Price 4/1/2010	Price 4/1/2011	% change	Dollar loss, $1,000 invested
Boeing	BA	$72.99	$74.01	1.4%	$13.97
Kellogg	K	$53.61	$54.00	0.7%	$7.27
Nucor	NUE	$45.95	$46.20	0.5%	$5.44
Procter & Gamble	PG	$63.36	$62.08	-2.0%	($20.20)
Pepsi	PEP	$66.68	$65.22	-2.2%	($21.90)
CVS Caremark	CVS	$36.23	$34.96	-3.5%	($35.05)
Target	TGT	$53.13	$50.36	-5.2%	($52.14)
Abbott	ABT	$52.28	$49.37	-5.6%	($55.66)
Sysco	SYY	$29.60	$27.88	-5.8%	($58.11)
Clorox	CL	$85.81	$80.52	-6.2%	($61.65)
Campbell Soup	CPB	$35.56	$33.22	-6.6%	($65.80)
Baxter	BAX	$58.23	$53.91	-7.4%	($74.19)
Northern Trust	NTRS	$56.64	$51.69	-8.7%	($87.39)
Johnson & Johnson	JNJ	$65.77	$59.49	-9.5%	($95.48)

TOP LOSERS, ONE-YEAR GAIN/LOSS, APRIL 1, 2010–APRIL 1, 2011

(continued)

Company	Symbol	Price 4/1/2010	Price 4/1/2011	% change	Dollar loss, $1,000 invested
Medtronic	MDT	$45.67	$39.50	-13.5%	($135.10)
Staples	SPLS	$23.70	$20.06	-15.4%	($153.59)
Entergy	ETR	$82.32	$67.64	-17.8%	($178.33)
Teva Pharmaceuticals	TEVA	$63.75	$50.54	-20.7%	($207.22)
Hewlett-Packard	HPQ	$53.24	$40.98	-23.0%	($230.28)
Best Buy	BBY	$42.57	$28.64	-32.7%	($327.23)

Out of 100 stocks, we had seventeen losers for the year, a slightly disappointing performance considering the overall positive tone of the markets. But with the exceptions of Hewlett-Packard and Best Buy, most of the losses were small, and centered in the health care industry and consumer staples, both of which acquired new risk factors this year in the form of health care legislation and rising commodity prices. HP and Best Buy, while still included in our *100 Best* 2012 list because of solid fundamentals, are also in our doghouse for management missteps and possible market shifts, and will be dropped in 2013 if their performance doesn't improve.

HALF FULL, OR HALF EMPTY?

Okay, why should you care about the losers? You check your portfolio, hoping not to find any of the losers we've listed here. Nope, good, done, time to move on? Not. These "losers" may actually be your biggest opportunities for next year, assuming they are retained on the *100 Best* list for 2012 (only losers Boeing and Entergy were dropped for next year). These "losers" are good companies too, or they wouldn't have been retained for the 2012 list, and they may have the most room to grow.

IS 20 PERCENT REALLY THAT MUCH BETTER THAN 13 PERCENT?

You may be wondering if it's worth buying this book and doing all this analysis simply to improve performance by 7 percent. In a phrase, you bet it is. Why? Because of compounding, which Einstein once referred to as the most powerful force in the universe.

Suppose you were lucky enough to invest $100,000 in the S&P 500 index and have it return 13 percent every year for ten years. Disregarding commissions, investment manager fees, taxes, and such, you would end up with a tidy sum of $339,456 at the end of ten years. Not bad. But if you had invested the same $100,000 in our *100 Best Stocks*, and again were fortunate enough to pull 20 percent returns every year for ten years, you'd end up with $619,173—almost twice as much.

Sound good? Well, now let's do the same for twenty years. Twenty years in the S&P 500 at 13 percent would get you to a healthy $1,152,308. In *100 Best Stocks* at 20 percent? Try $3,838,759. More than three times as much.

You can see where we're going with this. Invest in the S&P for thirty years at 13 percent, and you'd wind up with $3,911,589. Invest in the *100 Best Stocks* at 20 percent? How about $23,737,631? You'd be pretty darned happy with the $15.95 you had to shell out for this book each year.

Oh, by the way, in case you're curious—Warren Buffett, through his Berkshire Hathaway investment powerhouse, has achieved 30 percent returns for more than forty years. As you might guess, that's worth *billions*.

Sustainable Investing

So with the recent volatility and the speed of change becoming an increasingly permanent characteristic of today's markets, many financial journalists and pundits have recently noted the demise of long-term investing, specifically the so-called "buy-and-hold" strategy. Indeed, one wonders when such stalwarts as Citigroup and AIG and such long-term growth and income favorites as General Electric and BP run into trouble. The speed of change—change in technology and consumer tastes—and, in the case of BP, news-driven change—does indeed bring some concern to the idea of buying shares and locking them away in your safety deposit box. More than ever, you need to stay on your toes and watch for change.

What it really means is that you need to select companies that adapt well to change and can stay in front of changing markets. It also means that a periodic review of your investments—all of your investments—is more important than ever. Every stock you own should be evaluated from scratch—as though you were going to buy it again—at least once a year.

But that doesn't mean that long-term investing is dead. Great companies respond to change and find ways to continue to satisfy customers and make money, regardless of the mood and change of the day. Companies like

Procter & Gamble reinvent themselves constantly, not with a big house-cleaning (pardon the pun) and restructuring every few years. They get into cosmetics like Olay as the population ages and people become more conscious of their appearance, and as competitive pressure and lack of consumer interest drives profit margins on peanut butter steadily downward. (They did something about this, too, selling their Jif brand to new *100 Best Stocks* member J. M. Smucker, who knows a thing or two about both peanut butter and jelly.) As aging men become more concerned about their appearance, Procter developed Olay lines for men. You get the idea.

Some companies respond better to changes in the wind than others. Starbucks sailed in front of a huge tailwind, opening store after store until they had so many stores that they cannibalized each other and worse, lost their agility and brand cache. We now see that they learned from this mistake, and once again are a perennial favorite as well as a *100 Best Stocks* member based on brand strength, management excellence, balance sheet strength, and core business profitability. A fault once in a while is okay, but we tend to avoid companies that seem to be "restructuring" or "reinventing themselves" continuously.

Value—Now More Than Ever

The bottom line is this: For intelligent investors, chasing the latest fad doesn't work, neither does buying something and locking it away forever. Investors must make intelligent choices based on true value and follow those choices through time and change. It all points to taking a "value-oriented" approach to investing, and to staying modestly "active" with your investments.

The next obvious task is to define what we mean by a "value" approach. Essentially, it is to think of buying shares in a company as buying the company itself, it is about putting yourself in an entrepreneurial frame of mind, not just an investment frame of mind. Would you want to own that business? Why or why not? That's the first and biggest question that must be answered.

Fundamentally, whether or not you want to own the business depends on two factors: first, the returns you expect to receive on your investment in the near and long-term future and second, the risk you'll take in generating those returns. Fortunately, the third factor the prospective entrepreneur must consider—"do I have the time for this?"—isn't typically a consideration.

So you are looking for tangible value—tangible worth—for your precious, scarce, and hard-earned investment capital. Now, that return doesn't have to be immediate in the form of dividends or a share of the assets, as many in the traditional "value school" suggest. It can come in the form of growth for the longer term. If you realize your return in the form of owning a share of a larger company eventually, that's still a legitimate return. Cash flow received later in the form of a higher share price or a takeover is still cash return, it is just less certain because of the forces of change that may take place in the interim. It is also theoretically worth less because of the nature of discounting—a dollar received tomorrow is worth more than a dollar received twenty years in the future.

The point: Many investment experts distinguish between "value" and "growth" investing; in fact, mutual funds are often classified as being one or the other. We dismiss this separation; growth can be an essential component of a firm's value. Indeed, this is the key difference between the original 1930s Benjamin Graham school of value and the more evolved Warren Buffett take on it.

Value also implies safety. The safety comes in three forms. First is the fundamental quality and soundness of the firm's financial fundamentals, that is, income, cash flow, and the balance sheet. Value companies have plenty of reserves, a large enough *margin of safety*, to weather downturns and unforeseen events in the marketplace. Second, they have strong enough intangibles—brands, market position, supply chain strength, etc.—to maintain their position in that marketplace and generate future returns.

Thirdly, if you're really practicing value investing principles, you buy these companies at reduced prices, when the markets are down, when the company is out of favor. You're looking for situations where the price is less than what you perceive to be the value, although calculating the value that precisely is elusive. When you "buy cheap" you provide another margin of safety; that margin makes it less likely that the stock will drop further. It gives you room for error if you turn out to be wrong about a choice. Again, it's much like buying a business of your own—you want to pay as little as possible in case things don't turn out as you'd expect.

So taking a value approach provides greater confidence and safety, and is more likely to get you through today's volatile business and investing cycles.

YOU DON'T NEED TO BE A MATH GENIUS

Calculating "value" can be a daunting task, especially if one goes into the nuances of compounding, discounting, and all that business school stuff. Today's value investor doesn't ignore the numbers, but shuns complex mathematical formulas, which in the recent bust, tended not to work anyway; greater forces overtook almost all statistical and mathematical models for stock analysis, leaving many a "quant" scratching his or her head.

Buying companies is not a math-driven process, just as you can't evaluate a school based on its test scores alone. Warren Buffett and Charlie Munger have made this clear over the years and came back to the point with emphasis in the 2009 Berkshire Hathaway shareholders meeting. Buffett mused: "If you need to use a computer or a calculator to make the calculation, you shouldn't buy it." Reading between the lines: The story should be simple and straightforward enough to be obvious without detailed calculations.

Munger, Buffett's relatively more intrepid sidekick, added: "Some of the worst business decisions I've ever seen are those with future projections and discounts back. It seems like the higher mathematics with more false precision should help you, but it doesn't. They teach that in business school because, well, they've got to do something."

No need to read between the lines there.

Indeed, while the numbers are important, savvy value investors try to see where the puck is going. And that means a clear-eyed assessment of the intangible things that make companies great.

The 100 Best for 2012: A Few Comments

From mid-2009 through the early part of 2011, investors for the most part have had a noticeable tailwind, as the markets recovered from the deep troughs of 2009. Not only did the economy improve, helped along by a very accommodating Fed and interest rate environment, but the downturn also served as a huge wakeup call for companies, which hunkered down to refocus and cut costs wherever possible. It would be a stretch to say that investment success was like shooting fish in a barrel, but the environment was generally favorable aside from some brief spells of bad news and volatility. As we explained earlier, we think this sort of scenario is going to occur fairly regularly from here forward.

This year, as noted earlier in the introduction, we changed twelve companies, two fewer than last year. The changes should be characterized as adjustments—nothing taken off the list is "bad"; in fact, all but two increased in price during the year. We just felt certain other issues were more timely, and began to feel like the list was a bit over-weighted in food companies, which of course are excellent steady plays, but how many do you need? We also eliminated a few duplicates; that is, if there were two companies in the same niche we felt that we didn't need both of them, and narrowed the choice down to the company we felt had the best opportunity. We took Bunge off the list because we already had Archer Daniels

Midland; we cut Walgreens because we have CVS; we cut TJX because we felt that Ross already, and perhaps more effectively, covered the niche. Finally, we transferred four of our more aggressive picks—Chipotle, NetApp, Panera, and Peets—for coverage in our new *100 Best Aggressive Stocks You Can Buy 2012*. Table 3 below shows the twelve companies removed from the *100 Best Stocks* 2011 list.

▼ **Table 3: Stocks Removed from 2011 List**

Company	Symbol	Category	Sector
Boeing	BA	Aggressive Growth	Industrials
Bunge	BG	Conservative Growth	Consumer Staples
Dover	DOV	Aggressive Growth	Industrials
Entergy	ETR	Growth and Income	Utilities
Hormel	HRL	Conservative Growth	Consumer Staples
Kraft Foods	KFT	Conservative Growth	Consumer Staples
TJX	TJX	Aggressive Growth	Retail
Walgreen	WAG	Aggressive Growth	Retail

Stocks Transferred to *100 Best Aggressive* List

Company	Symbol	Category	Sector
Chipotle Mexican Grill	CMG	Aggressive Growth	Restaurants
NetApp	NTAP	Aggressive Growth	Technology
Panera	PNRA	Aggressive Growth	Restaurants
Peet's	PEET	Aggressive Growth	Restaurants

As we do each year, we took a hard look at all of our picks. The fact that we only changed twelve, and only eight for reasons other than moving to a more "aggressive" context, reflects the long-term quality we feel to be inherent in the picks made in previous years. As has become customary, our additions emphasized quality, safety, yield, and strong intangibles such as brand and competitive advantage

Table 4 shows additions to the *100 Best Stocks* list to arrive at the current 2012 version (which can be seen in its entirety at the beginning of Part II).

▼ **Table 4: Stocks Added for 2012**

Company	Symbol	Category	Sector
Aetna	AET	Conservative Growth	Health Care
Allergan	AGN	Aggressive Growth	Health Care
Amgen	AMGN	Conservative Growth	Health Care
Automatic Data Processing	ADP	Conservative Growth	Information Technology
Comcast	CMCSA	Aggressive Growth	Telecommunications Services
Illinois Tool Works	ITW	Conservative Growth	Industrial
McKesson	MCK	Conservative Growth	Health Care
Otter Tail Corp	OTTR	Growth and Income	Utilities/Industrial
Southwest Airlines	LUV	Conservative Growth	Transportation
Total S.A.	TOT	Growth and Income	Energy
Union Pacific	UNP	Conservative Growth	Transportation
Visa	V	Aggressive Growth	Business Services

To give a bit of a "big picture" view of our changes, Table 5 gives our annual summary of what changed by sector. Note the shift away from Consumer Staples (we probably had too many) and toward Health Care. Part of the shift to Health Care reflects the changes we envision particularly in the application of health-care technology; also, we feel that many health-care stocks have been relatively undervalued due to uncertainty arising from Federal health-care initiatives. That said, it would be a good bet that we'd trim health-care next year as events sort the best from the rest.

▼ **Table 5: Analysis of 2012 Best Stocks Change by Sector**

NUMBER OF COMPANIES

Sector	On 2011 List	Added for 2012	Cut from 2011	On 2012 List
Business Services	1		1	
Consumer Discretionary	3		3	
Consumer Staples	17		-3	14

NUMBER OF COMPANIES (continued)

Sector	On 2011 List	Added for 2012	Cut from 2011	On 2012 List
Energy	7	1		8
Financials	3			3
Health Care	13	4		17
Heavy Construction	1			1
Industrials	13	1	-2	12
Information Technology	8	2	-1	9
Materials	8			8
Restaurant	5		-3	2
Retail	11		-2	9
Telecommunications Services	2	1		3
Transportation	3	2		5
Utilities	5	1	-1	5

Yield Signs

In mid-2010, Standard and Poors (S&P) index expert Howard Silverblatt calculated that 136 of its S&P 500 companies had raised dividends by mid-2010 and only two had reduced or suspended dividends. That compares with 157 increases for all of 2009, feathered in with seventy-eight decreases or suspensions, fifty-seven of which came from the financial sector alone. Experts expect 2011 to be a banner year for dividends, although Silverblatt himself postulates that dividends won't recover to 2008 levels until 2013.

The fact that this is so at first glance sounds like a negative, but the chief reason appears to be restrictions placed by the Fed on dividends by financial institutions (which are slowly going away). Aside from that restriction, most agree that dividend increases will be in the double-digit range, as companies hold some 16 percent of their market value in cash, as investors clamor for greater returns, and as companies become more sensitive to that clamoring. Indeed, as reported earlier, ninety-five of our *100 Best* companies paid a dividend in 2010–2011, and fifty-nine of the eighty-six dividend-paying stocks on both the 2011 and 2012 lists *increased* their dividends during that period.

Indeed, Hewlett-Packard raised their dividend 50 percent and proclaimed "double-digit" increases for years to follow; Amgen paid dividends for the first time, and Iron Mountain raised its dividends from a pittance to something substantial, from 25 cents to 76 cents per year in one fell swoop. Not only did these companies catch our eyes, but also in general, as we examined stocks for this year's edition, we saw the same thing over and over—regular dividend increases throughout the past ten years and longer. It's like getting a raise every year; we like that a lot. If you buy a stock today paying, say, our average yield of 2.2 percent, and management manages to eke out a 10 percent increase every year for ten years—we'll do the math for you—that yield would expand to 5.7 percent if the stock price stayed exactly the same. Which it probably wouldn't; we'd expect the stock price to grow as well, reflecting the company's success. So you'd get both benefits—a 5.7 percent annual *return* on your original investment *plus* whatever return the stock generated through increases in share prices. Does that sound too good to be true? Hardly, in fact, the majority of our *100 Best Stocks* picks, if you look back through history, would have produced just this same sort of scenario. So we naturally circled our wagons around these stocks and others like them as a means to generate the same sort of dividend ecstasy moving forward. We think every investor should enjoy not only a decent current return, but also nice raises moving forward.

This scenario, in fact, has moved up to be one of our favored retirement planning and retirement investing scenarios. While we do expect markets overall, and our selected stocks in particular, to appreciate over time as good businesses capture more markets, become more efficient, and get better in general, stock price growth has become less dependable than in the past. The decades-long record of 10–11 percent annual growth, we think, will become more difficult to match. As a result, we think the more solid play is to invest for dividends, and particularly for dividend growth—and hey, if the stock price happens to grow too, so much the better.

Appendix B shows dividend yields for all *100 Best Stocks* for 2012. For this year, we added a column showing the dividend paid last year, so you could see the year-to-year change. Appendix C shows all *100 Best* companies, sorted by percentage yield, with the highest yielders at the top of the list. Interestingly, thirty-one of our *100 Best* picks pay a yield of 3 percent or higher.

Last year, we started to define "star" categories—groups of stocks, essentially the "best of the best" in five categories, we chose to highlight—Yield

Stars, Safety and Stability Stars, Growth Stars, Recovery Stars, and "Moat" Stars. This year we keep the same categories, and kick it off as we did last year with Yield Stars.

Table 6 below shows the top twenty stocks on our *100 Best* list by percentage yield as of mid-2011.

▼ **Table 6: Yield Stars**

TOP 20 DIVIDEND-PAYING STOCKS

Company	Symbol	Dividend	Yield %
Suburban Propane	SPH	$3.40	6.0%
AT&T	T	$1.72	5.6%
Duke Energy	DUK	$1.00	5.4%
Otter Tail Corporation	OTTR	$1.20	5.2%
Total S.A.	TOT	$3.16	5.1%
Verizon	VZ	$1.96	5.1%
Cincinnati Financial	CINF	$1.60	4.8%
Southern Company	SO	$1.84	4.8%
Dominion Energy	D	$1.96	4.4%
Kimberly-Clark	KMB	$2.80	4.3%
Paychex	PAYX	$1.24	3.9%
Abbott Laboratories	ABT	$1.92	3.9%
NextEra Energy	NEE	$2.10	3.8%
Sysco	SYY	$1.04	3.7%
Heinz	HNZ	$1.80	3.7%
Johnson & Johnson	JNJ	$2.16	3.6%
Campbell Soup	CPB	$1.16	3.5%
International Paper	IP	$1.04	3.4%
ConocoPhillips	COP	$2.64	3.3%
McDonald's	MCD	$2.44	3.2%

REMEMBER, THERE ARE NO GUARANTEES

While dividends and especially high yields are attractive, investors must remember that corporations are under no contractual or legal obligation to pay them! Interest payments on time deposits and bonds are much more clearly defined, and failure to pay can represent default. But with dividends, there is no such safety net. Companies can and do reduce or eliminate dividends in bad times, as most strikingly observed with BP in the wake of the Deepwater Horizon Gulf spill disaster. Dividend investors should therefore keep an eye out for changes in a company's business prospects and shouldn't put too many eggs in a single high-yielding basket. On the flip side—as investors become more conscious of returns—and as corporate management teams become more conscious of such investor consciousness— we've seen a lot of companies trumpet their recent dividend increases rather loudly to their investors and the investing public. It's a nice sound that we hope to continue to hear.

Dancing with the Stars

Readers have frequently asked us: "Out of your 100 Stocks, what are the best ones? What are your top ten picks?" Well, we don't actually rank our *100 Best Stocks* as one through 100. Why? Because different stocks serve different interests, needs, and risk tolerances, among other things, in a stock portfolio. And we're sure that if we name a "number one," everyone will follow our lead into it and some dumb thing will happen like the Gulf oil spill or some other more subtle unforeseen change in business conditions. The art and science of stock picking simply do not lend themselves to choosing an overall number one. Smart investors should buy groups of stocks to build a portfolio much as a diner in an à la carte restaurant picks several dishes to make a meal rather than looking for the single best dish on the menu.

With that in mind, we do believe we can create some value and interest by identifying the top ten stocks by certain attributes typically of common interest to investors, especially value-oriented investors. So this year we once again offer top ten lists in four categories. We call them our "stars" list, bringing the idea forward from our "Yield Stars" list above. The four categories are Safety Stars, Growth Stars, Recovery Stars, and Moat Stars.

Safety Stars

Safety stars are companies we think will hold up well in volatile and negative stock markets as well as recessionary economies. They have stable products and customer bases, and long traditions of being able to manage well in downturns. They are "sleep at night" stocks when the going gets tough. This list is unchanged from last year, although it wouldn't have been hard to pick a few more candidates, like Kellogg or Procter & Gamble, from the remainder of the *100 Best* list.

▼ **Table 7: Safety Stars**

TOP 10 STOCKS FOR SAFETY AND STABILITY

Company	Symbol	Dividend	Yield%
Becton, Dickinson	BDX	$1.64	2.0%
Campbell Soup	CPB	$1.16	3.5%
Clorox	CLX	$2.20	3.5%
Ecolab	ECL	$0.68	1.3%
General Mills	GIS	$1.12	3.1%
Heinz	HNZ	$1.80	3.7%
J. M. Smucker	SJM	$1.76	2.4%
Johnson & Johnson	JNJ	$2.16	3.6%
Kimberly-Clark	KMB	$2.80	4.3%
McCormick & Co.	MKC	$1.12	2.3%

Growth Stars

Looking at the other side of the coin, we picked ten stocks we feel are especially well positioned to grow, even in a negative economy and especially in a positive one. This year, because we moved Chipotle, NetApp, and Peet's to the *100 Best Aggressive Stocks You Can Buy* list and book, we identified three new candidates: Apache, St. Jude Medical, and Teva Pharmaceuticals.

▼ **Table 8: Growth Stars**

TOP 10 STOCKS FOR GROWTH

Company	Symbol	Dividend	Yield%
Apache	APA	$0.60	0.5%
Apple	AAPL	nil	nil
Carmax	KMX	nil	nil

TOP 10 STOCKS FOR GROWTH (continued)

Company	Symbol	Dividend	Yield%
Google	GOOG	nil	nil
NIKE, Inc.	NIKE	$1.24	1.6%
Nucor Corp	NUE	$1.44	3.1%
Perrigo	PRGO	$0.28	0.4%
St. Jude Medical	STJ	$0.84	1.6%
Teva Pharmaceuticals	TEVA	$0.88	1.7%
Tractor Supply Company	TSCO	$0.28	0.9%

Recovery Stars

As we continue to emerge from the 2008–2010 recession (assuming a normal course of economic recovery) we feel that certain companies will do especially well. The assessment is based both on top line revenues and their ability to cut costs during bad times. As good times return, these companies will be particularly well positioned to turn recovery into bottom line returns. Interestingly, you'll note that several stocks on this list—Alexander & Baldwin, Caterpillar, and Deere—also made our "Winners" list for best performers in the 2010–2011 performance assessment (see Table 1).

This year we will stay on the same horses that gave us a nice ride last year:

▼ **Table 9: Recovery Stars**

TOP 10 STOCKS FOR AN ECONOMIC RECOVERY

Company	Symbol	Dividend	Yield%
3M Company	MMM	$2.10	2.3%
Alexander & Baldwin	ALEX	$1.24	2.3%
Caterpillar	CAT	$1.76	1.6%
Deere	DE	$1.40	1.4%
Fluor	FLR	$0.48	0.7%
International Paper	IP	$1.04	3.4%
Johnson Controls	JCI	$0.64	1.5%
Norfolk Southern	NSC	$1.60	2.3%

TOP 10 STOCKS FOR AN ECONOMIC RECOVERY (continued)

Company	Symbol	Dividend	Yield%
Paychex	PAYX	$1.24	3.9%
Wells Fargo	WFC	$0.28	0.9%

Moat Stars

Finally, we get back to one of the basic tenets of value investing; the ability of a company to build a sustainable and unassailable competitive advantage. Value investing aficionados call such an advantage a "moat," for it represents a barrier to entry for competitors, likely to preserve advantage for some time. The moat can come in the form of technology, the use of technology, a brand, enduring customer relationships, channel relationships, size or scale, or simply a really big head start into a business making it hard or even impossible for competitors to catch up. The appraisal of a "moat" is hardly an exact science; here we give our top ten picks based on the size and strength (width?) of the moat.

This year we dropped Boeing from the *100 Best* list altogether because of continuing production problems, which to us signaled a less-than-ideal management climate, even though Boeing has one of the widest moats we can think of. We also dropped Patterson Dental from this list upon realization that there is more competition out there than we originally perceived, all chasing what's become a more competitive dental market. We added Starbucks (yes, there's Peet's, Caribou Coffee, and dozens of other coffee players, but oh, what a brand) and Visa (who would leave home without one?) to the Moat Stars list.

▼ **Table 10: Moat Stars**

TOP 10 STOCKS FOR SUSTAINABLE COMPETITIVE ADVANTAGE

Company	Symbol	Dividend	Yield%
Apple	AAPL	nil	nil
Carmax	KMX	nil	nil
Fair Isaac	FICO	$0.08	0.3%
Iron Mountain	IRM	$0.76	2.4%
McCormick	MKC	$1.04	2.7%

TOP 10 STOCKS FOR SUSTAINABLE COMPETITIVE ADVANTAGE (continued)

Company	Symbol	Dividend	Yield%
Starbucks	SBUX	$0.52	1.4%
Sysco	SYY	$1.04	3.7%
Valmont Industries	VMI	$0.68	0.6%
Visa	V	$0.60	0.1%
W. W. Grainger	GWW	$2.16	1.5%

Tenets, Anyone? The Essentials of Successful Investing

The 100 Best Stocks You Can Buy 2012 is designed to help you get started with picking stocks suitable for you. But rather than simply giving you fish (which may not be the freshest fish by the time they reach you), we feel it is also important to give you some investing groundwork to use in your own investing practice, as well as to help explain some of our guiding principles.

We do not intend to give a complete course on investing, or value investing, here. That probably wasn't the purpose you had in mind when you bought this book, and there isn't space here for a complete discussion anyway. For a more complete treatment of the topic, refer to Peter's title *Value Investing for Dummies* (second edition, Wiley, 2008).

At the risk of sounding "corporate," what makes sense here is to give a high-level overview of key investing "tenets" to keep top of mind and back of mind as you sift through the thousands of investment choices. By absorbing these principles, you'll gain a better understanding of the *100 Best Stocks* list and take away ideas to help with your own investment choices outside the list.

Buy Like You're Buying a Business

Already covered this one, but it's worth repeating: By buying shares of a corporation, you are really buying a share of a business. The more you can approach the decision as if you were buying the entire business yourself, the better.

Buy What You Know and Understand

Two of the most widely followed investment "gurus" of our age, Peter Lynch and Warren Buffett, have stressed the idea of buying businesses you know about and understand. This idea naturally follows the entrepreneurial idea of buying stocks as if you were buying a business; if you didn't understand the business, would you be comfortable buying it?

Peter Lynch, former manager of the enormous Fidelity Magellan fund and author of the well-known 1989 bestseller *One Up on Wall Street*, gave us the original notion of buying what you know. He suggests that the best investment ideas are those you see—and can learn about and keep track of—in daily life, on the street, on the job, in the mall, in your home. A company like Starbucks makes sense to Lynch because you can readily see the value proposition and how it extends beyond coffee, and can follow customer response and business activity at least in part just by hanging around your own neighborhood edition. And we hardly need to bring up the subject of iPods, iPads, and their use—and how they've turned Apple into the most valuable company in the world.

Buffett has famously stuck with businesses that are easy to understand—paint, carpet, electric utilities—with his investments (although he deals with the fantastically complicated businesses of casualty insurance and re-insurance in his core Berkshire Hathaway business). He has famously shunned technology investments because he doesn't understand them, and more than likely, because their value and consumer preference shifts too fast for him to keep up.

Both approaches make sense, and especially in hindsight, would have kept us farther from trouble in the 2008–2009 crash. Many, many investors didn't understand financial firms as well as they should have; the preponderance of evidence suggests that those financial firms didn't even understand themselves!

Clearly, you won't understand everything about the businesses you invest in—there's a lot of complexity and detail even behind the cooking and serving of hamburgers at McDonalds! Further, a sizeable amount of good knowledge is confidential so you likely won't ever get your hands on it. So you need to go with what you know and realize that the devil is in the details. When you analyze a company, if you can say "the more you know the better," instead of "the more you know the more you don't know," you'll be better off.

Greater Trends Are Important

Popular expressions abound about the idea of staying in touch with the big picture when you make any sort of decision. "Don't lose the forest in the trees," "keep an eye on the prize," and so forth. These phrases enjoy no finer hour than when tied in with the subject of investing.

We already covered the notion that technologies and consumer tastes change, and with them so do businesses—at least the good ones. Add to this the idea of change brought on by demographic trends (the aging of the population, for instance) and changes in law and policy (toward "green," for instance) and you end up with a wide assortment of "forest" influences that can affect your stock picks.

Sector analysis is employed by many investors as a starting point. Where sector analysis does make sense is in capturing and correctly assessing the larger trends in that sector or industry. The sector thus becomes the arena in which to appraise those trends, often by reading sector analyses published in the media or in trade publications in that sector. One can, and should, learn about the construction industry or health care industry before investing in a company in that industry.

Once the sector trends are understood, a selection of a company, or companies, in that sector can make more sense. A good example is offered by PC makers Hewlett-Packard (a *100 Best Stocks* choice) and Dell Computer (not a choice here, although, for different reasons, Dell appears on the *100 Best Aggressive Stocks* list). Dell was the darling of the sector for years, achieving high margins and return on equity, market share growth, and popular marketplace preference for years. The direct sales model seemed unbeatable as a way to reduce costs and avoid obsolescence, and the just-in-time supply chain model, using accounts payable as a primary financing mechanism, all seemed strategically right.

But change was in the air for the PC industry. Lower prices, greater standardization, and the migration to laptops all pointed to HP's retail-centric model. No longer was it necessary, or even advantageous, for customers to order direct from Dell. With more standardized computing applications and inexpensive technology, there was less need to customize computers. With laptops, displays, size, and the look and feel are more important than simple "speeds and feeds" and people wanted to see what they were buying. Finally, as costs came down, a PC, laptop or otherwise, was simply something to pick up at a local store. We predict PCs will soon sell in Walgreens, and if you don't believe that, consider that VCRs and DVD players also followed that thought-to-be-impossible path.

So HP ended up in the right place with their emphasis on the retail channel (Dell struggles as a latecomer) and further, was strategically correct in their emphasis on printers and high margin consumables that go with them, and in their emphasis on international markets. Dell has fallen by the wayside on counts—hence their 80 percent price drop from 2000 and 70 percent drop from their 2005 price peaks, respectively.

The ground continues to shift under both companies, really, as HP now faces the threat of tablets and smartphones (will their Palm acquisition helps them keep up with these changes?) and Dell reinvents itself as an enterprise and corporate supplier. And of course, the looming "cloud" may turn out to be either an opportunity or a threat; it remains too soon to tell. The upshot is that you must understand a company's marketplace position today, and be able to project it forward a few years as well.

So again the lesson, or "tenet," is to understand the greater trends in the economy, in the market, in the sector, and in the industry. If you buy a business, you want to know about the industry, right? Who the competitors are and how they compete, what the market and customer needs and customer tastes are, and how companies do business in that market. Right? You want to understand the *future* of that industry and market, right? It's no different when you buy shares.

One more thing to add: Most of the time we try to buy what we think to be the best company in the sector—best based on past, current, and expected future performance. But sometimes it makes sense, from an opportunity viewpoint, to "play the Avis game," that is, to buy a more nimble, more aggressive, less arrogant, or complacent number two competitor. Such a company is leaner, meaner, hungrier, and likely sells for a more reasonable price. Sometimes we'll buy both if we feel the industry or sector is large enough to support two strong competitors, and if there are large enough or strong enough niches available so they won't become cutthroat competitors.

For example, Peter owns Starbucks (a *100 Best* stock) and Caribou Coffee, a much smaller competitor located largely in the upper Midwest. There are two reasons for this choice. One, he felt that the Caribou brand cachet would work well in Minnesota and similar places. Second, and more importantly, he liked Caribou's franchising model as a contrast to Starbucks' company owned model (which now may be starting to change with the announcement of franchising for their own subsidiary Seattle's Best). Caribou just might do well capturing business with ambitious franchisees doing the work and understanding local markets best.

Niche and Get Rich

In understanding sectors, industries, and markets, it's important to consider success opportunities for niche players. A "niche" is a small captive market segment, usually too small for the biggest competitors to profitably consider, but still lucrative for a smaller, more nimble player. Niche players can define and play smaller markets based on product, location or geography, distribution channels, or other differentiators like language. Caribou is an example, capturing the franchising niche. Or McCormick & Co. (a *100*

Best stock) capturing the spice niche in a larger food and beverage industry. Or Pall Corporation, another *100 Best* stock, capturing the market for filtration systems in a variety of manufacturing industries.

For more on niche marketing, see *Niche and Get Rich—Practical Ways to Turn Your Ideas Into a Business* (Entrepreneur Press, 2003), a book Peter wrote with his former wife Jennifer back in 2003. It is aimed at small business, but (not by design) offers useful material for investing, too.

Stick to the Real Stuff

If you're familiar with accounting or the accounting profession, contrary to public perception, accounting for business assets and activity is not always a precise science. In fact, there can be quite a bit of art involved in accounting, especially for business assets and business income.

Why? Because, while the purchase *price* for most "physical" assets is known, the *value* of those assets over time is a subjective calculation. And there are many assets, like intellectual property, that elude precise evaluation altogether. How much is a patent worth? How much is an acquired business worth? Just like a stock you buy, you know what you paid for it, but how much is it really worth in terms of future returns to the acquiring company? It's a subjective number.

Likewise, reported net income can be fairly subjective, too. How much depreciation expense was taken against assets, and thus against income? How much "expense" was taken to write down intangible assets like patents and other intellectual property? How much "restructuring" expense was incurred? The rules give the accountants and corporate management quite a bit of flexibility to "manage" reported earnings, and asset values as well: What you see may not always be what you get.

The bottom line is this: While assets and income have at least some subjectivity in their valuation, debts are quite real, and so is cash. Debts must be paid sooner or later; there is no subjectivity or "art" to their valuation. Likewise, cash is cash, the stuff in the proverbial drawer, and is a take-it-or-leave-it, like-it-or-not fact of life or death for a business.

Thus, as value investors, we look at assets and income as important measures of business activity, but know that there's some subjectivity in those measures. At the same time, we look at debts, cash, and cash flow in and out of the business as absolute; neither cash nor debt lie. So we hang our valuation hats on cash and debt where we can.

Now, in particular, cash isn't an absolute measure of business success, either, for there are timing issues. Suppose you are running an airline, and decide this is the year to buy an airplane. A huge cash outflow, possibly matched by a cash inflow from borrowing. Are this year's cash flow statements fully representative of the firm's success or failure? No, because the airplane will be used over a number of years, and the cost of the airplane must be divvied up among those years and matched to airfares collected and other costs to truly understand performance. That's where conventional income accounting comes in—it helps to do that.

All that said, sharp value investors learn to look for companies that, over time, *produce* capital, in contrast to companies that *consume* it. As judged by the statement of cash flows, a company that produces more cash from operations than it consumes in investing activities (capital equipment purchases mainly) and in financing activities (repaying debt, dividends, etc.) is producing capital. When a company must always go to the capital markets to make up for a deficit in operating or investing cash flow, that's a sign of trouble, which is incidentally borne out by the other absolute measure—debt. If debt is high and increasing and especially if it is increasing faster than the business is growing—look out. Or at least, look for a story, like company XYZ is going through a known, understood, and rational expansion that needs to be funded. Going to the capital markets to fund operational cash deficits is an especially bad thing to do.

Thus, as an investor, you should always pay attention to assets and income, but even closer attention to cash and debt. This tenet was used in identifying the *100 Best Stocks*.

What Makes a Best Stock Best?

So now we get down to brass tacks. Now, the rubber meets the road. Just exactly what is it that separates the wheat from the chaff, the cream from the milk, the great from the merely good? What is it that defines excellence—*sustainable* excellence—among companies? That's been a topic of considerable debate for years, and with all the study that's gone into it, it's amazing that nobody has hit upon a single formula for deciphering undeniable excellence in a company.

That's largely because it isn't as scientific as most of us would like or expect it to be. It defies mathematical formulas. Take the square of net profits, multiply by the cosine of the debt-to-equity ratio, add the square root of the revenue-per-employee count, and what do you get? Some nice numbers, but not a clear picture of how it works together or how a company will sell its products to customers and prosper going forward.

Business and financial analysts study such fundamentals, as well they should. Fundamentals such as profitability, productivity, and asset efficiency tell us how well a company has done and by proxy, how well it is managed, and how well it has done in the marketplace. Fundamentals are about what the company has already achieved, and where it stands right now, and if a company's current fundamentals are a mess, stop right now, there isn't much point in going any farther.

In most cases, what really separates the great from the good is the intangibles, the "soft" factors—of market position, market acceptance, customer "love" of a company's products, its management, its aura—that really make the difference. These features create competitive advantage, or "distinctive competence" as an economist would put it, that cannot be valued. Furthermore, and most importantly, they are more about what a company is set up to achieve in the future.

Buffett put it best: Give me $100 billion, and I could start a company. But I could never create another Coca-Cola.

What does that mean? It means that Coke has already established a worldwide brand cachet, the distribution channels, customer knowledge, and product development expertise that cannot be duplicated at any cost. When companies have competitive advantages that cannot be duplicated at any cost, they have an enduring grip on their markets. They can charge more for their products. They have a "moat" that insulates them from competition, or makes it much more expensive for competitors to participate. They're perceived by loyal customers as being top-line products worth paying more for.

A company with exceptional intangibles can control price and in many cases, can control its costs.

A GREAT EXPERIENCE. BUT IS IT A GOOD INVESTMENT?

One way to learn a principle is to examine what happens when the principle does *not* apply. One industry where most of the fundamentals and almost all the intangibles work against it is the airline industry. Airlines cannot control price, because of competition, and because an airplane trip is an airplane trip. Aside from serving different snacks or offering better schedules, there is little an airline can do to differentiate their product, and almost nothing they can do to justify charging a higher price. Further, they have no control over costs—like fuel prices, union contracts, and airport landing fees. While some airlines offer good service, there is almost nothing they can do to distinguish themselves as excellent companies or excellent investments.

With these ills in mind, for two years we've resisted the temptation to put Southwest, one of the most efficient, customer-focused, and best-managed businesses we know of, on our *100 Best* list. Great company, bad industry. This year we decided to add them to the list anyway, as their business model and the continued floundering of their competitors should give them an edge that we feel investors may finally be willing to reward. We also think they've been so good for so long that many of their customers will be willing to pay somewhat higher prices to stick with their offering. Indeed, there's recent evidence that their average revenue per ticket has risen substantially. They've also introduced some effective revenue enhancers, like priority check-in, a much more customer-friendly revenue booster than the annoying baggage fees charged by other carriers. These guys still get it, and we feel that their approach will put them farther ahead of the competition and allow them to overcome some of the industry's worst ills. Fasten your seat belt. . . .

Strategic Fundamentals

Without any further ado, let's examine a list of "strategic fundamentals" that define, or keep score of, a company's success. This list can be used as a checklist, although it's hard to find a company that shows excellence in all of these areas.

Are Gross and Operating Profit Margins Growing?

We like profitable companies; who doesn't? But what really counts is the size of the margin and especially the growth. If a company has a gross margin (sales minus costs of goods sold) exceeding that of its competitors, that shows that it's doing something right, probably with its customers and/or with its costs. But competitive analysis is elusive; there is no dependable source of "industry" gross margins, and comparing competitors can be difficult because no two companies are exactly alike; it's easy to mix apples and oranges.

We like to see what direction gross margin is moving in—up or down. A growing gross margin also signals that the company is doing something right. That isn't perfect either; as the economy moved from boom to bust many excellent companies reported declines in gross and especially operating margins (sales – cost of goods sold – operating expenses) as they laid off workers and used less capacity. Still, in a steady state environment, it makes sense to favor companies with growing margins. In a declining market, companies that can *protect* their margins will come out ahead.

Does a Company Produce More Capital Than It Consumes?

Make no mistake about it—we like cash. And pure and simple—we like it when a company produces more cash than it consumes.

At the end of the day, cash generation is the simplest measure of whether a company is being successful, especially over the long term. Sure, if a company buys an airplane or opens a factory or a bunch of stores in a given quarter, it will be cash-flow negative. But that should be a temporary thing; over the long haul, it should produce, not consume cash. Companies that continually have to borrow or sell shares to raise enough cash to stay in business are on the wrong track.

So how do you determine this? You'll have to become familiar with the Statement of Cash Flows or equivalent in a company's financial reports. "Cash flow from operations" is usually positive and represents cash booked from sales less cost of goods sold, with adjustments for non-cash items like depreciation and for increases or decreases in working capital. In simple terms, it is the cash going into the cash register from the business.

"Cash used for investing purposes" or similar is a bit of a misnomer, and represents net cash used to "invest" in the business—usually for capital expenditures, but also for short-term non-cash investments like securities and a few other smaller items usually beyond scope. This figure is typically negative unless the company sells some part of its infrastructure. Over the long haul, cash generated from operations should well exceed cash used to invest in the business.

Companies in expansion mode may not show this surplus, and that's where "cash from financing activities" comes in. That's the cash generated from issuing debt or selling securities—or paying off debt or repurchasing shares, if things are going well, and dividends are included here as well. Again, a successful company will produce more cash—capital—from the business than it consumes, just as a successful household does the same, or else it goes into debt. Smart investors track this surplus over time.

Are Expenses Under Control?

Again, just like your household, company expenses should be under control, and anything else, especially without explanation, is a yellow flag.

The best way to test this is to check whether the "Selling, General and Administrative" expenses (SG&A) are rising, and more to the point, rising faster than sales. If so, that's a yellow, not necessarily a red, flag, but if it continues, it suggests that something is out of control, and it will catch up with the company sooner or later. In the recent downturn, companies that were able to reduce their expenses to match revenue declines scored more points, too.

Is Non-Cash Working Capital Under Control?

Working capital is a hard concept to grasp—even for small entrepreneurs who live with its ups and downs on a daily basis. Insufficient working capital is one of the biggest causes of death for small businesses, and working capital and especially changes in working capital can signal success or trouble.

Using a simplistic analogy, working capital is the circulatory lifeblood of the business. Money comes in, money goes out; working capital is what circulates in the veins in between. In its purest sense, it is cash, receivables, and inventory, less short-term debts. It's what you own less what you owe aside from fixed assets like plant, stores, and equipment.

If receivables are increasing, that sounds like a good thing—more people owe you more money. But if receivables are rising and sales aren't, that suggests that people aren't paying their bills, or worse, the business has to finance more to achieve the same level of sales. Similarly, a rise in inventory without a rise in sales means that it costs the business more money—more working capital—to do the same amount of business. That costs twice, because unless the firm is lucky, more inventory means more obsolescence and potentially more deep-discount sales or more write-offs down the road.

So a sharp investor will check to see that major working capital items—receivables and inventory—aren't growing faster than sales; indeed, a company that generates more sales with a decrease in working capital is becoming more productive.

Is Debt in Line with Business Growth?

Like many other "fundamentals" items, you can tear your hair out looking at debt figures and trying to decide whether they're in line with asset levels, equity levels, and industry norms. A simpler test is to check and see whether long-term debt is increasing or decreasing, and in particular, whether it is increasing faster than business growth. Gold stars go to companies with little to no debt, and to companies able to grow without issuing mountains of long-term debt.

Is Earnings Growth Steady?

We enter the danger zone here, because the management of many companies have learned to "manage" earnings to provide a steady improvement, always "beating the street" by a penny or two. So stability is a good thing for all investors, and companies that can manage toward stability get extra points, and it's worth checking for, but with the proverbial grain of salt.

Still, a company that is able to manage its sales, earnings, cash flow, and debt levels more consistently than competitors, and perhaps more consistently than what would be suggested by the ups and downs of the economy is desirable—or at least more desirable than the alternatives.

Is Return on Equity Steady or Growing?

Return on equity (ROE) is another of those hard-to-grasp concepts, and another measure subject to subjectivity in valuing assets and earnings. But at the end of the day, it's what all investors really seek, that is, returns on their capital investments.

And like many other figures derived from income statements and balance sheets, a pure number is hard to interpret—does a 26.7 percent ROE mean, in itself, that a company is excellent? The figure sounds healthy, to be sure—it's a heck of a lot better than investing your money in a CD or T-Bill. But because earnings and asset values are subjective, it may not represent true success. In fact, a company can increase ROE simply by borrowing money (yes!) and investing it into the business, even if it isn't invested as productively as other previous funds were invested. The math is complicated; we won't go into it here.

So the true test of ROE success is to check whether it is steady or increasing. Increasing—that makes sense. Why *steady*? Because if a company makes profits in a previous period and reinvests them in the business, that amount of money becomes part of equity (retained earnings). If the company reinvests productively, it will produce more returns, and ROE will at least keep up. If the company can't reinvest those earnings productively, ROE will drop—and perhaps it should be paying the earnings to you as dividends instead of investing them unproductively in the business. So if ROE is steady, the company still has good investments to make, and management is probably doing the right thing.

Does the Company Pay a Dividend?

Different people feel differently about dividends, and as we mentioned earlier, we're placing a greater emphasis on dividend-paying stocks this year. After all, save for the eventual sale of the company to someone else, a dividend is the only true cash that an investor will realize from buying a stock in a corporation, other than by selling the stock. And, at least in theory, investors should receive some compensation for their investments once in a while.

Yet, many companies don't pay dividends, or don't pay dividends that compete very effectively with fixed income yields. So why do investors put up with this? Because, in theory anyway, a company in a good business should be able to reinvest profits more effectively than the investor can (or else why would the investor have bought the company in the first place?). And, investors trust that reinvested profits will eventually bring the growth in company value that will be reflected in the share price, or eventual takeover or an eventual payment of a dividend or, better yet, growth in that dividend.

That's the theory, anyway. But there are still lots of companies that get away with paying no dividend at all. Can we tolerate this? Yes, if a company is really doing a great job with their retained profits, like Apple or Google. But we favor companies that offer at least something to their investors in the short term, some return on their hard-earned and faithfully committed capital. If nothing else, it keeps management teams honest, and shows that management understands that shareholder interests are up there somewhere on the list of priorities.

A dividend is a plus. Lack of a dividend isn't necessarily a showstopper, but it suggests a closer look. A dividend reduction—and there were many in the past year—suggests poor financial and operational health, because the dividend is usually the last thing to go, but in some cases, reflects management prudence and conservatism. Best question to ask yourself: Would you have reduced the dividend if you were running the company? And down the road, does the company bring back the dividend as times get better? A "no" to either of these questions is troubling.

Finally, dividend payouts should be examined over time. We've seen and included in our lists a number of companies that have steadily increased dividends, many for each of the eight previous years. We like this; it's just like getting an annual raise, and if you hold the stock long enough, the percentage return against your original investment can get quite large, even approaching 100 percent per year if the stock is held long enough and the dividend is raised persistently enough. Getting an ever-increasing dividend and owning a stock that has most likely appreciated because the dividend has increased is like having your cake and eating it too, a true favorite among investors.

ARE VALUATION RATIOS IN LINE?

One of the most difficult tasks in investing is determining the true value—and per share value—of a company. If this were easy, you'd just determine a value, compare it to the price, and if the price were lower than the value, push the buy button.

Professional investors try to determine what they call the "intrinsic value" of a company, which is usually the sum of all projected future cash flows of a company, discounted back to the present (remember, money received tomorrow is both less predictable and less valuable than money received now). They use complex math models, specifically, "discounted cash flow" or DCF models, to project, then discount, earnings flows. But those models—especially for the individual investor—depend too much on the crystal-ball accuracy of earnings forecasts, and the so-called discount rate is a highly theoretical construct beyond the scope of most individual investors. DCF models require a lot of estimates and number crunching, especially if multiple scenarios are employed as they should be. They take more time than it's worth for the individual investor. If you're an institutional investor buying multi-million-share stakes, we would conclude otherwise.

Valuation ratios are a shorthand way to determine if a stock price is acceptable relative to value. By far and away the most popular of these ratios is the so-called "price-to-earnings" (P/E) ratio, a measure of the stock price usually compared to "ttm," or trailing twelve months' earnings, but also sometimes compared to future earnings.

The P/E ratio correlates well to your expected return on an investment you might make in the company. For instance, if the P/E is 10, the price is ten times the past, or perhaps expected, annual earnings of the company. Take the reciprocal of that—1 divided by 10—and you get 0.10, or 10 percent. That's known as "earnings yield," the theoretical yield you'd get if all earnings were paid to you as dividends, as an owner. Ten percent is pretty healthy compared to returns on other investments, so a P/E of 10 suggests success.

But of course, the earnings may not be consistent or sustainable, or there may be substantial risk from factors intrinsic to the company, or there may be exogenous risk factors, like the total meltdown of the economy. The more risk, the more instability, the lower the expected P/E should be, for the earnings stream is less stable. If you think the earnings stream is solid and stable in the face of the risk, then the stock may be truly undervalued. Look for P/Es that 1) suggest strong earnings yield, and 2) are favorable compared to competitors and the industry.

Apart from P/E, the price-to-sales ratio (P/S), price-to-cash-flow (P/CF), and price-to-free-cash-flow (P/FCF) are often used as fundamental yardsticks. Like P/E, these measures also have some ambiguities, and it's best to think about them in real-world, entrepreneurial terms. Would you pay three times annual sales for a business and sleep well at night? Probably not—unless its profit margins were exceptionally high. So if a P/S ratio is 3 or above, look out; and opt for a business with a P/S of 1 or less if you can. Similarly, the price-to-cash-flow ratios can be thought of as true return going into your pocket for your investment; is it enough? Is it enough given the risk? And about the difference between "cash flow" and "free cash flow"? The difference is mostly cash laid out for capital expenditures, so it's worth making this distinction, although the lumpiness of capital expenditures makes consistent application of this number elusive. Incidentally, we don't regard price-to-book value (P/B) ratios as that helpful, because the book value of a company can be very elusive and arbitrary unless most of a company's assets are in cash or other easy-to-value forms.

Companies with high P/E, P/S, P/B, and P/CF ratios aren't necessarily bad investments, but you need to have good reasons to look beyond these figures if they suggest truly inadequate business results.

Strategic Intangibles

When you look at any company, perhaps the bottom line question follows the Buffett wisdom: If you had $100 billion in cool cash to spend (and we'll assume the genius intellect to spend it right), could you recreate that company?

If the answer is "yes," it may still be a great company, but it may not be great enough to fend off competition and keep its customers forever. If the answer is "no," the company truly has something unique to offer in the marketplace, difficult to duplicate at any cost. That distinctive competence, that sustainable competitive edge—whatever it is, a brand, a trade secret, a lock on distribution or supply channels, may be worth more than all the factories and high-rise office buildings and cash in the bank a company could ever have.

What we're talking about are the intangibles, the "soft" factors that make companies unique, that add up to more than the sum of their parts, the factors that ultimately drive future revenues. Intangibles not only define excellence, they define the future, while fundamentals mainly define the past. Seven key intangibles follow, although you'll think of more, and some industries may have some unique ones of their own, like intellectual property in the technology sector:

DOES THE COMPANY HAVE A MOAT?

A business "moat" performs much the same role as the medieval castle equivalent—it protects the business from competition. Whatever factors, some discussed below, create the moat, ultimately those are the factors that prevent you, with your $100 billion, from taking their business. Moats are usually a combination of brand, product technology, design, marketing and distribution channels, and customer loyalty all working together to protect a company. A moat doesn't just protect the existence of a company, it helps it command higher prices and earn higher profits.

Whether a company has a "narrow" moat, a "wide" moat, or none at all is a subjective assessment for you to make. However, you can get some help from Morningstar (*www.morningstar.com*) whose stock ratings include an assessment of the moat.

Coca-Cola has a moat because of the sheer impossibility of surpassing its brand and brand recognition worldwide. CarMax has a moat because it is farther along in putting retail-style dealerships on the ground and applying management information technologies to its business than anyone else is; it would take years for a competitor to catch up. The "Moat Stars" list presented earlier identifies the top ten stocks with a solid and sustainable competitive advantage.

DOES THE COMPANY HAVE AN EXCELLENT BRAND?

It's hard to say enough about brand, especially in today's fast-moving, highly packaged, highly national and international marketplace. A strong brand means consistency and a promise to consumers, and consumers sold on a brand will prefer it over any other, almost regardless of price. People still buy Tide; Starbucks is still synonymous with a high quality and ambience. Good brands command higher prices, and foster loyalty and identity and even customer "love." Again, using the Starbucks example, websites appeared soliciting customer appeals to not close stores during the recent store-closing initiative; when has anyone (other than a worker) offered so much resistance to closing a U.S. auto plant? Once a company has created a dominant brand (or brands, in the case of P&G) in the marketplace, aside from some major faux pas, they will endure and continue to create value for shareholders for years to come; a good brand is one of the most valuable (yet hard to value) long-term assets around.

Ask yourself if a company has a sought-after brand, a brand customers would pay extra to buy or align with, a brand that would be difficult to duplicate at any cost. Would customers rather fight than switch? Think about Starbucks, Coca-Cola, Heinz, Nike, or the brands within a house, like Frito-Lay (Pepsi) or Tide (P&G).

IS THE COMPANY A MARKET LEADER?

Market leadership usually—but not always—goes hand in hand with brand. The trick is to decide whether a company really leads in its industry. Often—but not always—that's a factor of size. The market leader usually has the highest market share, and the important point is that it calls the shots with regards to price, technology, marketing message, and so forth—other companies must play catch up and often discount their prices to keep up. Apple is a market leader in digital music, Intel is the market leader in microprocessors, and, despite a few setbacks, Toyota is emerging as the market leader in automobiles.

Excellent companies tend to be market leaders, and market leaders tend to be excellent companies. But this relationship doesn't always hold true—sometimes the nimble but smaller competitor is the excellent company—and will likely assume market leadership eventually. Examples like CarMax, Nucor, Perrigo, and Southwest Airlines can be found on our list.

DOES THE COMPANY HAVE CHANNEL EXCELLENCE?

"Channels" in business parlance means a chain of players to sell and distribute a company's products. It might be stores, it might be other industrial companies, it might be direct to the consumer. If a company is considered a top supplier in a particular channel, or a company has especially good relations with its channel, that's a plus.

Excellent companies develop solid channel relationships and become the preferred supplier in those channels. Companies like Dentsply, Patterson, Fair Isaac, McCormick, Nike, Pepsi, Procter & Gamble, and Sysco could all have excellent relationships with their channels through which they sell their product.

DOES THE COMPANY HAVE SUPPLY CHAIN EXCELLENCE?

Like distribution channels, excellent companies develop excellent and low-cost supply channels. They are seldom caught off guard by supply shortages and tend to get favorable and stable prices for whatever they buy. This is often not an easy assessment unless you know something about a particular industry. Hewlett-Packard and Nike are examples of companies that have done a good job managing their supply chains.

DOES THE COMPANY HAVE EXCELLENT MANAGEMENT?

Well, it's not hard to grasp what happens if a company *doesn't* have good management; performance fails and few inside or outside the company respect the company. It's not easy for an investor to determine if a management team does a good job or acts in shareholder interests. Clues can include candor and honesty and the ability of company management to speak in accessible, easily understood terms about the company and company performance (it's worth listening to conference calls as a resource). A management team that admits errors and eschews other forms of arrogance and entitlement (i.e., luxury perks, office suites, aircraft) is probably tilting his or her interests toward shareholders, as is the management team that can cough up some return to shareholders once in a while in the form of a dividend.

This may be the most subjective and elusive assessment of all, as few investors work with these folks on a daily basis. Still, over time, you can garner a strong hunch about whether a management team is effective and on your side.

ARE THERE SIGNS OF INNOVATION EXCELLENCE?

This question seems pretty obvious, but it's not just about the products that a company sells. True, if the company is leading the industry in innovation, that's usually a good thing, for "first to market" definitely offers business advantages.

The less obvious part of this question is whether the company makes the best *use* of technology to make operations and customer interfaces as efficient and effective as possible. Southwest Airlines may have missed our list in the past because of the difficulty of achieving excellence in an industry where players can't control prices or costs. But they do make our list today, not only because of brand and management excellence, but also innovation excellence. Why? Simply because, after all of these years, amazingly, they still have the best, simplest, easiest-to-use flight booking and check-in in the industry. Sometimes these sorts of innovations mean a lot more than bringing new, fancy products and bells and whistles to the market. And one can also look to Apple, Google, and CarMax on our list for more obvious examples of companies that have deployed technology and innovative customer interfaces to achieve sustainable competitive advantage.

IT PAYS TO FIND A SMART FRIEND IN THE BUSINESS

Most publicly traded companies are required to report their fundamentals on a quarterly and an annual basis through income statements, balance sheets, and statements of cash flows. That's good, because we as investors can easily see how the company is performing; we don't need to get on the phone with the CFO to check the progress of our investment.

But what about the intangibles? Companies are required to report exactly nothing of their brand strength, market position, new product pipeline, or management style. Sure, you may read a lot in an annual report, but it's as much a spin, a marketing message to investors, as it is the real "scoop" about what is or what's going to be.

So how do you fill this information gap? One way is to keep up with the trade press and trade publications of the industry you invest in. Like technology stocks? Read technology magazines and websites, and the technology sections of the *Wall Street Journal* and the *New York Times*. But if you really want the inside scoop, make friends with people who work in the industry. They are (or should be) experts in their business. They know the products and the competition. It's not so much that they'll divulge trade secrets about the company they work for; that isn't the point. Instead, they'll help you see where the puck is going for the industry, their company, and other players in their industry. The thousand words you get from a friend in the business can be worth far more than the picture in the annual report.

Choosing the 100 Best

So with all of this in mind, just how was this year's *100 Best Stocks* list actually chosen? It's probably about time, after pages and pages, to get to that.

The answer is a little more subtle than you might think. If we could give you a precise formula, you wouldn't need this book. You'd be able to do it yourself. In fact, every investor would be able to do it on his or her own. Our book would simply be the result of yet another stock screener. And every investor would invest in the same stocks. Is that a feasible or practical solution? Hardly. Everyone would scramble to buy the same *100 Best Stocks*. The prices would be sky high, and the price of other stocks would melt to nothing.

SIGNS OF VALUE

Following are a few signs of value to look for in any company. Not an exhaustive list by any means, but a good place to start:

>> Gaining market share
>> Can control price
>> Loyal customers
>> Growing margins
>> Producing, not consuming, capital (free cash flow)
>> Steady or increasing ROE
>> Management forthcoming, honest, understandable

SIGNS OF UNVALUE

... and signs of trouble, or "unvalue":

» Declining margins
» No brand or who-cares brand
» Commodity producer, must compete on price
» Losing market dominance or market share
» Can't control costs
» Must acquire other companies to grow
» Management in hiding, off message, making excuses, or difficult to understand

Fortunately or unfortunately, however you want to look at it, it isn't that simple. There are too many fundamentals, too many intangibles, and too many unknown and unknowable weighting factors to combine the fundamentals and intangibles that—well—it just wouldn't work. No screener could recreate the subtle judgment that gets applied to the cold, hard facts. It's that judgment, the interpretation of the facts and intangibles, that makes it worth spending money on a book like this.

While we didn't apply a specific formula or screener to the universe of stocks, we did take a few measurable factors into account to narrow the list from thousands to a few hundred issues. Those factors came from several sources, but at this point, we must tip our cap to Value Line and the research and database work they do as part of the Value Line Investment Survey. If you aren't familiar with Value Line, it's worth a look for any savvy individual investor, either online at *www.valueline.com* or, in many cases, at your local library. It is an excellent resource.

Anyway, here are some of the measured factors we looked into, most of which go beyond individual facts or items and instead are measures of strength or performance compiled from a number of factors. In this way, we gain some leverage for not having to deal with lots of little bits of individual data. Here are six metrics we use as a starting point to select and sort stocks for further review:

- *S&P Rating* is a broad corporate credit rating reflecting the ability to cover indebtedness, in turn reflecting business levels, business trends, cash flow, and sustained performance. It's a bit like the credit score you might use or might have used to determine your own personal credit risk.

- *Value Line Financial Strength Rating* is used much like the S&P rating except that it goes further into overall balance sheet and cash flow strength. It should be noted that several companies with "B" ratings were selected; these are typically newer companies that will grow into "A" companies or that may have been hit harder by the recession than others.
- *Value Line Earnings Predictability* is what it sounds like, a calculated tendency of companies to deliver consistent and predictable earnings without surprises.
- *Value Line Growth Persistence* is again what it sounds like—the company's ability to consistently grow even in weaker economic times.
- *Value Line Price Stability* reflects the stability and relative safety of a company. Again, we did not reject a company out of hand due to volatility; rather, if stability was low, we tried to make a case that the business, business model, and intangibles were worth the risk.
- *Dividends and Yield.* Companies that pay something are held in higher regard; however, again, it is not by any means an absolute criterion.

With these facts and figures in mind, the evaluation proceeded with a close eye on the "signs of value" and intangibles mentioned above. Some consideration was also given to diversification; we did not want to overweight any sector or industry, but rather to give you a healthy assortment of stocks to pick from across a variety of industries.

With these thoughts in mind, you can make more sense of the companies we picked. And of course, full disclosure and full disclaimer—we didn't do *all* the analysis. We couldn't have. It wouldn't have made any sense anyway, for things would have changed from the time we did it, and it might not match your preferences anyway. So it is of utmost importance for you to take our selections and analysis and make them yours—that is, do the due diligence to further qualify these picks as congruent with your investment needs.

The Surgeon General would label this book as "hazardous to your wealth" if you didn't.

Strategic Investing

Although this book is designed to help you pick the best stocks to buy, investing by nature goes well beyond simply buying stocks, just like owning an automobile goes far beyond buying it. Just as clearly, this book isn't about investing strategy, or about the personal financial strategies necessary to ensure retirement or a prosperous future. That said, we think a few words are in order.

We find that a lot of investors lose the forest in the trees, spending all of their energy trying to find individual stocks or funds without putting enough consideration into their overall investing framework. If they look at the big picture at all, they look at the formulaic covenants of asset allocation, a favorite subject of the financial planning and advisory community, as though the difference between 50 percent equities and 60 percent equities makes all the different in the world. Sure, it might in the world of pension funds and other institutional investments, where a 10 percent adjustment could move millions into or out of a particular asset class and more or less toward safety, but what about a $100,000 portfolio? Does $10,000 more or less in stocks, bonds, or cash make that much difference?

Perhaps not. And of course there's more to that story—doesn't it matter more which equities you invest in than just the fact that you're 60 percent in equities? So while asset allocation models make for nice pie charts, we prefer to approach big-picture portfolio constructs differently.

Start with a Portfolio in Mind

First, we'll make an assumption. That assumption is simply this: You are not a professional investor. You have other things to do with your time, and time is of the essence. You cannot spend forty, fifty, or sixty hours a week glued to a computer screen analyzing your investments.

To that assumption, we'll add another: that, as an individual investor, you're looking to beat the market. Not by a ton—20 percent sustained returns simply aren't possible without taking outlandish risks. But perhaps if the market is up 4 percent in a year, you'd like to achieve, 5, 6, perhaps 7 percent without taking excessive risks. Or if the market is down 20 percent, perhaps you cut your losses at 5 or 10 percent. You're looking to do *somewhat* better than the market.

Because of time constraints, and owing to your objective to do slightly better than average, we suggest taking a tiered approach to your portfolio. The tiers aren't based on the type of assets; they're based on the amount of activity and attention you want to pay to different parts of your portfolio. It's a strategic portfolio approach you would probably take if you were managing a small business—put most of your focus on the products and customers who might bring the greatest new return to your business; let the rest of your slow steady customer base function as it has for the long term.

We suggest breaking up your portfolio into three tiers or segments. This can be done by setting up specific accounts; or less formally by simply applying the model as a thought process.

We can't go much further without defining the three segments:

Active Portfolio Segmentation

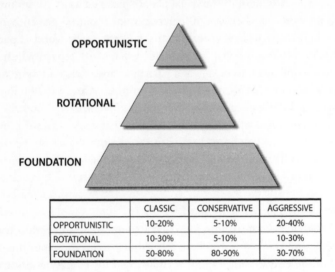

	CLASSIC	CONSERVATIVE	AGGRESSIVE
OPPORTUNISTIC	10-20%	5-10%	20-40%
ROTATIONAL	10-30%	5-10%	10-30%
FOUNDATION	50-80%	80-90%	30-70%

THE FOUNDATION PORTFOLIO

In this construct, each investor defines and manages a cornerstone foundation portfolio, which is long-term in nature and requires relatively less active management. Frequently, the foundation portfolio consists of retirement accounts (the paradigmatic long-term investment) and may include your personal residence or other long-lived personal or family assets, such as trusts, collectibles, and so forth. The typical foundation portfolio is invested to achieve at least average market returns through index funds, quality mutual funds, and some income-producing assets like bonds held to maturity. A foundation portfolio may contain some long-term plays in commodities or real estate to defend against inflation, particularly in such commodities as energy, precious metals, and real estate trusts. The foundation portfolio is largely left alone, although as with all investments it is important to check at least once in a while to make sure performance—and managers, if involved—are keeping up with expectations.

THE ROTATIONAL PORTFOLIO

The second segment, the rotational portfolio, is managed fairly actively to keep up with changes in business cycles and conditions. It is likely in a set of stocks or funds that might be rotated or remixed occasionally to reflect business conditions or to get a little more offensive or defensive. More than the other portfolios, this portfolio follows the rotation of market preference among different kinds of businesses and business assets. The portfolio is managed to redeploy assets among market or business sectors, between aggressive and defensive business assets, from "large cap" to "small cap" companies from companies with international exposure to those with little of the same, from companies in favor versus out of favor, from stocks to bonds to commodities, and so forth. Sector-specific exchange-traded funds are a favorite component of these portfolios, as are cyclical and commodity-based stocks like gold mining stocks.

Is this about "market timing"? Let's call it "intelligent" or "educated" market timing. Studies telling us that it is impossible to effectively time market moves have been around for years. It is impossible to catch highs and lows in particular investments, market sectors, or even the market as a whole. Nobody can find exact tops or bottoms. But by watching economic indicators and the pulse of business and the marketplace, long-term market performance can be boosted by well-rationalized and timely sector rotation. The key word is "timely." The agile active investor has enough of a finger on the pulse to see the signs and invest accordingly.

While the idea isn't new, the advent of "low-friction" exchange-traded funds and other index portfolios makes it a lot more practical for the individual investors. What does "low-friction" mean? They trade like a single stock—one order, one discounted commission. You don't have to liquidate or acquire a whole basket full of investments on your own to follow a sector. We should note that it's been possible to rotate assets in mutual fund families for years with a single phone call, but most funds in these families are less "pure" plays in their sector, and most families do not cover all sectors.

THE OPPORTUNISTIC PORTFOLIO

The opportunistic portfolio is the most actively traded portion of an active investor's total portfolio. The opportunistic portfolio looks for stocks or other investments that seem to be notably under- or overvalued at a particular time. The active investor look for shorter-term opportunities, perhaps a few days, perhaps a month, perhaps even a year, to wring out gains from undervalued situations.

The opportunistic portfolio also may be used to generate short-term income through covered option writing. Options are essentially a cash-based risk transfer mechanism whereby a possible, but low probability, investment outcome is exchanged for a less profitable but more certain outcome. A fee or "premium" is paid in exchange for transferring the opportunity for more aggressive gain to someone else. You collect this fee. Effectively, you as the owner of a stock can convert a growth investment into an income investment, paying yourself a dividend for the ownership of the stock by selling an option. Is this risky? Actually, it is less risky than owning the stock without an option.

Curiously, the main objective of this short-term portfolio is to generate income, or cash. Most traditional investors look at the long-term, more conservative components of a portfolio to generate income through bonds, dividend-paying stocks, and so forth. In this framework, the short-term opportunistic portfolio actually does the "heavy lifting" in terms of generating cash income. An active investor might look to trade those stocks with varying degrees of frequency or to sell some options to generate cash. These "swing" trades usually run from a few days to a month or so, and may be day trades if things work out particularly well and particularly fast. It should be emphasized again that day trades are not the active investor's goal nor their typical practice.

ARE RETIREMENT ACCOUNTS ALWAYS PART OF THE FOUNDATION?

The long-term objectives and nature of retirement accounts suggest normal inclusion as part of the foundation portfolio. In fact, retirement assets can be deployed as part of either the rotational or opportunistic portfolio. In fact, it might make a lot of sense. Why? Because returns generated are tax free, at least until withdrawn. Tax-free returns can compound much faster. Because of the importance of these assets, one should only commit a small portion to an actively managed opportunistic portfolio, but it can be a good way to "juice" the growth of this important asset base.

100 Best Stocks *and the Segmented Portfolio*

The next natural question is—"So how do I use the *100 Best Stocks* to construct my portfolio tiers?" The answer is really that selections from the *100 Best* list can be used in all tiers, depending on your time horizon and current price relative to value. If you see a stock on the *100 Best* list take a nosedive, and feel that nosedive is out of proportion to the real news and near-term prospects of the company, it may be a candidate for the opportunistic portfolio. If the stock makes sense as a long-term holding (as many on our list do), it's a good candidate for the foundation portfolio. Likewise, if you feel that, say, health care stocks are, as a group, likely to be in favor and are undervalued now, you can pick off the health care stocks on the *100 Best* list as a rotational portfolio pick. Similarly, if you feel that large-cap-dividend paying stocks will do well; again, you can use the *100 Best* list to feed into this hunch.

Not surprisingly, we feel the *100 Best* stocks are of the highest quality, and can be used with relatively less risk that most other stocks to achieve your objectives.

When to Buy? Consider When to Sell

If it's hard to figure out when to buy a stock, it's even harder to figure out when to sell. People "get married" to their investment decisions, feeling somehow that if it isn't right, maybe time will help, and things will get better. Or they're just too arrogant to admit that they made a mistake. There are lots of reasons why people hold on to investments for too long a time.

Here's the fundamental truth: Buying and selling should be much the same process. Let's look at it from the point of view of selling. When should you sell? Simply, when there's something else better to buy. Something else better for future returns, something else better for safety, something else better for timeliness or synchronization with overall business trends. That something else can be another stock, a futures contract, or a house. It can also be cash—sell that stock when . . . when what? When cash is a better investment. Or when you need the money, which is another way of saying that cash is a better investment.

Similarly, if you think of a buy decision as a best-possible deployment of capital, as a buy because there's no better way to invest your money, you'll also come out ahead. It really isn't that hard, especially if you've done your homework. And it's also made easier if you avoid rash over-commitments; that is, you avoid buying all at once in case you've made a mistake or in case better prices come later down the road.

Investing for Retirement

Most of us don't invest just for the sake of investing. We're not so much like players at a poker table who not only enjoy winning money but the process of winning. We're more interested in the *result* of investing than the process.

We may like to invest, like to do research, like to see things come out the way we had in mind. But the main reason we do it is to make money.

And why do we want to make money? Well, for some of us, it's about buying homes, paying for college, or just having a little extra spending money. But for a great many of us, especially those of us for whom there's no defined-benefit pension awaiting us when we retire, we invest because we want a more secure, comfortable retirement years down the road.

So how should one invest for retirement? Should one invest any differently than they would for any of the other objectives we just mentioned? Mostly, investing is investing, and the goal is to make money over the intended period of time one invests. Retirement investing isn't that much different, except there is a greater emphasis on the long term, and for many, a greater need for safety.

The retirement planning process starts with creating a goal, that is, estimating what you will need during retirement to live on. The "what you'll need" is referred to euphemistically as your "number an amount that will—with carefully planned withdrawals—service your needs net of government (Social Security) and other pensions until you and your spouse die. There are many ways to calculate this "number," and financial advisers have a bag of tricks and fancy spreadsheets. We like to use a permanent withdrawal rate rule of thumb—that is, you can draw down 4 percent of your asset base each year in retirement. So if you need $2,000 a month (plus Social Security) to live, that's $24,000 a year; $24,000 a year is 4 percent of (multiply by 25) $960,000 you'll need in your retirement account on Retirement Day 1. This number, however, assumes that market returns are steady and there won't be any severe market corrections during your retirement. The reality is that you can keep withdrawing a constant percentage; it may just be that the base amount, and thus your income, fluctuates. If you must keep your income steady, the 4 percent rule can be jeopardized in down or very volatile markets. You can see how complex the calculation can become.

But that's not the point of reading *100 Best Stocks*—the point is to get some tips on where and how to invest to achieve the number. We offer the following:

- *Stay diversified.* You've read about how Enron shareholders had their entire retirement tied up in company stock. If the company fails, you fail twice. It's probably best to not even invest most of your retirement assets in the same industry you work in. A good portfolio of stocks or funds (seven or so different stocks, three or so different funds) is probably optimal. But don't *over-diversify*—you can achieve the same returns at a lot less cost by simply buying an index fund.

- *Think long term.* Obvious, right? Well, today's market can bring some serious surprises to those who think they can simply buy and hold forever and capitalize on the growth of the American Way. The trick here is to buy individual companies that you think will not only be around when you retire, but will also be better than they are today. Try to visualize your company ten, twenty, or thirty years from now. And be prepared to bail out when things start to not look like you expected. There are a lot of GM shareholders and bondholders who wish they had done just that. The key word is "think."

- *Get at least some dividends.* Future appreciation is nice for retirement, but I believe that a bird in hand is worthwhile, especially if you can reinvest it in the stocks or funds held in your retirement accounts.

- *Dollar cost average.* If you keep reinvesting dividends and/or adding funds to your accounts consistently, you'll buy more shares when prices are low, bringing your average cost down. For most people, it's best to keep retirement contributions—and investments—as consistent as possible.

- *Use a portfolio strategy.* Like the one outlined above—create a strong, steady "foundation" and add some opportunistic investments. The opportunistic investments can be used to stretch returns a bit, and they work better in retirement accounts because capital gains taxes are deferred or avoided altogether. That said, you should opportunistically invest only what you can afford to lose. Most of the *100 Best Stocks* are suitable for foundation investments, and a few of the "aggressive growth" entries are good for opportunistic investments as well. Make some rules and stick by them.

So good luck, and we'll come visit you at your beach house.

When and How to Use an Adviser

To use a professional adviser, or not to use a professional adviser? That is the question almost all individual investors ask themselves at one time or another.

Individual investors are independent, self-starting, self-driven folks largely capable of accepting responsibility for their own decisions and actions. That's good, and I assume that if you're reading this book, you have at least some of that character. However, the world isn't so simple, and your time isn't so plentiful, and maybe business and investing stuff just isn't your cup of tea, anyway. You don't want to throw everything over the wall to a professional adviser (and pay the fees and lose control and all that) but you may want some help from time to time.

Just remember this—you, you only, and ultimately you are responsible for your own finances, just like a pilot flying an airplane is ultimately responsible for what happens to that airplane and its passengers. You are in charge. You are in charge whether or not you have someone else, like a broker or professional adviser, helping you out. You can (and should) think of advisers as more like a co-pilot, navigator, or air traffic controller—who will give you information and suggestions and help you interpret the information and remind you of the rules when necessary—but ultimately you're in charge.

Financial advisers come in many forms, and we won't go into the details here. What's important is to realize that no matter how much you outsource, you're still at the helm. You need to develop a good, two-way relationship with the adviser where he or she can bring value and help you bring value to the investment decisions and investment strategy. An adviser shouldn't tell you what to do, and shouldn't just be the "yes man" for everything you want to do. A lively, point-counterpoint discussion of any financial move with an adviser is healthy; two heads are better than one. Remember, if two people think the exact same way, you don't need one of them.

Don't be snowed by fancy terminology and concepts. Investing is a complex subject, but if the explanation sounds more complex than the task itself, look out below. Find an adviser who speaks your language, that is, plain English. Smart, experienced people make things simple, not complex, for others.

Also be clear what you want and what you expect from an adviser. If you aren't, he or she will give you the "standard" product, and it may be the same standard product given to the last client. Say that you want help constructing your portfolio and learning about, say, the tech and health care sectors, which you don't know enough about. Ask your adviser to help you understand the headlines and what's important about them for the banking industry. And so forth.

And of course, as Bernard Madoff has made so clear for so many—make sure you understand what your advisors are doing, if they're managing anything on your behalf. There is nothing worse than thinking everything is okay—when in fact it's completely off in the weeds.

Bottom line, an investment adviser should be a great partner, someone you'd hire into your business if you were trying to create a partnership in the investing business. Look for common sense, look for advisers to help you most with the things you're least comfortable with. Learn what they do (and have done) with other clients; if it sounds too good to be true, it probably is.

Here's another bottom line: Your adviser should make you sleep better at night. If you're waking up at 3 A.M. thinking about your investments, that's bad. If you're waking up at 3 A.M. thinking about your adviser, that's worse. In both cases, they're too risky for you.

Individual Stocks vs. Funds and ETFs

As long as we're sharing opinions on things like financial advisers and other help you can get with your investing, it makes sense to take a short detour into the world of managed investments. What are managed investments? Simply, they are individual investments where some intermediary buys and repackages individual investments, and sells you pieces of that package.

Intermediaries can be investment companies with professional managers choosing specific investments and otherwise looking after the portfolio. They can also be indexes, where groups of like stocks are accumulated into an index according to some sort of generally fixed formula. Either way, by buying into one of these intermediaries, you're giving up picking individual investments in favor of a packaged and sometimes professionally managed approach.

Of course, like any value proposition, you're giving up something in the interest of gaining something else. The "something else" you're trying to gain by using the packaged approach is usually a combination of the following:

- *Time*—You don't have the time to research individual stocks or to research individual stocks for 100 percent of your portfolio.
- *Expertise*—In the case of managed funds, you're getting a trained, experienced, investment professional. Some also prefer to hire others to do the work to take the emotion out of investing decisions.
- *Diversification*—By definition, both managed and index funds spread your investments so that you don't have too much wrapped up in a single company; this is generally good unless they diversify away any chance of outperforming the markets. Funds and ETFs also allow you to play in markets otherwise difficult to play in for lack of knowledge or time; e.g. Asian stocks, European currencies, etc.
- *Convenience*—It takes work to build and manage an investment portfolio. With funds you can move in and out of the markets with a single transaction; the administrative work is taken care of.

Of course, with any value proposition comes a downside, and the downsides of fund and index investing are often underappreciated by prospective clients:

- *Fees*—Not surprisingly, funds, and especially managed funds, charge money for the packaging and services they provide. Actively managed funds can take a half to over 2 percent of your asset value each year, whether they do well or not. If you understand compounding, you know that the difference between a 6 percent return and a 4 percent *net* return over time is huge. Index funds and ETFs are better in this regard, usually charging 0.10 to 0.50 percent, but it still puts a drag on your outcomes.

- *Tax efficiency*—When ordinary mutual funds sell shares, any gains flow through to you (unless you hold them in a tax-free or tax-deferred retirement account). You cannot control when this happens, and many "active" funds may roll their portfolios frequently, producing adverse tax consequences. Also, you need to watch when you enter the fund— you should buy in after capital gains are paid out, not before, or else you'll be paying for someone else's gains. Index funds and ETFs are far less likely to produce "unwanted" gains, for they tie their investments to the indexes, which don't change much.

- *Control*—With funds of any sort, you lose control, and as we said at the outset, there are few things more painful than having someone else lose your money for you. Particularly with managed funds, it is almost impossible to know what they are really doing with your money except in hindsight. We would support any initiative requiring funds to give you a more real-time accounting for what they do with *your* funds.

- *Tendency toward mediocrity*—One of the biggest criticisms of funds over time is the tendency for managers to follow each other and to follow standard business-school investing and risk-management formulas. The result you tend to get in practice is a herd instinct, known in the trade as an "institutional imperative." You can see this in many funds—pick almost any fund and the top ten holdings are GE, Microsoft, Exxon Mobil—you get the idea. Worse—and this is the biggie from our perspective—when you buy a fund and especially an index fund, you're getting *all* the companies in the industry—the mediocre players, the weak hands—not just the best ones.

So we suggest using funds where it makes sense to get some exposure to an industry or a segment of the market otherwise difficult to access or outside your expertise. Use funds to round out a portfolio or build a foundation or rotational portfolio, and to save yourself the time and bandwidth to focus more closely on other more "opportunistic" investments.

Part II

THE 100 BEST STOCKS
YOU CAN BUY

The 100 Best Stocks You Can Buy

Index of Stocks by Category

Company	Symbol	Industry	Sector	Category
—A—				
3M Company	MMM	Diversified	Industrials	Con Gro
Abbott Laboratories	ABT	Med. Supplies	Health Care	Gro Inc
Aetna*	AET	Insurance	Health Care	Con Gro
Air Products	APD	Gases	Materials	Aggr Gro
Alexander & Baldwin	ALEX	Transportation	Industrials	Gro Inc
Allergan*	AGN	Med Devices	Health Care	Aggr Gro
Amgen*	AMGN	Med Tech	Health Care	Con Gro
Apache Corporation	APA	Exploration	Energy	Aggr Gro
Apple	AAPL	Computer Tech	Consumer Discret	Aggr Gro
Archer Daniels Midland	ADM	Food	Consumer Staples	Con Gro
AT&T	T	Telephone	Telecomm.	Gro Inc
Automatic Data Processing	ADP	Business Svcs	Inform Tech	Con Gro
—B—				
Bard, C.R.	BCR	Hosp. Products	Health Care	Con Gro
Baxter	BAX	Med Equip	Health Care	Aggr Gro
Becton, Dickinson	BDX	Med Supplies	Health Care	Con Gro
Bed Bath & Beyond	BBBY	Household Pd	Retail	Aggr Gro
Best Buy	BBY	Electronics	Retail	Aggr Gro
—C—				
Campbell Soup	CPB	Packaged Foods	Cons Staples	Con Gro
CarMax	KMX	Auto, Truck	Retail	Aggr Gro
Caterpillar, Inc.	CAT	Machinery	Industrials	Aggr Gro
Chevron	CVX	Gas & Oil	Energy	Gro Inc
Church & Dwight	CHD	Household Pd	Consumer Staples	Aggr Gro
Cincinnati Financial	CINF	Financial	Financial	Income
Clorox	CLX	Household Pd	Cons Staples	Con Gro
Coca-Cola	KO	Beverages	Cons Staples	Con Gro
Colgate-Palmolive	CL	Household Pd	Cons Staples	Con Gro
Comcast*	CMCSA	Comm. Tech	Telecomm	Aggr Gro
ConocoPhillips	COP	Oil & Gas	Energy	Gro Inc
Costco Wholesale	COST	Warehouse Club	Retail	Aggr Gro
CVS/Caremark	CVS	Pharmacy	Retail	Con Gro

Index of Stocks by Category (continued)

Company	Symbol	Industry	Sector	Category
—D—				
Deere & Company	DE	Farm Equipment	Industrials	Aggr Gro
Dentsply Int'l	XRAY	Dental Products	Health Care	Con Gro
Dominion Resources	D	Gas & Electric	Utilities	Gro Inc
Duke	DUK	Gas & Electric	Utilities	Income
DuPont	DD	Chemicals	Materials	Gro Inc
—E—				
Ecolab	ECL	Specialty Chem.	Materials	Con Gro
ExxonMobil	XOM	Oil & Gas	Energy	Gro Inc
—F—				
Fair Isaac	FICO	Business Services	Inform Tech	Aggr Gro
FedEx Corporation	FDX	Air Freight	Transportation	Aggr Gro
Fluor	FLR	Heavy Construction	Industrials	Aggr Gro
FMC Corporation	FMC	Feeding World	Materials	Aggr Gro
—G—				
General Mills	GIS	Packaged Foods	Cons Staples	Gro Inc
Google	GOOG	Internet Tech.	Technology	Aggr Gro
Grainger, W. W.	GWW	Supplies	Industrials	Con Gro
—H—				
Harris Corp.	HRS	Communications	Inform Tech	Aggr Gro
Heinz	HNZ	Food	Consumer Staples	Gro Inc
Hewlett Packard	HPQ	Computers	Inform Tech	Aggr Gro
Honeywell	HON	Aerospace	Industrials	Aggr Inc
—I—				
IBM	IBM	Computers	Inform Tech	Con Gro
Illinois Tool Works*	ITW	Machinery	Industrials	Con Gro
International Paper	IP	Packaging	Materials	Con Gro
Iron Mountain	IRM	Business Services	Information Tech	Aggr Gro
—J—				
Johnson & Johnson	JNJ	Med Supplies	Health Care	Gro Inc
Johnson Controls	JCI	Elect. Equip.	Industrials	Con Gro
—K—				
Kellogg	K	Packaged Foods	Cons Staples	Gro Inc
Kimberly-Clark	KMB	Paper Products	Cons Staples	Gro Inc

Index of Stocks by Category (continued)

Company	Symbol	Industry	Sector	Category
—L—				
Lubrizol	LZ	Specialty Chem	Materials	Gro Inc
—M—				
Marathon Oil	MRO	Oil & Gas	Energy	Aggr Gro
McCormick & Co.	MKC	Spices	Cons Staples	Con Gro
McDonald's	MCD	Food	Restaurants	Aggr Gro
McKesson*	MCK	Pharmacy	Health Care	Con Gro
Medtronic	MDT	Med. Devices	Health Care	Aggr Gro
Monsanto	MON	Chemicals	Industrials	Aggr Gro
—N—				
NextEra Energy*	FPL	Power	Utilities	Gro Inc
NIKE	NKE	Apparel	Cons. Discret.	Aggr Gro
Norfolk Southern	NSC	Railroads	Transportation	Cons Gro
Northern Trust	NTRS	Bank	Financials	Con Gro
Nucor	NUE	Steel	Industrials	Aggr Gro
—O—				
Oracle	ORCL	Computer Software	Technology	Aggr Gro
Otter Tail*	OTTR	Utilities/Industrials	Energy	Gro Inc
—P—				
Pall	PLL	Gas Filtration	Industrials	Aggr Gro
Patterson Companies	PDCO	Dental	Health Care	Aggr Gro
Paychex	PAYX	Payroll Services	Inform Tech	Aggr Gro
PepsiCo	PEP	Beverages	Cons Staples	Con Gro
Perrigo	PRGO	Pharmacy	Health Care	Aggr Gro
Praxair	PX	Indust. Gases	Materials	Con Gro
Procter & Gamble	PG	Household Pd	Cons Staples	Con Gro
—R—				
Ross Stores	ROST	Clothing	Retail	Aggr Gro
—S—				
Schlumberger	SLB	Oilfield Services	Energy	Aggr Gro
Sigma-Aldrich	SIAL	Life Science	Industrials	Aggr Gro
J. M. Smucker	SJM	Packaged Food	Cons Staples	Gro Inc
Southern Co.	SO	Power	Utilities	Gro Inc
Southwest Airlines*	LUV	Airline	Transportation	Con Gro

Index of Stocks by Category (continued)

* New to this edition

3M Company

Ticker symbol: MMM (NYSE) □ S&P rating: AA– □ Value Line financial strength rating: A++ □
Current yield: 2.4%

Company Profile

The 3M Company, originally known as the Minnesota Mining and Manufacturing Co., is a $24 billion diversified manufacturing technology company with leading positions in industrial, consumer and office, health care, safety, electronics, telecommunications, and other markets. The company has operations in more than sixty countries and serves customers in nearly 200 countries. The company has such a broad reach that it is often looked to as a leading indicator for the general health of the world economy; it has proven its mettle in this regard both in the 2008–09 downturn and in the recovery commencing in 2010.

3M's operations are divided into six segments, approximate revenue percentages in parentheses:

- The Industrial and Transportation segment (31 percent) produces industrial tapes, a wide variety of abrasives, adhesives, specialty materials, filtration products, and products for the separation of fluids and gases. They supply markets such as paper and packaging, food and beverage, electronics, automotive (OEM), and the automotive aftermarket.

- The Health Care segment (19 percent) serves markets that include medical clinics and hospitals, pharmaceuticals, dental and orthodontic practitioners, and health information systems. Products and services include medical and surgical supplies, skin health and infection prevention products, drug delivery systems, dental and orthodontic products, health information systems, and antimicrobial solutions.

- The Safety, Security, and Protection Services segment (12 percent) serves a broad range of markets that increase the safety, security, and productivity of workers, facilities, and systems. Major product offerings include personal protection, safety and security products, energy control products, building cleaning and protection products, track and trace solutions, and roofing granules for asphalt shingles.

- The Consumer and Office segment (16 percent) serves

markets that include retail, home improvement, building maintenance, and other markets. Products in this segment include office supply products such as the familiar tapes and Post-It notes, stationery products, construction and home improvement products, home care products, protective material products, and consumer health care products.

- The Display and Graphics segment (14 percent) serves markets that include electronic display, traffic safety, and commercial graphics. This segment includes optical film solutions for electronic displays, computer screen filters, reflective sheeting for transportation safety, commercial graphics systems, and projection systems, including mobile display technology and visual systems products.

- The Electro and Communications segment (9 percent) serves the electrical, electronics, and communications industries, including electric utilities. Products include electronic and interconnect solutions, microinterconnect systems, high-performance fluids, high-temperature and display tapes, telecommunications products, electrical products, and touchscreens and touch monitors.

Value Line recently reclassified the company from "Diversified Chemical" to "Diversified Company," reflecting its broad range of products and businesses.

Financial Highlights, Fiscal Year 2010

FY2010 sales came in at $26.7 billion, a healthy recovery relative to the 2009 figure of $23.1 billion, which had been a drop of 8.5 percent from 2008. The figures suggest a 5–7 percent organic growth rate excluding the recession dip, a healthy rate for a company of this size and stability. Earnings for 2011 are projected to come in between $5.65 and $5.80 per share.

Reasons to Buy

3M manufactures a broad line of products for end user markets and for other manufacturing activities. We like the combination of manufacturing reach, innovation, and international presence (67 percent of sales are overseas). The company makes many products essential to the activities of other companies and organizations, and seemingly essential to most of us: e.g., Post-It notes and Scotch tape.

Aside from the attraction of the business itself, 3M offers a good combination of stability and innovation; financials are solid while adding a better-than-average growth prospect through its own innovations and expansion in overseas markets. While the company does dabble in acquisitions, we see 3M as less dependent on acquisitions to fuel growth than many of its "diversified company" competitors like GE or United Technologies. Dividends, earnings, and cash flow per share have all grown at healthy rates for a company of this size, and moderate but steady gains are likely for the future. With the exception of 2009, the company has stepped up dividend increases in recent years.

Reasons for Caution

3M is somewhat exposed to business cycles, and slowdowns in global manufacturing activity have tended to lead to down cycles in the share price. For the most part, these dips have proven to be buying opportunities. There is a risk that 3M may jump more aggressively into acquisitions if internal growth stalls.

SECTOR: **Industrials**
BETA COEFFICIENT: **.80**
10-YEAR COMPOUND EARNINGS PER SHARE GROWTH: **9.0%**
10-YEAR COMPOUND DIVIDENDS PER SHARE GROWTH: **6.0%**

	2003	2004	2005	2006	2007	2008	2009	2010
Revenues (Mil)	18,232	20,011	21,167	22,293	24,462	25,269	23,123	26,662
Net Income (Mil)	2,403	2,990	3,111	3,851	4,096	3,460	3,193	4,189
Earnings per share	3.09	3.75	3.98	5.06	5.6	4.89	4.52	5.75
Dividends per share	1.32	1.4	411.68	1.84	1.92	2	2.04	2.10
Cash flow per share	4.29	5.07	5.55	6.71	7.29	6.65	6.15	7.43
Price: high	85.4	90.3	87.4	88.4	97	84.8	84.3	91.5
low	59.7	73.3	69.7	67	72.9	50	40.9	68.0

3M Center
Building 225-01-S-15
St. Paul, MN 55144–1000
(651) 733–8206
Website: *www.MMM.com*

Abbott Laboratories

Ticker symbol: ABT (NYSE) ❑ S&P rating: AA ❑ Value Line financial strength rating: A++ ❑ Current yield: 3.7%

Company Profile

"A Promise for Life" is the slogan of Abbott Laboratories, founded in 1888 and one of the most diverse health care manufacturers in the world. Abbott is the third largest producer of pharmaceuticals in the United States, behind Johnson & Johnson and Pfizer and is the largest company in the nutritional products market. The company's products are sold in more than 130 countries, with about 40 percent of sales derived from international operations.

Abbott's major business segments include Pharmaceutical Products (particularly in immunology, cardiology, and infectious diseases), Diagnostic Products (laboratory and molecular diagnostics, diabetes, and vision care), Vascular Products (stents and closure devices), and Nutritional Products (infant, adult, and special needs). Pharmaceuticals accounted for just under 54 percent of FY2009 sales.

The company's leading brands include Freestyle (diabetes monitoring), Ensure (nutritional supplements for adults), Humira (rheumatoid arthritis), and Similac (infant formula).

The company has widespread respect among the medical and financial community as one of the most solid and diversified health-related names. In 2010, the company was named *Fortune*'s most admired company in the pharmaceutical industry, up from number four in 2008.

Financial Highlights, Fiscal Year 2010

Abbott turned in solid results for 2010 with double-digit growth for the year. The results included 20 percent–plus growth in the important Pharmaceutical and Vascular segments, reflecting both economic recovery and the $6.2 billion acquisition of Solvay in early 2010, which gave considerable lift and exposure to international and especially developing markets. The economic downturn had definite impact on the business as treatments were delayed, but this company has proven relatively immune to recession compared to many others.

The company's flagship product, Humira, remains a key growth driver with a 22 percent increase year-over-year in 2010 sales. Aside from a handful of new drugs, international growth is outpacing U.S. growth and is a key growth driver for the future. Operating margins have been on the increase in recent years, and the 3.7 percent dividend yield is safe and solid.

Reasons to Buy

This company continues to be a solid performer, and is well diversified both in product line and in geography. The company invests about 9 percent of sales in R&D and appears to get good results from those investments. The dividend yield is healthy and growing and gives good downside protection; overall financials are rock-solid. The company offers an attractive combination of income and long-term growth potential. ABT has paid consecutive quarterly dividends since 1924.

Humira continues to look like a blockbuster, and the company continues to believe that Humira is a platform for a number of future products addressing other autoimmune diseases, which if true, could mean several more years of a very strong product pipeline for Abbott. Humira itself remains under patent protection until 2016.

Reasons for Caution

While the long-term effects of the U.S. health care reform legislation passed in early 2010 are unknown, the early returns appear to be fairly neutral to the large pharmaceuticals. Earlier reform of Medicare drug policy under the Bush administration has settled out and seems to be carried forward under the new plan.

SECTOR: Health Care
BETA COEFFICIENT: .30
10-YEAR COMPOUND EARNINGS PER SHARE GROWTH: 8.0%
10-YEAR COMPOUND DIVIDENDS PER SHARE GROWTH: 9.0%

	2003	2004	2005	2006	2007	2008	2009	2010
Revenues (Mil)	19,681	19,680	22,337	22,476	25,914	29,528	30,764	35,167
Net Income (Mil)	3,479	3,522	3,908	3,841	4,429	4,734	5,745	6,500
Earnings per share	2.21	2.27	2.50	2.52	2.84	3.03	3.69	4.17
Dividends per share	0.98	1.04	1.10	1.18	1.30	1.44	1.60	1.76
Cash flow per share	3.01	3.05	3.42	3.51	4.05	4.32	5.00	5.90
Price: high	47.2	47.6	50.0	49.9	59.5	61.1	57.4	56.8
low	33.8	38.3	37.5	39.2	48.8	45.8	41.3	44.6

Abbott Laboratories
100 Abbott Park Road
Abbott Park, IL 60064–6400
(847) 937-3923
Website: *www.abbott.com*

Aetna Inc.

Ticker symbol: AET (NYSE) ❑ S&P rating: A– ❑ Value Line financial strength rating: A ❑ Current yield: 1.5%

Company Profile

Founded in 1853, Aetna is one of the nation's longest-lived insurers. However, that by itself doesn't qualify the company for our *100 Best Stocks* list. Today's Aetna, a product of a 1996 merger between Aetna Life and Casualty and U.S. Healthcare, is one of the largest and most important diversified health care, insurance, and benefits companies in the United States.

Today, the company has three businesses operated in three divisions. Health Care provides a full assortment of health benefit plans for corporate, small business, and individual customers, including PPO, HMO, point of service, vision care, dental, behavioral health, Medicare/Medicaid, and pharmacy benefits plans. The Group Insurance business provides group term life, disability, and accidental death and dismemberment insurance products primarily to the same sort of businesses that might sign up for its health plans. The Large Case Pensions business administers pension plans for certain existing customers.

The health care business is by far the largest segment and the focal point of our selection of this company. The business insures some 36 million individuals. Now with impending health care reforms, many of which are targeted at the insurance side of the industry, it would normally be hard to recommend such a company because of the uncertainty going forward and the general public dislike of health insurers. However, Aetna has proven itself to be a pacesetter among insurance providers, mainly through its support and innovations in the area of consumer directed health care.

For example, with Aetna's consumer-directed HealthFund plans, subscribers become responsible for a portion of their own health care costs, and are given the tools to shop health care alternatives and maximize preventive care. Aetna originally led the way with some of the first Health Savings Account compatible products in 2001. Since then the company has led the industry in developing tools, such as the Aetna Navigator price transparency tool, designed to help patients evaluate the cost and outcomes of procedures in different geographies. The company also has championed patient- and doctor-accessible medical records and other techniques for making health care delivery more efficient. These initiatives are meant not only to save money for end users, but also the businesses purchasing insurance plans; the company estimates a savings of $21.5 million per 10,000 customers over five years.

Financial Highlights, Fiscal Year 2010

Aetna's high-flying earnings growth subsided considerably in FY2009 as Medicare reimbursements dropped and the mix of business shifted unfavorably with the contraction of business and the loss of more profitable subscribers. Earnings dropped from $3.93 per share in 2008 to $2.75 a share in FY2009. While revenue growth has flattened as business recovers slowly and the effects of the new health care legislation gradually unfold, the company has redirected its efforts to streamlining and improved pricing and underwriting and to reducing administrative costs. Those efforts delivered a healthier $3.68 per share in earnings for FY2010, and Aetna has guided for $3.80–$3.90 per share in FY2011. The company also announced a $.60 per year dividend, a dramatic increase from its previous $.04-cent annual payout and more in line with its earnings and cash flow generation capacity. The company has also repurchased

a substantial number of shares, reducing share count from 610 million in 2003 to about 400 million currently.

Reasons to Buy

We feel that Aetna is ahead of the pack in terms of both business and technology innovation. Not only has this edge started to pay off in terms of increased profitability, it will also serve the company well going forward as it aligns the business to upcoming health care reforms. Many of the innovations the company has championed will also get a favorable ruling in the court of public opinion, which should help. The company has a solid brand and financials, and the new commitment to a reasonable dividend and ongoing share repurchases shows that it has shareholders' interests in mind as well.

Reasons for Caution

Public and governmental scrutiny of health insurers has never been higher, and burgeoning health care costs makes it difficult for even a company of Aetna's caliber to manage. It may become more difficult to pass cost increases on, and the cost of health insurance is simply knocking many potentially lucrative subscribers out of the market. Aetna investors will have to pay attention to ongoing and occasionally disruptive industry change.

SECTOR: **Health Care**
BETA COEFFICIENT: **1.27**
10-YEAR COMPOUND EARNINGS PER SHARE GROWTH: **12.5%**
10-YEAR COMPOUND DIVIDENDS PER SHARE GROWTH: **NM**

	2003	2004	2005	2006	2007	2008	2009	2010
Revenues (Mil)	17,976	19,904	22,492	25,146	27,600	30,951	34,765	34,246
Net Income (Mil)	934	1,215	1,344	1,602	1,842	1,922	1,236	1,555.5
Earnings per share	1.30	1.76	2.23	2.82	3.49	3.93	2.75	3.68
Dividends per share	.01	.01	.02	.04	.04	.04	.04	.04
Cash flow per share	1.86	2.38	2.73	3.63	4.36	5.07	3.83	5.20
Price: high	17.6	31.9	49.7	52.5	60.0	59.8	34.9	36.0
low	10.0	16.4	29.9	30.9	40.3	14.2	16.7	25.0

Aetna, Inc.
151 Farmington Avenue
Hartford, CT 17405–0872
(860) 273-0123
Website: *www.aetna.com*

Air Products, Inc.

Ticker symbol: APD (NYSE) ❑ S&P rating: A ❑ Value Line financial strength rating: A+ ❑ Current yield: 2.2%

Company Profile

Air Products and Chemicals produces and sells gases such as hydrogen, helium, nitrogen, and oxygen to industrial manufacturers and commercial end users worldwide. Gases are vital inputs to many manufacturing processes, and APD is one of the largest global bulk gas sellers. The company operates in more than forty countries and now derives about 54 percent of its sales from outside the United States.

After the Q1 2008 divestiture of the Chemicals business, APD reports revenues in four segments:

■ *Merchant Gases*—Industrial and medical customers throughout the world use oxygen, nitrogen, argon, helium, hydrogen, and medical and specialty gases for a wide array of applications. APD supplies most merchant gas in liquid form to small and larger customers delivered via tanker trucks and rail cars. APD provides smaller quantities of packaged gases for customers who require smaller quantities for their processes.

■ *Tonnage Gases*—Air Products supplies gases via large on-site facilities or pipeline systems to meet the needs of large-volume, or "tonnage" industrial gas users. AP either constructs a gas plant near the customer's facility or delivers product through a pipeline from an existing nearby facility. They also design and manufacture cryogenic and gas-processing equipment for air separation, hydrocarbon recovery and purification, natural gas liquefaction (LNG), and helium distribution equipment.

■ *Electronics and Performance Materials*—This segment specializes in delivery of products relevant to the electronics industry for the production of silicon, semiconductors, displays, and photovoltaic devices. They also provide performance chemical solutions for the coatings, inks, adhesives, civil engineering, personal care, institutional and industrial cleaning, mining, oil field, polyurethane, and other industries.

■ *Equipment and Energy*—This segment designs and sells equipment for energy production and partially owns and operates several small energy plants around the world. Equipment is sold worldwide to customers in a variety of industries, including chemical and petrochemical manufacturing, oil and gas recovery and processing, and steel and primary metals processing.

Financial Highlights, Fiscal Year 2010

APD's customer base is heavily weighted to industrial uses, more specifically manufacturing environments. This resulted in a not-unexpected softening of demand for APD's core products in 2009, but the emerging recovery in 2010 brought earnings up 24 percent from that dismal year. On February 5, 2010, APD announced a tender offer for the outstanding shares of Airgas, Inc. (ARG: NYSE), a producer and distributor of industrial, medical, and specialty gases based in Radnor, Pennsylvania. The offer of $60 per share was a 38 percent premium over ARG's share price on the day of the offer (valuing the deal at about $7 billion). The offer was rejected by Airgas but was extended several times, then sweetened twice

at the end of 2010 to an amount equivalent to $70 per ARG share. After a vigorous campaign by Airgas to maintain its position against the offer, and some court battles, APD withdrew the offer in February 2011.

Reasons to Buy

The Airgas acquisition would have filled some market niches not currently served by APD and would have provided some useful cost-reduction leverage. But even without the acquisition, APD's operating and net profit margins had been improving. Cost-reduction measures combined well with the recovering economy and growing overseas business. The company has delivered double-digit average compounded growth in earnings, dividends, and cash flow per share over the past five years. The company is a solid performer and good player in the global economic recovery.

Reasons for Caution

Without the ARG acquisition, organic growth in 2010 and 2011 will be moderate and cyclical at best. APD could be too dependent on an acquisition like Airgas to fuel growth. Now, however, without the acquisition, the company can focus on its core business; additionally, concerns about paying too much have gone away.

SECTOR: Materials
BETA COEFFICIENT: 1.17
10-YEAR COMPOUND EARNINGS PER SHARE GROWTH: 7.5 %
10-YEAR COMPOUND DIVIDENDS PER SHARE GROWTH: 10.0%

	2003	2004	2005	2006	2007	2008	2009	2010
Revenues (Mil)	6,297	7,411	7,768	8,850	10,038	10,415	8,256	9026
Net Income (Mil)	397	604	712	723	1,036	1,091	866	1,080
Earnings per share	1.78	2.64	3.08	3.18	4.4	4.97	4.06	5.02
Dividends per share	0.88	1.04	1.25	1.34	1.52	1.7	1.79	1.92
Cash flow per share	5.14	5.94	6.49	7.17	8.48	9.36	8.08	9.09
Price: high	53.1	59.2	65.8	72.4	105	106.1	85.4	81.4
low	37	46.7	53	58	68.6	41.5	43.4	64.1

Air Products and Chemicals, Inc.
7201 Hamilton Boulevard
Allentown, PA 18195–1501
(610) 481-5775
Website: *www.airproducts.com*

Alexander & Baldwin

Ticker symbol: ALEX (NASDAQ) □ S&P rating: BBB+ □ Value Line financial strength rating: B+ □
Current yield: 3.2%

Company Profile

An old Hawaiian company with origins dating back to the missionary days of the 1830s, Alexander & Baldwin, Inc., together with its subsidiaries, operates in Ocean Transportation, Real Estate, and Agribusiness. The company offers container ship freight services primarily between Long Beach, California; Oakland, California; Seattle; Hawaii; Guam; China; and other Pacific Islands. Its most recognizable carrier is the wholly owned subsidiary Matson Lines.

The company operates some of the fastest container ships in the Pacific Rim; it also has subsidiaries specializing in logistics, stevedoring, and port services in Hawaii, China, and on the U.S. mainland. Matson is one of the most technologically advanced shipping lines in the world with full Internet booking and shipment tracking capability. In many West Coast ports, Matson operates its own facilities, leading to further streamlining. The transportation business accounted for 86 percent of revenue and 97 percent of profits for 2009, a year in which other businesses struggled; that has

since changed as will be discussed below.

The Real Estate subsidiaries develop and sell residential and commercial property primarily in Hawaii, currently owning over 89,000 acres in the state. This business develops and sometimes owns and operates commercial, industrial, and residential facilities, often located on lands acquired over 100 years ago in use for sugar cane, primarily in Kauai and Maui. The Agribusiness segment specializes in sugar and the production, marketing, and distribution of coffee, and represents a relatively small share of the company's business at 7 percent of revenue. In 2009, the Agribusiness sector operated at a $29 million loss.

Financial Highlights, Fiscal Year 2010

The company earned $1.08 per share in 2009, its lowest tally in over fifteen years. The reasons are understandable with the global shipping slowdown and depressed commodity and real estate prices. The results could have been worse had the company not responded with cost controls as well as they did. A pickup in shipping demand and rising sugar prices combined to make 2010 a much better year than expected, with earnings through the first three quarters coming in at $1.74 versus the company's own forecast of $1.09. For the year, the company earned $2.22 per share, well ahead of 2009 and well ahead of forecast. ALEX is a cyclical business to be sure, but we feel that these results reflect more than just a return to prosperity, although earnings were over $3 during the height of the boom years in 2007.

Reasons to Buy

Alexander & Baldwin is a long-term play on the continued growth and importance of trans-Pacific shipping, combined with the growth and value of Hawaii, Hawaiian real estate, and agriculture. It is a diversified play with healthy niche businesses, strong cash flows, and healthy dividends.

The Jones Act provides that no non-U.S. flagged carrier can operate between Hawaii and other U.S. ports, giving Matson, by far the largest carrier serving Hawaii, a virtual monopoly on that business. Matson's fleet is nonetheless also competitive with Chinese carriers

servicing routes between Hawaii, Guam, and mainland China. Growth in China bodes well for the company, particularly given its strength in "fast" logistics and dedicated port facilities. This is a business where simple, dependable, and fast is good.

Reasons for Caution

The company fights economic cycles; all three of its primary businesses are vulnerable. That said, we think the Matson franchise is one of the best in the China trade and will remain strong in the future even during periods of soft demand. As recently as 2010, the sugar business looked bleak, with sugar prices far below breakeven points. The company considered getting out of sugar altogether, but commodity prices have strengthened overall and the decline of other sugar-producing assets worldwide for similar reasons has left Alexander & Baldwin in a better position today. In addition, we're optimistic that sooner or later, sugar-based ethanol will gain traction in the United States. While these arguments attenuate some of the negatives, Alexander & Baldwin is probably not the best stock to own for those who don't sleep well when economic storm clouds gather.

SECTOR: **Transportation**
BETA COEFFICIENT: **1.40**
10-YEAR COMPOUND EARNINGS PER SHARE GROWTH: **5.5%**
10-YEAR COMPOUND DIVIDENDS PER SHARE GROWTH: **3.0%**

	2003	2004	2005	2006	2007	2008	2009	2010
Revenues (Mil)	1,232	1,494	1,606	1,607	1,681	1,898	1,405	1,846
Net Income (Mil)	81	101	118.7	122	142	132	44.2	92.1
Earnings per share	1.94	2.33	2.7	2.81	3.3	3.19	1.08	2.22
Dividends per share	0.9	0.9	0.9	0.9	1.12	1.24	1.26	1.26
Cash flow per share	3.65	4.19	4.61	4.86	5.54	5.68	3.65	4.85
Price high	34.6	44.7	56.1	54.9	59.4	53.51	35.6	40.5
low	23.5	29	36.8	39.3	44.2	20.6	15.7	26.9

Alexander & Baldwin
822 Bishop Street
Honolulu, HI 96813–3924
(808) 525-6611
Fax: (808) 525-6652
Website: *www.alexanderbaldwin.com*

Allergan, Inc.

Ticker symbol: AGN (NASDAQ) ❑ S&P rating: A+ ❑ Value Line financial strength rating: A+ ❑ Current yield: 0.3%

Company Profile

Allergan is a health care products company making pharmaceutical, over the counter, and medical device items for the ophthalmic, neurological, dermatology, urology markets, and an assortment of aesthetic medical procedures such as breast aesthetics and obesity intervention, and other specialty medical markets. The company was founded in 1977 and originally marketed ophthalmic products for contact lens wearers and other products for eye inflammation and other disorders.

The company operates in two segments. The Specialty Pharmaceuticals Segment markets the ophthalmic products, including contact lens products, glaucoma therapy, artificial tears, and allergy and infection fighting products. Specialty Pharmaceuticals also sells Botox for a variety of medical conditions and for aesthetic use. Botox is used not only for the familiar skin wrinkle therapies, but also for neuromuscular disorders; recently it has been approved for use in treating chronic migraines, a new market with substantial potential. The segment also offers a number of popular skin care and acne medications for both acute care and aesthetic use.

The Medical Devices Segment makes and markets breast implants for augmentation, revision, and reconstructive surgery, and obesity intervention products including the "Lap-Band" system and the Orbera Intragastic Balloon System. The segment also markets other skin and tissue regenerative products for aesthetic and reconstructive purposes for burn treatment and other traumas.

The approximate business breakdown by revenue is 47 percent eye care, 30 percent neuromuscular including Botox, 11 percent breast and facial implants, 6 percent obesity implants, 1 percent urological, and 5 percent other. Foreign sales account for about 35 percent of the total.

Financial Highlights, Fiscal Year 2010

After a modest slowing of revenue and earnings growth during FY2009, the company resumed its growth pace in FY2010 with revenues of approximately $4.9 billion and earnings of

$3.13 per share, roughly a 13 percent increase from the previous year. Operating and net margins continued to expand as post-recession activity shifted customers toward more elective, and more profitable, treatments. Operating margins rose to 34 percent from the mid- to high-20s experienced through most of the previous decade. For FY2011, the company projects revenue between $5.02 billion and $5.22 billion and earnings in the range of $3.54–$3.60 per share.

Reasons to Buy

Allergan tends to be more economically sensitive and cyclical than other pharmaceutical and medical products companies because much of what they sell supports cosmetic, thus elective, and thus cash-paid (in contrast to insurance paid) procedures. Of course, this is a negative when the economy is soft, although the company sells enough regularly required products such as eye care products to not be hurt too much by bad times. We like the issue because it will do especially well in *good* times. Further, with aging and demographics we see a greater trend toward taking care of personal aesthetics through cosmetic procedures. At the same time, new technologies such as a "cohesive-gel" breast implant and others means that taking care of such issues is becoming safer, easier, and more mainstream, a trend that should make the business stronger going forward. New uses for Botox, such as the migraine treatments, overactive bladder symptoms, and others are also promising. We also think the company has strong potential in overseas markets.

Reasons for Caution

All pharmaceutical and medical device products come with an inherent risk of short- and long-term failure with painful financial and brand-image consequences. Cosmetic devices could be even more vulnerable—witness what happened to Dow Corning with breast implants in the 1970s. We also think the time will come soon, if not already, to give more back to the shareholders in terms of dividend and/or share repurchases; the stock price has followed and may have even preceded the company's prospects, which tends to mitigate yield and share repurchases and should make investors shop carefully for buying opportunities.

SECTOR: **Health Care**
BETA COEFFICIENT: **.91**
10-YEAR COMPOUND EARNINGS PER SHARE GROWTH: **4.0%**
10-YEAR COMPOUND DIVIDENDS PER SHARE GROWTH: **17.0%**

	2003	2004	2005	2006	2007	2008	2009	2010
Revenues (Mil)	1,755	2,046	2,318	3,063	3,939	4,403	4,503	4,883
Net Income (Mil)	305	371	477	452	575	786	850	975
Earnings per share	1.14	1.39	1.78	1.51	1.86	2.57	2.78	3.16
Dividends per share	0.18	0.18	0.20	0.20	0.20	0.20	0.20	0.20
Cash flow per share	1.40	1.67	2.07	1.98	2.58	3.46	3.65	4.03
Price: high	40.9	46.3	56.3	61.5	68.1	70.4	64.1	74.9
low	28.3	33.4	34.5	46.3	52.5	29.0	35.4	56.3

Allergan, Inc.
2525 Dupont Drive
Irvine, CA 92612
(714) 246-4500
Website: *www.allergan.com*

Amgen Inc.

Ticker symbol: AMGN (NASDAQ) ❑ S&P rating: A+ ❑ Value Line financial strength rating: A++ ❑ Current yield: Nil

Company Profile

Founded in 1980, Amgen is the world's largest and one of the first independent biotech medicines company. The company develops medicines and therapeutics based on advances in cellular and molecular biology, mainly for grievous or chronic illnesses such as cancer, kidney disease, rheumatoid arthritis, bone disease, inflammation, nephrology, and others.

Interestingly, the company generates most of its approximately $15 billion in revenues each year with nine major products, most of which you won't have heard of unless you have one of these diseases or are in the medical profession: Aranesp, Enbrel, EPOGEN, Neulasia, NEUPOGEN, Nplate, Prolia, Sinsipar, and Vectibix. The explanations of these products are far too technical for most of us to comprehend. Witness company literature describing its products: Neulasta (pegfulgrastim), a pegylated protein based on the Filgrastim molecule, and NEUPOGEN (Filgrastim) a recombinant-methionyl human granulocyte colony-stimulating factor, (G-SCF), both [of which]

stimulate the production of neutrophils (a type of white blood cell that helps the body fight infection)."

Get that? We didn't either, really. Ordinarily we'd be reluctant to recommend a company with only nine products—products we don't really understand—in such an R&D-intensive business and changing technology. But Amgen is an exception—maybe an exception for biotech in general—because it has turned these products into a cash machine. The company earned about $5 billion on that $15 billion in sales with about $6 billion in cash flow and $17 billion in cash on the balance sheet—not bad for a limited product assortment.

The company has made some acquisitions, and recently completed the acquisition of BioVex, a small outfit with a promising technology to stimulate immune system destruction of tumor cells.

Financial Highlights, Fiscal Year 2010

FY2010 revenues came in at just over $15 billion, 3 percent higher than FY2009, with earnings of

$5.15 per share. The company booked about $1.5 billion in net free cash flow to the cash account.

Amgen is part of the pool of drug and health care companies to be negatively affected by the recently passed health care reform legislation. The company estimates a hit of $400–$500 million in revenue, including $150–$200 million in excise fees under the act, compared to a total cost of $200 million in 2010. For FY2011 in total, the company projects revenues between $15.1–$15.5 billion, and earnings between $5.05–$5.20 per share.

Reasons to Buy

Amgen hasn't put any blockbuster new products on the market lately, and as a result, growth rates, once stellar, have moderated. Recent stock prices reflect that, and show what happens when a high-flying, emerging company matures. Yet, the company is regarded as the dominant player in this biotech niche, and has had success with R&D and approval processes thus far. The company just received approval for two new metastatic cancer treatments, and is excited about new prospects from the BioVex acquisition. With a

price-earnings ratio hovering near 10 and the aforementioned cash and cash-generation capability, any uptick in business or new product breakthrough will get the gravy train moving again in our opinion. Amgen is an unusual example of current value combined with a technology expertise and leadership giving strong growth potential for a next leg upward.

Reasons for Caution

With so much R&D and other expense going into a handful of products, any failure or FDA rejection can be very costly. The company, as mentioned, faces some impact from the new health care reform legislation, and initiatives to reduce health care costs could affect Amgen. And, we normally shy away from companies whose products we don't understand. Finally, while the company has very strong financials, there are no cash dividends being paid or any indication of any to come. We feel, especially if the product pipeline has really matured, that the cash and earnings position justifies some current shareholder return, and we hope the company avoids the temptation to make expensive acquisitions going forward.

SECTOR: **Health Care**
BETA COEFFICIENT: **0.45**
10-YEAR COMPOUND EARNINGS PER SHARE GROWTH: **17.0%**
10-YEAR COMPOUND DIVIDENDS PER SHARE GROWTH: **NA**

	2003	2004	2005	2006	2007	2008	2009	2010
Revenues (Mil)	8,356	10,550	12,420	14,268	14,771	15,093	14,642	15,053
Net Income (Mil)	2,259	2,885	3,710	4,181	3,761	4,196	4,931	4,941
Earnings per share	1.69	2.19	2.95	3.51	3.31	3.90	4.83	5.12
Dividends per share	–	–	–	–	–	–	–	–
Cash flow per share	2.30	2.87	3.72	4.41	4.57	5.03	6.01	6.39
Price: high	72.4	66.9	86.9	81.2	76.9	86.5	64.8	81.3
low	48.1	52.0	56.2	63.5	46.2	39.2	45.0	50.3

Amgen Inc.
One Amgen Center Drive
Thousand Oaks, CA 91320
(805) 447-1000
Website: *www.amgen.com*

Apache Corporation

Ticker symbol: APA (NYSE) ❑ S&P rating: A- ❑ Value Line financial strength rating: A ❑ Current yield: 0.5%

Company Profile

Established in 1954 with $250,000 of investor capital, Apache Corporation has grown to become one of the world's top independent oil and gas exploration and production companies and currently has a market cap over $30 billion. Today, Apache is a $43 billion "upstream" oil and gas producer with an effectively deployed strategic portfolio approach to diversification to reduce risk and maximize returns.

Apache's domestic operations focus on some of the nation's most important producing basins, including the Outer Continental Shelf of the Gulf of Mexico, the Anadarko Basin of Oklahoma, the Permian Basin of West Texas and New Mexico, the Texas-Louisiana Gulf Coast, and East Texas. Recently, the company acquired the Gulf Coast assets of Devon Energy and the Permian Basin and New Mexico assets of BP PLC among other acquisitions, giving rise to a 35 percent increase in production during 2010.

In Canada, Apache is active in British Columbia, Alberta, Saskatchewan, and the Northwest Territories. The company also has exploration and production

operations in Australia's offshore Carnarvon, Perth, and Gippsland basins; Egypt's Western Desert; the United Kingdom sector of the North Sea; China; and Argentina.

Apache's strategy is built on a portfolio of assets that provide opportunities to grow through a combination of original exploration, maximizing output on mature fields and acquisition activities. The company has seven core areas—two in the United States, and one each in Canada, Egypt, the North Sea (U.K.), Australia, and Argentina.

The company's portfolio is fairly well balanced in terms of gas versus oil, domestic and international production (in 2010 oil production was 54 percent overseas and 46 percent domestic), all to achieve moderate levels of geologic and political risk and healthy reserve life.

Revenues are 72 percent from oil and liquids and 28 percent from natural gas—a product mix that provides upside potential in either market. Each core area has significant producing assets and large, undeveloped acreage to provide running room for the future, but according to company documents and its philosophy, no single region contributes more than 25 percent of production or reserves. In each core area, the company's goal is to build critical mass that supports sustainable, lower-risk, repeatable drilling opportunities, balanced by higher-risk, higher-reward exploration.

Apache has increased reserves in each of the last twenty-one years and production in twenty-seven of the last twenty-eight years. Management believes the company's portfolio of assets provides a platform for profitable growth through drilling and acquisitions across industry cycles.

Financial Highlights, Fiscal Year 2010

A combination of higher oil prices, recovering demand, and acquisitions led to a healthy earnings recovery in 2010. While not quite approaching 2008 levels, earnings of $3 billion were sizably ahead of the $1.887 billion reported in FY2009, and revenues resumed a growth path. Higher energy prices and integration of recent acquisitions are now expected to deliver an FY2011 revenue total in excess of $15 billion and record earnings of over $4.5 billion, or almost $12.00 per share. With these figures, APA will establish themselves as one of the more profitable firms in the industry.

Reasons to Buy

Apache offers an attractive combination of growth and risk management with considerable earnings and cash flow strength. It may be one of the better-managed oil and gas producers. The company has attained its desired goal of "critical mass" in its major production centers, thus improving long-term profitability. We like the three-dimensional balance portfolio of oil and gas, domestic and international, and exploration versus mature field utilization. The strategies to avoid overconcentration in one region or field and to avoid areas of extreme political risk bode well. Additionally, the company will benefit from strengthening oil prices and from stronger gas prices if that happens, and we believe it will eventually. Apache has made a specialty of buying up older fields and finding ways to profitably extract additional production. This sort of talent will become increasingly useful as easy oil becomes more and more scarce. For the most part, we think Apache's acquisitions have made sense.

Reasons for Caution

Although the company is committed to avoiding overreliance on any particular producing region, almost a third of its 2009 oil production came from its Egyptian fields; this might be a cause for concern, except that 2010 acquisitions coming on line will, at least for now, bring this percentage back closer to 25 percent. The company is also exposed to reduced effectiveness and output from its mature field operation. Finally, in May 2010 the federal government instituted a widely publicized six-month moratorium on all deepwater drilling in U.S. territorial waters in the wake of the BP oil rig blowout in the Gulf of Mexico. Given Apache's recent acquisitions of Mariner's and Devon's deepwater operations in the Gulf, the company continues to be exposed to such moratoriums.

SECTOR: **Energy**
BETA COEFFICIENT: **1.17**
10-YEAR COMPOUND EARNINGS PER SHARE GROWTH: **32%**
10-YEAR COMPOUND DIVIDENDS PER SHARE GROWTH: **17.5%**

	2003	2004	2005	2006	2007	2008	2009	2010
Revenues (Mil)	4,190	5,333	7,584	8,289	9.978	12,389	8,615	12,092
Net Income (Mil)	1,246	1,670	2,618	2,552	2,812	3,912	1,887	3,000
Earnings per share	3.74	5.03	7.84	7.64	8.39	11.65	5.60	8.46
Dividends per share	0.22	0.26	0.36	0.50	0.60	0.60	0.60	0.60
Cash flow per share	7.36	8.80	12.21	13.19	15.48	19.19	12.72	15.81
Price: high	41.7	52.2	78.2	76.2	109.3	149.2	106.5	120.8
low	26.3	36.8	47.4	56.5	63	57.1	51	81.9

Apache Corporation
One Post Oak Central
2000 Post Oak Boulevard, Suite 100
Houston, TX 77056–4400
(713) 296–6662
Website: *www.apachecorp.com*

Apple Inc.

Ticker symbol: AAPL (NASDAQ) ❑ S&P rating: NA ❑ Value Line financial strength rating: A++ ❑ Current yield: nil

Company Profile

Apple Inc. designs, manufactures, and markets personal computers, tablet computers, portable music players, cell phones, and related software, peripherals, and services. It sells these products through its own retail stores, online stores, and third-party and value-added resellers. The company also sells a variety of third-party compatible products such as printers, storage devices, and other accessories through its online and retail stores, and digital content through its iTunes store.

The company's products have become household names: the iPhone, iPod, iPad, and MacBook are just some of the company's hardware products. And while the software may be less well-known, iTunes, QuickTime, and OSX are important segments of the business, each with their own revenue streams.

The company was incorporated in 1977 as Apple Computer, but has since changed its name to simply Apple. The name change in 2007 was the last step in a ten-year retooling that had already changed the company from a personal computer also-ran into one of the most recognizable and profitable consumer electronics brands in the world.

It's hard to imagine the current consumer tech landscape without Apple's presence at the top of the heap. Apple's iconic products have become so successful and its marketing so ubiquitous that if it didn't exist, it seems that we would have to invent something very much like it to fill in the void. Their product line, while comparatively narrow, is focused on areas where the user interface is highly valued, and Apple has leveraged this focus on the user experience into a business that is far and away the most profitable in the industry.

Enhancing the user experience is the industrial design. The Apple design ethic is extraordinarily well executed and is a large part of the value proposition for every product they release. Many of Apple's customers are uncomfortable with any tech product *not* designed around Apple's common content management interface. This overall focus on the user experience has been instrumental in creating an extremely loyal customer base and a brand cachet unequaled in the consumer electronics business. Apple was able to weather the downturn in consumer spending so well in part because many of its customers will forgo other expenditures in order to afford their next Apple purchase.

At various times during 2010 and 2011, Apple's extraordinary business and financial performance has vaulted it to the top of the heap, as the world's most valuable company in terms of market capitalization, even beyond ExxonMobil, Microsoft, and other heavyweights. Another fact: FY2010 earnings exceeded the highest 2004 share price. How many other companies can claim something like that? This is a testimonial to what can happen when a company creates extraordinary value through innovation and marketing excellence.

Financial Highlights, Fiscal Year 2010

Apple continued to fire on all cylinders in FY2010 and the first part of FY2011. Earnings for FY2010 came in at $15.15, almost 2.5 *times* the $6.29 reported for FY2009. Operating margins increased from 22.9 percent to 29.8 percent. For most companies, we're talking about single- or low double-digit increases in these numbers, not multiples! And incidentally, revenues were up just under 50 percent to $65.2 billion. The size and growth in these numbers go a long way toward justifying the high stock valuation, so long as things continue

along this path. In fact, Apple's ten-year earnings growth is 30 percent, a very healthy number when you consider the size of the company and the power of compounding.

This step-up in revenue and profits was due largely to the launch of the iPad and iPad 2 and the continued growth of the iPhone as the de-facto standard in the smartphone business. The momentum should persist, with earnings expected north of $22 per share in FY2011 on revenues north of $98 billion— another 50 percent increase.

Reasons to Buy

For the past five years, Apple has been the 800-pound gorilla of the consumer electronics space. Scratch that—they've been King Kong. Since 2006, revenues have more than tripled and profit has increased over seven-fold. While we here at *100 Best* tend to look favorably on a company that increases its margin by 20–30 basis points per year, Apple, over the five-year period, has increased its net margin by over 1,250 basis points (an average of 250 points per year).

Apple has accomplished this by taking fairly ordinary technology and relatively inexpensive components and putting them together with the utmost in user-centric and "cool" design to become the de facto, "gotta have one" standard. It has, by far, the most loyal customer base in the electronics industry, and it has capitalized on this by offering a regular "consumable" product in addition to its hardware offerings in the form of iTunes. High product margins plus even higher "consumable" margins spells success. It only remains to be seen what other markets, like home TV and home theater, it chooses to get into. If it redefines digital video the way it redefined digital audio, look out.

Reasons for Caution

When you're Number One, everybody wants a piece of the action, and who knows? Someone might succeed in crossing Apple's moat with a better, or at least less expensive, product. The Google Android smartphone operating system and the products that use it seem closest at this point, but that's like saying Mars is close to the Earth. There's still a lot of work to do. Also, it's hard to hit the buy button on such a high-priced stock, although the P/E is a modest 15 and appears to be on the decline as earnings continue to soar. Also, we, as many others, would like to see Apple pay a dividend.

SECTOR: **Consumer Discretionary**
BETA COEFFICIENT: **1.05**
10-YEAR COMPOUND EARNINGS PER SHARE GROWTH: **30%**
10-YEAR COMPOUND DIVIDENDS PER SHARE GROWTH: **Nil**

		2003	2004	2005	2006	2007	2008	2009	2010
Revenues (Mil)		6,207	8,279	13,931	19,315	24,006	32,479	36,537	65,225
Net Income (Mil)		76	276	1,254	1,989	3,496	4,834	5,704	14,013
Earnings per share		0.2	0.36	1.44	2.27	3.93	5.36	6.29	15.15
Dividends per share		0	0	0	0	0	0	0	0
Cash flow per share		0.26	0.54	1.72	2.59	4.37	5.97	7.12	16.42
Price:	high	12.5	34.8	75.5	93.2	203.0	200.3	214	326.7
	low	6.4	10.6	31.3	50.2	81.9	79.1	78.2	190.3

Apple Inc.
1 Infinite Loop
Cupertino, CA 95014
(408) 996-1010
Website: *www.apple.com*

Archer Daniels Midland Co.

Ticker symbol: ADM (NYSE) ❑ S&P rating: A ❑ Value Line financial strength rating: A ❑ Current yield: 2.0%

Company Profile

ADM is one of the largest food processors in the world. It buys corn, wheat, cocoa, oilseeds, and other agricultural products and processes them into food, food ingredients, animal feed and ingredients, and biofuels. It also resells grains on the open market. Rather than the finished consumer products most food processors are known for, ADM produces and distributes intermediate components for food product manufacture and is the largest publicly traded company in this business by far. Exports account for 46 percent of sales.

The company is highly vertically integrated and owns and maintains facilities used throughout the production process. It sources raw materials from sixty countries on six continents, transports them to any of their 230 processing plants via their own extensive sea/rail/road network, and then transports the finished products to the customer.

The company operates in three business segments: Oilseeds Processing, Corn Processing, and Agricultural Services. Revenue and profit percentages are in parentheses:

The Oilseeds Processing unit (43 percent/45 percent) processes soybeans, cottonseed, sunflower seeds, canola, peanuts, and flaxseed into vegetable oils and protein meals for the food and feed industries. Crude vegetable oils are sold as is or are further refined into consumer products, while partially refined oils are sold for use in paints, chemicals, and other industrial products. The solids remaining from this processing are sold for a number of applications, including edible soy protein, animal feed, pharmaceuticals, chemical, and paper.

The Corn Processing segment (13 percent/18 percent) milling operations (primarily in the United States) produce food products too numerous to list, but include syrup, starch, glucose, dextrose, and other sweeteners. Markets served include animal feeds and the vegetable oil market. Fermentation of the dextrose yields ethanol, amino acids, and other specialty food and feed products. The ethanol is processed for beverage stock or industrial use as the base for ethanol-blended gasoline and other fuels.

The Agricultural Services segment (36 percent/22 percent) is the company's storage and transportation network. This business is primarily engaged in buying, storing, cleaning, and transporting grains to/from ADM facilities and for export. It also resells raw materials into the animal feed and agricultural processing industries.

Financial Highlights, Fiscal Year 2010/2011

Fueled by worldwide demand for food products and biofuels, ADM has been on a roll for the past five years, with revenues, earnings, dividends, cash flows, and book value all turning in healthy double-digit increases. Volatility in agricultural commodity prices led to a surprise 25 percent operating profit drop in late 2010, but the core oilseed and corn businesses remained strong through this period. Most estimates suggest a P/E ratio under 10 and a price to cash-flow ratio between 6 and 7, solid figures for a strong player in this key agricultural business.

Reasons to Buy

Core businesses are strong and growing, and China and other emerging markets growth will be particularly strong. The company is and has been a strong player in the biofuels industry. While there are some uncertainties (discussed below) the company's experience and scale in ethanol and biodiesel are strong positives. The federal government recently paved the way to raising ethanol content in motor fuel from 10 percent to 15 percent. This business tends to do well when energy prices escalate, as they have recently. We like the solid track record for growth in shareholder value, which appears to be lagged by the growth in share price.

ADM continues to make acquisitions, most in the emerging markets of Asia and South America. Sales growth outside the United States has far outpaced domestic growth, and ADM's presence and extensive transportation capability give it a decided advantage over its smaller competitors, many of which are focused only in certain markets or certain industries. ADM's market and geographic breadth reduce its exposure to both climatic and political variables.

Reasons for Caution

ADM is heavily invested in the corn-ethanol-fuel processing chain. Continued concern about the efficiency of corn-based ethanol and its effects on food supply lead some to wonder whether the Republican-controlled Congress will abolish the forty-five-cent per gallon tax credit for ethanol production, and there is also concern that the tariff on imported Brazilian sugar-based ethanol may go away. Both would adversely affect ADM's ethanol business. While ethanol prices have strengthened moderately, corn and other commodity prices have risen and become more volatile, adding some risk to the business. That said, the relative price and earnings stability and the low 0.24 beta suggest a stock that lets you sleep at night.

SECTOR: **Consumer Staples**
BETA COEFFICIENT: **0.24**
10-YEAR COMPOUND EARNINGS PER SHARE GROWTH: **16.0%**
10-YEAR COMPOUND DIVIDENDS PER SHARE GROWTH: **11.0%**

	2003	2004	2005	2006	2007	2008	2009	2010
Revenue (Mil)	30,708	36,151	35,944	36,596	44,018	69,816	69,207	61,692
Net Income (Mil)	438	744	921	1,312	1,561	1,834	1,970	1,970
Earnings per share	0.68	1.16	1.40	2.00	2.38	2.84	3.06	3.08
Dividends per share	0.24	0.27	0.32	0.37	0.43	0.49	0.54	.58
Cash flow per share	1.68	2.20	2.44	3.00	3.51	3.97	4.21	4.49
Price:　　high	15.2	22.5	25.5	46.7	47.3	48.9	33.0	34.0
low	10.5	14.9	17.5	24	30.2	13.5	23.1	24.2

Archer Daniels Midland Co.
4666 Faries Parkway, Box 1470
Decatur, IL 62525
(217) 424-5200
Website: *www.admworld.com*

AT&T Inc.

Ticker symbol: T (NYSE) □ S&P rating: A- □ Value Line financial strength rating: A+ □ Current yield: 5.8%

Company Profile

Measured by revenue, AT&T continues to be the world's largest telecommunications holding company. It is the domestic market share leader in local and long-distance voice services, which is hardly a sexy business in the twenty-first century. More importantly, it is the largest provider of consumer, commercial broadband, and wi-fi services in the United States, and has become a large player in IP (Internet-based) television. But the largest portion of the business overall is its AT&T Wireless subsidiary, the leading and probably the most progressive cell phone service provider in the country. Beyond these consumer and commercial products, the company's servers and long-distance lines constitute a major part of the global Internet.

Its traditional wireline subsidiaries offer services in thirteen states, and the wireless business provides voice coverage primarily for traveling U.S. customers and U.S. businesses in 220 countries. It has approximately 150 million total Consumer Revenue Connections, with a sales revenue mix of approximately 49 percent wireless,

21 percent wireline data, 26 percent wireline voice, and 5 percent advertising and other. The company has long been focused on offering "one-stop-shop" services—wireline, data, wireless, and other services with one price on one bill. These efforts have had varying success, but the latest venture called U-verse, an IP-based bundling TV, data, and voice services turning the TV, the PC, and the cell phone into integrated display and transaction devices, is a particularly important development.

In late 2010, AT&T's largest wireless competitor Verizon finally boarded the iPhone and iPad gravy train, formerly the exclusive domain of AT&T. Whether that is a negative remains to be seen. However, in an effort to stay in a position of product and technology leadership, the company made a $2 billion commitment to buy wireless spectrum from Qualcomm Corporation to build out its 4G network for some 230 million potential customers in late 2010.

In early 2011, the company announced a blockbuster acquisition of Deutsche Telekom's T-Mobile subsidiary for $39 billion.

This acquisition, currently under regulatory review, would reduce the number of major wireless competitors from four to three (AT&T, Verizon, and Sprint), give the combined company access to 130 million subscribers, and add to AT&T's presence with budget-conscious "pay-as-you-go" customers. The combined unit could either expand that market or work to upsell them to more profitable smartphone services; the result will probably be a combination of the two. It remains to be seen how this big step in the company's wireless evolution will play out.

Financial Highlights, Fiscal Year 2010

AT&T reported moderate earnings declines through the recession and has seen some margin pressure from the competitive cell phone environment, as consumers migrated to less expensive or pay-as-you-go plans and handset subsidies increased. That said, a 9 percent compounded revenue growth over the last five years is healthy for a company of this size, and the company continues to forecast a 7 percent growth rate for 2011. Operating margins are healthy at 21 percent of revenues versus about 11.5 percent for the industry. Recent reported results show modest earnings growth, and the dividend, P/E ratio (12.4), and

price to cash flow of about 5 all suggest financial strength and steady income returns for customers.

Reasons to Buy

AT&T is particularly well positioned today to capitalize on its breadth and its recent investments. For now, the company is still the main provider of wireless services for the successful iPhone and iPad products and is working on a large 4G wireless network. The combination of technology innovation and product marketing leadership should bode well for the future; we continue to believe that U-verse is a very attractive product for customers in the digital transition—people who are in the process of rolling over to their first broadband connection, or those who are consolidating voice, data, and TV into one provider. It allows AT&T to retain what would have been lost AT&T customers and to capture new customers who are discarding their old wired voice service. In the process, AT&T trades one low-value voice connection for a very high value data link, through which they can provide upselling opportunities for additional services that cost very little more to deliver.

If AT&T is able to manage this rollover business well (and so far, it appears that they are), then their dull, boring, unprofitable wireline customers become a field of opportunity. Not only that, but many of the smaller regional carriers in the country with a similar customer base become attractive buyout opportunities as well.

Finally, the company may be able to find more value in its leadership as a wi-fi services provider, with its 23,000 hot spots in the United States and 125,000 worldwide.

Reasons for Caution

The wireless business continues to be very competitive, with service revenues per unit flat to slightly declining. The company's apparent attempts to upgrade as many wireless customers as possible to data-connected smartphone services

may have appeared more successful than they were because of the iPhone exclusivity, which will end soon. This may lead to an erosion in revenue and profitability unless the company is consistently able to deliver more value through its U-verse bundle, a successful 4G rollout, and broader perceptions of having the best and widest wireless network available. Wireline revenue has been declining for years as well, but those declines have lost momentum. Finally, while some of the cost of new wireless and data networks are already behind the company, AT&T will always face large capital investment requirements.

SECTOR: **Telecommunications Services**
BETA COEFFICIENT: **0.68**
10-YEAR COMPOUND EARNINGS PER SHARE GROWTH: **4.2%**
10-YEAR COMPOUND DIVIDENDS PER SHARE GROWTH: **5.5%**

	2003	2004	2005	2006	2007	2008	2009	2010
Revenues (Mil)	40,843	40,787	43,862	63,055	118,928	124,028	123,018	124,399
Net Income (Mil)	5,051	4,884	5,803	9,014	16,950	12,867	12,535	13,612
Earnings per share	1.52	1.47	1.72	2.34	2.76	2.16	2.12	2.35
Dividends per share	1.37	1.25	1.29	1.22	1.42	1.60	1.64	1.68
Cash flow per share	3.91	3.77	3.42	4.63	5.36	5.56	5.46	5.60
Price: high	31.7	27.7	26.0	36.2	43.0	41.9	29.5	29.6
low	18.8	23.0	21.8	24.2	32.7	20.9	21.4	23.8

AT&T Inc.
208 S. Akard Street
Dallas, TX 75202
(210) 821-4105
Website: *www.att.com*

Automatic Data Processing, Inc.

Ticker symbol: ADP (NYSE) ❑ S&P rating: AAA ❑ Value Line financial strength rating: A++ ❑
Current yield: 2.9%

Company Profile

"The Business behind Business" is the rather apt slogan employed by Automatic Data Processing, or ADP, as it is more widely known. ADP is the nation's largest provider of outsourced employer payroll, tax processing, employee benefits, and other automated and non-automated human resources (HR) and other business services.

The Employer Services unit accounts for about 72 percent of revenues and is engaged in payroll, tax, and other transaction processing for about 550,000 employers worldwide. These transactions include paychecks, direct deposit, FICA withholding tax payments, retirement and other benefits services, and reporting. About 80 percent of this business is in the United States, 13 percent in Europe, 5 percent in Canada, and 2 percent in Asia and Latin America.

The Professional Employer Organization Services unit provides a more complete, seamless HR back-end solution, branded as "TotalSource," for about 5,600 clients, including personal HR consultation for employees and retirement

plan administration. There are forty-seven TotalSource offices in twenty-two states. This unit accounts for about 14 percent of the business.

The remainder of ADP's business is primarily made up of the Dealer Services unit. Dealer Services provides a comprehensive and integrated dealership management solution (DMS), with bundled hardware and software designed to manage all dealership operations including sales management, inventory, HR, procurement, factory communications, warranty, accounting, and other functions. This DMS product is used by auto, truck, marine, motorcycle, and heavy equipment dealers, among others.

Recently the company has made a series of small acquisitions to expand into other vertical industries. A good example is AdvanceMD, a privately held provider of practice management and electronic health records systems for small and mid-sized medical practices. Another is Byte Software House S.p.A., an Italian payroll and HR software and service provider. Others include Cobalt; Workscape, Inc. DO2 Technologies; OneClick

HR; and others in the HR and office processing space.

Financial Highlights, Fiscal Year 2010

ADP's products and services are directly tied to the level of employment, so one wouldn't have been surprised to see a pretty substantial top and bottom line hit during the 2008-09 time period. Yet, the company didn't really see any sort of pullback but rather a flattening in both lines. Now, as employment gradually recovers, that should translate directly into demand for payroll and other employee services. The company earned $2.39 per share in FY2010, exactly the same figure as FY2009, on revenues of $8.9 billion, again almost flat revenues. ADP, like many of the companies it supports, learned how to streamline operations during this period. For FY2011, the company expects some acquisition costs, but also expects revenue to grow about 5 percent (9 percent including the acquisitions), with a 5 percent growth in earnings. The company also increased its dividend in late 2010 to an indicated $1.44 per share, and has been fairly aggressive in share buybacks, reducing share counts by about 100 million

shares, to 492 million shares, since 2004. The company has only $35 million in long-term debt, less than 0.5 percent of total capital.

Reasons to Buy

While not an exceptional growth business, ADP is a good, safe, and steady way to play the normal growth in the economy, with a bit of a short-term kicker in the form of the economic recovery. The company has a good brand in the business, and with the exception of PayChex (another *100 Best Stock*), has little substantial competition, and should own, or co-own, this niche for a long time to come. Outsourcing trends should push more business their way, while acquisitions make the offering more complete and achieve international expansion. The company has been fair to shareholders, giving them "raises" in the form of increased dividends in each of the last seventeen years.

Reasons for Caution

Aside from not being a growth star, the company is also somewhat vulnerable to economic downturns. That said, the most recent one didn't hurt them much.

SECTOR: **Information Technology**
BETA COEFFICIENT: **.64**
10-YEAR COMPOUND EARNINGS PER SHARE GROWTH: **8.0%**
10-YEAR COMPOUND DIVIDENDS PER SHARE GROWTH: **15 .0%**

		2003	2004	2005	2006	2007	2008	2009	2010
Revenues (Mil)		7,147	7,754	8,499	8,881	7,800	8,776	8,867	8,927
Net Income (Mil)		1,018	936	1,055	1,072	1,021	1,162	1,208	1,207
Earnings per share		1.67	1.56	1.79	1.85	1.83	2.20	2.39	2.39
Dividends per share		0.48	0.54	0.61	0.68	0.83	1.04	1.24	1.34
Cash flow per share		2.17	2,12	2.34	2.42	2.30	2.74	2.85	2.92
Price:	high	40.8	47.3	48.1	49.9	51.5	46.0	44.5	47.3
	low	27.2	38.6	40.4	42.5	43.9	30.8	32.0	28.5

Automatic Data Processing, Inc.
1 ADP Boulevard
Roseland, NJ 07068
(973) 974-5000
Website: *www.adp.com*

CONSERVATIVE GROWTH

C.R. Bard, Inc.

Ticker symbol: BCR (NYSE) □ S&P rating: A □ Value Line financial strength rating: A++ □ Current yield: 0.8%

Company Profile

Founded in 1907 by Charles Russell Bard, the company markets a wide range of medical, surgical, diagnostic, and patient-care devices. It markets its products worldwide to hospitals, individual health care professionals, extended care facilities, and alternate site facilities. Most of Bard's products fall into the category of consumables/supplies— intended to be used once and then discarded. The company operates in four core segments: Urology, Oncology, Vascular, and Surgery.

■ *Urology* (27 percent of sales)—The company offers a complete line of urological diagnosis and intervention products including Foley catheters (the market leader and their largest-selling product), procedure kits and trays, urethral stents, and specialty devices for incontinence.

■ *Oncology* (27 percent of sales)— Bard's products are designed for the detection and treatment of various types of cancer. Products include specialty access catheters and ports, gastroenterological products, and biopsy devices. The company's chemotherapy products serve a well-established market in which Bard holds a major market position.

■ *Vascular* (27 percent of sales)—The company's line of vascular diagnosis and intervention products includes peripheral angioplasty stents, catheters, guide wires, introducers and accessories, vena cava filters, and implantable blood vessel replacements. They also sell electrophysiology products such as cardiac mapping and laboratory systems, which support sales of the consumables.

■ *Surgical Specialties* (15 percent of sales)—Surgical specialties products include meshes for vessel and hernia repair; irrigation devices for orthopedic and laparoscopic procedures; and topical hemostatic devices.

Bard markets its products through twenty-two subsidiaries and a joint venture in over a hundred countries outside the United States, with international comprising about 31 percent of sales. Principal markets are Japan, Canada, the United Kingdom, and continental Europe.

Financial Highlights, Fiscal Year 2010

The company continued a steady march forward in sales and per-share earnings for 2010, although total earnings stalled a bit at $509 million for the year. Bard is also raising R&D expenditures in line with sales and has made a few pinpoint acquisitions to bolster its product lines. The company continued to do share buybacks, reducing outstanding share counts approximately 3 percent after a 5 percent reduction in 2009.

Reasons to Buy

Bard has a broad and well-diversified product line of consumables in a market that has been nearly recession-proof. No single segment dominates the business. Health care spending continues to grow ahead of inflation, and the majority of Bard's products fall into the area of non-discretionary purchases.

They have the number one or number two market position across nearly 80 percent of their product line, and their product line recognizes and addresses a number of compelling trends: an aging demographic and the shift

to lower-cost, patient-assisted (in-home) therapy.

The company has been successful with recent acquisitions, and remains well positioned to continue this strategy. They have large reserves of capital and low levels of debt. Bard has stated its intention to grow its R&D investment by up to 400 basis points (4 percent) through the next two to three years, and acquisitions have been one of the favorite tools.

We also like the company's stability, with a beta correlation of only 0.32, the shares are downdraft-resistant. Additionally, compared to many medical product manufacturers, Bard's products entail relatively little risk of recalls or events of that sort.

Reasons for Caution

Bard cannot afford to out-research their much larger competitors (St. Jude Medical, Boston Scientific, Johnson & Johnson) and so tends to acquire R&D properties on the open market. This is a more expensive method of funding R&D, to be sure, and it's an operating model that requires far more liquidity than internally developed IP might. The model works for Bard, but if for whatever reason maintaining this high liquidity becomes an issue, it could hamper Bard's top-line growth. We also feel the dividend, which lags sales and earnings growth considerably, could be a bit more generous given the industry, cash flow, and solid financials. While some cash is being used for share repurchases, the combination of cash flow and low dividends tends to signal "acquisition," which brings some risk to the business.

SECTOR: **Consumer Health Care**
BETA COEFFICIENT: **.60**
10-YEAR COMPOUND EARNINGS PER SHARE GROWTH: **17.0%**
10-YEAR COMPOUND DIVIDENDS PER SHARE GROWTH: **5.5%**

	2003	**2004**	**2005**	**2006**	**2007**	**2008**	**2009**	**2010**
Revenues (Mil)	1,433	1,656	1,771	1,985	2,202	2,452	2,535	2,720
Net Income (Mil)	204	263	327	352	406	455	510	509
Earnings per share	1.94	2.45	3.12	3.29	3.84	4.44	4.79	5.53
Dividends per share	0.45	0.47	0.5	0.54	0.58	0.62	0.66	0.70
Cash flow per share	2.4	3.03	3.76	4.14	4.85	5.5	6.29	6.55
Price: high	40.8	65.1	72.8	85.7	95.3	101.6	88.4	95.7
low	27	40.1	60.8	59.9	76.6	70	68.9	75.2

C.R. Bard, Inc.
730 Central Avenue
Murray Hill, NJ 07974
(908) 277–8413
Website: *www.crbard.com*

AGGRESSIVE GROWTH

Baxter International, Inc.

Ticker symbol: BAX (NYSE) ❑ S&P rating: A+ ❑ Value Line financial strength rating: A++ ❑ Current yield: 2.5%

Company Profile

Baxter International develops, manufactures, and markets biopharmaceuticals, drug delivery systems, and medical equipment. Their products are used to treat patients with hemophilia, immune deficiencies, infectious diseases, cancer, kidney disease, and other disorders. Based in the United States, Baxter has operations in over 100 countries and operates in three main segments: Bioscience, Medication Delivery, and Renal.

The Bioscience segment comprises 45 percent of the business and produces pharmaceuticals derived from blood plasma. The bulk of the product line is devoted to treatments for hemophilia and other bleeding disorders, and plasma-based therapies to treat immune deficiencies, burns and shock, and other chronic and acute blood-related conditions. It also includes biosurgery products and vaccines.

The Medication Delivery business is about 37 percent of the business and produces a wide range of equipment used to apply, inject, infuse, and otherwise deliver fluids and medications to the patient. Products include intravenous administration sets, premixed drugs and drug-reconstitution systems, and prefilled vials, syringes for injectable drugs, IV nutrition products, infusion pumps, inhalation anesthetics, and pharmacy compounding and packaging technologies.

The Renal business is about 18 percent of the total and is focused on the treatment of patients with kidney failure who are undergoing peritoneal dialysis treatment. They supply a range of products, including home PD machines and all of the accessories and disposables associated with them, as well as equipment and supplies for clinical dialysis facilities.

Product sales are split fairly evenly between the United States and Europe with the rest of world making up the balance. International sales are about 58 percent of the total.

Financial Highlights, Fiscal Year 2010

Despite the recession, Baxter had earnings in 2009 even with a modest 2 percent increase in revenues. Reduced hospital admissions and fewer surgical procedures have diminished the BioScience division somewhat, but the Medical Delivery segment continues strong. Earnings are on track for a 2011 EPS of $4.25, up from just $1.52 in 2005 and representing a healthy 14.5 percent compounded earnings growth rate over the past five years. Operating and net profit margins have increased steadily through this period.

Reasons to Buy

Baxter is a solid play on medical supplies for recurring or chronic diseases, and will do well as the population ages.

Over the past five years, Baxter's total shareholder return is nearly 85 percent, while the S&P 500's return over the same period is, not surprisingly, down 9 percent. What is surprising is Baxter's performance against the S&P Healthcare Sector, which over the past five years is up a rather paltry 5 percent. Why is Baxter beating its sector index? Baxter's focus on treatments for long-term, chronic, life-threatening conditions has largely insulated them from demand fluctuations; their international market presence has allowed them to serve the fastest growing markets; and their high market penetrations offer further protection from smaller, local competition.

The company has thirty products in its pipeline with targeted peak sales of $250 million each, and over half of those are already in Phase III clinical trials, including a treatment for some of the most debilitating symptoms associated with Alzheimer's disease. Baxter's steadily improving cash flow (up 18 percent in 2009) looks to be more than sufficient to grow its R&D budget while continuing to fund share repurchase and its steadily growing dividend.

The company's ADVATE product continues to gain momentum and reached sales of $2.05 billion in 2009. It holds leadership positions in the United States, Europe, Japan, and several other markets. Looking forward to continued growth, the company believes that some 70 percent of the world's hemophilia patients are currently undiagnosed and that only 25 percent of those diagnosed are receiving adequate care.

The company is gaining strength in the lucrative plasma market, and is hopeful to bring a major new Alzheimer's drug to market after trials expected to be completed in 2012.

Reasons for Caution

Health care reform and related spending slowdowns may cut into demand for some of Baxter's products. The company has at times had problems with some of its products, leading to recalls and softened demand.

SECTOR: **Health Care**
BETA COEFFICIENT: **0.51**
10-YEAR COMPOUND EARNINGS PER SHARE GROWTH: **10.5%**
10-YEAR COMPOUND DIVIDENDS PER SHARE GROWTH: **4.5%**

	2003	2004	2005	2006	2007	2008	2009	2010
Revenues (Mil)	8,916	9,509	9,849	10,378	11,263	12,348	12,562	13,056
Net Income (Mil)	922	1,040	958	1,464	1,826	2,155	2,330	2,368
Earnings per share	1.52	1.68	1.52	2.23	2.79	3.38	3.8	3.98
Dividends per share	0.58	0.58	0.58	0.58	0.72	0.91	1.07	1.18
Cash flow per share	2.4	2.66	2.46	3.13	3.8	4.52	5.02	5.25
Price: high	31.3	34.8	41.1	48.5	61.1	71.5	61	61.9
low	18.2	27.1	33.1	35.1	46.1	47.4	45.5	40.3

Baxter International, Inc.
1 Baxter Parkway
Deerfield, IL 60015
Website: *www.baxter.com*

CONSERVATIVE GROWTH

Becton, Dickinson and Company

Ticker symbol: BDX (NYSE) ❑ S&P rating: AA- ❑ Value Line financial strength rating: A++ ❑
Current yield: 2.0%

Company Profile

Becton, Dickinson is a global medical technology company broadly focused on improving drug delivery, enhancing the diagnosis of infectious diseases and cancers, and advancing drug discovery. The company develops, manufactures, and sells medical supplies, devices, laboratory instruments, antibodies, reagents, and diagnostic products through its three segments: BD Medical, BD Diagnostics, and BD Biosciences. These products are sold to health care institutions, life science researchers, clinical laboratories, the pharmaceutical industry, and the general public. International sales account for about 56 percent of the total. BD is a familiar brand both for observant patients in clinics, medical offices, and hospitals and for the nursing and medical community.

The company operates in three worldwide business segments: Medical (51 percent of FY 2010 sales), Biosciences (32 percent), and Diagnostics (17 percent).

The Medical segment produces a variety of drug delivery devices and supplies, including hypodermic needles and syringes, infusion therapy devices, intravenous catheters, insulin injection systems, regional anesthesia needles, and pre-fillable drug-delivery systems for pharmaceutical companies.

BD Diagnostics offers system solutions for collecting, identifying, and transporting blood and other specimens, as well as instrumentation for analyzing these specimens. Testing systems include those for sexually transmitted diseases, microorganism identification drug susceptibility, and certain types of cancer screening. The business also provides customer training and business management services.

BD Biosciences provides research tools and reagents to accelerate the pace of biomedical discovery. Clinicians and researchers use BD Biosciences' tools to study genes, proteins, and cells to understand disease, improve technologies for diagnosis and disease management, and facilitate the discovery and development of new therapeutics.

Financial Highlights, Fiscal Year 2010

In a year of difficult compares because of the H1N1 scare in the prior year, the company reported basically flat revenues and slightly increased earnings (3.6 percent) for FY2010. Comparisons were also difficult because of the divestiture of the Ophthalmic Systems, surgical blades, critical care, and extended dwell catheter businesses during the year, which netted a one-time gain but took approximately $200 million in revenue and $0.20 per share away from earnings. The published numbers reflect these changes, and the company has been making some other small acquisitions and resource commitments to fill the gap in a manner more aligned with the company's overall strategy. The company also announced an aggressive continuation of share repurchase activities, targeting $1.5 billion in buybacks in 2011 and $600 million in 2012.

Reasons to Buy

Becton, Dickinson continues to be as recession-proof as any stock on our list, while also offering decent growth potential, especially in earnings, cash flow, and dividends. The company has achieved double-digit growth in earnings, cash flow, dividends, and book value for the past ten years, and revenue growth has

only slightly missed that mark. Operating margins have steadily improved from about 25 percent ten years ago to about 30 percent currently. The company is well branded and well established in all of its markets, and it offers a solid way to play the long-term "health" of the health care industry. Share repurchases planned for 2011 and 2012 account for almost 10 percent of share float, a healthy figure. In this case, we think they suggest an above-average cash flow generation rather than a dearth of investment opportunities.

Reasons for Caution

Continued uncertainty surrounding the health care issue in the United States has to be considered when looking at any stock in this sector. Due to the basic and necessary nature of the bulk of their product line, we feel BD is well positioned to sail though these waters without getting swamped, but a re-evaluation of BD would make sense once the policy issues have been settled. There is also a general softening in elective and postponable medical procedures in response to the recession; it is still unclear whether these procedures will return to full volume any time soon.

SECTOR: **Health Care**
BETA COEFFICIENT: **.59**
10-YEAR COMPOUND EARNINGS PER SHARE GROWTH: **13.0%**
10-YEAR COMPOUND DIVIDENDS PER SHARE GROWTH: **14.5%**

	2003	2004	2005	2006	2007	2008	2009	2010
Revenues (Mil)	4,528	4,935	5,415	5,835	6,560	7,156	7,160	7,372
Net Income (Mil)	547	582	692	841	978	1,128	1,220	1,185
Earnings per share	2.07	2.21	2.66	3.28	3.84	4.46	4.95	4.94
Dividends per share	0.4	0.6	0.72	0.86	0.98	1.14	1.32	1.48
Cash flow per share	3.63	4.13	4.60	5.08	5.82	6.60	7.13	7.25
Price: high	41.8	58.2	61.2	74.2	85.9	93.2	80.0	80.6
low	28.8	40.2	49.7	58.1	69.3	58.1	60.4	66.5

Becton, Dickinson and Company
1 Becton Drive
Franklin Lakes, NJ 07417–1880
(201) 847–5453
Website: *www.bd.com*

Bed Bath and Beyond Inc.

Ticker symbol: BBBY (NASDAQ) ❏ S&P rating: BBB ❏ Value Line financial strength rating: A++ ❏
Current yield: Nil

Company Profile

Founded in 1971, Bed Bath &
Beyond (BB&B) and its subsidiaries sell a wide assortment of goods,
primarily domestics merchandise
and home furnishings, but including food, giftware, health and
beauty care items, and infant and
toddler merchandise. With over
1,100 stores in the United States,
Canada, and Mexico, the company
has strong geographic coverage and
a growing web presence—their
goal is to be the customer's first
choice for the merchandise categories offered. BB&B competes on
the breadth and depth of its product offerings, its focus on the home
and personal care, its customer service, new merchandise offerings,
and low prices.

The company also owns
(through acquisition) and operates
three other retail chain concepts.
Its CTS (Christmas Tree Shops)
chain counts sixty-one stores in
fifteen states. There are forty-five
Harmon stores in three states, and
twenty-nine buybuy BABY stores
in fourteen states. Additionally, the
web presence has grown through
BB&B's own website and emerging separate sites for buybuy BABY

and Harmon FaceValues Discount
Health & Beauty sites. The latter in
particular is worth a glance at *www
.facevaluesonline.com.*

The buybuy BABY stores offer
over 20,000 products for infants and
toddlers, including cribs, dressers,
car seats, strollers and highchairs,
feeding, nursing, bath supplies,
and everyday consumables, as well
as toys, activity centers, and development products. The stores are
equipped with private feeding and
changing rooms and offer home
delivery and setup on everything
they sell.

Founded on Cape Cod in
1970, Christmas Tree Shops is a
value-priced retailer of home décor,
giftware, housewares, food, paper
goods, and seasonal products. The
stores specialize in low-cost merchandise with frequent changes in
mix to generate continued interest.

These specialty stores thus far
account for only a small portion of
revenue and profits, although company documents don't break the
percentage down specifically. The
company is also dabbling in international markets, with stores in
Canada and Puerto Rico. In addition, the company is a partner in

a joint venture that operates two stores in the Mexico City market under the name Home & More.

Financial Highlights, Fiscal Year 2010

Boosted by the economic recovery and what we perceive to be effective management, the company achieved solid top line and especially bottom line growth during 2010 and early 2011.

Top line same-store sales grew at a 7 percent clip and were expected to continue that pace through 2011. Effective cost management resulted in an even faster growth in earnings. A reduction in SG&A from 28.7 percent to 27 percent of sales spurred a return of overall operating margins to 16 percent, up from just under 12 percent during the recession and closer to what was experienced during the economic boom.

Even more enticing is the company's aggressive share repurchase program, which reflects the strong cash and cash generation position it enjoys. The company repurchased 5 million shares in late 2010 and authorized a new $2 billion share repurchase program during that period, representing nearly 20 percent of its outstanding market capitalization. From 2004 through the fiscal third quarter of 2010, BB&B has returned approximately $2.6 billion to shareholders through share repurchases.

Reasons to Buy

Occasionally a retailer hits on a formula that works, and this one works well in its market and among other market participants. On the upper end are specialty shops like Restoration Hardware and Williams-Sonoma, competing on "fancy" with strong merchandising and shopping experiences but with high prices, relatively limited selection, and difficult mall access; at the low end lies Wal-Mart and others with assortments of name brand goods at low prices, but perhaps not such a complete assortment. BB&B fills the gap, stocking more products per category than its competitors and arranging its stores so as to emphasize the number of products per category. The BB&B format has not yet reached saturation levels, as there appears to be room for another 500 stores in the United States and Canada. The company's move into other formats, buybuy BABY in particular, comes along at just the right time, as BB&B is generating more than enough cash to fund its own expansion. The company plans to take CTS and buybuy BABY nationwide, and looks to be able to fund the expansion with free cash flow.

The exit of Linens 'N Things from the market in 2009 continues to benefit the company, and we continue to like BB&B's position in the market. The specialty stores and international markets give the company ample growth room in addition to its own branded stores. Finally, we like the management focus on profitability and shareholder value as demonstrated through the share repurchases. The Value Line "A++" financial strength rating is unusual for a retailer and a company with BB&B's growth potential.

Reasons for Caution

Two cautions that dog all specialty retailers: first, the concept may tire and get stale; consumers are fickle and may move on to something else. Second, a new competitor, not yet present on the horizon, may emerge to facilitate this process, much as Lowe's did to Home Depot several years back. Investors should consistently reaffirm this company's dominance in its niche.

SECTOR: **Retail**
BETA COEFFICIENT: **1.22**
10-YEAR COMPOUND EARNINGS PER SHARE GROWTH: **19.0%**
10-YEAR COMPOUND DIVIDENDS PER SHARE GROWTH: **Nil**

		2003	2004	2005	2006	2007	2008	2009	2010
Revenues (Mil)		4,478	5,147	5,810	6,617	7,049	7,208	7,829	8,759
Net Income (Mil)		400	505	573	611	563	425	600	791
Earnings per share		1.31	1.65	1.92	2.15	2.10	1.64	2.30	3.07
Dividends per share		–	–	–	–	–	–	–	–
Cash flow per share		1.61	2.05	2.43	2.68	2.78	2.31	2.98	3.65
Price:	high	45	44.4	47	41.7	43.3	34.7	40.2	50.9
	low	30.2	33.9	35.5	30.9	28	16.2	19.1	26.5

Bed Bath and Beyond Inc.
650 Liberty Avenue
Union, NJ 07083
(908) 688-0888
Website: *www.bedbathandbeyond.com*

AGGRESSIVE GROWTH

Best Buy Company

Ticker symbol: BBY (NASDAQ) ❑ S&P rating: BBB- ❑ Value Line financial strength rating: A ❑ Current yield: 1.8%

Company Profile

Best Buy is a multinational retailer of technology and entertainment products and services with 3,800 stores in the United States, Canada, Europe, China, Mexico, and Turkey. The company's retailers include Best Buy, with about 1,081 of the familiar "big-box" outlets in the United States, as well as Best Buy Mobile, Audiovisions, The Carphone Warehouse, Future Shop, Geek Squad, Jiangsu Five Star, Magnolia Audio Video, Napster, Pacific Sales, and The Phone House. The company has 180,000 employees working through retail locations, call centers, and websites, and providing in-home solutions and product delivery.

Founded in 1966, Best Buy's product portfolio is dominated by consumer electronics (about 40 percent) and home office products (about 33 percent). The company operates in two reporting segments, Domestic (all U.S.–based operations in all segments) and International.

The various retailers have up to six different revenue categories each, with U.S. Best Buy and the Canadian Future Shop stores offering the broadest selection of merchandise. Other stores offer a subset of the six categories, which include consumer electronics, home office, entertainment software, appliances, services, and other. The services revenue category consists primarily of service contracts, extended warranties, computer-related services, product repair, and delivery and installation for home theater, mobile audio, and appliances.

The company has a conscious strategy to create a successful total experience for its customers, with advice and assistance both for product purchase and for installation and support after the sale. The prominently branded "Geek Squad" in-store and mobile services are at the center of this effort. We like the company's mantra: "We make technology deliver on its promises."

Financial Highlights, Fiscal Year 2011 (ended February 2011)

After ringing sales, same-store sales, and gross margin gains through most of FY2011, the company reported a sharp and somewhat surprising slowdown at the end of calendar year 2010 just as the holiday shopping season got into full swing. Although the company met its profits targets in part due to share buybacks, same-store sales fell some 5 percent from a year earlier (an admittedly tough comparison because the Windows 7 rollout happening during the earlier period). Driven in part by decreasing prices and increased ease of buying flat screen televisions, the company cited loss of market share to discount retailer Wal-Mart and to Amazon.com. The company lowered its FY2011 guidance approximately 10 percent.

The company continues to be a prodigious generator of cash flow, especially for a relatively low margin retail business. Value Line projects cash flow of $6.65 per share in FY2011, a healthy sum for shares selling mainly in the 30s and 40s, and with capital needs for store expansion slowing. With the exception of a flat 2008, cash flow per share has increased steadily and substantially each year.

Reasons to Buy

Best Buy, more than most technology retailers, seems to have grasped the notion that they can increase the size of most tickets if the salesperson applies some expertise to what the customer is saying, and what customers really need beyond the product itself. The company wants to sell the *connectedness* of its products, and it seems that they are providing their salespeople with the proper tools and training to do so. The "Geek Squad" offering further supports this notion with an aptly branded configuration and tech support service. More than other retailers, Best Buy sells solutions, and customers have responded well while the company has expanded its margins as a result. We like this approach.

The company enjoyed a natural and fairly effortless gain in market share with the 2009 demise of Circuit City. Now the forces of Wal-Mart, Target, Amazon, and others give the company a challenge to hold onto that market share. We feel that these stores primarily compete in the low-end part of the market, where solutions and service are less important. These forces may drive Best Buy toward more upscale customers and vice versa, which might be a favorable outcome. The focus on solutions, plus continued expansion overseas, should help BBY weather the storm. The stock price "markdown" at the end of 2010 to the low to mid 30s, with a dividend approaching 2 percent, may have made the shares a true Best Buy. We think the company has the brand, the positioning, and the management talent to deal with, and capitalize on, the challenge.

Reasons for Caution

Those who can't stomach some uncertainty as the company strives to adapt to change and make solutions a bigger component of the business might want to steer clear. Additionally, the recent trend for shoppers with smartphones and "comparison apps" to comparison shop and order right from the store floor may be troubling short term, but smart retailers will learn to use this new connectivity to pitch their own specials. We expect Best Buy to figure this one out and lead the pack, and to "dive in headlong" as Chief Marketing Officer Barry Judge was recently quoted as saying.

SECTOR: **Retail**
BETA COEFFICIENT: **1.45**
10-YEAR COMPOUND EARNINGS PER SHARE GROWTH: **28.5%**
10-YEAR COMPOUND DIVIDENDS PER SHARE GROWTH: **11%**

	2003	2004	2005	2006	2007	2008	2009	2010
Revenues (Mil)	20,946	24,547	30,848	35,934	40,023	45,015	49,694	50,272
Net Income (Mil)	622	800	966	1,140	1,377	1,407	1,208	1,342
Earnings per share	1.27	1.63	1.91	2.27	2.79	3.12	2.88	3.15
Dividends per share	–	0.27	0.27	0.31	0.36	0.46	0.53	0.56
Cash flow per share	1.93	2.43	2.82	3.29	3.92	4.84	4.84	5.21
Price: high	35.8	41.8	41.5	53.2	59.5	53.9	53.0	45.6
low	11.3	15.8	29.2	31.9	43.3	41.8	16.4	24.0

Best Buy Company, Inc.
7601 Penn Avenue South
Richfield, MN 55423
(612) 291-1000
Website: *www.bestbuy.com*

Campbell Soup Company

Ticker symbol: CPB (NYSE) ❑ S&P rating: A ❑ Value Line financial strength rating: B++ ❑ Current yield: 3.4%

Company Profile

Campbell Soup Company is the world's largest soup maker. They also produce many other foods and beverages, but at least as far as we know, Andy Warhol never painted a jar of the company's Pace Pineapple Mango Chipotle Salsa, so the company is still best known for its ubiquitous soups. While there are twenty such brands under the Campbell roof, the original Campbell soup is still far and away the most important. The three top soups make up three of the top ten grocery products sold in the United States every week. Approximately 80 percent of U.S. households purchase the soup, and the average inventory on hand is six cans. Few brands have enjoyed such penetration and loyalty.

The company has four reporting segments: U.S. Soup, Sauces and Beverages; Baking and Snacking; International Soup, Sauces and Beverages; and North America Foodservice. Within each segment are the many familiar brands that constitute the business: Swanson, Prego, Pace, V8, Pepperidge Farm, Arnott's, Wolfgang Puck, and, of course, Campbell's.

Campbell's products are distributed to 120 countries worldwide and are sold through its own sales force and through distributors. U.S.–based operations accounted for 81 percent of revenue and 88 percent of earnings through FY2010. Products are manufactured in twenty principal facilities within the United States and in fourteen facilities outside the country, primarily in Australia, Europe, and Asia/Pacific. The vast majority of these facilities are company-owned.

Campbell's product strategy centers on three large, global categories—simple meals, baked snacks, and healthy beverages—which they feel are well aligned with broad consumer trends. The company's growth strategy has evolved toward greater innovation in product marketing and brand recognition and new packaging designed to broaden use in today's fast-paced economy, as well as a healthy dose of internationalization. New store displays and branding offer soups in four easily recognized categories: Classic Favorites, Healthy & Delicious, Taste Sensations, and Healthy Kids. We feel these categories move the brand forward without departing from core values. New microwaveable and heat-and-serve packages expand use into on-the-go environments. Finally, the core brand promise "Nourishing Peoples' Lives Every Day" should play well in the international space, a frontier the company is just beginning to capitalize on.

Financial Highlights, Fiscal Year 2009

Campbell has not been by any means a "growth star" for the last ten years, with compound annual sales, earnings, and cash flow all growing at around 1 percent. Recent performance has continued this trend, but cost cutting and the moderate innovations and international expansion should help move the company forward. The company is exposed, however, to commodity price increases.

Reasons to Buy

Brand strength is a key reason to stock a few shares of Campbell in your investment pantry. Campbell owns the number one or number two position in each of the product categories in which it participates. It dominates the $4 billion U.S. soup market with a 60-plus percent market share.

The company is investing heavily in Russia and China, which together account for half of the world's soup consumption. Russia and China have essentially no premade soups, so there is no in-place competition. Campbell's four largest current markets for premade soups (United States, Canada, France, and Germany) account for only 6 percent of the world's soup consumption, so opening up the Russia and China markets would create a tremendous growth opportunity. Just a 4 percent share of those markets would constitute a unit volume increase of over 10 percent. The company has invested $50 million per year for the past several years and has begun selling concentrated broths in both markets. Campbell expects to be profitable there within three years.

This is a fairly defensive stock with one of the lowest beta coefficients on our list at 0.28; non-cyclical, non-financial, low debt, and with a respectable yield. It's a good place to be if you're building a core of safe, well-established businesses that grow conservatively and occupy the top positions in their markets.

Reasons for Caution

It will be difficult for Campbell to organically grow market share for soups in the United States. The market is saturated and Campbell's customer base is an aging demographic that is not quick to adopt the new brands that Campbell will need to introduce to invigorate the portfolio. As others, like Coca-Cola, have found out over the years, there are risks inherent with tinkering with a long-established brand such as Campbell's.

SECTOR: **Consumer Staples**
BETA COEFFICIENT: **.28**
10-YEAR COMPOUND EARNINGS PER SHARE GROWTH: **2.5%**
10-YEAR COMPOUND DIVIDENDS PER SHARE GROWTH: **1.0%**

	2003	**2004**	**2005**	**2006**	**2007**	**2008**	**2009**	**2010**
Revenues (Mil)	6,678	7,109	7,548	7,343	7,867	7,998	7,586	7,676
Net Income (Mil)	626	652	707	681	771	798	771	842
Earnings per share	1.52	1.58	1.71	1.66	1.95	2.09	2.15	2.45
Dividends per share	0.63	0.64	0.69	0.74	0.82	0.88	1.00	1.05
Cash flow per share	2.12	2.24	2.42	2.41	2.78	3.07	2.87	3.25
Price: high	27.9	30.5	31.6	40	42.7	40.8	35.8	37.6
low	20	25	27.3	28.9	34.2	27.3	24.8	24.6

Campbell Soup Company
1 Campbell Place
Camden, NJ 08103–1799
(856) 342-6428
Website: *www.campbellsoupcompany.com*

AGGRESSIVE GROWTH

CarMax, Inc.

Ticker symbol: KMX (NYSE) □ S&P rating: NA □ Value Line financial strength rating: B+ □ Current yield: Nil

Company Profile

"The Way Car Buying Should Be." That's the slogan used by this clean-cut chain of used vehicle stores and superstores and its new big-box retail-like model for selling cars. Car-Max buys, reconditions, and sells cars and light trucks at 103 retail centers in forty-nine metropolitan markets, mainly in the Southeast and Midwest. The company specializes in selling cars that are under six years old with less than 60,000 miles; the cars are sold below Blue Book value in a no-haggle environment. The price is the price; the emphasis is on the condition of the vehicles and on a helpful and friendly sales and transaction process. Sales representatives are compensated for cars they sell, but not in such a way that it drives them to push the wrong car on a customer. The company sold some 357,129 used vehicles in FY2010 (which ended in February 2010) and most reports suggest they are gaining market share in the markets they serve with a high degree of customer satisfaction. Further, the health of the economy and consumer spending have swung car buying into a higher gear—but with newfound consumer prudence, many of these purchases are heading to the one-to-six year old used car sector of the business. In addition to "retail" used car sales, CarMax is a big player in auto wholesaling, having moved almost 200,000 units, mostly taken in trade last year.

CarMax also has service operations and web-based and other tools designed to make the car selection, buying, and ownership experience easier. The offering continues to be unique in the industry, and competitors would have a long way to go to catch up.

During the depth of the downturn, the company put its expansion plans on hold, but has opened five new stores recently and plans to resume store openings into the future. There is considerable geography in the United States not yet served by CarMax, including the Pacific Northwest, Colorado, and most of the Northeast.

Financial Highlights, Fiscal Year 2011 (FY2011 ends February 28)

CarMax ended their fiscal year 2011 in February 2011, so most of the results actually cover the calendar year 2010.

FY2010 saw a strong recovery for KMX. After being battered against the rocks for all of a dismal 2008, financial health was restored due to a number of factors. An improved credit market and pent-up demand drove sales through the entire year. The government's "cash for clunkers" program was a godsend for dealers, helping push new car sales and boosting consumer confidence. The sustained low interest rates with improved credit availability boosted financing profits. Tightened internal controls at CarMax reduced SG&A by $100 million on an annualized basis.

The result of the above is that CarMax's sales rebounded to 2006 levels and operating margin nearly tripled. Earnings increased fourfold to $255 million and net margin reached a record high of 3.4 percent. Share price went along for the ride, increasing over 200 percent, making CarMax one of our top performers from last year's portfolio.

Reasons to Buy

Quite simply, CarMax continues to be a stock to buy if you believe the traditional dealer model is broken, and if you believe people will continue to see value in late model used vehicles.

Additionally, CarMax brings the latest in business intelligence and analytic models to the car marketing process, in procurement, merchandising, pricing, and selling the vehicles. Do green Jeep Commanders sell well in Southern California? Then let's find some, and put them on the lot there, and set a market-based price. KMX is well ahead of the industry in making analysis-based supply and selling decisions.

In addition, a bigger picture and analytic tools allow CarMax to adjust inventories to business conditions more quickly; in the recent downturn, such inventory was reduced by tens of thousands of vehicles. That inventory is on the rise once again, prompting some analysts to raise eyebrows in late 2010, but the reality is that the company wouldn't have made this move if the business didn't warrant it. Similarly, the company has resumed hiring store help, another indicator of a solid future.

CarMax is clearly taking market share from "trad" used car dealers. There are close to 70,000 new and used car dealerships in the United States; that number will shrink over the next few years while CarMax builds brand strength and reputation in this important market and gains operational strength and experience to support it. The company is positioned well both for organic growth through market share and for geographic growth; additionally, earnings growth will be aided by increased market dominance, which should help both pricing and per-vehicle cost. CarMax is already the largest used car buyer in the world.

Reasons for Caution

CarMax will always be somewhat vulnerable to economic cycles, the availability of credit, and of quality used vehicles to resell. Used car supply has been a concern, especially with the downturn in new car sales and the scaling back in vehicle leasing seen in recent years. In addition, while international markets are a golden opportunity for most of our *100 Best Stocks*, it isn't clear how this company can grow internationally, although it is far from out of the question.

SECTOR: **Retail**
BETA COEFFICIENT: **1.31**
10-YEAR COMPOUND EARNINGS PER SHARE GROWTH: **9.0%**
10-YEAR COMPOUND DIVIDENDS PER SHARE GROWTH: **NA**

	2003	2004	2005	2006	2007	2008	2009	2010
Revenues (Mil)	4,052	4,597	5,260	6,560	7,466	8,200	6,974	7,400
Net Income (Mil)	94.8	116.5	112.9	148.1	198.6	182	59.2	255
Earnings per share	0.46	0.55	0.54	0.7	0.92	0.83	0.27	1.15
Dividends per share	0	0	0	0	0	0	0	0
Cash flow per share	0.53	0.64	0.64	0.83	1.08	1.05	0.52	1.4
Price: high	17	19.7	18.5	17.4	27.6	29.4	23	24.8
low	6.4	6.2	9	12.3	13.8	18.6	5.8	6.9

CarMax, Inc.
12800 Tuckahoe Creek Parkway
Richmond, VA 23238
(804) 747-0422
Website: *www.carmax.com*

AGGRESSIVE GROWTH

Caterpillar, Inc.

Ticker symbol: CAT (NYSE) □ S&P rating: A □ Value Line financial strength rating: A □ Current yield: 1.9%

Company Profile

Headquartered in Peoria, Illinois, Caterpillar is the world's largest manufacturer of construction and mining equipment, diesel and natural gas engines, and industrial gas turbines. It is a *Fortune* 50 industrial company with more than $40 billion in sales in a reasonably healthy economy. There are some 3 million of Caterpillar's distinctive yellow "Cat" branded machines in service in 180 countries around the world. International sales account for some 67 percent of the company's revenues.

Caterpillar's broad product line ranges from the company's line of compact construction equipment to hydraulic excavators, backhoe loaders, track-type tractors, forest products, off-highway trucks, agricultural tractors, diesel and natural gas engines, and industrial gas turbines. Cat products are used in the construction, road building, mining, forestry, energy, transportation, and material-handling industries.

Caterpillar products are sold, rented, and serviced through a notably loyal and effective dealer network. Products and components are manufactured in forty-one plants in the United States and forty-three more plants worldwide. The company has three operating segments: Machinery, Engines, and Financial Products.

Caterpillar's largest segment, the Machinery unit, makes the company's well-known earthmoving equipment. Machinery's end-markets include heavy construction, general construction, and mining quarry and aggregate, industrial, waste, forestry, and agriculture. End markets are very cyclical and competitive. Demand for Caterpillar's earthmoving equipment is driven by the health of global economies, commodity prices, and interest rates.

For decades, the Engine segment made diesel engines solely for the company's own earthmoving equipment. Now, Engine derives about 90 percent of sales from third-party customers, such as Paccar, Inc., the maker of well-known Kenworth and Peterbilt brand tractor/trailer trucks. Engine's major end markets are electric power generation, on-highway truck, oil and gas, industrial/OEM, and marine.

The Financial Products segment, which provides 7.6 percent of revenues but 20 percent of operating profits, primarily provides financing to Caterpillar dealers and customers. Financing plans include operating and finance leases, installment sales contracts, working capital loans, and wholesale financing plans.

Financial Highlights, Fiscal Year 2010

Towards the middle of the year, the company really started to regain traction after a very soft 2009, which saw a stunning cyclical decline of 37 percent of sales and 75 percent in earnings.

The downturn was the worst for the company since the 1940s. In response to the downturn, the company went into cost-control mode, while at the same time, doing what it could to prop up the dealer network, including allowing dealers to cancel orders for the first time. One cost-control measure was the expansion of overseas manufacturing in Brazil, India, and China. These moves, as with many companies during the recession and recovery, but more so with Caterpillar, led to greater strength when the recovery finally took hold. At the end of 2010, earnings, and the stock price, were quite healthy; CAT was one of the best-performing stocks in the Dow Jones Industrial Average.

Reasons to Buy

Caterpillar is the world's largest supplier of heavy equipment. The company continues to be a strong player in international business and exports, the expansion of mining and the rebuilding of U.S. infrastructure, and the building of new infrastructure, particularly in Latin America and Asia. The company enjoys a solid brand strength and reputation worldwide. Stated goals to increase earnings to $10 per share seem on track, assuming the economy stays reasonably healthy. The strength and loyalty of the dealer network, coupled with the in-house financing business, are pluses. The company acquired rail locomotive maker Electro-Motive Diesel, formerly owned by GM, in 2010. This acquisition will produce $1.8 billion in new sales and makes Cat a dominant player in the lucrative rail market.

We like the combination of brand excellence, management excellence, and continued growth prospects in infrastructure creation and replacement. The company has been on a long and successful triple play, experiencing double-digit sales, earnings, and cash flow growth for the past ten years, which with the exception of 2009, accelerated sharply in the past five years. The company seems to be on the right track, assuming healthy global economic fundamentals.

Reasons for Caution

Caterpillar is irretrievably tied to the economic cycle, although as we've seen in the last recession, economic downturns can lead to greater spending on infrastructure, which can help Cat even during these lean times. While foreign markets are a strength, we are also concerned about foreign competition from companies like Kubota and Komatsu, makers of mainly smaller, more compact equipment that is cheaper to acquire and operate. The share price has responded well to the recovery; new investors would be encouraged to wait and buy on dips. Because of the cyclical nature, dividend payout and increases have been relatively modest compared to gains in earnings and cash flow.

SECTOR: **Industrials**
BETA COEFFICIENT: **1.74**
10-YEAR COMPOUND EARNINGS PER SHARE GROWTH: **8.5%**
10-YEAR COMPOUND DIVIDENDS PER SHARE GROWTH: **10.5%**

	2003	2004	2005	2006	2007	2008	2009	2010
Revenues (Mil)	22,763	30,251	36,339	41,517	44,958	51,234	32,396	42,588
Net Income (Mil)	1,099	2,035	2,854	3,537	3,541	3,557	895	2,700
Earnings per share	1.57	2.88	4.04	5.17	5.37	5.71	1.43	4.15
Dividends per share	0.72	0.78	0.96	1.2	1.32	1.62	1.68	1.72
Cash flow per share	3.62	5.00	6.46	8.03	8.64	9.25	5.17	7.82
Price: high	42.5	49.4	59.9	82	87	86	61.3	113.9
low	20.6	34.3	41.3	57	58	32	50.5	92.3

Caterpillar, Inc.
100 N. E. Adams Street
Peoria, IL 61629–5310
(309) 675-4619
Website: *www.cat.com*

Chevron Corporation

Ticker symbol: CVX (NYSE) ❑ S&P rating: AA ❑ Value Line financial strength rating: A++ ❑ Current yield: 3.7%

Company Profile

Chevron is the world's fourth largest publicly traded, integrated energy company based on oil-equivalent reserves and production. It is engaged in every aspect of the oil and gas industry, including exploration and production, refining, marketing and transportation, chemicals manufacturing and sales, and power generation.

Active in more than 180 countries, Chevron, formerly Chevron-Texaco from the 2001 merger, has reserves of 11.9 billion barrels of oil and gas equivalent and daily production of 2.7 million barrels. In addition, it has global refining capacity of more than 2 million barrels per day (bpd) and operates more than 22,000 retail outlets (including affiliates) around the world. The company also has interests in thirty power projects now operating or being developed.

Its downstream (refining/retailing) businesses include four refining and marketing units operating in North America, Europe, West Africa, Latin America, Asia, the Middle East, and southern Africa. Downstream also has five global businesses: aviation, lubricants, trading, shipping, and fuel and marine marketing.

The company's global refining network comprises twenty-three wholly owned and joint-venture facilities that process more than 2 million barrels of oil per day. Gasoline and diesel fuel are sold through more than 22,000 retail outlets under three well-known consumer brands: Chevron in North America; Texaco in Latin America, Europe, and West Africa; and Caltex in Asia, the Middle East, and southern Africa.

Chevron is the number one jet fuel marketer in the United States and third worldwide, marketing 550,000 barrels per day in eighty countries. The company's fuel and marine marketing business is a leading global supplier and marketer of fuels, lubricants, and coolants to the marine and power markets, with about 500,000 barrels of sales per day.

Financial Highlights, Fiscal Year 2010

Chevron's sales in 2009 fell 36.8 percent to $167 billion, while net income fell 56.2 percent to $10.5 billion. Ouch. The overall decline in the worldwide economy drove down volumes significantly, leading to a large oversupply of both petroleum and gas products. As a result, benchmark prices for West Texas Intermediate crude fell 38 percent (full-year average) and natural gas prices experienced a similar decline, with prices falling 58 percent. If you're a vertically integrated oil company, those numbers pretty much tell you how your year is going to go.

As crude prices rose slowly through 2009, Chevron's refining operations were squeezed between higher input costs and reduced retail demand for gasoline. As a result, the downstream operations saw dramatically reduced earnings, falling from $3.5 billion in 2008 to $500 million in 2009.

Reasons to Buy

Chevron will be following the lead of Exxon with regard to its less-profitable downstream business. The company will limit its refining business to forty markets, down from ninety-three markets in 2009. Overall, Chevron is cutting refining capital expenditures 23 percent this year and will be combining their refining and chemical operations in 2010 to better leverage costs. They also plan to reduce the number of retail filling stations from 3,200 down to 1,900. Upstream operations are more profitable (and are becoming ever-more expensive), so the money is better spent there.

Successful production has begun at several new fields, including Angola (142,000 bpd), Brazil (72,000 bpd), and the United States (135,000 bpd). New finds during the year include significant deposits in Angola, the United States, and the Republic of the Congo. In Australia, Chevron has finalized delivery agreements for the output of a very large liquid natural gas platform in Western Australia that should produce on the order of 8.6 million metric tons of liquefied natural gas (LNG) annually.

Chevron is one of the world's largest producers of heavy crude oil, which represents about one-third of the world's hydrocarbon reserves. Industry production of heavy oil is projected to grow by 30 percent by the end of this decade.

Reasons for Caution

The April 2010 BP well blowout in the Gulf of Mexico and the consequent loss of life, the sinking of a TransOcean floating rig, and the resulting environmental damage have cast a pall over the entire industry. BP's full exposure is yet to be determined, but we continue to expect that this incident will substantially increase the cost of any and all future deepwater operations in the Gulf and could substantially damage the value of the leases there. Chevron currently derives 10 percent of its production from the Gulf.

SECTOR: Energy
BETA COEFFICIENT: .90
10-YEAR COMPOUND EARNINGS PER SHARE GROWTH: 17.5%
10-YEAR COMPOUND DIVIDENDS PER SHARE GROWTH: 7.5%

	2003	2004	2005	2006	2007	2008	2009	2010
Revenues ($B)	121.8	150.9	198.2	210.1	220.9	273	172.6	204.9
Net Income ($B)	7.2	13	14.1	17.1	18.7	23.9	10.5	19.0
Earnings per share	3.48	6.14	6.54	7.8	8.77	11.67	5.24	8.48
Dividends per share	1.43	1.53	1.75	2.01	2.32	2.53	2.66	2.84
Cash flow per share	5.9	8.67	8.96	10.09	12.11	16.69	10.95	15.99
Price: high	43.5	56.1	66	76.2	95.5	104.6	79.8	92.4
low	30.7	41.6	49.8	53.8	65	55.5	56.1	66.8

Chevron Corporation
6001 Bollinger Canyon Road
San Ramon, CA 94583–2324
(925) 842–5690
Website: *www.chevrontexaco.com*

Church & Dwight

Ticker symbol: CHD (NYSE) ❑ S&P rating: BBB- ❑ Value Line financial strength rating: A ❑ Current yield: 1.0%

Company Profile

Church & Dwight is the world's largest producer of sodium bicarbonate, but that hardly tells the whole story. The story is really about how this company built a brand and series of products based on sodium bicarbonate, known to most of us as baking soda. These well-known products are marketed under the Arm & Hammer brand, a brand that is deployed across several product categories. The company has sold this iconic product continually since its founding in 1846—the product's longevity owing to its versatility. Sodium bicarbonate is used in the chemical industry, baking, cleaning, agriculture (as both a soil and feedstock amendment), medicine, and the paper industry. It's an abrasive, a deodorizer, a leavening agent, a water purifier, an antacid, a dialysate (treatment for kidney failure), a blowing agent for plastics . . . the list goes on and on.

Church & Dwight is a fairly quiet, low profile company that has gradually learned the ropes of contemporary consumer staple marketing. Sodium bicarbonate is not the company's only product, but it is at the core of most of its businesses.

These businesses are divided into two basic groups, Consumer and Specialty, with the Consumer group further divided into Domestic and International segments. The Domestic Consumer segment accounted for 74 percent of the company's FY2009 net sales, Consumer International 16 percent, and Specialty the remaining 10 percent.

The company has eight key brands, which constitute 80 percent of its Consumer sales. About 40 percent of the company's U.S. consumer products are sold under the brand name Arm & Hammer and derivative trademarks, such as Arm & Hammer Dental Care Toothpaste and Arm & Hammer Super Scoop Clumping Cat Litter. But fueled by acquisitions mostly since 2001, the brand portfolio extends well past Arm & Hammer. The other seven are Trojan, Oxiclean, Spinbrush, First Response, Nair, Orajel, and Xtra. Of the eight brands, all but Arm & Hammer have been added since 2001 through acquisition, and all except Xtra occupy the top position in their product segment.

In 2003, the company acquired the former Unilever oral care business in the United States and

Canada, comprising the Metadent, Pepsodent, and Aim Toothpaste brands, and exclusive licensing rights to Close-Up Toothpaste. Late in 2005, the company expanded its oral care business with the acquisition of the Spinbrush battery-operated toothbrush business from Procter & Gamble. In August 2006, the company expanded its household brand portfolio with the acquisition of the net assets of Orange Glo International.

The company claims the Arm & Hammer brand appears in more grocery aisles than any other brand, and that the brand appears in over 90 percent of American homes. The company, and particularly the Arm & Hammer brand, are positioned for value, that is, quality and strength at an attractive price point, although the company has recently expanded some of its higher-priced premium brands.

Financial Highlights, Fiscal Year 2010

FY2010 was consistent with the company's very steady long-term growth. Top line organic sales growth came in at about 5 percent. But the company continues to enjoy gross and net margin increases, exiting the year with an operating margin of 21 percent, well above the 14–16 percent range exhibited 2003–2007. Acquisitions and cost-cutting measures paid off, and earnings were some 14 percent ahead of 2009, which was some 23 percent ahead of 2008. The company has achieved a ten-year triple play of sales, earnings, and cash flow growth well into the double digits. Not surprisingly, CHD has shown a steady up and to the right performance in stock price; the ten-year stock price chart is one of the cleanest and steadiest we've seen with hardly a blip for the 2008–09 downturn.

Reasons to Buy

Ten years ago, Church & Dwight had one iconic consumer brand and its net sales were less than $1 billion. They now have over eighty brands and $2.5 billion in annual sales. The growth in their base of core brands has accelerated over the past five years and the company is in terrific position for further acquisitions. They've done an excellent job of integrating the acquired brands into the core business, as well as leveraging their core brand into new products. If they can repeat this sort of performance, they could start acquiring even larger and stronger brands.

The company's brand base is split 60/40 between premium and value brands, providing a fair amount of protection during shifting economic environments.

Church & Dwight feels there is room for further growth in its gross margin and has several supply chain initiatives underway to make improvements through 2011. From a common sense point of view, the $5 billion market cap makes this company a good value; one to own if, say, we had $5 billion to invest, and that may get some of its larger rivals thinking about owning it too.

Reasons for Caution

While core brand expansion has been very successful, and while recent acquisitions have been successful, we tend to be cautious about companies that tend to overly rely on acquisitions as a growth strategy. It's easy to make a mistake, even though the company has had an excellent track record so far. Without acquisitions, the enviable growth rates will inevitably slow. The company has also had a relatively conservative dividend policy, probably due at least in part to its acquisition strategy.

SECTOR: **Consumer Staples**
BETA COEFFICIENT: **0.42**
10-YEAR COMPOUND EARNINGS PER SHARE GROWTH: **18.5%**
10-YEAR COMPOUND DIVIDENDS PER SHARE GROWTH: **8.0%**

		2003	2004	2005	2006	2007	2008	2009	2010
Revenues (Mil)		1,057	1,462	1,737	1,946	2,221	2,422	2,521	2,589
Net Income (Mil)		78.5	88.8	123	143	169	201	249	286
Earnings per share		1.24	1.37	1.83	2.07	2.47	2.86	3.48	3.98
Dividends per share		0.21	0.23	0.24	0.26	0.26	0.34	0.46	0.62
Cash flow per share		1.78	2.02	2.64	2.97	3.41	3.89	4.73	5.02
Price:	high	27.7	33.7	39.6	43.6	57.2	65.5	62.4	71.0
	low	18.4	25.6	32.1	32.7	42.4	47.6	45.4	59.1

Church & Dwight Co., Inc.
469 North Harrison Street
Princeton, NJ 08543
(609) 683-5900
Website: *www.churchdwight.com*

INCOME

Cincinnati Financial

Ticker symbol: CINF (NASDAQ) ❑ S&P rating: BBB ❑ Value Line financial strength rating: B++ ❑
Current yield: 5.1%

Company Profile

Cincinnati Financial Corporation (CFC), founded in 1968, is engaged primarily in property casualty insurance marketed through independent insurance agents in thirty-seven states. The company, one of the twenty-five largest property and casualty insurers in the nation, operates in four segments: Commercial Lines Property Casualty Insurance, Personal Lines Property Casualty Insurance, Life Insurance, and Investments. Commercial lines account for about 70 percent of premium revenues; personal lines about 30 percent, and all insurance products are sold through independent agencies.

At year-end 2010, the company owned 100 percent of three subsidiaries: the Cincinnati Insurance Company, CSU Producer Resources Inc., and CFC Investment Company. In addition, the parent company owns an investment portfolio and the headquarters property, and is responsible for corporate borrowings and shareholder dividends.

Its standard market property casualty insurance group includes two subsidiaries: the Cincinnati Casualty Company and the Cincinnati Indemnity Company. This group writes a range of business, homeowner, and auto policies.

The two non-insurance subsidiaries of Cincinnati Financial are CSU Producer Resources, which offers insurance brokerage services to CFC's independent agencies so their clients can access CFC's excess and surplus lines insurance products; and CFC Investment Company, which offers commercial leasing and financing services to CFC's agents, their clients, and other customers.

Financial Highlights, Fiscal Year 2010

While FY2010 continued to be a difficult year for insurers because of exceptionally low interest rates and thus diminished investment returns, FY2010 results showed some profit improvement, mostly due to reduced insurance losses (69 percent of premiums versus 77 percent a year earlier). The company earned $1.68 per share, ahead of FY2009's $1.32, placing earnings once again ahead of the $1.56 per share dividend, a good sign (cash flow is $3.20 per share, so the dividend is well covered regardless). For FY2011, earnings are likely to continue soft with low investment returns and a lackluster sales environment as business customers work to cut costs, and recent storm activity in early 2011 does not bode well for loss coverage. However, the company noted some pricing improvement, or at least less resistance from its customer base when premium increases were announced.

Reasons to Buy

CINF enjoys both a loyal customer base and a loyal agency base. Measured by premium volume, the company is ranked as the number one or number two carrier among 75 percent of the agencies that have represented them for the past five years. Working to improve that measure further, during 2009, the company rolled out three major new technology platforms for their writers, with the goal of improving efficiency in quoting, billing, and payment across all business and personal lines.

The company is on firm financial footing with a well-covered dividend and a relatively low 14 percent long-term debt as a percentage of total capital. Despite the recent financial storm, dividend payouts have increased slowly and steadily, and at an average 10.5 percent rate over the past ten years, a nice bonus. Any return to normal investment return rates, and any resurgence in policy writing and pricing will figure well for this solid insurance play, and may add some growth to the already attractive yield.

Reasons for Caution

Interest rates on the industry's traditional investment instruments continue to be weak, although recent signs that the Fed will finally allow interest rates to rise some will help the company. That said, as its current bond investments come due, the company will be forced to invest at subpar rates of return for at least the near term. Competition is stiff, and a year of substantial casualty losses could hurt.

SECTOR: **Financial**
BETA COEFFICIENT: **0.95**
10-YEAR COMPOUND EARNINGS PER SHARE GROWTH: **5.0%**
10-YEAR COMPOUND DIVIDENDS PER SHARE GROWTH: **10.5%**

	2003	**2004**	**2005**	**2006**	**2007**	**2008**	**2009**	**2010**
Total Assets (Mil)	15,509	16,107	16,003	17,222	16,637	13,369	14,440	15,095
Net Income (Mil)	386	524	562	496	610	344	215	273
Earnings per share	2.17	2.94	3.17	2.82	3.54	2.10	1.32	1.68
Dividends per share	0.91	1.00	1.21	1.34	1.42	1.53	1.57	1.59
Loss/Prem Earned	.71	.63	.63	.64	.59	.73	.77	.69
Price: high	38.0	53.5	45.9	49.2	48.4	40.2	29.7	32.3
low	30.0	36.6	38.4	41.2	36.0	13.7	17.8	25.3

Cincinnati Financial Corporation
6200 S. Gilmore Road
Fairfield, OH 45014
(513) 870-2000
Website: *www.cinfin.com*

The Clorox Company

Ticker symbol: CLX (NYSE) ❏ S&P rating: BBB+ ❏ Value Line financial strength rating: B++ ❏ Current yield: 3.5%

Company Profile

A leading manufacturer and marketer of consumer products, Clorox markets some of consumers' most trusted and recognized brand names, including its namesake bleach and cleaning products, Green Works natural cleaners; Fresh Step and Scoop Away cat litter; Kingsford charcoal; Hidden Valley and K C Masterpiece dressings and sauces; Brita water-filtration systems; Glad bags, wraps, and containers; and Burt's Bees natural personal care products. By sales, the more mundane liquid bleach products, trash bags, and charcoal dominate sales, contributing 13, 11, and 11 percent of sales respectively. With approximately 8,300 employees worldwide, the company manufactures products in more than two dozen countries and markets them in more than 100 countries. International sales account for about 21 percent of the total.

The company's home-care cleaning products are primarily comprised of disinfecting sprays and wipes, toilet bowl cleaners, carpet cleaners, drain openers, floor mopping systems, toilet and bath cleaning tools, and premoistened towelettes.

Clorox also provides professional products for institutional, janitorial, and foodservice markets, including bleaches, disinfectants, food-storage bags, and bathroom cleaners. Citing a poor fit to its core business, the company recently divested itself of its Armor All and STP auto care brands. The company's Lifestyle Division offers food products, including salad dressings, seasonings, sauces, and marinades. Clorox sells its products to grocery stores and grocery wholesalers primarily through a network of brokers; and through a direct sales force to mass merchandisers, warehouse clubs, and military and other retail stores in the United States. It also sells its products outside the United States through subsidiaries, licensees, distributors, and joint-venture arrangements with local partners.

The company was founded in 1913 as Electro-Alkaline Company. It has been known as the Clorox Company since 1957.

Financial Highlights, Fiscal Year 2010

Fiscal year 2010 earnings, ending June 2010, started out healthy and ahead of expectations, then gradually sagged as the year progressed. While this softening affected the entire industry in established markets such as the United States, Clorox is decidedly less international than many of its competitors—21 percent versus Colgate-Palmolive's (75 percent of sales,) and Procter & Gamble's (62 percent of sales)—thus amplifying the softness and attenuating the opportunity to make up for it elsewhere. In early 2011 the company scaled back the top end of its 2011 sales projection from "flat to 2 percent" growth to "flat to 1 percent" growth, and scaled back earnings guidance by $.15 to $4.05–$4.20 from $4.20–$4.35.

The divestiture of the auto care businesses had an impact too. Those businesses were large enough—$300 million in sales and $0.55 in per share earnings—to make sequential sales and earnings comparisons tricky, but the company set out to repurchase about 10 percent of its shares with the proceeds to negate the dilution.

Finally, the company has admitted to being stung by the 2007 Burt's Bees acquisition, having paid some $925 million for the firm. The company announced a $250 million goodwill write-down related to the acquisition.

Reasons to Buy

Even in a slowing consumer market, Clorox, due to its strong brand

position (number one or two positions in the market with 88 percent of its products) has proven itself able to increase prices in the past. That said, many consumers have switched away from name brand products; just how many remains to be seen as Clorox has proven itself as a strong and shareholder-oriented defensive player. During the 2008–09 recession, the company increased its dividend by 25 percent, and has grown its dividend by 10 percent compounded over the past ten years. The stock has tended to trade in a very tight range even with negative news; it is a safety and stability play.

The company's brands remain strong, and we especially like the emerging Green Works brand, which, unlike many "green" products, seem to work and have become a standard on store shelves.

Reasons for Caution

We continue to be concerned about the lack of international exposure, although that could also be viewed as an opportunity with a strong brand campaign and distribution channels in key markets. The company is exposed to higher commodity prices, although thus far has been able to recover them with price increases. With Burt's Bees, the company has also learned a lesson about overreaching with acquisitions; the beauty care maker may turn out to have been a fad not worth chasing, but we are concerned that the company could be tempted again into poor acquisitions to spur growth. It's just too hard to grow demand and market share for bleach, trash bags, and charcoal. While we considered dropping Clorox from the list, we feel that core brand strength, good management, and orientation toward shareholder returns continue to earn its stripes. One more gut check: At an $8.5 billion market cap, Clorox may be one of those companies that we'd buy if we had that kind of money—and others may be thinking the same.

SECTOR: **Consumer Staples**
BETA COEFFICIENT: **.42**
10-YEAR COMPOUND EARNINGS PER SHARE GROWTH: **9.0%**
10-YEAR COMPOUND DIVIDENDS PER SHARE GROWTH: **10.0%**

		2003	2004	2005	2006	2007	2008	2009	2010
Revenues (Mil)		4,144	4,324	4,388	4,644	4,847	5,273	5,450	5,534
Net Income (Mil)		514	546	517	443	496	461	537	603
Earnings per share		2.33	2.43	2.88	2.89	3.23	3.24	3.81	4.24
Dividends per share		0.88	1.08	1.1	1.14	1.31	1.66	1.88	2.05
Cash flow per share		3.3	3.49	4.66	4.17	4.55	4.82	5.22	5.68
Price:	high	49.2	59.4	66	66	69.4	65.3	65.2	69.0
	low	37.4	46.5	52.5	56.2	56.2	47.5	59	59.0

The Clorox Company
1221 Broadway
Oakland, CA 94612
(510) 271-2270
Website: *www.clorox.com*

The Coca-Cola Company

Ticker symbol: KO (NYSE) □ S&P rating: A+ □ Value Line financial strength rating: A++ □ Current yield: 2.8%

Company Profile

The Coca-Cola Company is the world's largest beverage company. For more than 100 years, the company has mainly produced concentrates and syrups, which it then sells to independent bottlers worldwide. These bottlers add water (still or carbonated, depending on the product), sugar, and other (often local) ingredients, then bottle and distribute the products to restaurants, retailers, and other distributors. The company owns the brand and is responsible for consumer brand marketing initiatives, while the distributors handle all downstream merchandising. The company operates in over 200 countries and markets nearly 500 brands of concentrate. These concentrates are then used to produce over 3,000 different branded products, including Coca-Cola.

In 2010, the company took a big step toward full integration of its supply chain with the purchase of the North American operations of Coca-Cola Enterprises (CCE), the largest of its network of bottlers, for some $12.4 billion, including debt assumption. The acquisition was expected to streamline distribution and marketing, give greater control of pricing, and cut about $350 million in redundant costs. At the same time, Coke sold distribution in Norway, Sweden, and a future in Germany back to CCE, reaffirming the third-party bottler model in international, or at least European, markets.

The company has also been striving to expand its beverage offerings beyond the traditional carbonated soda drinks. Major brands besides Coke include Minute Maid juices, Dasani and Evian bottled water, Powerade and Full Throttle sports beverages, and Nestea iced teas.

The total numbers are staggering: 570 billion servings per year, 1 billion beverages consumed per day, 18,000 servings per second, unit growth in 2008 equivalent to the entire Japanese market, processed through over 300 bottlers, and all handled through the world's largest beverage distribution system. Some 74 percent of the company's sales are overseas, and overseas markets are where the growth is.

Financial Highlights, Fiscal Year 2010

Coke rebounded well from the 2008–09 recession, resuming its

5–7 percent top line growth rate after a dip in 2009. Some of the 2009 dip was related to demand softness, some to currency fluctuations, and the company remains exposed, good or bad, to ups and downs in the U.S. dollar.

In late 2010, the company resumed its share buyback program with a commitment to repurchase some $1.5 billion in 2011. This isn't large with respect to the total market cap of $140 billion, but does show the company's commitment to returning cash to shareholders.

Operating margins were also flat in this period, but may start to notch upward with the consolidation of the supply and distribution chain and with continued progress in overseas markets.

Reasons to Buy

Coca-Cola has global category leadership in soft drinks, juices, and juice drinks, and ready-to-drink coffees and teas. They're number two globally in sports drinks, and number three in packaged water and energy drinks. In Coca-Cola, Diet Coke, Sprite, and Fanta, they own four of the top five brands of soft drink in the world. They're everywhere, and with so many popular brands, the local bottlers can "test the waters," choosing among hundreds of products for the right ones for their area.

Although the company has lagged the market in terms of non-CSD (carbonated soft drink) product offerings, the growth of those products in Coke's developing markets is very encouraging. Coke has targeted moving forward, particularly in the growing economies of India, Indonesia, and China. The growth in the consumption of non-alcoholic ready-to-drink beverages tracks the per-capita growth in disposable income, and the company has identified key cities with the most promising demographics for its marketing efforts. If Coke could realize the success in China, which is currently at about 20 per capita consumption (PCC), or beverages consumed per capita per year, that it has in Mexico (660 PCC), the effects would be huge.

The Coca-Cola name is probably the most recognized brand in the world, and is almost beyond valuation. Warren Buffett once uttered the classic line about brand strength and intangibles in reference to Coke: "If you gave me $100 million and said take away the soft drink leadership in the world from Coke, I'd give it back to you and say it can't be done."

Coke has traditionally been a steady hedge stock, and offers a solid dividend with a steady track record of dividend growth (11 percent over the last ten years). It is also as close to a pure play on international business as you'll find in a U.S. company.

Reasons for Caution

The per capita consumption (PCC) map is quite interesting (see *www* *.thecoca-colacompany.com/our* *company/ar/map.html#/per-capita-consumption* on the company's website) and reveals a big opportunity on the global stage. But the slight decline in U.S. PCC, from 396 in 1999 to 382 in 2009, is unnerving and may reflect the ongoing publicity and buzz about health, child obesity, and so forth. Unit volume in the United States has been flat (pardon the pun) for years, and an aging U.S. population doesn't help. The company is combating this with non-soda lines and offerings like Coke Zero, but it remains to be seen whether Coke can enjoy consumption growth on this continent anytime soon.

As Coke consumers ourselves, we're continuously disappointed at the erosion of Coke products in favor of Pepsi in many restaurants and fast food chains. We realize that PepsiCo owns a number of fast food chains and has a captive market there, but we wonder how and why Coke is losing this important distribution and brand recognition channel, especially as far more people seem to specify Coke than Pepsi when ordering their cola. It makes us wonder whether there are larger elephants in their sales and marketing room. It also serves as an example of what you, as an astute individual investor, can yourself observe about your companies in the course of daily life.

SECTOR: **Consumer Staples**
BETA COEFFICIENT: **0.61**
10-YEAR COMPOUND EARNINGS PER SHARE GROWTH: **7.0%**
10-YEAR COMPOUND DIVIDENDS PER SHARE GROWTH: **9.5%**

		2003	2004	2005	2006	2007	2008	2009	2010
Revenues (Mil)		21,044	21,962	23,104	24,088	28,857	31,944	30,990	35,123
Net Income (Mil)		4,790	5,014	5,196	5,568	5,981	7,050	6,824	8,144
Earnings per share		1.95	2.06	2.17	2.37	2.57	3.02	3.05	3.49
Dividends per share		0.88	1	1.12	1.24	1.36	1.52	1.64	1.76
Cash flow per share		2.31	2.45	2.59	2.81	3.08	3.58	3.6	4.18
Price:	high	50.9	53.3	45.3	49.3	64.3	65.6	59.4	65.9
	low	37	38.3	40.3	39.4	45.6	40.3	37.4	37.4

The Coca-Cola Company
One Coca-Cola Plaza
Atlanta, GA 30313
(404) 676-2121
Website: *www.coca-cola.com*

Colgate-Palmolive Company

Ticker symbol: CL (NYSE) ❑ S&P rating: AA- ❑ Value Line financial strength rating: A++ ❑ Current yield: 2.7%

Company Profile

Colgate-Palmolive is the second-largest domestic manufacturer of detergents, toiletries, and other household products. The company manages its business in two straight-forward segments: Oral, Personal and Home Care; and Pet Nutrition. The Oral, Personal and Home Care division produces and markets a number of familiar brands and products: Ajax, Palmolive, Irish Spring, Softsoap, Mennen, and SpeedStick, as well as the familiar Colgate brand of oral care products. These brands dominate the business, but Colgate is also one of the leaders in the pet nutrition market; its Hill's pet food brand represents 17 percent of its total sales.

Colgate is also strong in the global consumer products market, with a presence in over 200 countries and territories. About 75 percent of its business is international, with particular strength in Latin America.

Financial Highlights, Fiscal Year 2010

The recession brought flat revenue for FY2009, which is typical of such a consumer staples company. Even in that "off" year, the company was able to deliver an eye-popping 21 percent growth in earnings per share due mostly to cost-cutting measures, price strength in key product lines, and a modest reduction in share count. Operating margins improved from 23.2 percent in 2008 to 26.2 percent in 2009.

The company got off to a good start in FY2010, with revenues for the first three quarters up 3 percent from FY2009 and earnings up 13.6 percent. The upward path reversed a bit in the fourth quarter, when a 1 percent unit volume increase was wiped out by an unfavorable foreign exchange climate, which had a negative 3.5 percent impact versus the FY2009 fourth quarter. With Colgate's high international exposure, such fluctuations have more impact. More intense competition with Procter & Gamble and GlaxoSmithKline, especially in the oral care space, brought some price decreases and additional marketing expenses. The combined impact resulted in FY2010 sales of $15.564 million, about $80 million off earlier projections, and earnings per share of $4.31, slightly off the FY2009 number.

Citing market share gains in oral care in Latin America, China, and India, the company is fairly optimistic about FY2011 gross margins, sales, and earnings, but has guided earnings growth only in the low single digits for the year. Higher marketing costs to bring new products to market was cited as one reason.

Reasons to Buy

Colgate is the predominant global market leader in toothpastes. Nearly half of all toothpaste sold worldwide in 2009 was a Colgate product. Market acceptance for toothpastes in the United States is nearly 100 percent, but outside the country toothpaste is still a rapidly growing market. Analysts suggest that worldwide, consumer oral care products are barely at 50 percent market penetration. Given this healthy potential for market growth, along with the improving demographics of a health-conscious and appearance-conscious pool of consumers, globalization gives a Colgate investor a lot to smile about.

Looking at the bigger picture, Colgate is probably a safer, steadier alternative in this consumer staple marketplace than Procter & Gamble (another *100 Best Stock*), as it is less prone to reach for new, rapidly changing markets like cosmetics, and less apt to try to grow through acquisitions. This company is about slow, steady returns with little risk and little market volatility in bad times. We like the fact that Colgate has been able to grow earnings and dividends faster than sales; the focus on operational efficiency has paid off. We also like the company's focus on international markets, although currency adjustments create another source of volatility.

Reasons for Caution

Colgate participates in an increasingly competitive market, requiring more frequent new product rollouts and related marketing expenses just to keep up. Also, the Colgate business will not "fascinate" anyone and will probably not be a favored choice for more aggressive investors.

SECTOR: **Consumer Staples**
BETA COEFFICIENT: **.50**
10-YEAR COMPOUND EARNINGS PER SHARE GROWTH: **10.5%**
10-YEAR COMPOUND DIVIDENDS PER SHARE GROWTH: **11.5%**

	2003	2004	2005	2006	2007	2008	2009	2010
Revenues (Mil)	9,903	10,584	11,397	12,238	13,790	15,330	15,327	15,564
Net Income (Mil)	1,421	1,327	1,351	1,353	1,737	1,957	2,291	2,203
Earnings per share	2.46	2.33	2.43	2.46	3.2	3.66	4.37	4.31
Dividends per share	0.9	0.96	1.11	1.28	1.44	1.56	1.72	2.03
Cash flow per share	3.2	3.18	3.42	3.71	4.21	4.54	5.29	5.14
Price: high	61	59	57.2	67.1	81.3	82	87.4	86.1
low	48.6	42.9	48.2	53.4	63.8	54.4	54.5	73.1

Colgate-Palmolive Company
300 Park Avenue
New York, NY 10022–7499
(212) 310-2291
Website: *www.colgate.com*

Comcast Corporation

Ticker symbol: CMCSA (NASDAQ) □ S&P rating: BBB+ □ Value Line financial strength rating: B+
□ Current yield: 0.6%

Company Profile

Comcast is one of the nation's leading providers of communications services and information and entertainment content passed through those services. The core business is Comcast Cable, the familiar cable TV network that has evolved into a "pipe" for delivering bundled high-speed Internet services, phone services, and on-demand content. This business, which serves some 24 million subscribers in thirty-nine states, has up until recently represented 95 percent of the total business.

The company has been evolving its information and entertainment business over the years through its ownership of regional sports networks and national channels such as the Golf Channel, E! (an entertainment channel), fandango.com, and others. The company took a major leap forward as a content provider with the early 2011 closing of the acquisition of 51 percent of NBC Universal (GE still owns the other 49 percent), almost instantly turning the company into not only a connectivity powerhouse but a media powerhouse as well. With that acquisition, Comcast is now regarded as the largest integrated content development and distribution business in the United States.

Most likely in an attempt to evolve and to overcome the legacy of negative public opinion about cable operators, the company has been building its Xfinity brand to compete with satellite operators and such offerings as AT&T U-verse and Verizon FiOS. Customers can buy bundles of service including TV, including new on-demand video and, as an emerging offering, on-demand TV. (The company owns a stake in the leading free TV website Hulu, a new on-demand TV service that bears watching.) With Xfinity, customers can also get up to 105Mbps Internet service, probably the best service for downloading large chunks of video content. Through the Xfinity package and brand, Comcast also announced a new Internet 2go wireless Internet service through a 4G network. In short, Comcast has evolved from being a lackluster cable TV service to a full-scale communications utility with some of the highest performance products on the market.

The vast majority of Comcast customers are residential, although the company also offers a "Business

Class" service to meet the needs of small and mid-sized organizations. The company also owns the Philadelphia 76ers and Flyers and a series of Universal theme parks through the NBC Universal subsidiary.

Financial Highlights, Fiscal Year 2010

For many years until about 2005, Comcast was a fairly lackluster company with lackluster financial performance; earnings bounced back and forth between losses and very modest profits. The growth in the Internet and, most likely, the ability to bundle high speed Internet service in contrast to satellite providers, served as an awakening for the company in the marketplace and financially. In the past five years, compounded revenues have risen 15 percent, earnings 47.5 percent, and cash flow 21.5 percent. In FY2010, the company posted $1.29 in earnings, almost flat from the year before but burdened with acquisition costs, on revenues of about $37.7 billion. Projections call for resumed earnings growth to $1.50 per share in FY2011 and in the $1.70–$1.75 range in FY2011. Annual revenue growth is estimated at about 13 percent. In early FY2011, the company raised its dividend to $.45 a share and beefed up its share repurchase program some 75 percent over FY2010 to $2.1 billion.

Reasons to Buy

Comcast is one of those companies that has spent years building its product and infrastructure, and is now finally figuring out how to utilize it more profitably while at the same time offering a better value proposition to customers. Although there are some risks in entering the oft-fickle media business, we generally like Comcast's efforts to make the most of its network. What really intrigues us at this point is the on-demand services for both video and TV. While NetFlix and others are bringing such services to market, because of bandwidth and other considerations, they probably make the most sense to deliver through the extremely high bandwidths of a cable system. Comcast owns the largest such system and is putting it to use—and starting to question whether the competitors should be able to use its network. While such restrictive thinking can annoy customers and bring out the antitrust regulators, it should serve to build business, and the Xfinity offering makes this offering much more consumer friendly. In short, Comcast is doing a lot of the right things both in the marketplace and financially.

Reasons for Caution

In most people's minds, Comcast is still a cable company, and people don't like cable companies. If the company becomes too aggressive in the media content market, and particularly if it restricts others from using its "last mile" of cable, that could bring some grief in the court of public opinion, not to mention regulation. The company faces extreme competition in most of its markets, although it may have at least a temporary bandwidth advantage at present. Finally, scenarios where the top two executives make over $50 million combined and have a controlling interest in the voting Class B shares can turn out to be a negative.

SECTOR: **Telecommunications**

BETA COEFFICIENT: **.85**

10-YEAR COMPOUND EARNINGS PER SHARE GROWTH: **NM percent**

10-YEAR COMPOUND DIVIDENDS PER SHARE GROWTH: **22.0%**

	2003	2004	2005	2006	2007	2008	2009	2010
Revenues (Mil)	18,348	20,307	22,255	24,966	30,895	34,256	35,756	37,937
Net Income (Mil)	(218)	970	1,098	2,235	2,287	2,701	3,638	3,535
Earnings per share	(.07)	0.29	0.33	0.47	0.74	0.91	1.26	1.29
Dividends per share	–	–	–	–	–	0.25	0.27	0.38
Cash flow per share	1.25	1.69	1.84	1.48	2.82	3.10	3.57	3.89
Price: high	22.0	23.6	22.8	28.7	29.6	22.5	17.3	21.2
low	15.0	17.3	17.0	16.2	17.3	12.1	10.3	14.3

Comcast Corporation

One Comcast Center

Philadelphia, PA 19103

(215) 665-1700

Website: *www.comcast.com*

GROWTH AND INCOME

ConocoPhillips

Ticker symbol: COP (NYSE) ❑ S&P rating: A ❑ Value Line financial strength rating: A++ ❑ Current yield: 4.0%

Company Profile

ConocoPhillips is the third-largest U.S.–based integrated energy company and the sixth largest worldwide based on market capitalization. It is also the second largest petroleum refiner in the United States and the fifth largest refiner in the world. ConocoPhillips has the eighth-largest stock of proven petroleum reserves in private hands. Their businesses span the hydrocarbon value chain from wellhead through refining, marketing, transportation, and chemicals.

ConocoPhillips is best known for its technological expertise in deepwater exploration and production, reservoir management and exploitation, 3-D seismic technology, high-grade petroleum coke upgrading, and sulfur removal.

Headquartered in Houston, Texas, ConocoPhillips operates in more than forty countries with about 30,000 employees worldwide and annual revenues approaching $180 billion.

The company has four core activities worldwide:

■ *Petroleum exploration and production.* This segment, approximately 25 percent of revenues, primarily explores for, produces, transports, and markets crude oil, natural gas, and natural gas liquids on a worldwide basis. The company's E&P operations are geographically diverse, pro- ducing in the United States (including a large presence in Alaska's Prudhoe Bay), Norway, the United Kingdom, Canada, Australia, offshore Timor-Leste in the Timor Sea, Indonesia, China, Vietnam, Libya, Nigeria, Algeria, and Russia.

■ *Petroleum refining, marketing, supply, and transportation.* This segment, approximately 71 percent of revenues, purchases, refines, markets, and transports crude oil and petroleum products, mainly in the United States, Europe, and Asia. In the U.S. marketplace, COP products are mainly marketed under the familiar Phillips 66, Conoco, and 76 brand names.

■ *Midstream.* This segment, about 3 percent of revenues, gathers, processes, and markets natural gas produced by ConocoPhillips and others, and fractionates and markets natural gas liquids, predominantly in the United States and Trinidad. The Midstream segment primarily consists of a 50 percent equity investment in DCP Midstream, LLC, but also includes a 30.3 percent interest in Duke Energy Field Services, LLC.

■ *Chemicals/Emerging Businesses/ other.* This 1 percent segment manufactures and markets petrochemicals and plastics on a worldwide basis. The Chemicals segment consists of a 50 percent equity investment in Chevron Phillips Chemical Company LLC (CPChem). There are also investments in power generation, waste hydrocarbon recovery, and other energy technologies.

Financial Highlights, Fiscal Year 2010

Aided by the 2010 recovery in oil prices, revenues and earnings continued to grow at a double-digit pace. At the end of that year, that growth rate slowed considerably as asset sales and slightly diminished E&P results came into play. At the same time, refining margins improved, keeping sales and earnings steady, if not spectacular.

Last year we mentioned the company's intent to divest itself of $10 billion of its current asset base and use the proceeds for share buyback. That actually happened, and in late 2010, the company completed a spinoff of approximately three-quarters of the 20 percent interest owned in LUKOIL, the Russian energy conglomerate, for a gain of approximately $2.4 billion. That cash was primarily used to repurchase shares, and the company announced a $6 billion continuation of its share buyback program in 2011. In short, the company is on a path to "right size" itself and spin off proceeds to shareholders.

In early 2010, Conoco announced their intention to sell off, over a period of three years, their 20 percent share in LUKOIL, The announcement was not met with joyous acclaim by the Russian government, but the government has said they will not attempt to block or hamper the sale in any way. This sale is independent of Conoco's other planned asset sale.

Reasons to Buy

Oil and gas stocks have historically been cyclical with long-term growth as a trend. We like COP's business mix and track record, and we applaud the "right sizing," a refreshing change from the usual pedal-to-the-metal growth strategies we see in place around the industry. The company has solid financials with an excellent earnings, cash flow, and dividend track record, in fact, a rare "quintuple play" with sales, earnings, cash flow, dividends, and book value all growing in double digits over the past ten years. This and the share buybacks suggest a focus on shareholder value not always found in the energy industry.

Reasons for Caution

The dominance of the refining business means that operating margins will be volatile, and indeed, they have been over the past five years—from the mid-20 percent range in 2006–07 to less than 1 percent in 2008 to a more "normal" 16–17 percent in 2010. While the company is well diversified and appears to manage these ups and downs well, they do add some risk. The ambiguities of exploration and geopolitics add a bit more uncertainty to the risk profile.

SECTOR: Energy
BETA COEFFICIENT: **1.16**
10-YEAR COMPOUND EARNINGS PER SHARE GROWTH: **20.5%**
10-YEAR COMPOUND DIVIDENDS PER SHARE GROWTH: **10.5%**

	2003	2004	2005	2006	2007	2008	2009	2010
Revenues ($Bil)	104.2	135.1	179.4	183.7	187.4	240.8	149.3	189.4
Net Income ($Bil)	4.59	8.11	13.64	15.55	11.89	15.86	5.35	9.8
Earnings per share	3.35	5.79	9.55	9.66	9.14	10.66	3.59	5.92
Dividends per share	0.82	0.9	1.18	1.44	1.64	1.88	1.91	2.16
Cash flow per share	5.91	8.28	10.27	14.19	14.86	16.8	9.85	12.50
Price: high	33	45.6	71.5	74.9	90.8	96	57.4	68.6
low	22.6	32.2	41.4	54.9	61.6	41.3	34.1	48.5

ConocoPhillips
600 North Dairy Ashford
Houston, TX 77079–1175
(212) 207-1996
Website: *www.conocophillips.com*

Costco Wholesale Corporation

Ticker symbol: COST (NASDAQ) □ S&P rating: A+ □ Value Line financial strength rating: A+ □
Current yield: 1.2%

Company Profile

Costco Wholesale Corporation operates a multinational chain of membership warehouses, mainly under the Costco Wholesale name, that carry brand-name merchandise at substantially lower prices than are typically found at conventional wholesale or retail sources. The warehouses are designed to help small to medium-sized businesses reduce costs in purchasing for resale and for everyday business use, but as most know, the individual consumer has been their big growth driver. The company capitalizes on size and operational efficiencies, like "cross-docking" shipments directly from manufacturers to stores, to achieve attractive pricing to its customers. Costco is the largest membership warehouse club chain in the world based on sales volume and is the fifth largest general retailer in the United States.

Costco carries a broad line of product categories, including groceries, appliances, television and media, automotive supplies, toys, hardware, sporting goods, jewelry, cameras, books, housewares, apparel, health and beauty aids,

tobacco, furniture, office supplies, and office equipment. The company also operates self-service gasoline stations at a number of its U.S. and Canadian locations. Approximately 56 percent of sales come from food, beverages, alcohol, sundries, and snacks, and the rest from an assortment of hard and soft lines.

Additionally, Costco Wholesale Industries, a division of the company, operates manufacturing businesses, including special food packaging, optical laboratories, meat processing, and jewelry distribution.

Costco is open only to members of its tiered membership plan. As of August 2010 Costco has 566 locations, 416 in the United States and Puerto Rico, 79 in Canada, 32 in Mexico, 22 in the United Kingdom, 22 in Asia, and one in Australia.

Financial Highlights, Fiscal Year 2010

Like all retailers, Costco felt the effects of the worldwide recession and turned in their first-ever year-over-year decline in revenues in 2009, down 1.5 percent versus 2008.

Most of this was due to a decrease in comparable sales, partially offset by sales at new warehouses. The company fared well in the recovery, however, and returned sales to a steady track. Same-store sales had risen 4 percent in mid-2009, aided by more frequent visits, but not necessarily larger transactions. Membership fees continued their momentum, with higher fees and upgrades being absorbed by a very loyal customer base. Per share earnings likewise regained their momentum.

Reasons to Buy

Costco is in an attractive best-of-both-worlds niche: They are a price leader consistent with the attitudes of today's more frugal consumer, yet they enjoy a reputation for being more upscale than their competition. We also like the international expansion, and think the formula will play well overseas. Anyone who has hosted a visitor from abroad knows that Costco is a favored destination during the visit. The company has a strong brand in a highly competitive sector, and is gaining market share.

Costco has completed the coveted triple play—double-digit compounded sales, earnings, and cash flow growth over the past ten years. We like the commitment to dividend growth though the yield isn't so high at present.

Reasons for Caution

One concern is the dependence on low margin food and sundry lines. With the ramp-up of Wal-Mart and Target groceries and stiff competition elsewhere, Costco may not always be the food source of choice. That said, food does get customers into the store. We are also concerned about the company's not surprisingly razor-thin 1.7 percent net profit margins—even a small change in supply/demand economics or cost structure can wipe out profitability. Most retail concepts run out of steam eventually as they run out of opportunities to expand, although Costco's international expansion attenuates this concern somewhat. With these concerns in mind, recent share prices may be a bit rich.

SECTOR: **Retail**
BETA COEFFICIENT: **.74**
10-YEAR COMPOUND EARNINGS PER SHARE GROWTH: **9.0%**
10-YEAR COMPOUND DIVIDENDS PER SHARE GROWTH: **NM**

	2003	2004	2005	2006	2007	2008	2009	2010
Revenues (Mil)	41,693	48,107	52,935	60,151	64,400	72,483	71,422	77,946
Net Income (Mil)	721	882	989	1,103	1,083	1,283	1,086	1,307
Earnings per share	1.53	1.85	2.03	2.3	2.37	2.89	2.57	2.93
Dividends per share	0	0.2	0.45	0.49	0.55	0.61	0.68	0.77
Cash flow per share	1.53	1.86	2.03	2.31	2.63	2.89	4.16	4.85
Price: high	39	50.5	51.2	57.9	72.7	75.2	61.3	73.2
low	27	35	39.5	46	51.5	43.9	38.2	53.4

Costco Wholesale Corporation
999 Lake Drive
Issaquah, WA 98027
(425) 313-8203
Website: *www.costco.com*

CVS/Caremark Corporation

Ticker symbol: CVS (NYSE) ❑ S&P rating: BBB+ ❑ Value Line financial strength rating: A ❑ Current yield: 1.0%

Company Profile

Stanley and Sid Goldstein were distributing health and beauty products in the early 1960s when they decided to branch out into retailing, opening their first Consumer Value Store in Lowell, Massachusetts, in 1963. The CVS chain had grown to forty outlets by 1969, the year they sold the business to Melville Shoes. Melville underwent a restructuring in the mid-1990s, spinning off CVS and other retail units.

CVS Corporation is now the largest domestic drugstore chain, based on store count. CVS operates over 7,000 retail and specialty pharmacy stores in forty states and the District of Columbia. The company holds the leading market share in thirty-two of the 100 largest U.S. drugstore markets, more than any other retail drugstore chain.

Stores are situated primarily in strip shopping centers or free-standing locations, with a typical store ranging in size from 8,000 to 12,000 square feet. Most new units being built are based on either a 10,000 square foot or 12,000 square foot prototype building that typically includes a drive-thru pharmacy. The company says that about

one-half of its stores were opened or remodeled over the past five years.

The Caremark acquisition in 2007 transformed CVS from a retailer into the nation's leading manager of pharmacy benefits, the middlemen between pharmaceutical companies and individuals with drug benefit coverage. The Caremark acquisition forms the core of the company's Pharmacy Benefits Management (PBM) operations, which now make up about 65 percent of sales.

CVS' purchase of Long's Drugs in 2008 vaulted the company into the lead position in the U.S. drug retail market, ahead of Walgreen's. Long's is only the most recent in a series of acquisitions by CVS in recent years, including Minute-Clinic, Osco Drugs, and Sav-On Drugs in 2006, Caremark (for $26.5 billion) in 2007, and finally Long's (for $2.6 billion) in 2008. Earnings over the period have nearly tripled, although per share earnings have grown a somewhat more modest 55 percent.

MinuteClinic is especially interesting in today's climate of examining health care costs, with 569 clinics in twenty-five states offering basic health services like flu shots and such in a convenient retail environment. All but twelve of these clinics are located in CVS stores, naturally serving to drive traffic into the stores and vice versa.

Financial Highlights, Fiscal Year 2010

Softness in the Pharmacy Benefits segment, unfortunately, brought a dip of approximately 2 percent in total 2010 sales. The decline was attributed to generic drugs and the loss of a few key contracts. FY11 results should improve, however, with a new $8 billion deal signed with Aetna and increased Medicare Part D business. Per share earnings stayed relatively flat largely due to share buybacks. Operating margins continue to be challenged by the PBM business, down to 22–23 percent from 26–27 percent prior to the acquisition. The company faces some challenges with PBM but should fare well with cost cutting and innovation efforts.

Reasons to Buy

People who shop CVS regularly can see the difference between these stores and the ubiquitous competitors, especially Walgreen's. These stores are essentially big-box convenience stores, but we think the company does a notably good job of merchandising, offering a good mix of convenience merchandise,

food, and health care products to truly capitalize on its convenient retail format.

That goes beyond the typical positives seen for this industry: the graying of the population, and the rather effortless spending on health care that still goes on. The company continues to feel that its leadership in sun-belt states will capitalize on this megatrend. The recent federal health care overhaul left Medicare Part D basically untouched, which at the end of 2009, provided prescription coverage to 27 million Americans who would otherwise not be eligible. Medicare Part D also encourages caregivers to use generic drugs whenever possible, and generics, while cheaper overall, generate higher margins for the pharmacy. Over the next five years, more than $50 billion in branded drugs will lose patent protection, creating further opportunities for generics and driving pharmacy margins even higher.

We are also behind its acquisitions of well-run smaller companies in the same business, Osco in particular, and we think the Minute-Clinic idea will gain significant traction. Finally, the company has scored a quintuple play over the past ten years with double-digit compounded sales, earnings, cash flow, dividend, and book value growth over the period. That said, the dividend yield remains modest.

Reasons for Caution

The PBM business continues to be challenging from both a sales and profitability standpoint. It may be too big, and it may be defocusing. It does seem that CVS is well managed in general, but PBM may stretch this to the limit. At the same time, if the company succeeds in optimizing the PBM business, shareholders could be rewarded considerably.

SECTOR: Retail
BETA COEFFICIENT: 0.82
10-YEAR COMPOUND EARNINGS PER SHARE GROWTH: 13.5%
10-YEAR COMPOUND DIVIDENDS PER SHARE GROWTH: 9.0%

		2003	2004	2005	2006	2007	2008	2009	2010
Revenue (Mil)		26,588	30,594	37,006	43,814	76,330	87,472	98,413	96,413
Net Income (Mil)		847	959	1,225	1,369	2,637	3,589	3,662	3,427
Earnings per share		1.03	1.15	1.45	1.6	1.92	2.44	2.63	2.67
Dividends per share		0.12	0.13	0.14	0.16	0.24	0.26	0.3	0.35
Cash flow per share		1.49	1.75	2.15	2.5	2.59	3.37	3.73	3.75
Price:	high	18.8	23.7	31.6	36.1	42.6	44.3	38.3	37.8
	low	10.9	16.9	22	26.1	30.5	23.2	23.7	26.8

CVS/Caremark Corporation
One CVS Drive
Woonsocket, RI 02895
(914) 722-4704
Website: *www.cvs.com*

AGGRESSIVE GROWTH

Deere & Company

Ticker symbol: DE (NYSE) ❑ S&P rating: A ❑ Value Line financial strength rating: A++ ❑ Current yield: 1.6%

Company Profile

Founded in 1837, Deere & Company grew from a one-man blacksmith shop into a worldwide corporation that today does business in more than 160 countries and employs more than 40,000 people around the globe. Deere has a diverse base of operations reporting in two broad categories following a 2009 restructuring: Equipment Operations and Financial Services.

Equipment Operations includes the signature Agriculture and Turf Equipment segment, comprising about 85 percent of the business, and the Construction and Forestry Equipment segment, both segments being bolstered in the marketplace by the Financial Services segment. Deere has been the world's premier producer of agricultural equipment for nearly fifty years. If it's used on a farm and requires an engine, Deere likely offers it. With the Construction and Forestry segment, Deere is also the world's leading manufacturer of forestry equipment, and a major manufacturer of heavy construction equipment (Caterpillar being the market leader in the heavy construction segment). They're also the world leader in premium turf-care equipment and utility vehicles in both the commercial and consumer markets.

The Financial Services segment includes John Deere Credit, which is one of the largest equipment finance companies in the United States, with more than 1.8 million accounts and a managed asset portfolio of nearly $16 billion. It provides retail, wholesale, and lease financing for agricultural, construction and forestry, commercial and consumer equipment, including lawn and ground care, and revolving credit for agricultural inputs and services. These services are available in all of Deere's largest markets, including Argentina, Australia, Brazil, Canada, France, and Germany. Overall, international sales account for about 42 percent of the total.

Financial Highlights, Fiscal Year 2010

Deere has clearly emerged from the slowdown with its main line businesses intact; in addition, it became leaner and meaner during hard times with a reduced cost structure. During the first half of 2010, sales continued to lag, but earnings were up 20 percent from the year before. During the latter part of the year, sales continued at a brisk clip and earnings tracked some 40-plus percent higher than 2009, in part due to a ten-year high operating margin exceeding 13 percent. Restructuring appears to have been effective in reducing costs without negatively affecting delivery of product or taking too large a bite out of the company's underlying finances.

Reasons to Buy

"Nothing runs like a Deere" is the company's apt slogan, and as far as industrial companies go, Deere has achieved almost unparalleled excellence over the years. They have an outstanding brand (and one of the most popular logos for hats, jackets, and so on, worn by people who have never seen a farm field!) and reputation in the agriculture industry, and we see the ag industry as strong and strategic far into the future. Farm incomes are on the rise, with a 3.5 percent growth projected for 2011. The company is making good progress in developing markets, particularly in Brazil and India.

Beyond its products, Deere has established an almost unassailable brand leadership with its services and customer-centered innovations. Deere, more than others, puts its people in the field (literally) to figure out what agriculture professionals really need, and they work with their customers closely to sell their products through a solid dealer network, not unlike Caterpillar in the construction market.

Reasons for Caution

The company is, and always will be, vulnerable to business cycles and particularly cycles in the farm sector. While agricultural commodities are once again on the rise, that can turn on a dime, and the company's 1.55 beta reflects this long-term volatility. Recent public-sector belt tightening both at the federal and state level may hurt the farming business, as will any protracted rise in energy prices. Finally, many investors have noticed Deere's excellent track record, and outside the 2008–09 downturn, the shares have tended to be relatively expensive related to fundamentals.

SECTOR: **Industrials**
BETA COEFFICIENT: **1.55**
10-YEAR COMPOUND EARNINGS PER SHARE GROWTH: **12.5%**
10-YEAR COMPOUND DIVIDENDS PER SHARE GROWTH: **9.5%**

	2003	**2004**	**2005**	**2006**	**2007**	**2008**	**2009**	**2010**
Revenues (Mil)	13,349	17,673	19,401	19,884	21,489	25,804	20,756	23,573
Net Income (Mil)	643	1,406	1,447	1,453	1,822	2,053	1,198	1,885
Earnings per share	1.32	2.78	2.94	3.08	4.01	4.7	2.82	4.35
Dividends per share	0.44	0.53	0.61	0.78	0.91	1.06	1.12	1.16
Cash flow per share	2.02	3.54	3.85	4.09	5.12	6.01	4.05	5.72
Price: high	33.7	37.5	37.4	50.7	93.7	94.9	56.9	84.9
low	18.8	28.4	28.5	33.5	45.1	28.5	24.5	46.3

Deere & Company
One John Deere Place
Moline, IL 61265
(309) 765–4491
Website: *www.deere.com*

Dentsply International, Inc.

Ticker symbol: XRAY (NASDAQ) ❑ S&P rating: A– ❑ Value Line financial strength rating: B++ ❑
Current yield: 0.6%

Company Profile

Dentsply is the largest dental products company in the world. The company designs, develops, manufactures, and markets a broad range of products for dentists, orthodontists, and dental laboratories, including dental prosthetics, precious metal dental alloys, dental ceramics, endodontic instruments and materials, pastes, sealants, scalers, and crown and bridge materials. They are the leading United States manufacturer and distributor of dental x-ray equipment, dental handpieces, intraoral cameras, dental x-ray film holders, film mounts, and bone substitute/grafting materials. Finally, they are also a leading worldwide manufacturer or distributor of dental injectable anesthetics, impression materials, orthodontic appliances, dental cutting instruments, and dental implants. In all, the company produces or resells over 120,000 SKUs, protected by more than 2,000 patents.

Dentsply has a presence in more than 120 countries, though its main operations take place in the United States, Canada, Germany, Switzerland, the United Kingdom, Japan, and Italy. The company has an extensive sales network of over 2,100 sales representatives, distributors, and importers. Its products are manufactured in or distributed from facilities around the world and include well-established brand names such as Caulk, Cavitron, Ceramco, Dentsply, Detrey, Midwest, R&R Rinn, and Trubyte. International sales account for more than 60 percent of the total.

Financial Highlights, Fiscal Year 2010

You would think dental care is a necessity largely unaffected by a recession, but that has proven not to be the case. Particularly since most dental insurance only provides partial coverage and many aren't insured at all, people delay or postpone routine or reconstructive dental procedures to the extent possible. In FY2009 Dentsply's net sales declined 1.5 percent—the first year-over-year decline in sales in over fifteen years—although the shortfall was small enough that when precious metal content is removed from the calculation (precious metal costs are passed through to customers without margin), sales were essentially flat. Gross margin fell

200 basis points (2 percent) because of unfavorable product mix and unfavorable currency movements.

During that year, the company put expense controls in place in response to the downturn in the economy and was able to shave 100 basis points off of SG&A. Additional savings were gained via headcount reduction and restructuring, and operating margins remained relatively strong at 21.2 percent, but in the end, earnings fell 2 percent, or $.04/share versus 2008. As bad years go, though, this was not all that bad.

The year 2010 was much the same story, with sales still off the 2008 pace and essentially flat earnings. The company continues to seek operational improvements but growth will really be driven by the economy making people more willing to pursue dental work. The base level of demand, meanwhile, remains secure.

Cash flow is ample, and the company has been repurchasing shares, reducing share counts from approximately 160 million in 2004 to an estimated 140 million in 2010.

Reasons to Buy

We feel that the base level of demand is solid, and any economic recovery will bring healthy earnings and cash flow growth to a relatively leaner and meaner Dentsply. We feel that

the chickens will come home to roost from a couple of years of relative dental neglect: sugar and bacteria simply didn't get the memo to hold back on tooth decay during the recession. Demographics, at least in the domestic market, continue to work in the company's favor. Older people tend to spend more on dental care, and every office visit, whether it be for a simple cleaning or full endodontic repair, uses Dentsply consumables. A larger percentage of the population are retaining their natural teeth, and are doing so far longer than they used to, and natural teeth require relatively more dental care.

Trends in the global economy also favor Dentsply. As per capita and discretionary incomes rise in the emerging nations of the Pacific Rim, Latin America, and Eastern Europe, improved health care, and dental care in particular, become a priority. Dental care spending in India and China is growing far faster than in the mature U.S. market.

The company is nearly debt-free and has cash to support both share repurchase and acquisitions, should opportunities arise.

Reasons for Caution

Dentistry in North America and Western Europe has changed focus over the years from treating pain, infections, and poor overall dental health toward a practice with an increased emphasis on preventive care and cosmetic dentistry. Cosmetic dentistry includes many high-value procedures, but cosmetic procedures are elective in nature and are often not covered under insurance programs. In general, dental insurance coverage is on the decline. These factors lead to reduced and deferred dental care, which will hurt the top line at least short term.

SECTOR: **Health Care**
BETA COEFFICIENT: **1.03**
10-YEAR COMPOUND EARNINGS PER SHARE GROWTH: **13.5%**
10-YEAR COMPOUND DIVIDENDS PER SHARE GROWTH: **10.0%**

		2003	2004	2005	2006	2007	2008	2009	2010
Revenues (Mil)		1,571	1,694	1,715	1,810	2,010	2,194	2,160	2,221
Net Income (Mil)		173	196	216	224	260	286	276	278
Earnings per share		1.07	1.2	1.34	1.41	1.68	1.88	1.84	1.90
Dividends per share		0.1	0.11	0.12	0.14	0.16	0.19	0.2	0.20
Cash flow per share		1.38	1.52	1.69	1.8	2.03	2.3	2.32	2.45
Price:	high	23.7	28.4	29.2	33.8	47.8	47.1	36.8	38.2
	low	16.1	20.9	25.4	26.1	29.4	22.8	21.8	27.8

Dentsply International, Inc.
P.O. Box 872
221 West Philadelphia Street
York, PA 17405–0872
(717) 849-4243
Website: *www.dentsply.com*

Dominion Resources, Inc.

Ticker symbol: D (NYSE) ❑ S&P rating: A- ❑ Value Line financial strength rating: B++ ❑ Current yield: 4.3%

Company Profile

Dominion is one of the nation's largest producers and distributors of energy, with 27,000 megawatts of power generation, 6,000 miles of electric transmission lines, 12,000 miles of natural gas transmission, gathering, and storage pipeline, and 1.3 trillion cubic feet equivalent of natural gas reserves. Included in these assets is the nation's largest underground natural gas storage system with about 942 billion cubic feet of storage capacity serving retail energy customers in twelve states. Dominion's strategy is to be a leading provider of electricity, natural gas, and related services to customers in the energy-intensive Midwest, Mid-Atlantic, and Northeast regions of the United States, a potential market of 50 million homes and businesses where 40 percent of the nation's energy is consumed.

As of 2010, Dominion operates in three reporting segments:

Dominion Generation (44 percent of revenue, 59 percent of profits) includes the generation operations of Dominion's merchant fleet and regulated electric utility, as well as energy marketing and price risk management activities for its generation assets. Their utility generation operations primarily serve the supply requirements for the Dominion Virginia Power segment's utility customers. Their generation mix is diversified and includes coal, nuclear, gas, oil, and renewables. DG produced 60 percent of the company's earnings in 2009.

Dominion Energy (30 percent of revenue, 24 percent of profits) includes Dominion's Ohio regulated natural gas distribution company, regulated gas transmission pipeline, and storage operations, regulated liquefied natural gas (LNG) operations, and Appalachian natural gas Exploration & Production (E&P) business. Dominion Energy also includes producer services, which aggregates natural gas supply, engages in natural gas trading and marketing activities and natural gas supply management, and provides price risk management services to Dominion affiliates.

The gas transmission pipeline and storage business serves gas distribution businesses and other customers in the Northeast, Mid-Atlantic, and Midwest.

Dominion Virginia Power (26 percent of revenue, 18 percent of profits) is responsible for all regulated electric distribution and electric transmission operations in Virginia and North Carolina. It is also responsible for Dominion Retail and all customer service, as well as its non-regulated retail energy marketing operations. DVP's electric transmission and distribution operations serve residential, commercial, industrial, and governmental customers in Virginia and northeastern North Carolina.

The company's utility revenue breakdown (2009) was 45 percent residential, 33 percent commercial, 8 percent industrial, and 14 percent other. The generation mix was 33 percent coal, 32 percent nuclear, 25 percent purchased, 9 percent gas, and 1 percent oil.

Financial Highlights, Fiscal Year 2010

Dominion's net revenue continued to decline slightly with the 2010 divestiture of its gas exploration and distribution operations. Earnings came in at $2.89 per share versus an acquisition-adjusted $2.64 per share on revenues of $15.2 billion. For 2011, the company forecast a dip in earnings to about $3.15 per share for the year.

In late 2010, the company not only raised its dividend 7.7 percent, from $1.83 to $1.97 per share, but it also announced a change in dividend policy, whereby 60–65 percent of net earnings would be paid to shareholders, up from the previous 55 percent.

In early 2011, Duke Energy announced a $13.7 billion acquisition bid for Progress Energy to create what would be the country's largest regulated public utility. Both companies operate as virtual neighbors to Dominion, and it was rumored that Dominion had started this round of mergers with its own quest for Progress or even possibly Duke. This situation bears watching as an indicator of whether authorities support another round of mergers and consolidations in the industry.

Reasons to Buy

Dominion has exited the natural gas exploration and production business, having sold off its remaining assets in early 2010 (the divestiture began in 2006). The company felt that the business, although profitable, was too volatile and far from the core business. This was viewed as a negative among the traditional utility and large institutional investors. In the meantime, the company's core businesses are healthy and located in areas of solid recovery and growth potential, particularly in the Eastern Seaboard areas. The acquisition winds are blowing, and the effects on Dominion bear watching.

Reasons for Caution

The year 2011 looks to be one of higher energy prices, and naturally, Dominion is exposed to such price increases. That said, the company has enough nuclear capacity in its portfolio to diversify away from some of this risk. And that said in turn, those who avoid nuclear energy should probably avoid this issue.

SECTOR: **Utilities**

BETA COEFFICIENT: **.70**

10-YEAR COMPOUND EARNINGS PER SHARE GROWTH: **7.5%**

10-YEAR COMPOUND DIVIDENDS PER SHARE GROWTH: **2.0%**

		2003	2004	2005	2006	2007	2008	2009	2010
Revenues (Mil)		12,078	13,972	17,971	16,482	15,674	16,290	15,131	15,197
Net Income (Mil)		1,261	1,425	1,033	1,704	1,414	1,781	1,585	1,724
Earnings per share		1.96	2.13	1.5	2.4	2.13	3.04	2.64	2.89
Dividends per share		2.58	1.3	1.34	1.38	1.46	1.58	1.75	1.83
Cash flow per share		3.97	4.18	3.71	4.91	5.08	5.07	4.82	5.10
Price:	high	33	34.5	43.5	42.2	49.4	48.5	39.8	45.1
	low	25.9	30.4	33.3	34.4	39.8	31.3	27.1	36.1

Dominion Resources, Inc.

P.O. Box 26532

Richmond, VA 23261–6532

(804) 819–2156

Website: *www.dom.com*

Duke Energy

Ticker symbol: DUK (NYSE) ❑ S&P rating: A- ❑ Value Line financial strength rating: A ❑ Current yield: 5.4%

Company Profile

Duke Energy Corporation is a utility provider and operator working primarily in the Southeast and Midwest but with operations outside those areas. The company has three segments: U.S. Franchised Electric and Gas, Commercial Power, and International Energy. The company was reformed into a new company in 2007 after spinning off most of its gas business into a new company called Spectra Energy.

The Franchised Electric and Gas segment generates, transmits, distributes, and sells electricity in central and western North Carolina, western South Carolina, southwestern Ohio, Indiana, and northern Kentucky including the Greater Cincinnati area; and transports and sells natural gas in southwestern Ohio and northern Kentucky. This segment supplies electric service to approximately 4 million residential, commercial, and industrial customers with approximately 151,600 miles of distribution lines and a 20,900-mile transmission system. The company is relatively heavily invested in nuclear power, with some 35 percent of its power provided this way (55 percent coal, 10 percent other).

The Commercial Power segment offers onsite energy solutions and utility services for large customers. This segment owns, operates, and manages power plants; and handles all procurement and services around these plants; it also develops customized energy solutions for these customers.

The International Energy segment operates and manages power generation facilities and sells and markets electric power and natural gas outside the United States. This segment provides services and consulting for retail distributors, electric utilities, independent power producers, marketers, and industrial and commercial companies. It also develops, owns, and operates a fiber optic communications network, primarily in the Southeast United States, serving wireless, local, and long-distance communications companies, as well as Internet service providers, and other businesses and organizations. The company was founded in 1916 and is based in Charlotte, North Carolina.

In early 2011, Duke announced a $13.7 billion takeover of Progress Energy, which operates in adjacent markets and would make the combined company the largest public utility in the United States. Aside from direct impacts on the company and its operations, the acquisition is viewed as a referendum on public regulator acceptance of a new round of "mega" mergers in the utility industry.

Financial Highlights, Fiscal Year 2010

The 2007 spinoff makes long-term comparisons difficult. The year 2010 saw a moderate earnings increase to $1.40 per share from $1.13 a year before, due to an unusually hot summer, but 2011 earnings were forecast to stay in the $1.30–$1.40 range. The company continues to bring new generating capacity online in its most vibrant markets in the Carolinas. The company continues to generate cash flow almost double reported earnings.

Reasons to Buy

Duke has always been a well-managed utility operating in solid markets with a growing customer base. The North Carolina customer base is diverse and especially attractive as more companies and individuals move there to enjoy lower costs of living and costs of doing business. The company should also stand to benefit, perhaps more than its peers, from an economic recovery.

We actually like its nuclear exposure as we do think nuclear power will return to the electricity generating stage in a bigger way. Duke will have the advantage of experience and existing infrastructure. Because it's a relatively new concern in its current form, and perhaps because of its nuclear exposure, the dividend is about 1 percent higher than the average for similar companies. That said, it is well covered by current cash flows.

Reasons for Caution

For many, nuclear power is a reason for caution, and we certainly would want to diversify utility holdings to avoid overexposure to utilities with nuclear facilities. Like most utilities, Duke depends on regulatory rate relief to grow revenues, and so the regulatory environment is critical. The Progress acquisition would create size and critical mass but may also consume a lot of cash and make the company too big and perhaps too reliant on acquisitions to fuel growth. That said, the company seems well enough managed to take on such an endeavor.

SECTOR: **Utilities**
BETA COEFFICIENT: **0.41**
10-YEAR COMPOUND EARNINGS PER SHARE GROWTH: **NA**
10-YEAR COMPOUND DIVIDENDS PER SHARE GROWTH: **NA**

	2003	2004	2005	2006	2007	2008	2009	2010
Revenues (Mil)	-	-	-	10,607	12,720	13,207	12,731	14,272
Net Income (Mil)	-	-	-	1,080	1,522	1,279	1,461	1,771
Earnings per share	-	-	-	.92	1.20	1.01	1.13	1.34
Dividends per share	-	-	-	-	.86	.90	.94	.97
Cash flow per share	-	-	-	2.62	2.70	2.45	2.53	2.70
Price: high	-	-	-	21.3	20.6	17.9	17.5	18.6
low	-	-	-	16.9	13.5	11.7	15.9	15.5

Duke Energy Corporation
526 South Church Street
Charlotte, NC 28202–1803
(704) 594-6200
Website: *www.duke-energy.com*

E. I. DuPont De Nemours

Ticker symbol: DD (NYSE) ❑ S&P rating: A ❑ Value Line financial strength rating: A++ ❑ Current yield: 5.3%

Company Profile

"The miracles of science" is the slogan and rallying cry of this $30 billion–plus science and technology juggernaut originally founded in 1802 to make gunpowder. Although the company is known to many as a cyclical "diversified chemical" company making a host of rather lifeless chemical products and ingredients, many by the tank car load, today's DuPont is reawakening as a world leader in science and technology with important end product ingredients in a range of disciplines, including biotechnology, electronics materials and science, safety and security, and synthetic fibers. The company has taken on a newly found pride, referring to their business as "market-driven science," reflected in 2009's introduction of over 1,400 new products and more than 2,000 patent grants. The company has always been a technology leader with such well-known inventions as Nylon and Rayon in earlier years, and Teflon and Kevlar more recently, but at least until recently has been taken in more as a commodity producer than an innovator. We see signs of change in that reputation.

In 2009, the company strategically realigned its businesses into several market- and technology-focused growth platforms. Included are:

- Agriculture and Nutrition—a rapidly growing segment seen to approach 28–30 percent of sales with brands like Pioneer seeds and a host of insect protection and other systems. The Pioneer acquisition happened twelve years ago; most don't observe DuPont as an ag company either. But the 2011 acquisition announcement for Denmark's Danisco for $6.3 billion, a major producer of food ingredients, additives, and enzymes, signals rapid growth for the ag business, now projected at 35 percent of sales going forward.
- Safety and Protection makes protective fibers and clothing, including bulletproof apparel and disinfectants.
- Health Care & Medical specializes in protection apparel, disinfectants, and protective building surfaces.

- Electronic and Communications makes a line of high-tech materials for the semiconductor industry, including ceramic packages and LCD materials.
- Building Materials sells such ubiquitous brands as Tyvek housewrap and Corian countertops.

And the core businesses:

- Performance Chemicals
- Performance Materials
- Performance Coatings

The company has operations in ninety countries worldwide and about 60 percent of consolidated net sales are made to customers outside the United States. Worldwide subsidiaries and affiliates of DuPont conduct manufacturing, seed production, or selling activities, and some are distributors of products manufactured by the company.

DuPont has one of the largest R&D budgets of any company in the world and operates more than seventy-five R&D centers worldwide. DuPont's core research is concentrated at its Wilmington, Delaware, facilities. DuPont's modern research is focused on renewable bio-based materials, advanced biofuels, energy-efficient technologies, enhanced safety products, and alternative energy technologies.

Financial Highlights, Fiscal Year 2010

A few years ago, the company projected 2012 earnings at $3.50 per share, up from the mid-$1 range. At the time, at least one pundit suggested that top management should take a drug test. But the truth of the matter? The company appears on track to meet the goal a year early. Core businesses are rebounding with the rebound in the auto industry and others, and the newer businesses and products are growing and making a steadily larger contribution. One analyst now estimates some half of 2012 business will come from "growth" businesses and products.

Further, the CEO now projects annual revenue growth of 7 percent and earnings growth of 12 percent during the 2010–2015 timeframe.

Reasons to Buy

DuPont seems to be succeeding in its efforts to reinvent itself as an innovation leader, and to capitalize equally on innovation and product leadership in established categories. Not that this company doesn't have experience with innovation—quite the opposite, in fact—the problem seems to be in getting recognized for its innovation. The product pipeline continues to be full, individual product margins remain strong, and the company's biggest moneymakers still dominate their markets.

The company now visualizes itself as a "fast growing science company" set to capitalize on "global megatrends"—population growth, alternative energy production, and so forth. The improvement of worldwide food production is at the center of its new growth initiatives. Alternative energy will also get the spotlight: The Danisco acquisition is, among other things, a major play in the synthetic cellulosic biofuels market with its Genencor industrial enzymes business. The U.S. government has mandated some 30 billion gallons of annual cellulosic biofuel production by 2017.

In short, this company is firing on all cylinders, especially in terms of capitalizing on existing brands and technology leadership. The 3.3 percent dividend yield provides an added measure of safety and opportunity to wait for things to really come together.

Reasons for Caution

For whatever reason—anemic marketing may be one of them—the company has seldom been able to capitalize on its "science and technology" positioning, and is viewed as a commodity producer instead. We'll see if it's any different this time. The stock price has woken up to these brighter prospects, and has been relatively strong, particularly in comparison to its 2009 low of $16. Buyers should look for dips.

SECTOR: Materials
BETA COEFFICIENT: 1.37
10-YEAR COMPOUND EARNINGS PER SHARE GROWTH: –1.0%
10-YEAR COMPOUND DIVIDENDS PER SHARE GROWTH: 2.0%

	2003	2004	2005	2006	2007	2008	2009	2010
Revenues (Mil)	26,996	27,340	26,639	28,982	30,653	30,529	26,109	31,505
Net Income (Mil)	1,607	2,390	2,100	3,148	2,988	2,477	1,769	3,032
Earnings per share	1.65	2.38	2.32	2.88	3.22	2.73	2.04	3.28
Dividends per share	1.4	1.4	1.46	1.48	1.52	1.64	1.64	1.64
Cash flow per share	3.19	3.75	3.97	4.4	4.89	4.25	3.4	4.80
Price: high	46	49.4	54.9	49.7	53.9	52.5	35.6	50.2
low	34.7	39.9	37.6	38.5	42.3	21.3	16	31.9

E. I. DuPont De Nemours
1007 Market Street
Wilmington, DE 19898
(800) 441-7515
Website: *www.dupont.com*

CONSERVATIVE GROWTH

Ecolab, Inc.

Ticker symbol: ECL (NYSE) ❑ S&P rating: A ❑ Value Line financial strength rating: A ❑ Current yield: 1.5%

Company Profile

Ecolab is the global leader in commercial products and services used for cleaning, sanitizing, food safety, and infection prevention. Founded in 1923 and headquartered in St. Paul, Minnesota, Ecolab serves customers in more than 160 countries across North America, Europe, Asia and the Pacific, Latin America, the Middle East, and Africa, and employs more than 26,000. The company delivers comprehensive programs and services to industries such as foodservice, food and beverage processing, hospitality, health care, government and education, retail, vehicle care, pest elimination, and facilities maintenance.

The company conducts its domestic business under these segments:

- Institutional Division is the leading provider of cleaners and sanitizers for utensils, laundry, kitchen cleaning and general housecleaning, product-dispensing equipment and dishwashing racks and related kitchen sundries to the foodservice, lodging, and

health care industries. It also provides products and services for pool and spa treatment.

- Food & Beverage Division offers cleaning and sanitizing products and services to farms, dairy plants, food and beverage processors, and pharmaceutical plants.

- Kay Division is the largest supplier of cleaning and sanitizing products for the quick-service restaurant, convenience store, and food retail markets.

Ecolab also sells janitorial and health care products; textile care products for large institutional and commercial laundries; vehicle care products for rental, fleet, and retail car washes; and water-treatment products for commercial, institutional, and industrial markets. Other domestic services include institutional and commercial pest elimination and prevention, and commercial kitchen equipment repair services.

The company operates directly in nearly seventy countries, with about 47 percent of sales originating abroad. In addition, the company reaches customers in more than 100 countries through distributors, licensees, and export operations, with more than fifty state-of-the-art manufacturing and distribution facilities worldwide.

Financial Highlights, Fiscal Year 2010

FY2009 was a rough period for the restaurant and hospitality industries, which are two of Ecolab's core markets. During that year, the company didn't fare too badly, taking about a $200 million, or 4 percent, hit to the top line, which has since recovered. Improved operating efficiencies actually resulted in an earnings gain for the year. In FY2010, the recovery in the restaurant and hospitality industries lagged the rest of the economy (these businesses are doing a lot of cost cutting, too), and earnings came in at $2.23 per share, a nice 11 percent gain despite revenues flat from two years ago. The company prides itself on efficiency, noting that it has achieved double-digit earnings gains for nine of the past ten years despite relatively modest revenue increases.

For FY2011, the company expects earnings in the $2.48 to $2.53 range, keeping the double-digit tradition alive. Strong sales in Asia Pacific and Latin America and an accelerated restructuring in Europe will offset continued sluggish results in the U.S. cleaning and sanitizing businesses. An accelerated recovery in the restaurant, hospitality, and textile sectors would help considerably. The company is focused on total shareholder return, retiring about 8 percent of outstanding shares since 2004 and raising the dividend—albeit modestly—for nineteen consecutive years.

Reasons to Buy

Ecolab is the largest participant (with a 10 percent share) in what is estimated to be a $45 billion global cleaning and sanitation market, and Ecolab's operating margin is three times that of its largest competitor, DiversyJohnson. Overall, the market is not especially cyclical and has a built-in growth component as governments improve and modify regulations regarding cleanliness for public and private institutions and commercial buildings—the 4 percent revenue swing in 2008–2010 bears that out.

The company is not simply a distributor, as many other smaller players tend to be;—they have over 4,500 patents on their branded products. Many of their products are cleaning systems, which once in place, tend to stay in place and then require Ecolab-branded consumables throughout their life.

In light of several well-publicized food contamination

incidents over the past two years, Ecolab's customers have a renewed focus on cleanliness and sanitation in food preparation and serving, which is the heart of Ecolab's Institutional business. Ecolab is leveraging this positive attention by growing their presence in mainland China, where they have found a receptive customer base and huge opportunity. The company is simply the largest and most efficient player in a large and essential market niche, and that niche is expanding, particularly overseas.

Reasons for Caution

The stock has recently been trading at multiples in the mid-twenties while the stock has been flirting with all-time highs. That's okay if there's support for those valuations, but it isn't clear that growth opportunities support such valuations, particularly if the company runs out of efficiency measures to deploy. Companies under the gun to grow when the core business has matured tend to expand through acquisitions, and such behavior has its risks.

SECTOR: **Materials**
BETA COEFFICIENT: **0.7**
10-YEAR COMPOUND EARNINGS PER SHARE GROWTH: **12.5%**
10-YEAR COMPOUND DIVIDENDS PER SHARE GROWTH: **10.5%**

		2003	2004	2005	2006	2007	2008	2009	2010
Revenues (Mil)		3,762	4,185	4,535	4,896	5,470	6,138	5,901	6,090
Net Income (Mil)		277	310	320	369	427	464	447	530.3
Earnings per share		1.06	1.19	1.23	1.43	1.7	1.86	1.99	2.23
Dividends per share		0.29	0.33	0.35	0.4	0.52	0.52	0.56	0.62
Cash flow per share		1.96	2.18	2.27	2.54	2.87	3.38	3.43	3.78
Price:	high	27.9	35.6	37.2	46.4	52.8	52.3	49.7	52.5
	low	23.1	26.1	30.7	33.6	37	29.6	40.7	40.7

Ecolab, Inc.
370 Wabasha Street North
St. Paul, MN 55102–1390
(651) 293-2809
Website: *www.ecolab.com*

GROWTH AND INCOME

ExxonMobil Corporation

Ticker symbol: XOM (NYSE) ❑ S&P rating: AAA ❑ Value Line financial strength rating: A++ ❑ Current yield: 2.3%

Company Profile

ExxonMobil is the world's largest publicly traded oil company. They are engaged in the exploration, production, manufacture, transportation, and sale of crude oil, natural gas, and petroleum products. They also have a stake in the manufacture of petrochemicals, packaging films, and specialty chemicals.

Divisions and affiliated companies of ExxonMobil operate or market products in the United States and some 200 other countries and territories. Their principal business is energy, involving exploration for, and production of crude oil and natural gas; manufacture of petroleum products; and transportation and sale of crude oil, natural gas, and petroleum products.

The company is a major manufacturer and marketer of basic petrochemicals, including olefins, aromatics, polyethylene, and polypropylene plastics and a wide variety of specialty products. It also has interests in electric power generation facilities.

ExxonMobil conducts oil and gas exploration, development, and production in every major accessible producing region in the world. They have the largest energy resource base of any non-government company and are the largest non-government natural gas marketer and reserves holder. They're the world's largest fuels refiner and manufacturer of base stocks used for making motor oils. They have refining operations in twenty-six countries, 42,000 retail service stations in more than 100 countries, and lubricants marketing in almost 200 countries and territories. They market petrochemical products in more than 150 countries, and 90 percent of the company's petrochemical assets are in businesses that are ranked number one or number two in market position.

The XTO acquisition, completed in 2010, is a strong indication of Exxon's shift toward more profitable upstream operations, as well as a play in the likely future upside in natural gas prices. Since then, the company has been relatively quiet on the acquisition front, but we may see more activity, especially in the natural gas business.

Financial Highlights, Fiscal Year 2010

Not too surprisingly, Exxon is rebounding well from the economic and energy price lows of 2009. FY2010 sales came in at $342 billion, well ahead of 2009's $275 billion but short of the energy heyday high of $425 billion in 2008. Earnings came in at $6.22/share, compared to $3.98 for the full year 2009 and a stellar $8.69 for 2008. It's interesting to observe the impact of the price of a few commodities on a company's business. Most predict earnings and margins will stabilize closer to numbers seen in 2005–06. The company appears headed toward a more balanced mix of revenue and profitability in oil and gas, exploration, production, distribution, and chemical manufacturing segments.

Reasons to Buy

ExxonMobil and Apple Inc. vie for the number one and number two spots in total market capitalization, that is, the total value of shares outstanding. A decision to buy Exxon-Mobil over a company like Apple is essentially the decision to own a company with 23 billion barrels of oil equivalent in the ground and the means to bring them to market as high value add products, in contrast to owning a company with outstanding products, market acceptance, and innovation. It's an interesting choice.

Exxon is a huge generator of cash, and they've used considerable amounts of that cash to buy back

shares. Outstanding shares dropped from 6.1 billion in 2005 to an estimated 4.8 billion at the end of 2011. This is a significant move and long-term benefit for shareholders.

Finally, Exxon is the largest publicly traded oil company in the world, and in the oil business, there are strategic advantages that accrue to size. Having the resources to bring to bear on an opportunity can mean the difference between winning and losing an exploration or development award. Despite the company's enormous size, it has managed to return double-digit growth over the past ten years in sales, earnings, and cash flow, although these might be tied more to energy prices than operational excellence.

Reasons for Caution

ExxonMobil is the biggest and the best at a lot of things in a key strategic industry. But there can be such a thing as too big, and if any integrated energy company is to suffer for being too big, this may be the one. While we applaud the share buybacks, we would like to see a higher dividend payout, although the recently low yields reflect a resurgence in the stock price—also not a positive for entering investors. We don't expect XON to outperform the market to any great extent, but it should continue to be a solid cornerstone holding.

SECTOR: **Energy**
BETA COEFFICIENT: **.48**
10-YEAR COMPOUND EARNINGS PER SHARE GROWTH: **14.5%**
10-YEAR COMPOUND DIVIDENDS PER SHARE GROWTH: **7.0%**

	2003	2004	2005	2006	2007	2008	2009	2010
Revenues (Bil)	211	264	328	335	359	425	276	342
Net Income (Bil)	17	25.3	36.1	39.1	40.6	45.3	19.3	30.4
Earnings per share	2.56	3.89	5.71	6.62	7.28	8.69	3.98	6.22
Dividends per share	0.98	1.06	1.14	1.28	1.37	1.55	1.66	1.74
Cash flow per share	3.97	5.48	7.19	8.82	9.82	11.58	6.60	9.08
Price: high	41.1	52	66	79	95.3	96.1	82.7	73.7
low	31.6	39.9	49.2	56.4	69	56.5	61.9	55.9

ExxonMobil Corporation
5959 Las Colinas Boulevard
Irving, TX 75039-2298
(972) 444–1538
Website: *www.exxonmobil.com*

AGGRESSIVE GROWTH

Fair Isaac Corporation

Ticker symbol: FICO (NYSE) ❑ S&P rating: NA ❑ Value Line financial strength rating: B++ ❑
Current yield: 0.3%

Company Profile

Fair Isaac Corporation provides decision support analytics, software, and solutions to help businesses improve and automate decision making and risk management. The most well-known and best example of these solutions is the "FICO score"—an analytic single-figure estimate of a consumer's creditworthiness used in the credit industry and for other purposes such as employment and insurance.

FICO provides its analytic solutions and services to a variety of financial and other service organizations, including banks, credit reporting agencies, credit card processing agencies, insurers, retailers, marketers, and health care organizations. It operates in three segments: Applications, Scores, and Tools. The Applications segment provides decision and risk management tools, market targeting products, and fraud detection tools and associated professional services. The Scores segment includes the business-to-business scoring solutions, as well as myFICO solutions delivering FICO scores for consumers and associated professional services. The Tools segment provides software products and consulting services to help organizations build their own analytic tools.

About 76 percent of the company's revenues are derived from transaction and unit-priced products, such as the access and sale of a FICO score. About 71 percent of revenues are derived from the consumer credit, financial services, and insurance industries. Overseas revenue has grown from 29 percent to 33 percent of total revenues in the past three fiscal years.

Financial Highlights, Fiscal Year 2010

As most of its leading customers are in the financial and financial services industries, FICO suffered among other suppliers of products and services to this industry during the downturn. Loan and transaction volumes declined, businesses closed or downsized, and those still left tightened budgets. Revenues and earnings dropped more than 25 percent from their 2007 peak, reaching a low in 2010. Company efforts to improve products for the financial sector, including a new formulation for the FICO score and a special version for the mortgage industry, and deeper penetration into areas like fraud prevention and ID theft analytics for all industries are helping the business in 2011. The company is expected to earn $1.65 a share in 2011, on par with 2008 before the lights went out.

Reasons to Buy

There are a number of companies, large and small, in the analytics business. But few have the brand reputation and leadership enjoyed by FICO. FICO is the gold standard for this type of product, and has built its leadership, and really a pretty large moat, on its brand. We also think a stabilizing financial industry with new rules, fewer workers, and a greater recognition for risk and risk management will bode well for the FICO product suite. FICO products offer a good combination of streamlining and sophistication to financial and other decision making. Long term, we can easily see their modeling approaches being extended to analyzing customer behavior and providing decision support for insurability, employability, acceptance into schools, and other areas well beyond a consumer's ability to repay extended credit. International demand for FICO's products continues to grow. Although the percentage of revenue generated from international orders has remained relatively flat at approximately one-third of total revenues over the last three years, new products, a growing market acceptance of analytics, and a focus on the international market is expected to provide increased leverage here.

Although revenues and earnings have fallen for two consecutive years, the company is well capitalized and has maintained respectable operating margins, due in large part to effective cost controls and restructuring efforts. And although the company has divested itself of some operations and is a bit leaner, its core businesses are well funded and well positioned for growth as the smoke clears from the recent recession.

Reasons for Caution

Most of the changes afoot in the credit card and financial services industry bode well for FICO, but we wonder if credit demand will ever be what it was in 2004–07. The company's business is still heavily tied to transaction volumes. There is some public concern that scoring models oversimplify lending and insurability decisions and should not be used or relied on so heavily.

SECTOR: Information Technology
BETA COEFFICIENT: 1.43
10-YEAR COMPOUND EARNINGS PER SHARE GROWTH: 110.0%
10-YEAR COMPOUND DIVIDENDS PER SHARE GROWTH: 13.0%

	2003	2004	2005	2006	2007	2008	2009	2010
Revenues (Mil)	629.3	706.2	798.7	825.4	822.2	744.8	630.7	605.6
Net Income (Mil)	107.2	108.9	134.5	103.5	104.7	81.2	65.1	64.5
Earnings per share	1.41	1.49	1.86	1.5	1.82	1.64	1.34	1.42
Dividends per share	0.05	0.08	0.08	0.08	0.08	0.08	0.08	0.08
Cash flow per share	2.18	2.24	2.91	2.57	3.03	2.49	2.15	2.36
Price: high	43.1	41.5	48.5	47.8	41.8	32.2	24.5	27.0
low	28	23.7	32.3	32.5	32.1	10.4	9.8	19.5

Fair Isaac Corporation
901 Marquette Avenue Suite 3200
Minneapolis, MN 55402–3232
Phone: 612-758-5200
Website: *www.fairisaac.com*

FedEx Corporation

Ticker symbol: FDX (NYSE) ❑ S&P rating: BBB ❑ Value Line financial strength rating: B++ ❑ Current yield: 0.5%

Company Profile

FedEx Corporation is the world's leading provider of guaranteed express delivery services, and is a major player in the overall small shipment and small package logistics market. The corporation is organized as a holding company, with individual businesses that compete collectively and operate independently under the FedEx brand. The company offers a wide range of express delivery services for the time-definite transportation of documents, packages, and freight. The company also offers freight services for less time-sensitive items and small or less than truckload (LTL) shipments under the FedEx Ground and FedEx Freight brands. Finally, the company has ventured into more comprehensive business services with its 2004 acquisition of Kinko's copy and office centers, now operating under the "FedEx/Kinko's" brand.

The company's operations include:

- The world's largest express transportation company (FedEx Express)
- North America's second-largest ground carrier for small-package business shipments (FedEx Ground)
- The largest U.S. regional less-than-truckload freight company (FedEx Freight)
- A "24/7" option for urgent shipments, providing nonstop, door-to-door delivery in the contiguous United States, Canada, and Europe (FedEx Custom Critical)
- The largest-volume customs filer in the United States, providing freight forwarding, advisory services, and trade technology (FedEx Trade Networks)

The infrastructure supporting these businesses is enormous. For example, the FedEx Express business alone operates 135,000 ground vehicles and 664 aircraft and employs 265,000 people. In addition, they maintain over 700 World Service Centers, over 1,800 FedEx Office locations, nearly 7,000 authorized ShipCenters, and over 43,000 Drop Boxes. They serve over 375 airports in over 200 countries. In FY2010, the Express segment accounted for 62 percent of revenues, Ground 21 percent, Freight 12 percent, and Services 5 percent.

Financial Highlights, Fiscal Year 2010/2011

FedEx's revenues during and shortly after the recession took an expected dip due to the slowdown in worldwide trade. Revenue declines were offset somewhat by absorption of some business from DHL, which ceased domestic express operations in 2008. Driven by a resurgent global economy, revenues are expected to top $38 billion in 2011 (ending May 2011), an all-time high. Operating efficiencies are expected to raise operating margins slightly and deliver EPS in the $5.10–$5.20 range, short of 2007's $6.67, but good historically. Cash flow has been and will be more than double EPS, a good sign for the true health of the business.

Reasons to Buy

FedEx has a strong brand and offers a diverse set of services, really a complete logistics solution, for a large group of customers. The resurgence in the economy and growth in online shopping and delivery will certainly help volumes and pricing, and a resumption of strong U.S. exports not only helps volume but also helps fill up planes traveling from the United States. The logistics business is always ripe for innovation, and FedEx has long been an innovator in the transportation and small package shipment business; we expect this to continue. As pointed out, strong cash flows are also an attraction, and some of that is cautiously being paid back to shareholders.

Reasons for Caution

FedEx is obviously vulnerable to fuel price increases, and the same economic factors that create business growth can lead to growth in costs, so efficiency is Job Number One. The company has recently been investing in its ground businesses, which to a large degree compete head to head with UPS. These are relatively low margin businesses that we feel will succeed the most if effectively integrated—and marketed—with other services into a total solution. FedEx/Kinko's hasn't worked out as well financially as the company had hoped, although some of the integration we just spoke of has happened. Yes, you can have a FedEx Ground shipment held at FedEx/Kinko's for you to pick up, but too few people know about such services. Most still perceive FedEx/Kinko's as a good place to get copies. FedEx could do a better job of marketing what they really do to the general public, and perhaps, to businesses.

SECTOR: **Transportation**
BETA COEFFICIENT: **1.18**
10-YEAR COMPOUND EARNINGS PER SHARE GROWTH: **7.5%**
10-YEAR COMPOUND DIVIDENDS PER SHARE GROWTH: **8.0%**

		2003	**2004**	**2005**	**2006**	**2007**	**2008**	**2009**	**2010**
Revenues (Mil)		22,487	24,710	29,363	32,294	35,214	37,953	35,497	34,734
Net Income (Mil)		830	838	1,449	1,885	2,073	1,821	1,173	1,184
Earnings per share		2.74	2.76	4.82	5.98	6.67	5.83	3.76	3.76
Dividends per share		0.20	0.24	0.29	0.33	0.37	0.40	0.44	0.44
Cash flow per share		7.31	8.15	9.74	11.13	12.39	12.13	10.09	10.01
Price:	high	78	100.9	105.8	120	121.4	99.5	92.6	97.8
	Low	47.7	64.8	76.8	96.5	89.5	53.9	34	69.8

FedEx Corporation
942 South Shady Grove Road
Memphis, TN 38120
(901) 818–7200
Website: *www.fedex.com*

Fluor Corporation

Ticker symbol: FLR (NYSE) ◻ S&P rating: A- ◻ Value Line financial strength rating: A++ ◻ Current yield: 0.7%

Company Profile

Fluor is one of the world's largest publicly owned engineering, procurement, construction, maintenance, and project management companies. They provide a diverse portfolio of large-scale infrastructure and infrastructure services, primarily for five industry segments:

- **Oil & Gas** (37 percent of revenues, 55 percent of gross profit in 2010), where they serve all facets of the traditional energy industry, including upstream, downstream, and petrochemical markets, including oilfields, refineries, and pipelines.
- **Industrial and Infrastructure** (33 percent of revenue, 27 percent of profits) is their most diverse organization, which includes transportation, mining, life sciences, telecom, manufacturing, and commercial and institutional projects. This segment also covers the emerging alternative energy projects, including major windmill farm developments.
- **Government** (9 percent of revenue, 9 percent of profits)

addresses the U.S. Departments of Energy, Defense, and Homeland Security.
- **Global Services** (9 percent of revenue, 11 percent of profits) provides operations and maintenance, supply chain, equipment services, and contract staffing.
- **Power** (6 percent of revenue, 10 percent of profits) designs, builds, commissions, and retrofits electric generation facilities using coal, natural gas, and nuclear fuels.

Financial Highlights, Fiscal Year 2010

Fluor's revenues continued to fall slightly from an already diminished 2009, with gross revenue of $20.8 billion compared to a 2008 peak of $22.3 billion. Needless to say, the recession cut into construction activity across virtually all sectors, and since these projects are long in decision and in duration, the effects of the downturn lag the actual low point of the recession. Earnings held steady in 2009, however, but fell considerably in 2010 to 1.98 per share due to, of all things, a major cost overrun on a contracted offshore wind farm in the United Kingdom.

The rest of the business remains firm and with healthy prospects for 2011 and beyond. At the end of 2010, the company reported a $33 billion backlog, the highest since December 2008, including a company record $9.3 billion in new orders placed in the second quarter of 2010.

Reasons to Buy

For investors tolerant of some economic risk, Fluor's shares represent a solid way to play an economic recovery. General large-scale construction should regain health across all industries including oil and gas as the construction cycle becomes more favorable. In our view, there are two growth "kickers" not to be ignored: one is their presence in the alternative energy industry; the other is their presence in the utility infrastructure industry. Both will see waves of new investment to capitalize on new energy technologies; in addition, there are thousands of miles of old water pipes, electric lines, and other infrastructure that is due, or overdue, for replacement. These two megatrends will boost Fluor's business for quite some time to come.

Reasons for Caution

Fluor is more cyclical and more responsive to economic trends than most companies, as is clear from its relatively high beta of 1.28. A ten-year stock price chart shows how the company hit a wall in 2008. Additionally, the company's ten-year growth rates in revenues, earnings, dividends, and cash flows are relatively anemic compared to other companies on our list; that said, the most recent five years have been considerably stronger.

SECTOR: Industrials
BETA COEFFICIENT: 1.28
10-YEAR COMPOUND EARNINGS PER SHARE GROWTH: 13.0%
10-YEAR COMPOUND DIVIDENDS PER SHARE GROWTH: 1.5%

		2003	2004	2005	2006	2007	2008	2009	2010
Revenues (Mil)		1,433	1,656	1,771	1,985	2,202	2,452	2,199	2,085
Net Income (Mil)		180	178	227	264	410	673	685	357.5
Earnings per share		1.12	1.08	1.31	1.48	2.25	3.67	3.75	1.98
Dividends per share		0.32	0.32	0.32	0.32	0.4	0.5	0.5	0.50
Cash flow per share		1.58	1.58	1.9	2.21	3.14	4.61	4.85	3.11
Price:	high	20.4	27.6	39.6	51.9	86.1	101.4	50.5	67.3
	low	13.3	18	25.1	36.8	37.6	28.6	41.7	41.2

Fluor Corporation
6700 Las Colinas Blvd
Irving, TX 75039
Tel: (469) 398-7000
Website: *www.fluor.com*

AGGRESSIVE GROWTH
FMC Corporation

Ticker symbol: FMC (NYSE) ❑ S&P rating: BBB+ ❑ Value Line financial strength rating: A ❑ Current yield: 0.7%

Company Profile

FMC Corporation is a diversified chemical company serving global agricultural, industrial, and consumer markets. The company, founded in 1883, employs some 4,800 people throughout the world. FMC operates its businesses in three segments: Agricultural Products, Specialty Chemicals, and Industrial Chemicals. The company is one of the world's largest producers of strategic materials like phosphorus, hydrogen peroxide, and lithium compounds.

FMC Agricultural Products provides crop protection and pest control products for worldwide markets. The business offers a portfolio of insecticides and herbicides, and is considered an industry leader for its innovative packaging.

In the Specialty Chemicals Group, FMC BioPolymer is the world's leading producer of alginate, carrageenan, and microcrystalline cellulose, which are key thickening, texturing, stabilizing, and fat substitute ingredients used in the food industry. FMC Lithium is one of the world's leading producers of lithium-based products and is recognized as the technology leader in

specialty organolithium chemicals and related technologies.

In the Industrial Chemicals Group, FMC Alkali Chemicals is the world's largest producer of natural soda ash and is the market leader in North America. Downstream products include sodium bicarbonate, sodium cyanide, sodium sesquicarbonate, and caustic soda. FMC Hydrogen Peroxide is the market leader in North America with manufacturing sites in the United States, Canada, and Mexico. FMC Active Oxidants is the world's leading supplier of persulfate products and a major producer of peracetic acid and other specialty oxidants. Based in Barcelona, Spain, FMC Foret is a major chemical producer supplying customers throughout Europe, the Middle East, and Africa with a diverse range of products including hydrogen peroxide, peroxygens, phosphates, silicates, zeolites, and sulfur derivatives.

Financial Highlights, Fiscal Year 2010

Given FMC's large customer base of industrial users, the company took a modest revenue and earnings dip in 2009, but has largely regained its footing to prerecession 2008 levels. Revenues in 2010 of $3.11 billion were slightly below 2008 but well ahead of prior years; earnings per share of $4.83 were just ahead of 2008's $4.63 and well ahead of 2007's $3.40. On the basis of higher volumes, higher prices, and higher margins, the year 2011 is expected to produce $6.81 per share. Volume growth and rebounds occurred fairly evenly across all sectors of the business. The company has also been able to increase prices in key markets for the first time in a while as demand has strengthened.

Reasons to Buy

FMC is well positioned in several areas of relative strategic importance in the chemical industry, in particular the lithium compounds business. The strength of the economic rebound combined with these leadership positions in specialty markets bode well for the company. Pricing strength, improving margins, and strong international sales (63 percent of sales in 2010) all add to a promising picture.

As an example of FMC's strategic portfolio, the company is well positioned as the leading supplier of lithium-based compounds used in the lithium-ion battery industry. Lithium batteries are used extensively in technology products such as laptops, music players, and soon, electric cars. Every current hybrid car currently in production uses nickel metal hydride (NiMH) battery chemistry, but lithium batteries appropriate for automobile usage are not far off. Lithium's unparalleled power-to-weight ratio and rapid recharge cycle time make cars lighter and more amenable to typical usage patterns.

FMC is a key player in a broad consortium of U.S.–based companies working to establish a dominant domestic lithium battery industry. Lithium battery technology is the key to the future of the automotive industry, and some have said that the country that makes the batteries will make the cars.

Reasons for Caution

While the company occupies a leadership position in several important chemical and ingredient markets, FMC can't get away completely from its role as a commodity producer, particularly in such compounds like soda ash. As such, competition and business cycles will always play a role in growth and stability. Additionally, while the company did start paying dividends in 2006, cash returns and long-term growth are relatively modest.

SECTOR: **Materials**
BETA COEFFICIENT: **1.04**
10-YEAR COMPOUND EARNINGS PER SHARE GROWTH: **4.0%**
10-YEAR COMPOUND DIVIDENDS PER SHARE GROWTH: **NM**

	2003	2004	2005	2006	2007	2008	2009	2010
Revenues (Mil)	1,921	2,051	2,150	2,347	2,633	3,115	2,826	3,116
Net Income (Mil)	67.5	135.2	171.9	216.4	132.4	351	305	353
Earnings per share	0.95	1.60	2.20	2.74	3.40	4.63	4.15	4.83
Dividends per share	-	-	-	0.36	0.42	0.48	0.50	.50
Cash flow per share	2.72	3.64	4.00	4.54	5.25	6.55	6.00	6.81
Price: high	17.4	25.3	31.9	39	59	80.2	63.3	82.0
low	7.1	16.5	21.6	25.9	35.6	28.5	34.9	50.8

FMC Corporation
1735 Market Street
Philadelphia, PA 19103
(215) 299-6000
Website: *www.fmc.com*

General Mills, Inc.

Ticker symbol: GIS (NYSE) ❑ S&P rating: BBB+ ❑ Value Line financial strength rating: A+ ❑
Current yield: 3.2%

Company Profile

General Mills is the second-largest domestic producer of ready-to-eat breakfast cereals and the sixth-largest food company in the world. Their sales are broken out into three major segments: U.S. Retail ($9.1 billion), International ($2.6 billion), and Bakery and Food-stuffs ($2.0 billion). They also have unconsolidated net sales in the Joint Venture segment ($1.2 billion).

Major cereal brands, most of which bear the Big G label, include Cheerios, Wheaties, Lucky Charms, Total, and Chex. The company owns Pillsbury, which it acquired in 2001. Other consumer packaged food products include baking mixes (Betty Crocker and Bisquick); meals (Betty Crocker dry packaged dinner mixes); Progresso soups; Green Giant canned and frozen vegetables; Hamburger Helper; snacks (Pop Secret microwave popcorn, Bugles snacks, grain, and fruit snack products); Pillsbury refrigerated and frozen dough products including Pillsbury Doughboy, frozen breakfast products, and frozen pizza and snack products; and organic foods and other products, including Nature Valley, Yoplait, Go-gurt, and Colombo yogurt. The company's holdings include many other brand names, such as Haagen-Dazs ice cream and a host of joint ventures.

The company's international businesses consist of operations and sales in Canada, Europe, Latin America, and the Asia/Pacific region. In those regions, General Foods sells numerous local brands, in addition to internationally recognized brands, such as Haagen-Dazs ice cream, Old El Paso Mexican foods, and Green Giant vegetables. Those international businesses have sales and marketing organizations in thirty-three countries.

Financial Highlights, Fiscal Year 2010

For the fiscal year ended May 31, 2010, General Mills net sales grew at a scant 0.7 percent to 14.8 billion, while year-to-year per share earnings grew at a healthier 15.6 percent to 42.30 from $1.99 in FY2009. Internal efficiencies, operating leverage, and moderating ingredient costs caused net profit margin to exceed 10 percent for the first time in recent history. The rise in ingredient costs in the latter two thirds of calendar 2010 brought an essentially flat performance in the company's early FY2011 performance.

Reasons to Buy

General Mills continues to enjoy solid brand strength and a competitive position in a very competitive cereal and packaged food market. Recent trends have pointed to brand leveraging (e.g., Chocolate Cheerios, Wheaties Fuel) and the results have been encouraging. There's evidence that the recession "taught" more people to eat at home, and those folks are starting to return to more premium brands found on store shelves. Finally, while the company has developed some international markets, notably in Latin America and the Caribbean, and generates about 24 percent of its sales overseas, we feel that additional international expansion may bring some opportunity.

Earnings, operating margins, and cash flows have all followed a steady track modestly upward and in tune with management guidance. The company has continued its policy of share repurchase, further reducing the number of outstanding shares by 2.5 percent. Since 2004, the company has reduced its share count from 758 million to about 640 million. The company also raised the dividend 10 percent in 2010 and has boosted its dividend "raises" in recent years. Finally, General Mills is a notably safe and stable stock with a beta of 0.20, one of the lowest on our list.

Reasons for Caution

As a food products producer, the company is vulnerable to spikes in commodity prices; recent commodity price trends have given some cause for worry, especially as they are not easy to pass on to consumers in a competitive and recessionary environment.

SECTOR: **Consumer Staples**
BETA COEFFICIENT: **.20**
10-YEAR COMPOUND EARNINGS PER SHARE GROWTH: **8.5%**
10-YEAR COMPOUND DIVIDENDS PER SHARE GROWTH: **5.0%**

	2003	**2004**	**2005**	**2006**	**2007**	**2008**	**2009**	**2010**
Revenues (Mil)	10,506	11,070	11,244	11,640	12,442	13,652	14,691	14,796
Net Income (Mil)	917	1,055	1,100	1,090	1,144	1,288	1,367	1,571
Earnings per share	1.33	1.43	1.37	1.45	1.59	1.78	1.99	2.30
Dividends per share	0.55	0.55	0.62	0.67	0.72	0.79	0.86	0.96
Cash flow per share	1.85	1.97	2.09	2.13	2.30	2.50	2.78	3.09
Price: high	24.8	25.0	26.9	29.6	30.8	36.0	36.0	39.0
low	20.7	21.5	22.3	23.5	27.1	25.5	23.2	33.1

General Mills, Inc.
Post Office Box 1113
Minneapolis, MN 55440–1113
(763) 764-3202
Website: ***www.generalmills.com***

AGGRESSIVE GROWTH

Google Inc.

Ticker symbol: GOOG (NASDAQ) □ S&P rating: AA- □ Value Line financial strength rating: A++ □ Current yield: Nil

Company Profile

Google operates the world's leading Internet search engine. The vast majority of its income (96 percent in 2010) is derived from the delivery of targeted advertising through the Google AdWords and Google AdSense products. Sales of advertising management services and the licensing of its search technology (Google Search Appliance) to other companies generates the remainder of its revenue.

The operational model is simple, elegant, and provides for timely and thorough customer and client management. Google's AdWords scans the HTML code that's displayed on a user's screen, searching for keywords. When keywords are found, ads relevant to the keywords are displayed on the page as well. Advertisers select their own target keywords and pay when customers click on their ads. Google and the advertiser are notified of every click, and other tracking information relevant to the click is transmitted as well.

Advertisers get targeted ads without a great deal of up-front cost, and the ads appear on pages from Google's large roster of partners, from AOL to the *Washington* *Post.* Partners in turn receive a share of the advertising revenue when ads on their pages are clicked.

The company also provides, free of charge, a number of worthwhile programs. Google Docs, for example, mimics most of the popular commercial office suites. They also provide, at no charge, their own browser, 3D modeling software, image manipulation software, website authoring software, mapping software, mail portal, and personal search engine. Google also owns and operates YouTube, one of the most popular social media sites on the Internet.

For the first six months of 2010, the company offered its Nexus One mobile phone for sale direct to consumers on the Google website, but that business has been discontinued. But that doesn't diminish Google as a player in the mobile and tablet market; its Android operating system is catching on as a serious competitor to the highly successful iPhone.

Financial Highlights, Fiscal Year 2010

Revenues rose 24 percent over 2009, reflecting both an improved business environment and the continued migration of advertising revenues from offline to online media. The company realized improved earnings on this growth due to a shift in traffic volume away from partner sites and toward company-owned sites, where margins are significantly higher. The company says this pattern has accelerated over the past few years and they expect it to continue "for the foreseeable future." Good news for the company and great news for value investors.

Reasons to Buy

Last year we wrote that Google, in losing the bidding war for wireless spectrum space (to Verizon), managed to win a battle. They were able to persuade the federal regulators to include in the final issuance documents some common-carrier provisions that appeared to be very beneficial to Google's longer-term plans: support for context and location-sensitive search and ad placement. Google's win last year now has the potential to pay off in a big way, as the scenario described above is no longer speculative. Google's most recent annual report includes the following statement of their position on the mobile ad space: "Google Mobile extends our products and services by providing mobile-specific features to mobile device users. Our mobile-specific search technologies include search by voice, search by sight, and search by location. In 2010, we acquired AdMob, Inc., which offers effective ad units and solutions for application developers and advertisers. We continue to invest in improving users' access to Google services through their mobile devices." This sounds to us like the mobile space holds a fair amount of promise for Google's traditional ad-based revenue and the potential for new developments.

The company's recent (and rather tentative) moves to monetize media content on YouTube have gone reasonably well, but will require some critical mass to compete with NetFlix. The company has said they will move faster in this space, but this remains to be seen.

We like the recently announced management changes. A lot. Google has done some tremendous things in their space, but they've begun to look very cautious, and we think that's really just the effect of overlapping responsibilities and the inability to reach consensus at the top of the organization. Three very bright, very confident young men will not always agree and will not always agree to disagree. Having more clearly defined roles and responsibilities will lead to a more dynamic company and faster decision-making.

Finally, while the $600-plus share price might spook a lot of investors, the ratios of price to earnings and price to cash flow are actually more reflective of a more conservative "value" stock. We feel that if Google would split its stock, with its strong growth-oriented business and investment profile, the stock could actually command a higher price per unit of earnings. This company is the epitome of the growth equals value premise mentioned in our introduction. By the way, we don't necessarily recommend a split, for there is no "real" change to a share's value or its prospects. But it's an intriguing possibility going forward.

Reasons for Caution

It's a nice problem to have, but we have to wonder what the company plans to do about the cash situation. Even though they've been in acquisition mode seemingly from day one, the fact is they spent about one month's earnings on all of last year's acquisitions. The increases of $10 billion per year for the past two years give us pause: Are the opportunities they take a pass on really that bad? Can't they afford to be just a wee bit more aggressive, particularly during a period such as we saw recently where share valuations were as low as they're ever likely to be? As long as the company remains dependent on a single revenue stream, the big bankroll looks a bit like lost opportunities.

SECTOR: **Technology**
BETA COEFFICIENT: **0.9**
10-YEAR COMPOUND EARNINGS PER SHARE GROWTH: **NA**
10-YEAR COMPOUND DIVIDENDS PER SHARE GROWTH: **Nil**

	2003	2004	2005	2006	2007	2008	2009	2010
Revenues (Mil)	1,465	3,189	6,138	10,604	16,594	21,795	23,650	29,321
Net Income (Mil)	106	406	1,518	2,941	4,204	5,299	6,519	8,505
Earnings per share	0.41	1.49	5.20	9.50	13.29	16.69	20.41	26.31
Dividends per share	–	–	–	–	–	–	–	–
Cash flow per share	0.64	1.93	5.97	11.12	16.00	20.66	24.45	29.90
Price: high	–	201.6	446.2	513	747.2	697.4	626	630.8
low	–	85	437	331.5	437	247.3	282.8	433.6

Google Inc.
1600 Amphitheater Parkway
Mountain View, CA 94043
(650) 253-0000
Website: *www.google.com*

W. W. Grainger, Inc.

Ticker symbol: GWW (NYSE) ❑ S&P rating: AA+ ❑ Value Line financial strength rating: A++ ❑
Current yield: 1.6%

Company Profile

If you're running a production operation and have a sudden and urgent need for a hand truck, a "Keep Out" sign, a positive displacement pump, or a pair of safety glasses, who do you call? You certainly can't afford to send someone out to Home Depot or some such, and no "big-box" retailer would stock even a small fraction of the 1 million items that W.W. Grainger stocks anyhow.

Grainger is North America's largest supplier of maintenance, repair, and operating supply (MRO) products. They sell more than a million different products through a network of over 600 branches, eighteen distribution centers, and several websites, with a catalog containing some 307,000 items (a fascinating read if you like this sort of thing). Grainger also offers repair parts, specialized product sourcing, and inventory management supplies. Grainger sells principally to industrial and commercial maintenance departments, contractors, and government customers. The company has nearly 2 million customers, most in North America.

Their Canadian subsidiary is Canada's largest distributor of industrial, fleet, and safety products. They serve their customers through 166 branches, five distribution centers, and offer bilingual websites and catalogs. Grainger, S.A. de C.V. is Mexico's leading facilities maintenance supplier, offering customers more than 40,000 products.

Grainger's customer base includes governmental offices at all levels, heavy manufacturing customers (typically textile, lumber, metals, and rubber industries), light manufacturing, transportation (shipbuilding, aerospace, and automotive), hospitals, retail, hospitality, and resellers of Grainger products. Grainger owns a number of trademarks, including Dayton motors, Dem-Kote spray paints, and Westward tools.

Many of Grainger's customers are corporate account customers, primarily *Fortune* 1000 companies that spend more than $5 million annually on facilities maintenance products. Corporate account customers represent about 25 percent of Grainger's total U.S. sales. Both government and corporate account customer groups typically sign multi-year contracts for facilities maintenance products or a specific category of products, such as lighting or safety equipment. In 2009, the company averaged 95,000 transactions per day.

The Grainger strategy is centered on the idea of being easy to do business with. Customers can interact with a direct sales force, interact with one of the 400 distribution outlets in the United States, or order through an e-commerce website. Released quietly during the dot.com boom, *www.grainger .com* handles some $1.5 billion, or about 25 percent of the company's U.S. business each year, a solid e-commerce success story.

Financial Highlights, Fiscal Year 2010

Grainger's FY2010 sales and earnings rebounded smartly and beyond expectations from the recession lows. Revenues were up 15 percent from 2009, while earnings were up some 30 percent from $5.33 per share to $6.92. Some one-time factors were in play, including the BP Gulf oil spill and resulting cleanup. For FY2011, the company projects sales growth continuing at a 5–9 percent clip, with earnings coming in the $7.15–$7.90 range. Cost cutting measures, such as consolidating two of its largest operating segments, and other measures have driven operating margins up from the 10–11 percent range to the low 13 percent range.

The company took on $500 million in debt, ostensibly to finance further expansion/acquisitions. It has a clean balance sheet with no other significant long-term debt. Cash flow has been strong, and that cash has been used among other things to repurchase shares. Since 2004, the company has retired 20 million of the 90 million-plus shares it had outstanding at the time; that figure was 106 million in 1994. The company has also raised its dividend in each of the last thirty-nine years.

Reasons to Buy

Grainger is far and away the biggest presence in the MRO world. Their only broad-line competitor is one-quarter their size and the rest of the market is highly fragmented (Grainger has 4–5 percent market share). They also have the deepest catalog by far. It's estimated that 40 percent of purchases in the MRO market are unplanned, so having the broadest inventory and having it in stock is a big advantage for Grainger.

Even with its size and scope, the company estimates that it has only 4 percent of the U.S. MRO market, leaving a large growth opportunity. International sales are less than 20 percent of the total, and Grainger has established only a foothold in Mexico, China, Japan, Korea, Columbia, and Puerto Rico with less than 1 percent of those markets. The company has a larger presence in Canada. Especially with so much manufacturing relocated overseas, the international opportunity looks rich for Grainger.

The share repurchases and dividend increases reflect a better-than-average orientation to shareholder value, and shareholder value is indeed one of the stated goals of the company. We find it refreshing to see it not only stated but also delivered upon.

Reasons for Caution

Grainger will always be vulnerable to economic cycles and manufacturing displacement, especially so long as it remains concentrated on U.S. soil. International expansion will help alleviate this concern. Over the past five years, the share price has reflected most of the good news, mandating either careful price shopping for the stock or reliance on incremental growth opportunities in the United States and especially overseas market share.

SECTOR: Industrials
BETA COEFFICIENT: 0.96
10-YEAR COMPOUND EARNINGS PER SHARE GROWTH: 11.5%
10-YEAR COMPOUND DIVIDENDS PER SHARE GROWTH: 11.0%

		2003	2004	2005	2006	2007	2008	2009	2010
Revenues (Mil)		4,667	5,050	5,527	5,884	6,418	6,850	6,222	7,182
Net Income (Mil)		227	227	346	383	420	479	402	502
Earnings per share		2.46	3.02	3.78	4.25	4.94	6.09	5.25	6.81
Dividends per share		0.74	0.79	0.92	1.16	1.4	1.55	1.78	2.08
Cash flow per share		3.47	4.14	4.97	5.79	6.95	8.28	7.60	9.40
Price:	high	53.3	67	72.4	80	98.6	94	102.5	139.1
	low	41.4	45	51.6	60.6	68.8	58.9	59.9	96.1

W. W. Grainger, Inc.
100 Grainger Parkway
Lake Forest, IL 60045
(847) 535-0881
Website: *www.grainger.com*

Harris Corporation

Ticker symbol: HRS (NYSE) ❏ S&P rating: BBB+ ❏ Value Line financial strength rating: A ❏ Current yield: 1.9%

Company Profile

Harris is an international communications and information technology company serving government and commercial markets in more than 150 countries. Founded in Ohio in 1895, the company was primarily a supplier of printing equipment until the mid-1950s when it began to focus on electronics. Over the next two decades, the electronics segment grew much faster than the print segment, and the company exited the printing business entirely in 1983. Now headquartered in Melbourne, Florida, the company has over 15,000 employees, including nearly 7,000 engineers and scientists. Harris develops communications products, systems, and services for global markets, including government communications, broadcast communications, and wireless transmission network solutions.

Its major business units include:

■ Government Communications Systems conducts advanced research studies, develops prototypes, and produces and supports communications and information systems for mission-critical applications for military and government customers. These activities also provide a research base for commercial products and services. GCS accounts for approximately 50 percent of revenue.

■ RF (radio frequency) Communications supplies tactical radio communication products, systems, and networks to military and government organizations, and provides high-security encryption solutions. These solutions address the requirements of U.S., NATO, and Partnership for Peace forces, as well as government agencies and embassies around the world. RFC accounts for approximately 40 percent of revenue.

■ Broadcast Communications provides content delivery solutions, including advanced digital transmission, automation, asset management, digital media, network management, and video infrastructure solutions to commercial broadcasters in radio, television, and digital satellite broadcast markets. BC accounts for approximately 10 percent of revenue.

In total, government contracts, sales, and services account for about 51.5 percent of FY2010 revenue.

Financial Highlights, Fiscal Year 2010

After a lackluster FY2009, reflecting a divestiture and some one-time goodwill impairment, Harris's FY2010 performance returned to a growth track, albeit with revenues still slightly off 2008's peak. FY2010 revenues came in at $5.2 billion, up about 4 percent from FY2009, while earnings per share climbed to $4.48 from $3.87, reflecting among other things an improvement in operating margins. FY2011 projections call for a healthy increase in revenues and per share earnings, to $6 billion and $4.85 respectively.

Reasons to Buy

Over the past five years, Harris has doubled its share of the ground-based tactical radio market to 42 percent. This is a $3.8 billion dollar worldwide market that is growing at 11 percent per year. Current backlogs still reflect a substantial business in this segment.

The RF addressable radio market, currently valued at $8 billion, is expected to grow to nearly $18 billion in calendar year 2012, of which Harris's current and planned products are expected to cover over 90 percent.

The company has been able to capture sales in foreign markets, notably in Australia and Pakistan, adding new business to a fairly solid U.S. base. The company has been able to translate acquisitions and design wins into income at an impressive rate. Over the past five years, Harris's earnings compound annualized growth rate (CAGR) is a healthy 35 percent, and products introduced in the past three years have revenue CAGR of 49 percent.

The company has great cash flow (up 8 percent in FY2010 after rising 12 percent in FY2009) and a sound capital structure. In addition to funding nearly $1 billion in R&D in 2009 ($250 million internal, $750 million under government contract), the company continues to buy back shares and has repositioned themselves as a bit of an income play with an $.88 dividend, up from $.44 in 2007 and $.32 in 2006. They're well positioned for their acquisition plans and will continue to repurchase shares and boost dividends.

In June 2009, the company rejected preliminary buyout offers in the neighborhood of $10 billion, saying that it was under an expected offer of $75–$85/share.

Reasons for Caution

Questions remain about the eventual value of the F-35 strike fighter contract. Actual delivered quantities may be far lower than originally discussed. Harris is the prime contractor for three of its avionics and communication subsystems, with a projected value of $4 billion over the life of the program. The company is, and always will be, vulnerable to cuts in defense spending.

SECTOR: **Information Technology**
BETA COEFFICIENT: **1.00**
10-YEAR COMPOUND EARNINGS PER SHARE GROWTH: **17.5%**
10-YEAR COMPOUND DIVIDENDS PER SHARE GROWTH: **7.5%**

	2003	2004	2005	2006	2007	2008	2009	2010
Revenues (Mil)	2,093	2,519	3,001	3,475	4,243	5,311	5,005	5,206
Net Income (Mil)	90	126	202	310	391	462	513	562
Earnings per share	0.68	0.94	1.46	2.22	2.8	3.39	3.87	4.28
Dividends per share	0.16	0.2	0.24	0.32	0.44	0.6	0.80	0.88
Cash flow per share	1.1	1.36	2.06	3.07	4.06	4.75	5.27	5.71
Price: high	19.7	34.6	45.8	49.8	66.9	66.7	48.3	54.5
low	12.7	18.9	26.9	37.7	45.9	27.6	26.1	40.2

Harris Corporation
1025 West NASA Boulevard
Melbourne, FL 32919
(321) 727-9383
Website: *www.harris.com*

H.J. Heinz Company

Ticker symbol: HNZ (NYSE) ❑ S&P rating: BBB ❑ Value Line financial strength rating: A+ ❑ Current yield: 3.8%

Company Profile

H.J. Heinz Company manufactures and markets food products such as condiments and sauces, frozen food, soups, desserts, entrées, snacks, frozen potatoes, appetizers, and others for consumers and commercial customers. The company's best-known product, its ketchup, has a 60 percent market share in the United States, 70 percent in Canada, and nearly 80 percent in the United Kingdom. Condiments and sauces (including ketchup) account for approximately 42 percent of the company's revenue, with meals and snacks producing 45 percent, and Infant/Nutrition making up the remainder. Ore-Ida frozen potato products, Classico pasta sauces, and SmartOnes meals are among the more well-known Heinz brands.

The Heinz portfolio includes 150 brands that hold the number one or number two market share positions in their categories, with presence on five continents and in more than fifty countries. The company sells its products through its own direct sales organizations, through independent brokers and agents, and to distributors to retailers and commercial users. The company has operations in North America, Africa, Latin America, Europe, Asia Pacific, and the Middle East. About 56 percent of Heinz's sales are from overseas, and the company estimates that 18 percent of sales are from emerging markets; these markets, including China and Russia, are growing rapidly. As part of the international expansion strategy, in 2010 the company completed the acquisition of Foodstar, a maker of soy sauces and fermented bean curd in China. In early 2011, the company announced the purchase of 80 percent of Brazil's S.A. Industrias Alimenticias, which is expected to double Heinz's overall Latin America sales.

Heinz's laboratories develop the company's recipes, which are then duplicated at one of the seventy-nine company-owned factories or one of several leased factories. Most of the bulk raw products are sourced locally when possible, and are purchased against futures contracts in order to stabilize pricing, while other ingredients are purchased on the spot market.

Financial Highlights, Fiscal Year 2010 (ended April 27, 2011)

Heinz reported low single-digit sales gains all through the 2008–09 recession, and kept the trend going in FY2010 with a strong exit to that year. In an investor conference, Chairman William R. Johnson noted the company delivered its twenty-sixth consecutive quarter of organic sales growth, with that growth in the 2 percent range. Interestingly, the organic growth of the top fifteen brands came in at 4 percent, a departure from what one would expect in such a business. The organic sales gains were especially notable in China, India, Indonesia, and Russia, with gains of 14 percent in those countries. The company earned $3.10 per share for the year, and raised the dividend for the eighth consecutive year.

Reasons to Buy

The resilience of Heinz's strong brands was apparent during the recession as the company maintained growth in sales and earnings over each of the past three years, and it appears that those brands are continuing to perform well, especially in emerging markets. The company looks to be a solid and steady play in a steady industry with a growth "kicker" in the form of its international business and international expansion. Heinz has been successful recently with its new brand introductions, leveraging its Global Innovation and Quality Center. Part of the company's product development goal is to derive 15 percent of revenues from products introduced within the previous thirty-six months.

For investors looking for steady and solid shareholder returns, both current and future, Heinz is an attractive choice.

Reasons for Caution

Growth in emerging markets will come at a cost. Many of the brands we take for granted will require large investments in marketing to establish presence and familiarity. Heinz can also expect to see higher acquisition costs for established local brands as competitors move into this arena, and international acquisitions in particular can be tricky. Finally, higher commodity prices will produce some headwinds, especially in the near term.

SECTOR: **Consumer Staples**

BETA COEFFICIENT: **0.57**

10-YEAR COMPOUND EARNINGS PER SHARE GROWTH: **1.5%**

10-YEAR COMPOUND DIVIDENDS PER SHARE GROWTH: **2.0%**

	2003	2004	2005	2006	2007	2008	2009	2010
Revenues (Mil)	8,414	8,913	8,643	9,002	10,070	10,148	10,495	10,650E
Net Income (Mil)	779	823	750	792	845	923	915	1,005E
Earnings per share	2.2	2.34	2.18	2.38	2.63	2.9	2.87	3.10E
Dividends per share	1.08	1.14	1.2	1.4	1.52	1.66	1.71	1.80E
Cash flow per share	2.86	3.11	3.06	3.28	3.63	3.82	3.83	4.00E
Price: high	36.8	40.6	39.1	46.8	48.8	53	43.8	50.8
low	28.9	34.5	33.6	33.4	41.8	35.3	30.5	40.0

H.J. Heinz Company

One PPG Place

Pittsburgh, PA 15222

(412) 456-5700

Website: *www.heinz.com*

AGGRESSIVE GROWTH

Hewlett Packard

Ticker symbol: HPQ (NYSE) ❑ S&P rating: A ❑ Value Line financial strength rating: A++ ❑ Current yield: 0.7%

Company Profile

Hewlett-Packard is a global technology solutions provider to consumers, businesses, and institutions. The company's offerings span IT infrastructure, services, business and home computing, and imaging and printing.

The company is organized around six reporting segments:

- Personal Systems Group (32 percent of revenue, 16 percent of profits) is the world's leading provider of personal computers based on unit volume shipped and annual revenue. PSG provides commercial PCs, consumer PCs, workstations, handheld computing devices, calculators and other related accessories, plus software and services for the commercial and consumer markets.
- Imaging and Printing Group (21 percent of revenue, 27 percent of profits) is the leading imaging and printing systems provider in the world for consumer and commercial printer hardware, printing supplies, printing media, and scanning devices. IPG is also

focused on imaging solutions in the commercial markets, including managed print services solutions, commercial printing, industrial applications, outdoor signage, and the graphic arts business.

- Enterprise Storage and Servers (17 percent of revenues, 20 percent of profits) provides solutions for both the enterprise and the small business markets. ESS provides products in a number of categories, including entry-level and mid-range servers, and business-critical systems such as the fault-tolerant Integrity servers.
- HP Services (27 percent of revenues, 33 percent of profits) is HP's consulting arm, providing multi-vendor IT services, technology services, consulting and integration and outsourcing services. HPS also offers industry-specific services for communications, media and entertainment, manufacturing and distribution, financial services, health and life sciences, and the public sector, including government services. HPS collaborates with the HP

business units as well as with third-party system integrators and software and networking companies to bring solutions to HP customers. EDS, the large integrator and consulting concern that the company acquired in 2008, makes up most of this segment.

- HP Software (2 percent of revenues, 5 percent of profits) is a provider of enterprise and service provider software and services, including IT management software, business reporting solutions, and integrated voice/data development platforms. Despite the small percentage of the HP total business, HP Software is a big player, especially in enterprise IT and network management software.

- HP Financial Services (1 percent of revenues, 2 percent of profits) offers leasing, financing, utility programs, and asset recovery services, as well as financial asset management services for large global and enterprise customers.

The company has experienced unusual levels of change and upheaval recently. CEO Mark Hurd departed unexpectedly and under somewhat mysterious circumstances in August 2010; his replacement, Leo Apotheker, started that November and has only weighed in slightly on his plans. Some internal restructuring and a greater orientation to software and services and a wholehearted effort to be part of the "cloud" computing model is in the plans. Notably, Mr. Apotheker, a former CEO of SAP Inc., comes from the software world. The company also reshuffled its board of directors recently; it remains to be seen what the outcome of that move might bring. Finally, the company went on an acquisition spree in 2010, acquiring Palm Inc., networker 3Com, storage technology role player 3PAR, and a few other niche acquisitions to fill holes in its product line and become a bigger player in corporate security and cloud infrastructure. It remains to be seen what these acquisitions will mean to the overall business.

Financial Highlights, Fiscal Year 2010

Despite the executive suite and acquisition dramas, HP delivered solid results in 2010. Bolstered by a recovery in the economy and particularly in corporate IT spending, HP reported earnings of $3.69 per share, a 14 percent gain from $3.48, on revenues just exceeding $126 billion, a 10 percent increase over FY2009. These numbers reflect recovery and acquisitions but also signal that the company is still growing well for a company of its size. Projections call for continued revenue growth in the 4–6 percent range with earnings growth to about $4.35 per share, diluted. Cash flow is still huge at nearly $13 billion a year and one of the strengths of the company. The company has also retired almost 900 million shares since issuing about 1 billion shares to complete the 2002 Compaq acquisition—nice to finally pay in full for this purchase, which accounts for some $40–50 billion in annual sales (international sales make up about 65 percent of the total).

Reasons to Buy

We will admit to being frustrated with our call on HP. The company continues to make the *100 Best* list despite some obvious missteps. As a pure value play, the fundamentals are there. The price-to-earnings ratio has hovered somewhere near 10 and has been below 10 at times as the company wrestles with CEO and boardroom shenanigans—a multiple unheard of in this industry. Cash flow is enormous, and the company occupies a number one position in many of its key markets. HP still has a pure cash cow in the printing business, and has learned to make money (albeit still not that much) in the PC business. CEO Mark Hurd brought tremendous operational efficiencies, cost reductions, and focus, bringing a leaner

and meaner company with a resurgent brand. All of that has been put into question with his departure, although most in the business see little true impact on the strong HP brand. Bottom line: With some management stability, a real return from the "cloud" strategy, and with a good showing for recent acquisitions, as well as moderate base business growth expectations, the stock may be positioned for solid advances. But . . .

Reasons for Caution

. . . HP continues to skate closer to the brink with what seems like an uncoordinated acquisition strategy. How 3Com, 3PAR, and Palm all fit together, we do not know. These acquisitions will dilute focus at a time when a new CEO is coming on board—with his own ideas—while new board members assume their seats, and while competitive pressures mount. Mark Hurd's arrival at Oracle to run their hardware business (formerly, Sun) makes them a suddenly formidable competitor, as if there wasn't enough competition already. HP has never succeeded in the software business, so new ventures there add as much risk as reward in our opinion. Finally, we've long been annoyed by the company's conservative dividend policy, which brought no increases in eleven years, a clear contrast to most of the companies on our *100 Best* list and surprising for a company that could have afforded more. The company just announced its intentions to give "double digit increases" for the foreseeable future, although the dollar amounts involved will be small. In short, HP has done a lot to mystify, and frankly, alienate shareholders, but that said, prospects are bright should the company get its ducks in a row.

SECTOR: **Information Technology**
BETA COEFFICIENT: **1.03**
10-YEAR COMPOUND EARNINGS PER SHARE GROWTH: **8.5%**
10-YEAR COMPOUND DIVIDENDS PER SHARE GROWTH: **Nil**

	2003	2004	2005	2006	2007	2008	2009	2010
Revenues (Bil)	73.06	79.91	86.67	91.66	104.3	118.4	114.5	126
Net Income (Bil)	3,557	4,067	4,708	6,198	7,264	8,329	7,660	8,761
Earnings per share	1.16	1.33	1.62	2.18	2.68	3.25	3.14	3.69
Dividends per share	0.32	0.32	0.32	0.32	0.32	0.32	0.32	.32
Cash flow per share	2	2.22	2.49	2.97	3.86	4.84	5.26	6.16
Price: high	23.9	26.3	30.3	41.7	53.5	51	52.9	54.8
low	14.2	16.1	18.9	28.4	38.2	28.2	25.4	37.3

Hewlett-Packard Company
3000 Hanover Street
Palo Alto, CA 94304
(866) 438-4771
Website: *www.hp.com*

Honeywell International, Inc.

Ticker symbol: HON (NYSE) □ S&P rating: A □ Value Line financial strength rating: A++ □ Current yield: 2.7%

Company Profile

Honeywell is a diversified technology and manufacturing company, developing, manufacturing, and marketing aerospace products and services (40 percent of sales); control technologies for buildings, homes, and industry (31 percent); automotive products (15 percent); and specialty materials (14 percent).

Honeywell operates in four business segments: Aerospace, Automation and Control Solutions, Specialty Materials, and Transportation Systems.

The Aerospace segment primarily makes cockpit controls, power generation equipment, and wheels and brakes for commercial and military aircraft. It also makes jet engines for regional and business jet manufacturers. Products include avionics, auxiliary power units (APUs), aircraft lighting, and landing systems. Demand for the company's aircraft equipment is driven primarily by expansion in the global jetliner fleet, particularly jets with 100 or more seats. Since 1993, the global airliner fleet has grown at a 3 percent annual pace. The Aerospace segment is also a major player in the $35 billion global aircraft maintenance, repair, and overhaul industry, which is growing at a 2.2 percent annual rate.

Honeywell's Automation and Control Solutions segment is best known as a maker of home and office climate controls equipment. It also makes home automation systems, sensing and combustion controls for heating, A/C and other environmental controls, lighting controls, security systems and sensing products, and fire alarms. This segment produces most of the components of what is known in the trade and advertising lingo as a "smart building."

The Specialty Materials operation makes specialty chemicals and fibers, which are sold primarily to the food, pharmaceutical, and electronic packaging industries.

The Transportation System segment consists of a portfolio of brand name car-care products, such as Fram filters, Prestone antifreeze, Autolite spark plugs, and Simoniz car waxes. The unit also manufactures braking systems for large trucks and service vehicles.

Financial Highlights, Fiscal Year 2010

Honeywell is in several economically sensitive businesses, and that showed up big in 2009 results, which in terms of revenue were almost 20 percent below 2008. As many of the company's products serve "long cycle" businesses like aircraft and commercial building construction, FY10 sales were up but still remained more than $3 billion, or more than 10 percent off the 2008 peak. Not surprisingly, earnings "troughed" in a similar manner, except that 2010 was worse than 2009 and almost a third lower than 2008. Orders and business trends started to pick back up in the second quarter of 2010, and 2011 guidance, while short of 2008 levels, is close to 2007 and historically strong. During the downturn, the bulk of the earnings declines were in the Aerospace and Transportation segments; the Automation and Control segment remained fairly steady despite its dependence on the large-scale construction industry.

Reasons to Buy

We like where Honeywell is positioned with regard to the growing awareness of the value of energy efficiency. Over the next few years we see a lot of movement toward green practices in building design and use, and no one has a stronger portfolio of lighting and temperature control systems than Honeywell. Over half of the company's portfolio, across all four segments, is in the area of energy efficiency. The company also has a valuable distribution network and existing customer base, as they've been in this business longer than anyone else. If Honeywell can leverage their position here with the right message (and assuming the construction market begins to turn around), the company could experience strong growth, particularly in the Automation and Controls segment.

Honeywell will be part of the consortium responsible for the development and deployment of the next-generation air traffic control system commissioned by the FAA. This is a long-term program and Honeywell is not the primary contractor, but this system will likely be the model for the modernization of air traffic systems worldwide.

The company has a solid balance sheet and participates almost exclusively in high-margin businesses. Economic recovery should further accelerate HON's earnings growth.

Reasons for Caution

Honeywell has a lot of competition, particularly in the aerospace and transportation sectors, and is sensitive to economic cycles, especially in these industries. Many of the industries Honeywell sells to—in particular, the aerospace industry—are and probably will always be low-growth businesses. These segments dilute our excitement about the building controls industry and its implied play on energy efficiency.

SECTOR: **Industrials**
BETA COEFFICIENT: **1.34**
10-YEAR COMPOUND EARNINGS PER SHARE GROWTH: **3.5%**
10-YEAR COMPOUND DIVIDENDS PER SHARE GROWTH: **6.5%**

	2003	2004	2005	2006	2007	2008	2009	2010
Revenues (Mil)	23,103	25,601	27,653	31,367	34,589	36,556	30,908	33,370
Net Income (Mil)	1,344	1,281	1,736	2,083	2,444	2,792	2,153	2,153
Earnings per share	1.56	1.49	1.92	2.52	3.16	3.75	2.85	3.00
Dividends per share	0.75	0.75	0.83	0.91	1.00	1.10	1.21	1.21
Cash flow per share	2.25	2.27	2.93	3.59	4.39	5.03	4.07	4.27
Price: high	33.5	38.5	39.5	45.8	62.3	63	41.6	53.7
low	20.2	31.2	32.7	35.2	43.1	23.2	23.1	36.7

Honeywell International, Inc.
101 Columbia Road
P. O. Box 2245
Morristown, NJ 07962–2245
(973) 455-2222
Website: *www.honeywell.com*

IBM

Ticker symbol: IBM (NYSE) ❑ S&P rating: A+ ❑ Value Line financial strength rating: A++ ❑ Current yield: 1.68%

Company Profile

Big Blue is the world's leading provider of computer hardware and services. IBM makes a broad range of computers, mainframes, and network servers. But the company has morphed over the years into a software and services company; the company is number two behind Microsoft in the software business. IBM is also an innovation and new product development leader, for the past seventeen years leading the world in the number of U.S. patents issued.

In 2009, IBM derived over 75 percent of its revenue and 82 percent of its income from the Software and Services businesses. Although now only 17 percent of the business, the company continues to design and produce mainframes and has its label on five of the top ten supercomputers in the world. They also produce high-margin commercial servers and enterprise-level installations, but in recent years they have exited the lower-margin hardware businesses, such as consumer PCs, laptops, and hard drives.

Financial Highlights, Fiscal Year 2010

Although the company didn't reach the $104 billion revenue high point of 2008, they did resume modest revenue growth, reaching almost $100 billion from a 2009 lull of $95.8 billion. The good news is per share earnings and cash flow, which both rose through the three year period as if there were no "glitch" in revenues whatsoever. FY2010 per share earnings rose almost 11.5 percent to $11.52, making 2010 the eighth consecutive year of double-digit EPS growth at the company. IBM's shift to higher-margin businesses continues to account for the higher earnings in the face of relatively steady sales.

Cash flow continues to excel, with a double-digit increase to $16.01 per share in FY2010. Over the past nine years, Big Blue has generated over $100 billion in free cash flow and has used a significant portion to repurchase shares, retiring some 75 million in 2010 and some 500 million since 2002 to reach today's 1.2 billion shares outstanding, all while paying a healthy and growing dividend. Improving margins have been part of the IBM success story. Led by the software and services businesses, operating margins have improved from the 16–20 percent range through 2008 to 23 percent currently, while net margins have improved from 9–11 percent to the 13 percent range.

Reasons to Buy

Once viewed as a teetering giant of the computer industry, with a massive intellectual property portfolio but with an uncertain product strategy, IBM has, over the last decade, successfully reinvented itself as a powerhouse in the Software and Services sector. Further, IBM seems positioned "where the puck is going" in the IT world, a fact not lost on HP and other competitors trying to emulate the business model. Not long ago, many companies felt they had to have in-house information technology departments to service their IT needs. Now, most have found that it's far more efficient to contract those services out to someone who can provide data warehousing, website development and maintenance, regional/national/global IT infrastructure, etc., without requiring a commitment in fixed assets. This is where IBM has leveraged their expertise, and as this trend continues and as businesses

increase their reliance on these services, IBM benefits. As the common architecture becomes more "cloudlike," we also feel IBM will benefit.

IBM has traditionally led in the development of international IT markets, and today, international business represents about 64 percent of the total. While international has been the fastest growing marketplace for years, U.S. growth recently resumed a positive direction after seven quarters in the red during the recession.

They continue to innovate and are in a great position to acquire whatever technology they choose not to develop internally. They have world-class semiconductor design and production facilities and license design, manufacturing, and packaging services and products.

While all IT companies are vulnerable to economic cycles, IBM services income is largely based on long-term contracts, which are not as subject to the vagaries of the world economy as would be sales of hardware.

Finally, the company has an exceptionally strong cash and cash flow position, and has shown the propensity to turn this into shareholder return, both through buybacks and a 15.5 percent annual dividend increase rate for the past ten years.

Reasons for Caution

IBM has carved out a very large chunk of the outsourced IT business. Innovation in this area can be rapid and disruptive, and margins can shrink precipitously as a result. IBM will have to stay ahead of the curve with innovative and compelling products and defensive product strategies in order to maintain revenue growth.

Competition in the services area is heating up, with Hewlett-Packard's purchase of EDS and Oracle's acquisition of Sun Microsystems. These two moves have created competitors with strong synergies and a compelling sales pitch to new and existing customers.

Finally, IBM has a larger exposure to governments and government contracts than many of its competitors. While this can be stabilizing in hard times, this time we feel that a massive and widespread public sector belt tightening could hurt the company.

SECTOR: **Information Technology**
BETA COEFFICIENT: **0.77**
10-YEAR COMPOUND EARNINGS PER SHARE GROWTH: **10.5%**
10-YEAR COMPOUND DIVIDENDS PER SHARE GROWTH: **16.5%**

	2003	2004	2005	2006	2007	2008	2009	2010
Revenues (Mil)	89,131	96,503	91,134	91,424	98,786	103,630	95,758	99,870
Net Income (Mil)	7,583	8,448	7,934	9,492	10,418	12,334	13,425	14,833
Earnings per share	4.34	4.39	4.91	6.06	7.18	8.93	10.01	11.52
Dividends per share	0.66	0.7	0.078	1.1	1.5	1.9	2.15	2.50
Cash flow per share	7.27	8.24	8.71	9.56	11.28	13.28	13.9	16.01
Price: high	94.5	100.4	99.1	97.4	121.5	130.9	132.3	147.5
low	73.2	81.9	71.8	72.7	88.8	69.5	81.8	116.0

International Business Machines Corporation
New Orchard Road
Armonk, NY 10504
(800) 426-4968
Website: *www.ibm.com*

Illinois Tool Works

Ticker symbol: ITW (NYSE) ❑ S&P rating: A+ ❑ Value Line financial strength rating: A++ ❑ Current yield: 2.5%

Company Profile

Illinois Tool Works is a longstanding multinational conglomerate involved in the manufacture of a diversified range of industrial products, mainly components, fasteners, and other "ingredients" for other manufacturers. Customers include the automotive, machinery, construction, food and beverage, and general industrial markets. The company currently operates some 850 decentralized business units in fifty-four countries, employing approximately 65,000. Some of the products are branded and familiar, like Wolf and Hobart kitchen equipment and DeVilbiss air power tools; some are obscure and only known to others in the industry.

The businesses are organized into seven major segments, each contributing fairly equally to revenue:

■ Industrial Packaging includes steel, plastic, and paper products used for bundling, shipping, and protecting goods in transit. Primary brands include Acme, Signode, Pabco, and Strapex. Major end markets served are primary metals,

general industrial, construction, and food/beverage.

■ Power Systems and Electronics produces equipment and consumables associated with specialty power conversion, metallurgy, and electronics. Their primary products include arc-welding equipment and consumables, solder materials and equipment and services for electronics assembly. Primary brands include AXA Power, Hobart, Kester, and Weldcraft.

■ Transportation includes transportation-related components, fasteners, fluids, and polymers, as well as truck remanufacturing and related parts and service. Major end markets are automotive OEM and automotive aftermarket.

■ Food Equipment produces commercial food equipment and related service, including professional kitchen ovens, refrigeration, mixers, exhaust, and ventilation systems. Major brands include Hobart, Traulsen, Vulcan, and Wolf.

■ Construction Products concentrates on tools, fasteners, and other products for construction applications. Their major end markets are residential, commercial, and renovation construction.

■ Polymers and Fluids businesses produce adhesives, sealants, lubrication, and cutting fluids, and hygiene products. Their primary brands include Futura, Kraft, Devcon, and Rocol.

■ Decorative Services produces a line of countertops, flooring, and laminates primarily for the commercial and retailing markets.

Finally, the remaining ITW brands include a cornucopia of businesses addressing a dozen or more markets. Brands well known to industrial users (and probably not many others) include Chemtronics, Magnaflux, and Texwipe.

Financial Highlights, Fiscal Year 2010

Mainly because of the economic downturn and an uncertain recovery cycle, we dropped ITW from our 2011 *100 Best* list. This year, with the economic recovery gaining some steam and the relative health of many U.S. manufacturing sectors including automotive, the company has made the list again.

With exposure across most of the hardest hit industrial sectors, the company fared worse than most in FY2009, experiencing a 13 percent drop in revenues and a 37 percent skid in earnings per share. But the company gained almost all of that back in FY2010, with a 14 percent increase in sales to $15.9 billion and a recovery in earnings per share to near parity with FY2008. Without out the effects of an FY2009 tax adjustment, "organic" earnings for FY2010 Q4 were actually 30 percent ahead of the prior year.

For FY11 the prospects of continued recovery bode well, and ITW expects a healthy 10 percent revenue gain to $17.4 billion with per share earnings in the $3.60–$3.84 range. The businesses are doing well and generating solid positive cash flow, which is being used to repurchase shares. The company has retired some 127 million of 617 million shares since 2003, and raised its dividend to an effective $1.36 per share annually.

Reasons to Buy

Buying shares of ITW is like buying a mutual fund covering the entire U.S. and world manufacturing sector. The company is well diversified and serves many markets, some with end products, some with components, some in cyclical industries like automotive and construction, some in "steady-state" industries like food processing and packaging. We should note that foreign sales accounted for 57 percent of the total—a healthy figure for an industrial goods company. The company has solid models for making acquisitions, and seems to do better than most conglomerates historically in choosing candidates and then managing them once they're in the fold. The company seems to do an equally good job of turning opportunity into cash flow and using that cash flow to enhance shareholder returns, as exemplified by the steady record of dividend increases each year since 1994.

Reasons for Caution

ITW is by nature tied to some of the more volatile elements of the business cycle, and so may not be the best pick for investors living in fear of the next downturn. Conglomerates are notoriously difficult to manage (it's hard enough to manage one business, let alone 850 of them); any sign of cracks in this structure should be taken seriously. While acquisitions are part of the growth strategy, the company, thus far, keeps them small and does not depend on acquiring other big names, but the disruptions of a big acquisition could pose problems.

SECTOR: **Industrials**
BETA COEFFICIENT: **1.10**
10-YEAR COMPOUND EARNINGS PER SHARE GROWTH: **7.5%**
10-YEAR COMPOUND DIVIDENDS PER SHARE GROWTH: **15.0%**

	2003	2004	2005	2006	2007	2008	2009	2010
Revenues (Mil)	10,036	11,371	12,922	14,055	16,169	15,869	13,876	15,870
Net Income (Mil)	1,040	1,340	1,494	1,717	1,826	1,583	969	1,527
Earnings per share	1.69	2.20	2.60	3.01	3.36	3.05	1.93	3.03
Dividends per share	0.47	0.50	0.61	0.71	0.91	1.15	1.24	1.27
Cash flow per share	2.18	2.90	3.34	3.87	4.44	4.56	3.27	-
Price: high	42.3	48.3	47.3	53.5	60.0	55.6	51.2	52.7
low	27.3	36.5	39.3	41.5	45.6	28.5	25.6	40.3

Illinois Tool Works, Inc.
3600 West Lake Avenue
Glenview, IL 60026
(847) 724-7500
Website: *www.itwinc.com*

International Paper Company

Ticker symbol: IP (NYSE) □ S&P rating: BBB □ Value Line financial strength rating: B+ □ Current yield: 2.6%

Company Profile

International Paper Company (International Paper), incorporated in 1941, is a global paper and packaging company complemented by a North American merchant distribution system with primary markets and manufacturing operations in North America, Europe, Latin America, Russia, Asia, and North Africa.

At the end of 2009, the company operated twenty-one pulp, paper, and packaging mills; 146 converting and packaging plants; nineteen recycling plants; and three bag facilities. Production facilities in Europe, Asia, Latin America, and South America included nine pulp, paper, and packaging mills; fifty-two converting and packaging plants; and two recycling plants.

The company operates in six segments: Printing Papers, Industrial Packaging, Consumer Packaging, Distribution, Forest Products, and Specialty Businesses and Other. The Printing Papers segment produces uncoated printing and writing papers, including papers for use in copiers, desktop and laser printers, and digital imaging. Market pulp is used in the manufacture of printing, writing, and specialty papers, towel and tissue products and filtration products. Pulp is also converted into non-paper products such as diapers and sanitary napkins.

The Industrial Packaging segment produces containerboard, including linerboard, whitetop, recycled linerboard, and saturating crafto. About 70 percent of the company's production is converted into corrugated boxes and other packaging. The company also recycles a million tons of corrugated, mixed, and white paper through twenty-one recycling plants.

The Consumer Packaging segment produces somewhat finer materials including bleached sulfate board for making packaging applications like food, cosmetics, pharmaceuticals, etc. Subsidiaries such as Shorewood Packaging Corporation form containers and add graphics for specific customers.

Xpedx, the company's North American merchant distribution business, provides distribution services and products to a number of customer markets. Xpedx supplies commercial printers with printing papers and graphic pre-press, presses, and post-press equipment, building services and away-from-home markets with facility supplies, and manufacturers with packaging supplies and equipment.

The company suffered a major swing in fortunes in 2008 as demand softened and costs escalated. Earnings dropped 55 percent, the dividend was cut 70 percent, and the stock price reached a nadir just under $4 per share. The company acquired the containerboard, packaging, and recycling businesses of Weyerhaeuser that year, and set out to continue a restructuring into 2009 and 2010, including the divestiture of most of its 200,000 acres of U.S. forestland and an international growth initiative spearheaded by the acquisition of SCA Packaging Asia in 2010. The company is becoming more aggressive in achieving scale, becoming more focused, and modernizing its product mix.

Financial Highlights, Fiscal Year 2010

Aided by strengthening customer demand, a better product mix, and better-than-expected results from the Weyerhaeuser acquisition, the FY2010 transition was mostly a success. Revenue at the end of 2010 was running 7 percent ahead of comparable periods in 2009; Q4 earnings were almost triple the year-ago period. Capping it off, the company announced a 50 percent dividend increase to $.1875 per share per quarter, exceeding what analysts had hoped for and bringing the company halfway back to the $1.00 per share paid for years up until the 2008 down cycle.

Reasons to Buy

Based on the sharp drop in 2008–09, it was an exercise in patience to keep this company on the *100 Best Stocks* list. It turned out to be the best performer on our 2010 list, but one must consider where it started. That said, the company has done a good job of turning itself around, and, like some patients finally undergoing long-awaited surgery, we think it is emerging stronger and better for the experience. The company has added to its dominance in key commodity and value-add paper and packaging markets, exited low-margin businesses, and has increased operating margins substantially as a result. We think the company is well managed and is a solid player in a fairly steady industry. A return of the dividend to the $1.00 level would provide a decent income for shareholders as well.

Reasons for Caution

For the most part, IP is in a commodity business with a high reliance on corrugated boards and raw packaging materials. To the extent that the company can find ways to add value to its products and deliver finished paper and packaging to end consumers, and develop international markets, the company will overcome the negatives of being a commodity producer. We're also concerned that IP's customers, in efforts to cut costs and be more environmentally sensitive, might cut or trim packaging consumption. We also believe that enhanced Internet experiences and devices like iPads may be reducing the amount of computer-generated printing. More aggressive investors will definitely not find this to be a sexy business.

SECTOR: Materials
BETA COEFFICIENT: 2.20
10-YEAR COMPOUND EARNINGS PER SHARE GROWTH: 4.0%
10-YEAR COMPOUND DIVIDENDS PER SHARE GROWTH: -2.5%

	2003	2004	2005	2006	2007	2008	2009	2010
Revenues (Mil)	25,179	25,548	24,097	21,995	21,890	24,829	23,366	25,179
Net Income (Mil)	382	634	513	635	1,168	829	378	644
Earnings per share	0.80	1.30	1.06	2.18	2.70	1.96	0.88	1.48
Dividends per share	1.00	1.00	1.00	1.00	1.00	1.00	0.33	0.40
Cash flow per share	4.21	4.51	3.85	3.63	4.15	5.02	4.27	4.78
Price: high	43.3	45	42.6	38	41.6	33.8	27.8	29.3
low	33.1	37.1	27	30.7	31	10.2	3.9	19.3

International Paper Company
400 Atlantic Street
Stamford, CT 06921
(901) 419-4957
Website: *www.internationalpaper.com*

AGGRESSIVE GROWTH

Iron Mountain Incorporated

Ticker symbol: IRM (NYSE) ❑ S&P rating: BB- ❑ Value Line financial strength rating: B ❑ Current yield: 2.9%

Company Profile

The name implies security and invulnerability, and as such, Iron Mountain is the world's leading provider of secure record, document, and information-management services. Businesses that require or desire off-site, secure storage and/or archiving of data in physical or electronic form contract with IRM for whatever level of service meets their needs.

In general, IRM provides three major types of service: records management, data protection and recovery, and information destruction. All three services include both physical and electronic media.

Revenues accrue to the company through two streams—storage and services. Storage revenues consist of recurring per-unit charges related to the storage of material or data. The storage periods are typically many years, and the revenues from this service account for just over half of IRM's total revenue over the past five years. Service revenue comes from charges for any number of services, including those related to the core storage service and others such as temporary access, courier operations, secure destruction, data recovery, media conversion, and the like.

Although its roots are in document management, the company recently expanded its operations in the area of digital records management. Digital archiving and services are analogous to the services done for paper, except that they are done for e-mail, e-statements, images, and other forms of electronic documents. It also includes web-based archiving of computer, server, and website data, as well as storage of backup or disaster recovery digital media. The company also offers tailored industry-specific services for industries like health care. The company also offers value-add services in organizing, indexing, and facilitating search through documents and records.

IRM's client base is deep and diverse. They have over 90,000 clients, including 93 percent of the *Fortune* 1000 and over 90 percent of the FTSE 100. They have over 900 facilities in 165 markets worldwide, and they are six times the size of their nearest competitor.

Financial Highlights, Fiscal Year 2010

Iron Mountain has had a couple of soft years. First, there was the normal 2008–09 downturn that affected everybody. Less business means less paper and fewer records; that, combined with increasing cost containment on the part of many clients, led to a slight revenue and profit dip in 2009, nothing to be too worried about. Then the announcement of a $255 million write-down of the digital records storage venture ($1.24 per share) hit in September 2009 and IRMs shares were found on the new fifty-two-week lows list at a time when few other companies were there in sympathy. On top of that, Warren Buffett's Berkshire Hathaway sold its entire 8 million-share holding.

That turned out to be a pretty good entry point, for the company has rebounded smartly with $1.13 per share 2010 earnings on $3.14 billion in sales and operating margins at a new high of 30 percent. As evidence of the company's confidence in the future and in cash generation potential, it began paying dividends in early 2010, and raised that dividend 200 percent to an indicated $.75 per share per year during the fourth quarter.

Reasons to Buy

Iron Mountain's business strategy for the past fifteen years has been one of becoming by far the biggest in the business with the strongest and most recognizable brand. Much of this growth and dominance has been achieved through acquisition and integration, buying smaller businesses and consolidating their operations and, more importantly, their customer base. Customers in this business tend to stay with a known quantity, and over the years, no one has become more known than IRM. This strategy has worked very well for them, and now IRM is the clear market leader. Their large, predictable revenue stream gives them the flexibility to maintain their policy of strategic acquisition while funding the resulting restructuring internally.

A common observation of IRM's critics is that paper records are dying off and most data is now generated and stored electronically, creating opportunity for competitors like IBM and EMC. This is true, but it ignores a couple of facts: Existing paper still needs to be stored for a long time, and there's a lot of it. Nearly 75 percent of IRM's revenue comes from paper storage, but this percentage is declining as IRM's customers are storing far more electronic data now.

It also ignores a number of other important points. For one, IRM's current customers would need a very good reason to split their data storage business between two vendors, one doing only electronic storage and the other doing electronic storage plus everything else as well. Second, if competitors for the electronic storage business become a problem, IRM can price their electronic storage below market and still be quite profitable. And last, for the customer base that IRM serves, this is not a burdensome expense. Changing vendors could likely cost them more than they might ever hope to save. For now, IRM has a pretty good moat.

Finally, it's hard to ignore the new and recently initiated dividend; the payout of nearly 3 percent is quite attractive for a company with a solid future and decent growth prospects.

Reasons for Caution

Although many of its services are required for compliance to various record-keeping laws and norms, IRM is vulnerable to economic dips. Further, the company still hasn't completely found its way in the digital space, which should prove to be its biggest growth area moving forward. It remains to be seen whether digital storage and services are as profitable as their paper counterparts.

SECTOR: **Information Technology**
BETA COEFFICIENT: **1.00**
5-YEAR COMPOUND EARNINGS PER SHARE GROWTH: **29.4%**
10-YEAR COMPOUND DIVIDENDS PER SHARE GROWTH: **NM**

	2003	**2004**	**2005**	**2006**	**2007**	**2008**	**2009**	**2010**
Revenues (Mil)	1,501	1,817	2,078	2,350	2,730	3,055	3,014	3,127
Net Income (Mil)	84.6	94.2	114	129	153	152	195	230
Earnings per share	0.44	0.48	0.57	0.64	0.76	0.78	0.96	1.15
Dividends per share	–	–	–	–	–	–	0.75	.19
Cash flow per share	1.12	1.32	1.52	1.69	2.01	2.19	2.55	2.75
Price: high	18.1	23.4	30.1	29.9	38.8	37.1	24.9	28.5
low	13.4	17.2	17.8	22.6	25	16.7	21.3	19.9

Iron Mountain Incorporated
745 Atlantic Avenue
Boston, MA 02111
Website: *www.ironmountain.com*

GROWTH AND INCOME

Johnson & Johnson

Ticker symbol: JNJ (NYSE) ❑ S&P rating: AAA ❑ Value Line financial strength rating: A++ ❑
Current yield: 3.6 percent

Company Profile

Johnson & Johnson is the largest and most comprehensive health care company in the world, with 2010 sales of approximately $62 billion. JNJ offers a broad line of consumer products and over-the-counter drugs, as well as various other medical devices and diagnostic equipment.

The company has three reporting segments: Consumer Health Care, Medical Devices and Diagnostics, and Pharmaceuticals. In those segments, Johnson & Johnson has more than 200 operating companies in fifty-four countries, selling some 50,000 products in more than 175 countries. Among Johnson & Johnson's premier assets are its well-entrenched brand names, which are widely known in the United States as well as abroad. And as a marketer, JNJ's reputation for quality has enabled it to build strong ties to commercial health care providers.

The company has a stake in a wide variety of health segments: anti-infectives, biotechnology, cardiology and circulatory diseases, diagnostics, gastrointestinals, minimally invasive therapies, nutraceuticals, orthopedics, pain management, skin care, vision care, women's health, and wound care.

The company's vast portfolio of well-known trade names includes Band-Aid adhesive bandages; Tylenol; Stayfree, Carefree, and Sure & Natural feminine hygiene products; Mylanta; Pepcid AC; Neutrogena; Johnson's baby powder, shampoo, and oil; Listerine; and Reach toothbrushes.

The company has recently expanded acquisitions in key health care categories. In September 2009, JNJ, through a new subsidiary JANSSEN Alzheimer Immunotherapy, acquired most all of the assets and rights of Elan, plc related to its Alzheimer's Immunotherapy Program. In September 2010, JNJ acquired Micrus Endovascular, a global provider of minimally invasive devices for hemorrhagic and ischemic stroke.

Financial Highlights, Fiscal Year 2010

Johnson & Johnson has a dominant and stable franchise in a secure and lucrative industry. We like the model of steady, recurring income from solid consumer brands such as Tylenol combined with more aggressive and lucrative ventures into pharmaceuticals and surgical products. Yet the company's earnings performance has been tepid of late, in part due to a series of expensive recalls, liability lawsuits, and plant shutdowns. As examples, the company had recalls of Tylenol, Benadryl, and Zyrtec during 2010, and in early 2011 a $420 million class action suit was filed against subsidiary DuPuy Orthopedics for hip replacement devices.

Revenues slackened a bit during the recession from a $63.7 billion level in 2008 to $61.7 billion in 2009, and back to just over $62 billion in 2010. Earnings during that period remained almost flat, and rose slightly on a per share basis as the company repurchased about 100 million shares of its approximately 2.8 billion shares outstanding. Because of continued costs of these recalls and lawsuits, management guided earnings slightly lower for 2011 to $4.80–$4.90 per share from previous estimates of $4.99–$5.05 because of the "near term pressures on the business."

The company continued to expand its global footprint, building new research and manufacturing operations in Brazil, Russia, India, China, and other developing markets. International markets account for about 50 percent of sales.

The company also received a nice $1 billion bump from a legal settlement involving patent infringement on cardiac stents with Boston Scientific in January 2010, and another $700 million in January 2011 from the same settlement.

Reasons to Buy

JNJ has made a lot of headlines recently for its stumbles in manufacturing and in certain consumer and professional markets, yet its core business remains solid and intact. Earnings and cash flow are steady, and when you combine the healthy dividend and share repurchases, shareholder returns have been healthy even during the slight period of "sickness" experienced by the company. Once the current "sniffles" are out of the system, the company will likely resume a steady growth rate in the 5 percent range. Acquisitions and a healthy new drug pipeline will likely add a bit to margins.

International sales continue to be a solid growth path. As standards of medical care rise internationally and as the potential for health care funding reform in the United States increases, J&J's growth outside the United States is particularly appealing. The world health care market is expected to grow 5 percent per year over the next five years, and J&J participates in over 30 percent of those markets.

Despite the size, some softness in consumer spending, and the

aforementioned problems, the company has delivered a solid double-
digit growth triple play in ten-year
earnings, cash flow, and dividend
growth, despite sales growth nar-
rowly missing double digits at 9.5
percent. We feel that JNJ is rock
solid with modest growth prospects
and little long-term downside.

Reasons for Caution

While JNJ is a "steady Eddie" in a
steady health care segment, investors aren't likely to strike it rich on
this company due to its size and
relative steadiness of the markets it
serves. Even a blockbuster drug or
acquisition isn't likely to move the
needle very much.

There may be some concern
that regulators and litigators, now
having seen JNJ as a juicy target for
action, will step up these actions,
or short of that, watch JNJ through
a microscope creating a distraction
for management. Worse, these
events could damage consumer
perception and brand strength if
they continue. However, we think
these blemishes will likely heal and
won't be contagious to long-term
performance.

SECTOR: **Health Care**
BETA COEFFICIENT: **.57**
10-YEAR COMPOUND EARNINGS PER SHARE GROWTH: **12.5%**
10-YEAR COMPOUND DIVIDENDS PER SHARE GROWTH: **14.0%**

	2003	2004	2005	2006	2007	2008	2009	2010
Revenues (Mil)	41,862	47,348	50,514	53,324	61,095	63,747	61,897	61,587
Net Income (Mil)	7,197	8,509	10,411	11,053	10,576	12,949	12,906	13,279
Earnings per share	2.4	2.84	3.35	3.73	4.15	4.57	4.63	4.76
Dividends per share	0.93	1.1	1.28	1.46	1.62	1.8	1.93	2.11
Cash flow per share	3.36	3.84	4.25	4.6	5.23	5.70	5.69	5.90
Price: high	59.1	64.2	70	69.4	68.8	72.8	65.9	66.2
low	48	49.2	59.8	56.6	59.7	52.1	61.9	56.9

Johnson & Johnson
One Johnson & Johnson Plaza
New Brunswick, NJ 08933
(800) 950-5089
Website: *www.jnj.com*

CONSERVATIVE GROWTH

Johnson Controls, Inc.

Ticker symbol: JCI (NYSE) ❑ S&P rating: BBB+ ❑ Value Line financial strength rating: A ❑ Current yield: 1.6%

Company Profile

Johnson Controls is a fairly low-profile U.S. manufacturer with three principal businesses that just now happen to all be in favor for the first time in years. JCI is a large manufacturer of automotive parts and subassemblies, heating ventilation and air conditioning (HVAC) and other energy controls, and an assortment of battery technologies and products. Their products are found in over 200 million vehicles, 12 million homes, and 1 million commercial buildings. Their business operates in three segments: Automotive Experience, Building Efficiency, and Power Solutions.

Their automotive business is one of the world's largest automotive suppliers, providing seating and overhead systems, door systems, floor consoles, instrument panels, cockpits, and integrated electronics. Customers include virtually every major automaker in the world, including newer start-ups and plants in China. The company now plans a third plant in that country. The business produces automotive interior systems for original equipment manufacturers (OEMs) and operates in twenty-nine countries worldwide.

Additionally, the business has partially owned affiliates in Asia, Europe, North America, and South America. In fiscal 2010, the automotive business accounted for 48 percent of the company's consolidated net sales and 46 percent of profits.

Building Efficiency is a global leader in delivering integrated control systems, mechanical equipment, services, and solutions designed to improve the comfort, safety, and energy efficiency of non-residential buildings and residential properties with operations in more than 125 countries. Revenues come from facilities management, technical services, and the replacement and upgrade of controls/HVAC mechanical equipment in the existing buildings and "smart buildings" market. In fiscal 2009, Building Efficiency accounted for 42 percent of the company's consolidated net sales and 30 percent of profits.

The Power Solutions business produces lead-acid automotive batteries, serving both automotive original equipment manufacturers and the general vehicle battery aftermarket. They also offer Absorbent Glass Mat (AGM), nickel-metal-hydride, and lithium-ion battery technologies to power hybrid vehicles. Sales of automotive batteries generated 14 percent of the company's fiscal 2009 consolidated net sales and 24 percent of profits.

Financial Highlights, Fiscal Year 2010

Johnson Controls suffered with the rest of the economy in FY2009 as a large supplier to the automotive and construction industries. FY2010 has been a different story.

A recovery in the auto industry and especially the U.S.–based auto industry, combined with greater emphasis on energy-efficient buildings and focus on new battery technologies for electric vehicles have combined to not only bring JCI out of the doldrums but to bring in revenues and profits steadily beating forecasts. Revenues at the Automotive Experience group were 18 percent ahead of 2009, while Power Systems surged 19 percent and Building Efficiency logged a cool 10 percent increase.

Business is good, and a strong international component is making it better. The company raised 2011 guidance for a 12 percent sales increase with earnings in the $2.50–$2.55 range compared to $2.00 in FY2010.

Reasons to Buy

As previously noted, JCI is hitting on all cylinders right now, with a resurgent automotive manufacturing climate, strong demand for energy-efficient buildings, and even stronger demand for effective battery technologies for current and future applications.

JCI will be a major participant in the coming automotive applications of lithium battery technology. They are already in the 2009 Mercedes S-class hybrid and are the exclusive suppliers to the upcoming (2012) Ford plug-in hybrid for its battery and battery controls. Johnson's joint venture with Saft Advanced Power Solutions (JCS) is also providing lithium-ion batteries to the Dodge Sprinter development program. JCI's subsidiary Varta has set up a JCS development center in Hanover, Germany, to support the European market.

Finally, we see plenty of opportunities to expand into overseas markets that, until recently, haven't held much promise for the company.

Reasons for Caution

Needless to say, the automotive and building efficiency businesses can be intensely cyclical and economically sensitive; in fact, the construction industry is still in its doldrums or else JCI would be making even greater revenue and earnings gains. Also, JCI is a leader in the race for the next automotive power technology, but there's no guarantee that lithium will be the clear winner.

Other technologies are making progress as well, and the politics of lithium sourcing are far from settled. Finally, operating margins in the 7 percent range don't leave much room for error.

SECTOR: **Industrials**
BETA COEFFICIENT: **1.81**
10-YEAR COMPOUND EARNINGS PER SHARE GROWTH: **11.5%**
10-YEAR COMPOUND DIVIDENDS PER SHARE GROWTH: **12.5%**

	2003	**2004**	**2005**	**2006**	**2007**	**2008**	**2009**	**2010**
Revenues (Mil)	22,646	25,363	27,883	32,235	34,624	38,062	28,497	34,305
Net Income (Mil)	683	818	909	1,028	1,252	1,400	281	1,365
Earnings per share	1.2	1.41	1.5	1.75	2.09	2.33	0.47	2.00
Dividends per share	0.24	0.28	0.33	0.37	0.44	0.52	0.52	0.52
Cash flow per share	2.28	2.5	2.6	2.95	3.34	3.63	1.48	3.00
Price: high	19.4	21.1	25.1	30	44.5	36.5	28.3	40.2
low	12	16.5	17.5	22.1	28.1	13.6	8.4	25.6

Johnson Controls, Inc.
P. O. Box 591
Milwaukee, WI 53201–0591
(414) 524-2375
Website: *www.johnsoncontrols.com*

Kellogg Company

Ticker symbol: K (NYSE) □ S&P rating: BBB+ □ Value Line financial strength rating: A □ Current yield: 3.2%

Company Profile

Founded in 1906, Kellogg is the world's leading producer of breakfast cereal and a leading producer of convenience foods, including cookies, crackers, toaster pastries, cereal bars, frozen waffles, meat alternatives, pie crusts, and cones.

The company's brands include Kellogg's, Keebler, Pop-Tarts, Eggo, Cheez-It, Nutri-Grain, Rice Krispies, Special K, Murray, Austin, Morningstar Farms, Famous Amos, Carr's, Plantation, and Kashi.

The company operates in two segments: Kellogg North America (NA) and Kellogg International, with NA generating just under two-thirds of the company's revenue. NA operations are further divided into Cereals, Snacks, and Frozen/Specialty categories. International operates as three regional entities: Europe, Latin America, and Asia Pacific. The company produces more than 1,500 different products, manufactured in nineteen countries and marketed in more than 180 countries around the world.

Kellogg is a conservatively run company, emphasizing long-term thinking and leveraging existing brand strengths while keeping a sharp focus on cost savings. They've created and manage to several internal measures of financial performance that are geared toward sustainable long-term growth.

Financial Highlights, Fiscal Year 2010

Kellogg hit a bit of a flat spot during the 2009–10 period, as increased competition from Ralcorp ("Post" brand) and a recall of some Eggo frozen waffle products hit the bottom line. Competition and some price cutting pressure in both the United States and Europe led to 5 percent sales declines, and in combination with increased marketing costs, led to as much as a 14 percent drop in earnings during FY2010 quarters. For 2011, the company projected a currency-neutral sales growth in the low single digits, a flat to slightly off net profit performance, and a low single-digits growth in earnings per share. Flat profits with EPS growth, of course, suggests stock repurchases, and the company has been fairly aggressive with them, buying back between

10 and 20 million shares per year and some 50 million of its 2004 reported 413 million share count since that year.

Reasons to Buy

Kellogg owns just over a third of the U.S. market for ready-to-eat cereals, which makes them the most recognized brand and market leader in probably the most mature food category in the world. But, having invented it over a hundred years ago, they continue to respond to customer demand for new and interesting products, many with a health bent. In 2009, for instance, they released Special K Chocolatey Flakes, and added dietary fiber to Corn Pops, Apple Jacks, and Froot Loops. In 2010, they rolled out Eggo Thick & Fluffy waffles, Frosted Flakes with Fiber, "Scrabble" Junior Fruit Flavored Snacks, and three flavors of Special K cracker chips,

Kellogg's strategy since 2001 has been to "win in cereal and expand snacks," meaning "hold onto market share in the mature segment and grow the newer segment with product innovation." This has worked well for them, as 25 percent of their revenues are from cereals, and snacks have grown (organically and through acquisition) to 30 percent of overall revenue. If they continue to succeed with this strategy we can expect to see continued steady growth in the top line; in addition they are working toward the stated goal of $1 billion in cost savings by the end of 2011.

We like Kellogg's growth in international markets. As discretionary income rises, so does consumption of prepared foods, and the international markets will reward companies that have the right products. Special K, for example, is growing at double-digit rates internationally and at triple-digit rates in India.

The company has a compelling history of slow but steady growth. Kellogg has been accelerating dividend growth in recent years; combined with share buybacks, the total shareholder return package and inherent safety make Kellogg a stock that will let you sleep at night.

Reasons for Caution

Particularly in a soft economy, Kellogg faces threats from generic and store-branded products, especially on the cereal aisle. Price competition is intense and required advertising and marketing spending can further eat into profits. Growth prospects beyond the single digits for this type of company are unlikely. The company also faces some exposure to commodity price increases, although they are well hedged for such increases.

SECTOR: Consumer Staples
BETA COEFFICIENT: .44
10-YEAR COMPOUND EARNINGS PER SHARE GROWTH: 8.0%
10-YEAR COMPOUND DIVIDENDS PER SHARE GROWTH: 4.0%

	2003	2004	2005	2006	2007	2008	2009	2010
Revenues (Mil)	8,812	9,614	10,177	10,907	11,776	12,822	12,575	12,397
Net Income (Mil)	787	891	980	1,004	1,103	1,148	1,212	1,247
Earnings per share	1.92	2.14	2.26	2.51	2.76	2.99	3.17	3.30
Dividends per share	1.01	1.01	1.06	1.14	1.24	1.3	1.43	1.56
Cash flow per share	2.83	3.15	3.39	3.41	3.78	3.99	4.35	4.48
Price: high	38.6	45.3	47	51	56.9	58.5	54.1	56.0
low	27.8	37	42.4	42.4	48.7	35.6	35.6	47.3

Kellogg Company
One Kellogg Square
P. O. Box 3599
Battle Creek, MI 49016–3599
(269) 961-6636
Website: *www.kelloggcompany.com*

GROWTH AND INCOME

Kimberly-Clark

Ticker symbol: KMB (NYSE) ◻ S&P rating: A ◻ Value Line financial strength rating: A++ ◻ Current yield: 4.3%

Company Profile

Kimberly-Clark develops, manufactures, and markets a full line of personal care products, mostly based on paper and paper technologies. Well known for their ubiquitous Kleenex brand tissues, KMB also is a strong player in bath tissue, diapers, feminine products, incontinence products, industrial and health care–related paper products, and others.

The company operates in four segments: Personal Care, Consumer Tissue, K-C Professional & Other, and Health Care. The Personal Care segment provides disposable diapers, training and youth pants, and swimpants; baby wipes; and feminine and incontinence care products, and related products. Brand names include Huggies, Pull-Ups, Little Swimmers, Good-Nites, Kotex, Lightdays, Depend, and Poise. The Consumer Tissue segment offers facial and bathroom tissue, paper towels, napkins, and related products for household use under the Kleenex, Scott, Cottonelle, Viva, Andrex, Scottex, Hakle, and Page brands. The K-C Professional & Other provides paper products for the away-from-home,

that is, commercial/institutional marketplace under Kimberly-Clark, Kleenex, Scott, WypAll, Kimtech, KleenGuard, Kimcare, and Jackson brand names. The Health Care segment offers disposable health care products, such as surgical drapes and gowns, infection control products, face masks, exam gloves, respiratory products, pain management products, and other disposable medical products.

To give an idea of what drives growth at KMB, in the first quarter of 2010, Personal Care sales grew 8.1 percent, consumer tissue grew 2 percent, K-C Professional & Other products grew 12.1 percent, and Health Care products grew at a 23.2 percent rate.

The company sells its products to a variety of retailers, mass merchandisers, and distributors. Wal-Mart accounts for some 13 percent of sales. Sales have been centered in the United States, but the company is reaching out to foreign markets. The company was founded in 1872 and is headquartered today in Dallas, Texas, with a historical, technology, and manufacturing base in the Fox River Valley in Wisconsin.

Financial Highlights, Fiscal Year 2010

Kimberly-Clark experienced a moderate drop in revenues in 2009 as consumers became more thrifty and steered clear of premium brands. Organic revenue growth came in slightly lower than earlier projections, but the company regained a low single-digits growth pace with $19.7 billion in revenues. Price increases and strong international sales continued to be a big part of the story. On the profit front, the company reported FY2010 earnings of $4.45 per share, slightly off from $4.52 in 2009. Earnings were aided by ongoing cost-cutting efforts stemming from its rather bluntly named "Project FORCE"—Focus on Reducing Costs Everywhere—program. These costs cuts were offset by higher raw pulp and other commodity prices, which will bear watching going forward.

For FY2011, the company is expecting earnings growth in the 3–5 percent range, or $4.90–$5.05, on revenues of $20.4 billion. More encouraging was the announcement of the latest dividend increase, to $2.80 per year from the previously indicated $2.64. The dividend has doubled since 2003; on top of that, the company has retired about 20 percent of its outstanding shares since that time.

Reasons to Buy

Kimberly-Clark has shown itself to be a steady business in all kinds of economic climates. The high yield and strong track record of raising dividends and buying back shares is a definite plus. Strong cash flow has financed these initiatives as well as funding international expansion and enhanced marketing efforts. With a dividend well over 4 percent and growing, share buybacks, and steady performance, the company seems to make shareholder interests a priority.

The company has stellar brands, and should do well expanding them into overseas markets, a relatively untapped frontier compared to some of its peers. Also, compared to some peers, especially Procter & Gamble, the company is less inclined to go for "glamour" markets such as cosmetics, choosing instead to add to margins through operating efficiencies and scale. Safety-oriented investors may find this approach preferable. In addition, Value Line gives the company an "A++" for financial strength and a top rating for safety, the latter of which it has maintained since 1990.

Reasons for Caution

While the paper products business is steady, it isn't easy to see where growth would come from. The company, rightly so, is targeting international expansion, but competition and currency fluctuation make the results far from certain. The cost of pulp and paper raw materials can also be highly volatile. Investors should focus on income and safety with this issue; any growth would be a plus.

SECTOR: **Consumer Staples**
BETA COEFFICIENT: **0.42**
10-YEAR COMPOUND EARNINGS PER SHARE GROWTH: **4.0%**
10-YEAR COMPOUND DIVIDENDS PER SHARE GROWTH: **9.0%**

	2003	2004	2005	2006	2007	2008	2009	2010
Revenues (Mil)	14,348	15,083	15,903	16,747	18,266	19,415	19,115	19,746
Net Income (Mil)	1,716.7	1,800.2	1,803.7	1,844.5	1,861.6	1,698.0	1,884.0	1,843
Earnings per share	3.38	3.61	3.78	3.90	4.25	4.14	4.52	4.45
Dividends per share	1.36	1.60	1.80	1.96	2.08	2.27	2.38	2.58
Cash flow per share	4.91	5.39	5.74	6.10	6.34	5.98	6.40	6.53
Price: high	59.3	69.0	68.3	68.6	72.8	69.7	67.0	67.2
low	42.9	56.2	55.6	56.6	63.8	50.3	43.1	58.3

Kimberly-Clark
P.O. Box 619100
Dallas, TX 75261
(972) 281-1200
Website: *www.kimberly-clark.com*

Lubrizol Corporation

Ticker symbol: LZ (NYSE) ❑ S&P rating: BBB+ ❑ Value Line financial strength rating: A ❑ Current yield: 1.3%

Company Profile

Lubrizol has been "taken out" by Berkshire Hathaway in a $9.7 billion deal ($135 per share) announced March 14, 2011, meaning that you are no longer able to invest directly in this company. However, we retain the issue on our *100 Best* list for now, first, because the transaction isn't complete and second, and more importantly, to present a good model for what Warren Buffett seeks in companies he acquires.

Lubrizol produces and supplies specialty chemicals and other materials that improve the quality and performance of its customers' products in the global transportation, industrial, and consumer markets. Typical applications include fluid additives for engine oils, gasoline, and diesel fuel; machine lubricants; and additives, coatings, thickeners, and other performance, consistency, and protective additives for pharmaceuticals and specialty materials. A maker of everything from hydraulic fluid to polymer thickeners for skin cream, the company could be easily described as a "high tech"

chemical company, as exemplified by the recent press release "Permax 805 Vinylidene Chloride Emulsion Provides APE-Free, Corrosion Resistant Solutions for Metal Substrates." Pretty sexy stuff—if you're in the right industrial/commercial audience.

The company is geographically diverse, with global manufacturing, supply chain, technical, and commercial infrastructure targeted to serve a technically advanced audience. They operate production and/ or laboratory facilities in twenty-seven countries, in key regions around the world. Lubrizol sells its products in more than 100 countries.

The company reports results from two segments—Lubrizol Additive and Lubrizol Advanced Materials.

The company's key strategic focus to achieve top line and earnings growth includes driving organic growth and product innovation, new products, and new applications. The company will also focus on selective acquisitions in either specialty chemicals or industrial fluids, complementing Lubrizol's existing business lines.

Financial Highlights, Fiscal Year 2010

For years, the company was an ordinary and rather unsexy chemical concern until the mid-2000s; then a number of factors led to an impressive and accelerating top and bottom line growth that continues to this day. Ten-year compounded earnings growth is 5.5 percent, but for the past five years, it has been 12 percent, and Value Line estimates a 16.5 percent earnings growth range from 2008 through 2015. Lubrizol has established itself as a high-margin niche player supplying key ingredients to an assortment of industries, including transportation, manufacturing, consumer products, personal care, health care, and a number of others. Niche dominance is evidenced by operating margins, which have risen from the 13–15 percent range in the mid-decade to an estimated 23.5 percent in 2010. The company has been able to raise prices and plans to do so in the near future.

The company raised its own guidance nearly every quarter in 2010, and finished the year with EPS of $9.91, some 31 percent ahead of 2009. That compares to earnings of $4.06 for 2007 and $2.50 for 2005. It's been quite a run, especially when you consider the recessionary interlude along the way.

Reasons to Buy

Regardless of the effects of the Berkshire acquisition, Lubrizol has figured out how to unlock value in a relatively mundane industry, and future prospects are bright. The company has a lot of earning and cash generation power, and has begun to deploy that, not only for strategic acquisitions but also to buy back shares, of which there are only 65 million in the first place. The company recently authorized repurchase of up to 10 percent of its shares.

Reasons for Caution

Additives are a moderate-growth segment, but are very profitable at the moment. This could change if oil prices spike up, but as long as material costs remain reasonable and Lubrizol is effectively hedged, the company's cost structure looks solid. In part due to earnings momentum, the shares have behaved recently like a momentum stock, with lots of new money piling in, and relatively small supply. This can change quickly with bad news, so LZ might be better suited for more aggressive investors or investors who have the time to pay close attention.

SECTOR: Materials
BETA COEFFICIENT: 1.45
10-YEAR COMPOUND EARNINGS PER SHARE GROWTH: 5.5%
10-YEAR COMPOUND DIVIDENDS PER SHARE GROWTH: 1.5%

	2003	2004	2005	2006	2007	2008	2009	2010
Revenues (Mil)	2,049	3,156	3,622	4,041	4,499	5,027	4,586	5,418
Net Income (Mil)	91	139	189	106	283	281	521	682
Earnings per share	2.04	2.48	2.36	2.62	4.05	4.09	7.55	9.91
Dividends per share	1.04	1.04	1.04	1.04	1.16	1.23	1.24	1.36
Cash flow per share	3.71	4.36	5.17	5.45	6.52	6.75	10.09	13.29
Price: high	34.4	37.4	44.5	50.8	69.9	61.4	97.8	116.3
low	26.5	29.4	35.2	38	48.8	23.6	68.9	68.9

Lubrizol Corporation
29400 Lakeland Boulevard
Wickliffe, OH 44092–2298
(440) 347-1206
Website: *www.lubrizol.com*

AGGRESSIVE GROWTH

Marathon Oil Corporation

Ticker symbol: MRO (NYSE) □ S&P rating: A+ □ Value Line financial strength rating: A+ □ Current yield: 1.9%

Company Profile

Marathon Oil is a vertically integrated producer, refiner, and marketer of petroleum and natural gas products. It sells crude to other refiners, but its primary revenue stream is through the sale of its refined petroleum products to resellers and to end consumers via company-owned retail locations.

Marathon had long operated in four segments: Exploration and Production; Oil Sands Mining; Refining, Marketing, and Transportation; and Integrated Gas. E&P is a worldwide producer and marketer of liquid hydrocarbons and natural gas. OSM mines, extracts, and transports bitumen from deposits in Alberta, Canada, and upgrades it to produce synthetic crude. RM&T refines, markets, and transports petroleum products throughout the Midwest and southeastern regions of the United States. Finally, IG transports liquefied natural gas and methanol worldwide.

In 2011, the company announced its intentions to spin off the RM&T refining and distribution business into a separate entity, Marathon Petroleum Corporation. MPC would operate Marathon branded outlets as well as the Speedway chain of 1,300 service stations and convenience stores. The separated unit will also run the pipeline operations. The idea is to improve focus and "right size" the resulting companies; as of mid-2011 the plan hadn't been fully put into place. We continue to identify the current MRO as a *100 Best* stock, and would continue to recommend the two derivative companies in the proposed proportions of 1 share of the current MRO E&P business plus 0.5 share MPC per share of MRO owned. Naturally, next year we will revisit the eligibility of both spinoffs for the *100 Best* list.

The company has exploration rights/interests in the United States, Angola, Norway, Indonesia, Equatorial Guinea, Libya, Canada, and the United Kingdom. The bulk of their U.S. activities are in the Gulf Coast region. Overall, at the end of 2010, their reserves were distributed as follows: 40 percent in Africa, 35 percent in Canada, 18 percent in the United States, and 7 percent in Europe.

Marathon, via acquisition, holds a 20 percent outside-operated interest in the Athabasca Oil Sands

Project in Alberta, Canada. Oil sands mining bears no resemblance to any of Marathon's other oil production processes. Oil sands operations more closely resemble a coal surface mine. Output from these operations is on the order of 30,000 barrels of synthetic crude per day, with significantly higher than normal refining costs.

Financial Highlights, Fiscal Year 2010

FY2010 was a comeback year for the company. Depressed refining margins hurt the company through 2009, but stronger fuel demand and stable crude prices brought higher margins and volume from this business. Earnings doubled from the low in 2009 of $1.67 per share. FY2011 will no doubt be strengthened by the boom in oil prices, with projected earnings in the $4.50 per share range.

Reasons to Buy

MRO's exploration is oriented toward oil, as opposed to natural gas, and that's a good thing in today's oil and gas price environment. Refining margins (known as "crack margins") have improved dramatically from a few years ago. The two subsidiaries will emerge strong and independent, as the current refining business only gets 5 percent of its input from MRO's current exploration business. The company continues to be successful with its recent exploratory wells, finding developable assets in 96 percent of its holes in 2009 and over 86 percent in the past three years.

Reasons for Caution

The split could be a distraction and could incur some costs, but it will most likely be a "blip" in the course of business. Oil prices could decline as demand/supply balance is once again achieved in the futures markets as well as actual shipments. And refining margins can be a big question mark. The share price has advanced to the point where the current dividend yield lags some other similar companies, like Total S.A. and ConocoPhillips (both *100 Best Stocks*) come to mind.

SECTOR: Energy
BETA COEFFICIENT: 1.18
10-YEAR COMPOUND EARNINGS PER SHARE GROWTH: 12.0%
10-YEAR COMPOUND DIVIDENDS PER SHARE GROWTH: 8.5%

	2003	2004	2005	2006	2007	2008	2009	2010
Revenues (Mil)	36,678	45,135	58,596	59,917	59,389	72,128	48,456	67,113
Net Income (Mil)	1,012	1,314	3,051	4,636	3,755	3,528	1,184	2,568
Earnings per share	1.63	1.94	4.22	6.42	5.43	4.95	1.67	3.61
Dividends per share	0.48	0.52	0.61	0.77	0.92	0.96	0.96	0.99
Cash flow per share	3.52	3.65	6.01	8.85	7.56	8.08	5.38	8.80
Price: high	16.8	21.3	36.3	49.4	67	63.2	33.1	37.2
low	9.9	15	17.8	30.2	41.5	19.3	20.2	27.6

Marathon Oil Corporation
5555 San Felipe Road
Houston, TX 77056
(713) 629-6600
Website: *www.marathon.com*

CONSERVATIVE GROWTH

McCormick & Company, Inc.

Ticker symbol: MKC (NYSE) ❑ S&P rating: A- ❑ Value Line financial strength rating: A ❑ Current yield: 2.5%

Company Profile

McCormick manufactures, markets, and distributes spices, herbs, seasonings, and flavors to the global food industry. They are the largest such supplier in the world. Customers range from retail outlets and food manufacturers to foodservice businesses.

Industrial customers include foodservice, food-processing businesses, and retail outlets. The Industrial segment was responsible for 42 percent of sales and 19 percent of operating profits. A majority of the top 100 food companies are MKC's customers.

McCormick's U.S. Consumer business (58 percent of sales and 81 percent of operating profits), its oldest and largest, manufactures consumer spices, herbs, extracts, proprietary seasoning blends, sauces, and marinades. Spices are sold under an assortment of recognizable brand names: McCormick, Lawry's, Zatarain's, Thai Kitchen, Simply Asia, Clubhouse, Billy Bee, Produce Partners, Golden Dipt, Old Bay, and Mojave.

Many of the spices and herbs purchased by the company, such as black pepper, vanilla beans, cinnamon, herbs, and seeds must be imported from countries such as India, Indonesia, Malaysia, Brazil, and the Malagasy Republic. Other ingredients such as paprika, dehydrated vegetables, onion, and garlic, and food ingredients other than spices and herbs originate in the United States.

The company was founded in 1889 and has approximately 7,500 full-time employees in facilities located around the world. Major sales, distribution, and production facilities are located in North America and Europe. Additional facilities are based in Mexico, Central America, Australia, China, Singapore, Thailand, and South Africa. International sales account for about 42 percent of the total. The company has recently deployed more informative print and web content with recipes and other information to spur cooking with spices. We also like a new packaging initiative to sell prepackaged spices set to cook a particular meal called "Recipe Inspirations"; this launch has been initially successful.

Financial Highlights, Fiscal Year 2010

The spice and ingredient business is a fairly slow, steady business at most times, but, aided by a growing number of people eating at home to control expenses in response to the recession, McCormick had a good FY2010, and the stock price performed accordingly. Earnings during the year rose 15.1 percent from the comparable FY2009 period.

Through innovations and other measures (no pun intended), the company has also improved profitability, with operating margins, long stuck in the 15–16 percent range, rising to 18 percent in 2009 and projected in the low 20s going forward.

FY2011 is projected to keep the same trends afloat, with the top line projected to grow between 5 and 7 percent in local currency, and a bottom line earnings projection of $2.80–$2.85, again putting growth in the 16 percent range.

Reasons to Buy

McCormick's is about as "pure" a play as there is in this book. They make seasonings (spices/herbs/flavorings), a few specialty foods, and nothing else. They're the largest branded producer of seasonings in North America, and they're the largest private-label producer of seasonings in North America, giving them

a substantial level of price protection. McCormick is not just a producer/supplier, however—they also create new seasoning products. In fact, every year since 2005, between 13 percent and 18 percent of their industrial business sales have come from new products launched in the preceding three years. Keeping up with changing tastes requires McCormick to produce that new, hot flavor and to come up with new and interesting flavors and blends of existing seasonings.

On the consumer side, as amateur cooks ourselves, we have long felt that people would use more spices if they only knew how to use them. The new information outlets, and the prepackaged Recipe Inspirations meal kits will serve well to get the less experienced cooks "across the chasm" of using spices effectively in their own cooking. In our view, these initiatives, combined with continuing growth in the health-conscious segment by learning to replace fat flavoring with spice flavoring, will add to a solid business base for the company.

McCormick's sales have increased every year for the past fifty years, and the company has paid a dividend every year since 1925. In 2010, they raised the dividend for the twenty-fifth consecutive year. As further evidence of improved profitability, the company has achieved double-digit compounded ten-year earnings, cash flow, and dividend growth despite growing sales only 6.5 percent for the period. This profitability surge and the stability and defensive nature of the company and its business present an attractive combination for investors.

Reasons for Caution

Real reasons for caution are few and far between. Top line growth is likely to remain moderate except by acquisition. Additionally, without significant innovations the current surge in profitability is likely to plateau at some point.

SECTOR: **Consumer Staples**
BETA COEFFICIENT: **.42**
10-YEAR COMPOUND EARNINGS PER SHARE GROWTH: **11.0%**
10-YEAR COMPOUND DIVIDENDS PER SHARE GROWTH: **10.5%**

	2003	2004	2005	2006	2007	2008	2009	2010
Revenues (Mil)	2,270	2,526	2,592	2,716	2,916	3,177	3,192	3,339
Net Income (Mil)	199	214	215	202	230	282	311	356.3
Earnings per share	1.4	1.52	1.56	1.72	1.92	2.14	2.35	2.65
Dividends per share	0.46	0.56	0.64	0.72	0.8	0.88	0.96	1.04
Cash flow per share	1.93	2.1	2.24	2.45	2.64	2.83	3.08	3.39
Price: high	30.2	38.9	39.1	39.8	39.7	42.1	36.8	47.8
low	21.7	28.6	29	30.1	33.9	28.2	28.1	35.4

McCormick & Company, Inc.
18 Loveton Circle
P. O. Box 6000
Sparks, MD 21152–6000
(410) 771-7244
Website: *www.mccormick.com*

AGGRESSIVE GROWTH

McDonald's Corporation

Ticker symbol: MCD (NYSE) ❑ S&P rating: A ❑ Value Line financial strength rating: A++ ❑ Current yield: 3.3%

Company Profile

McDonald's Corporation operates and franchises the ubiquitous "golden arches" McDonald's restaurants. At 2010 year-end, there were approximately 32,737 restaurants in 118 countries, over 26,000 of which were operated by franchisees and 6,200 were operated by the company. Franchisees pay for and own the equipment, signs, and interior of the businesses, and are required to reinvest in same from time to time. The company owns the land and building or secures leases for both company-operated and franchised restaurant sites.

Revenues to the company come in the form of sales from company-owned stores and rents, fees, royalties, and other revenue streams from the franchisees. The company is primarily a franchisor and has recently begun to sell off more of its company-owned stores, in the process realizing benefits to cash flow, reduced operational costs, and reduced exposure to commodities prices.

McDonald's completely dominates the fast food hamburger restaurant market segment with a 35 percent market share. Burger King and Wendy's are the next largest competitors at 4 percent market share each. In the overall fast food segment, McDonald's is still the single biggest player with a 19 percent market share by revenue, followed by Doctor's Associates, Inc. (Subway) with a 10 percent share.

The company generates about 65 percent of its revenue outside the United States.

Financial Highlights, Fiscal Year 2010

It's hard for us to summarize MCD's 2010 any better than they did, so here is an excerpt of their earnings press release in early 2011:

Global comparable sales increase of 5.0 percent, with positive comparable sales across all geographic segments for every quarter.

- Consolidated revenues up 6 percent (5 percent in constant currencies) to a record-high $24 billion
- Combined operating margin increase of 90 basis points to 31.0 percent
- Consolidated operating income increase of 9 percent (9 percent

in constant currencies) with the U.S. up 7 percent, Europe up 8 percent (12 percent in constant currencies) and APMEA up 21 percent (11 percent in constant currencies)

- Earnings per share of $4.58, up 11 percent (11 percent in constant currencies)
- Return of $5.1 billion to shareholders through share repurchases and dividends paid

The reasons for their success include new menu offerings and a continuing drive to move more stores to a franchising model. The latter in particular is responsible for the operating margin increases. Rents and royalty incomes are a low cost and very stable revenue stream with low capital requirements, and we expect this refranchising trend to continue even as McDonald's opens new locations. The company has also benefited from "reimaging" its stores, particularly in Europe, and plans to add 1,100 stores and reimage a comparable number in 2011.

The expansion in financial performance slowed somewhat toward the end of FY2010, with sales only 4 percent and earnings only 5 percent ahead of the year ago period. The company did say it was off to a good start in FY2011 with a same-store sales growth projection of 4–5 percent, which should lead to a larger figure for overall top line growth.

The company also raised its dividend 11 percent during FY2010.

Reasons to Buy

In the early part of the decade, McDonald's had been adding mainly company-owned stores in an effort to boost revenues, they aren't as profitable, and there were signs that people were becoming tired of the menu and more concerned about health. In 2003, McDonald's initiated a new strategy that called for increasing sales at its existing stores by expanding menu options, expanding store hours, and renovating stores. They also began franchising a higher percentage of its stores, driving revenue with reduced capital expense. The strategy has paid off handsomely—revenues have grown by 40 percent, which would be impressive on its own, but operating margins have grown from the mid-20s to the mid-30s, with most of that increase coming in the 2008–2010 timeframe, and not surprisingly, net income has increased more than two and a half times in that same period. At the same time, share buybacks have reduced share counts from 1.26 billion down to about 1.05 billion. These factors have produced substantial shareholder returns, much of which is actually getting returned to shareholders, as the dividend has climbed from 40 cents per share to $2.44 per share in the eight-year period—nearly 150 percent over the same period. As a result, the share price is six times its 2003 low.

McDonald's has an exceptionally strong international franchise, and is growing particularly well in China. Local menus continue to evolve, and the convenience that fast food provides is highly valued.

McDonald's' menu additions are proving very popular, and consumers are welcoming the novelty of the newer menu items like McCafe, brewed teas, smoothies, McRib sandwiches, the Angus burger line, and expanded salad selections.

Reasons for Caution

Concerns over childhood obesity have drawn attention to dietary factors, and fast food restaurants will likely be central to most conversations on the topic. Some states are requiring the posting of signs with caloric content next to item price, but it's not clear that this will lead to a decline in sales in the near term. The stock has also enjoyed a long-run higher compatible with the steady earnings growth; similar growth in the near future may be harder to attain.

SECTOR: Restaurants
BETA COEFFICIENT: 0.49
10-YEAR COMPOUND EARNINGS PER SHARE GROWTH: 11.0%
10-YEAR COMPOUND DIVIDENDS PER SHARE GROWTH: 25.5%

		2003	2004	2005	2006	2007	2008	2009	2010
Revenues (Mil)		17,141	19,065	20,460	21,586	22,787	23,522	22,745	24,075
Net Income (Mil)		1,831	2,358	2,509	2,873	3,522	4,201	4,451	4,970
Earnings per share		1.43	1.93	1.97	2.3	2.91	3.67	4.11	4.60
Dividends per share		0.4	0.55	0.67	1.00	1.50	1.63	2.05	2.26
Cash flow per share		2.36	2.88	2.98	3.43	4.06	4.85	5.2	5.95
Price:	high	27	33	35.7	44.7	63.7	67	64.8	80.9
	low	12.1	24.5	27.4	31.7	42.3	45.8	50.4	61.1

McDonald's Corporation
One McDonald's Plaza
Oak Brook, IL 60523
(630) 623-3000
Website: *www.mcdonalds.com*

McKesson Corporation

Ticker symbol: MCK (NYSE) ❑ S&P rating: A– ❑ Value Line financial strength rating: A+ ❑ Current yield: 0.9%

Company Profile

McKesson Corporation is America's oldest and largest health care services company, and engages in two distinct businesses to support the health care industry. Pharmaceutical and medical supply distribution is the first and by far the largest business: The company is the largest such distributor in North America. The company delivers to approximately 40,000 pharmaceutical outlets as well as hospitals and clinics throughout North America.

Second and not to be ignored is a technology solutions business that provides clinical systems, analytics, supply chain management, and connectivity solutions to hospitals, pharmacies, and an assortment of health care providers. While the distribution business, at $105 billion for FY2010, provides 97 percent of the company's revenue, the information technology business is no less important and is a $3 billion business all by itself. McKesson's software and hardware IT solutions are installed in some 70 percent of the nation's hospitals with more than 200 beds.

The company offers products and services covering most aspects of pharmacy and drug distribution, including not only physical distribution and supply chain services but also a line of proprietary generics and automated dispensing systems, record keeping systems, and outsourcing services used in retail and hospital pharmacy operations.

In late 2010, the company completed a $2.16 billion acquisition of U.S. Oncology, a distributor of products targeted to the cancer care industry. With that acquisition, McKesson becomes the leading supplier of materials, technology, and operational platforms to the oncological community.

Financial Highlights, Fiscal Year 2010

The McKesson business is about as close to recession-proof as one can become. Sales flattened only slightly in FY2010 (ending March 2010) to $108.7 billion, while earnings continued a nice upward run at $4.58 per share, up 12.5 percent from the previous year and up from $2.18 per share in 2004.

During this period, the company benefited somewhat from the H1N1 flu scare and vaccine distribution volume, so FY2011 revenue comparisons are relatively flat. With operational improvements and the integration of the U.S. Oncology business, the company expects to earn between $4.90 for FY2011. In 2010, the company raised its dividend 50 percent to $0.72 per share, and authorized a $1 billion stock buyback—both easily afforded in light of the company's strong cash flows.

Reasons to Buy

The distribution business has proven to be rock solid and will likely continue that way. Demographics and the addition of millions to the "insured" health-care rolls will keep demand moving in the right direction. McKesson dominates its niche. Additionally, hospitals and other care providers are starting to get the memo that it is time to improve operational efficiency, and McKesson's technology solutions are hard to ignore, although many might do so at first glance as they are only 3 percent of the business. As most distributors do, McKesson operates on very thin margins; the expansion of technology services and generic equivalent drugs should help. The company has reduced its share count about 16 percent since 2005 and will continue to buy back shares.

Reasons for Caution

Some, and perhaps much, of the optimism previously mentioned has already been priced into the stock; the company will have to continue to seek growth opportunities to keep the earnings momentum going. That could result in more acquisitions, and while the U.S. Oncology buyout has been favorably received by investors, that is no guarantee that all such moves will be. Additionally, and as mentioned, the company does operate on thin margins and as such has a low tolerance to mistakes or major changes in the health care space that could be brought on by legislation or regulation.

SECTOR: **Health Care**
BETA COEFFICIENT: **.74**
10-YEAR COMPOUND EARNINGS PER SHARE GROWTH: **12.0%**
10-YEAR COMPOUND DIVIDENDS PER SHARE GROWTH: **11.6%**

	2003	**2004**	**2005**	**2006**	**2007**	**2008**	**2009**	**2010**
Revenues (Mil)	42,288	69,506	80,515	88,050	92,977	101,703	106,632	108,702
Net Income (Mil)	572	646	653	737	881	1,021	1,194	1,251
Earnings per share	1.96	2.19	2.18	2.34	2.89	3.43	4.28	4.58
Dividends per share	0.24	0.24	0.24	0.24	0.24	0.48	0.48	0.72
Cash flow per share	2.63	2.99	3.02	3.30	3.99	5.03	6.03	6.37
Price: high	37.1	35.9	52.9	55.1	68.4	68.4	65.0	71.5
low	22.6	22.6	30.1	44.5	50.5	28.3	33.1	57.2

McKesson Corporation
One Post Street
San Francisco, CA 94104
(415) 983-8300
Website: *www.mckesson.com*

AGGRESSIVE GROWTH

Medtronic, Inc.

Ticker symbol: MDT (NYSE) ❑ S&P rating: AA- ❑ Value Line financial strength rating: A++ ❑ Current yield: 2.3%

Company Profile

Medtronic is the world's largest manufacturer of implantable medical devices and is a leading medical technology company, providing lifelong solutions to "alleviate pain, restore health and extend life," primarily for people with chronic diseases. The seven business segments are (with contribution to FY2010 revenues in parenthesis):

- Cardiac Rhythm Disease Management (33 percent) develops products that restore and regulate a patient's heart rhythm, as well as improve the heart's pumping function. This segment markets implantable pacemakers, defibrillators, monitoring and diagnostic devices, and cardiac resynchronization devices, including the first implantable device for the treatment of heart failure.
- Medtronic Cardiovascular (18 percent) develops products and therapies that treat a wide range of vascular diseases and conditions. These products include coronary, peripheral, and neuro-vascular stents, stent graft systems for diseases

and conditions throughout the aorta, and distal protection systems. The segment also develops products that are used in both arrested and beating heart bypass surgery, and markets the industry's broadest line of heart valve products for replacement and repair, plus autotransfusion equipment and disposable devices for handling and monitoring blood during major surgery.

- Medtronic Spinal and Biologics (22 percent) develops and manufactures products that treat a variety of disorders of the cranium and spine, including traumatically induced conditions, deformities, herniated discs and other disc diseases, and tumors. The Biologics business is the global leader in biologics regeneration and pain therapies across a variety of musculoskeletal applications including spine, orthopedic trauma, and dental.
- Medtronic Neurolmodulation (10 percent) employs many technologies used in heart electrical stimulation to treat diseases of the central nervous

system. It offers therapies for movement disorders, chronic pain, urological and gastroenterological disorders, and psychological diseases, including incontinence, benign prostatic hyperplasia (BPH), enlarged prostate, and gastroesophageal reflux disease (GERD).

- Medtronic Diabetes (8 percent) offers advanced diabetes management solutions, including insulin pump therapy, glucose monitoring systems, and treatment management software.
- Medtronic Surgical Technologies (6 percent) develops and markets products and therapies for ear, nose, and throat–related diseases and certain neurological disorders; among them are precision image-guided surgical systems.

Financial Highlights, Fiscal Year 2010 (FY2010 ended April 30, 2011)

Medtronic's revenues grew 8 percent year/year to $14.6 billion, while non-GAAP (our standard for this company) earnings rose 9 percent to $3.58 billion. Per share earnings grew 10 percent.

Fourth-quarter revenues broke $4 billion, a first for Medtronic. The final number, $4.2 billion, represents a 10 percent increase over 4Q2009 revenues. Earnings for the

quarter were $986 million, up 8 percent over the prior year.

International revenue grew 15 percent for the year, representing 41 percent of the company's total revenue. International's fourth quarter revenue grew 20 percent over 4Q2009.

Dividends were increased 34 percent to $.85/share, and the company bought back 25 million shares of stock, or approximately 2.3 percent of the outstanding shares.

Reasons to Buy

Medtronic has a dominant market share in three of its six core lines (ICD, Diabetes, and Neurological). Although the company saw some near-term slowdowns in its businesses due to the economy and delayed treatments for certain medical conditions, the company is well-positioned to take advantage of the aging demographic and increased use of technology to provide long-term care solutions.

The company is a pioneer, technology leader, and a successful innovator in many surgical and implant technologies, including the restoration of normal brain function and chemistry to millions of patients with central nervous system disorders. The company's DBS (Deep Brain Stimulation) systems treat disorders by modulating the nervous system with electrical stimulation, chemicals, and biological agents delivered in precise amounts to specific sites in the brain and spinal cord. This system has been used successfully to treat the most severe symptoms of conditions such as Parkinson's disease, and in March of 2010, Medtronic received FDA approval for techniques employing DBS devices for treatment of epilepsy.

Medtronic has enjoyed steady growth and has achieved the quintuple-play—double-digit compounded ten-year growth in revenues, earnings, cash flow, dividends, and book value. The dividend, relatively generous for a "tech" company of this sort, has almost tripled in six years. The stock price has been relatively flat during this period, offering reasonable entry points.

Reasons for Caution

Medtronic may be entering the "mature" life-cycle phase in many of its product lines, meaning future growth opportunities may be harder to come by. The company has also relied on small acquisitions for a lot of its growth, a somewhat riskier strategy than growing "organically."

SECTOR: **Health Care**
BETA COEFFICIENT: **.89**
10-YEAR COMPOUND EARNINGS PER SHARE GROWTH: **14.0%**
10-YEAR COMPOUND DIVIDENDS PER SHARE GROWTH: **117%**

	2003	2004	2005	2006	2007	2008	2009	2010
Revenues (Mil)	7,665	9,087	10,055	11,292	12,299	13,515	14,599	15,817
Net Income (Mil)	1,600	1,959	2,270	2,687	2,798	2,984	3,282	3,577
Earnings per share	1.3	1.63	1.86	2.21	2.41	2.61	2.92	3.22
Dividends per share	0.25	0.28	0.31	0.36	0.41	0.47	0.63	0.85
Cash flow per share	1.75	2.02	2.26	2.8	2.96	3.22	3.45	3.85
Price: high	49.7	52.9	53.7	58.9	59.9	58	57	44.9
low	32.5	42.2	44	48.7	42.4	44.9	28.3	24.1

Medtronic, Inc
710 Medtronic Parkway N. E.
Minneapolis, MN 55432–5604
(763) 505-2692
Website: *www.medtronic.com*

AGGRESSIVE GROWTH

Monsanto Company

Ticker symbol: MON (NYSE) ❑ S&P Rating: A+ ❑ Value Line financial strength rating: A ❑ Current yield: 1.5%

Company Profile

Monsanto was once a major chemical company with a broad pedigree ranging from saccharine to sulfuric acid to Agent Orange and DDT. Monsanto was absorbed into Pharmacia Upjohn in 2000, which kept its pharmaceutical products and spun off the agricultural products business into a "new" Monsanto in 2002. Today's Monsanto provides a set of leading-edge, technology-based agricultural products for use in farming in the United States and overseas. The company broadly views its business as providing better quality foods and animal feedstocks while reducing the costs of farming.

The company has two primary business segments: Seeds and Genomics, and Agricultural Productivity.

The Seeds and Genomics segment produces seeds for a host of crops, most importantly corn and soybeans, but also canola, cotton, and a variety of vegetable and fruit seeds. Most of the seed products are bioengineered to provide greater yields and to be more resistant to insects and weeds. Familiar to many consumers, especially those who travel in the Midwest, is the DeKalb seed brand, but there are many others.

The Agricultural Productivity segment offers glyphosate-based herbicides, known as Roundup to most of us, for agricultural, industrial, and residential lawn and garden applications. Beyond this market-leading product, the division also offers other selective herbicides for control of pre-emergent annual grass and small seeded broadleaf weeds in corn and other crops. The company owns many of the major brands in both seed and herbicide markets.

The company also partners with other agricultural and chemical companies like Cargill, BASF, and Biotechnology, Inc., to develop other high-tech agricultural and food-processing solutions.

Financial Highlights, Calendar Year 2010 (Fiscal Year ended August 31)

Monsanto had an especially weak and discomforting 2010. Weakening demand in many agricultural markets, which started in 2009, continued into the year. Worse, expiring patents on the glyphosate products, news of immunity to the chemical developing in certain weeds, and new competition, especially in cheaper foreign substitutes, turned into a top-line rout—a decline of 10 percent in sales for the year. Earnings softened to $2.41 per share from $4.41 from the previous year with deficits in two of the four quarters (as a seasonal company, this isn't as alarming as it sounds), as gross margins collapsed from about 34 percent to the 24 percent range. Guidance calls for a gradual earnings recovery to $2.75–$2.80 per share for FY2011, with revenues recovering about half of what was lost in 2010.

Reasons to Buy

The expiration of the Roundup "monopoly" combined with news of its attenuated effectiveness was a double whammy, especially for a company whose profits were so dependent on the product and its combination sales with glyphosate-resistant seed stocks. The company was forced to lower product prices to keep market share. This is the bad news; the bigger picture shows Monsanto still as a market leader in technology-based agricultural products with a strong track record for innovation and a big head start on most competitors. The company is stressing its biotechnology-rich Seeds and Genomics products while the Agricultural Productivity unit brings new formulations to market and reduces costs on the glyphosate products to bring them in line with the newer, lower prices. The stock dropped from the 80s to the mid-40s during the FY2010 consolidation period, but recovered quickly. We still feel this is a premier technology company aimed at a sector of primary global importance—that is, agriculture—and is a good place for invested capital, especially long term.

Reasons for Caution

Clearly, Monsanto didn't anticipate the negative effects of the adverse news on the glyphosate products. The strong lock they had on their markets seemed to disappear overnight, and they were caught with their proverbial overalls down. Lesson learned, we hope. Monsanto's future success will continue to depend on agricultural innovation—but also on being the best player in competitive markets with a diverse product portfolio. Astute investors must hold them to that standard and walk away if they become too dependent on one product or system once again.

SECTOR: **Industrials**
BETA COEFFICIENT: **0.85**
10-YEAR COMPOUND EARNINGS PER SHARE GROWTH: **37.0%**
10-YEAR COMPOUND DIVIDENDS PER SHARE GROWTH: **26.0%**

	2003	2004	2005	2006	2007	2008	2009	2010
Revenues (Mil)	4,936	5,457	6,294	7,344	8,563	11,365	11,724	10,502
Net Income (Mil)	334	434	565.7	722.1	1,027	1,895	2,448	1,327
Earnings per share	0.64	0.61	1.05	1.31	1.98	3.39	4.41	2.41
Dividends per share	0.24	0.28	0.34	0.34	0.55	0.83	1.01	1.08
Cash flow per share	1.5	1.73	2.06	2.28	2.85	4.5	5.49	3.57
Price: high	14.5	28.2	39.9	53.5	116.3	145.8	93.4	87.1
low	6.8	14	25	37.9	49.1	63.5	66.6	44.6

Monsanto Company
800 North Lindbergh Boulevard
St. Louis, MO 63167
Phone: 314-694-1000
Web Site: *www.monsanto.com*

GROWTH AND INCOME

NextEra Energy, Inc

Ticker symbol: NEE (NYSE) ❑ S&P rating: A- ❑ Value Line financial strength rating: A ❑ Current yield: 3.7%

Company Profile

FPL Group, formerly Florida Power & Light, changed its name to Next-Era Energy, Inc. in May of 2010. Such a name change is hardly a first in the corporate world, but it does reflect how the company operates and how it sees itself: as one of the cleanest existing energy providers with an eye (and a subsidiary) dedicated to the future of large scale alternative energy.

NextEra is a leading energy holding company with 2010 revenues of more than $15 billion, approximately 43,000 megawatts of generating capacity, and more than 15,000 employees in twenty-eight states and Canada. Headquartered in Juno Beach, Florida, FPL Group's principal operating subsidiaries are NextEra Energy Resources, LLC, and Florida Power & Light Company, one of the largest rate-regulated electric utilities in the country. FP&L serves 4.5 million customer accounts in Florida. Through its subsidiaries, FPL Group collectively operates the third largest U.S. nuclear power generation fleet.

NextEra Energy Resources, LLC (formerly FPL Energy, LLC),

FPL Group's competitive energy subsidiary, is a leader in producing electricity from clean and renewable fuels, and, unlike many other alternative-energy driven businesses, is a viable standalone business entity. It has 115 facilities in twenty-six states and 4,700 employees, and operates solar and wind farms, nuclear energy facilities, and has gas infrastructure operations. With 2010 revenues just over $4.6 billion, the subsidiary accounts for nearly a third of NextEra's total revenue—and nearly half of its profits. The subsidiary has 8,298 megawatts of wind generation capacity alone, representing about 20 percent of the company's total generation capacity. The generating assets of NextEra represent over 18,000 megawatts of capacity. FPL Fiber-Net, LLC, provides fiber-optic services to FPL and other customers, primarily telecommunications companies in Florida.

FP&L is recognized as one of the "cleaner" producers in the United States, with just over half of its generation coming from natural gas, about 21 percent from nuclear sources, and less than 15 percent coming from coal and oil. By contrast, coal makes up 50 percent of the fuel mix for electricity generation nationwide. Additionally, NextEra Energy is the largest owner and operator of the wind and solar generating facilities in the United States.

Financial Highlights, Fiscal Year 2010

Revenues in FY2010 declined slightly to $15.3 billion while earnings per share rose about 19 percent from $3.97 to $4.74. The decline in revenue is due primarily to the decrease in usage by residential customers. Going back to FY2000, FPL's average annual customer growth has been 1.8 percent, but starting in 2007, that growth has essentially stopped, likely due to the credit/housing crisis that affected many fast-growth real estate markets such as south Florida. For 2011, the company is absorbing the costs of bringing some new capacity online and a one-time mark-to-market benefit in 2010, and now expects earnings in the $4.25–$4.55 per share range for the year. The company also stated that it expects earnings to grow in the 5–7 percent range from 2009 through 2014.

Reasons to Buy

For those who believe that alternative energy is the future for large-scale power generation, NextEra is the best play available. The Recovery Act of 2009 contains a number of tax incentives for the deployment and use of renewable and nuclear sources, and NextEra is well positioned to take advantage. Its total current investment in wind resources is over $12.5 billion, and it added 1,238 megawatts of wind generation in 2010 with plans to add 1,000–1,500 megawatts in each of 2011 and 2012. Solar energy projects, including a large one in Spain, are also coming on line, with a recent California Public Utilities Commission agreement to buy 250 megawatts from a project known as "Genesis" being one recent win.

NextEra is the largest provider in a growing alternative energy market, and has been one of the best-performing stocks in the utility market over the past several years.

Reasons for Caution

The company's FP&L subsidiary is still a regulated utility, and has run into some trouble with Florida regulators, particularly in passing on the costs of a new $900 million gas-fired plant. An agreement was reached but allowed no further rate increases until 2012. Adding some additional headwind is the state of the Florida real estate market and overall economy. The dividend yield, while still healthy for a company with future growth prospects in an up and coming industry, is still low by current utility standards—reflecting in part the fact that investors have already put a lot of energy into this stock and the price accounts for its prospects. Buyers should look for good entry points.

SECTOR: Utilities

BETA COEFFICIENT: .59

10-YEAR COMPOUND EARNINGS PER SHARE GROWTH: 7.0%

10-YEAR COMPOUND DIVIDENDS PER SHARE GROWTH: 6.0%

	2003	2004	2005	2006	2007	2008	2009	2010
Revenues (Mil)	9,630	10,522	11,846	15,710	15,263	16,410	15,646	15,317
Net Income (Mil)	883	887	885	1,261	1,312	1,639	1,615	1,957
Earnings per share	2.45	2.46	2.32	3.23	3.27	4.07	3.97	4.74
Dividends per share	1.2	1.3	1.42	1.5	1.64	1.78	1.89	2.00
Cash flow per share	5.36	5.6	6.18	6.77	6.85	8.03	8.75	9.60
Price: high	34	38.1	48.1	55.6	72.8	73.8	60.6	56.3
low	26.8	30.1	35.9	37.8	53.7	33.8	41.5	45.3

NextEra Energy, Inc.

700 Universe Boulevard

Juno Beach, FL 33408

(561) 694-4697

Website: *www.investor.fplgroup.com*

NIKE, Inc.

Ticker symbol: NKE (NYSE) □ S&P Rating: A+ □ Value Line financial strength rating: A++ □
Current yield: 1.5%

Company Profile

NIKE's principal business activity is the design, development, and worldwide marketing of footwear, apparel, equipment, and accessory products. NIKE is the largest seller of athletic footwear and athletic apparel in the world, but a big part of the story is how they are extending beyond traditional footwear and apparel. Their products are sold to retail accounts, through NIKE-owned retail outlets, and through a mix of independent distributors and licensees in over 180 countries around the world.

NIKE does no manufacturing—virtually all of their footwear and apparel are manufactured by independent contractors outside the United States, while equipment products are produced both in the United States and abroad.

NIKE's shoes are designed primarily for athletic use, although a large percentage of these products are worn for casual or leisure purposes. Their shoes are designed for men, women, and children for running, training, basketball, and soccer use, although they also carry brands for casual wear.

NIKE sells apparel and accessories for most of the sports addressed by their shoe lines, as well as athletic bags and accessory items. NIKE apparel and accessories are designed to complement their athletic footwear products, feature the same trademarks, and are sold through the same marketing and distribution channels.

NIKE has a number of wholly owned subsidiaries, including Cole Haan, Converse, Hurley, and Umbro that variously design, distribute, and license dress, athletic and casual footwear, sports apparel, and accessories. In FY2009, these subsidiary brands together with NIKE Golf accounted for approximately 43 percent of total revenues.

The company has more than 23,000 retail accounts in the United States. The company makes substantial use of a "futures" ordering program, which allows retailers to order five to six months in advance of delivery with the commitment that their orders will be delivered within a set time period at a fixed price. In FY2009, 87 percent of their U.S. wholesale footwear shipments of NIKE-branded products were made under the futures program. About 50 percent of the company's total sales are overseas, and

NIKE is one of the strongest U.S. consumer brands abroad.

Financial Highlights, Fiscal Year 2010

NIKE's sales declined just a shade in FY2010, in what was an off year for most of the garment and athletic wear industry due to decreased discretionary spending (we should also note that the fiscal year ends May 31, so FY10 actually included a lot of calendar 2009). The company projects returns to a high single-digit revenue growth in FY2011, bolstered by international sales and the release of important new products and brands, such as the LeBron line of footwear. Backlogs are strong and retail futures orders have exceeded projections, and the company has been increasing production rates. Revenues are projected at $20.4 billion for FY2011, with earnings in the $4.40 range. The company also increased its dividend 15 percent in late 2010. The company has almost no debt—long-term debt is $440 million against a market capitalization of $41 billion.

Reasons to Buy

Why buy NIKE? In a word, brand. The NIKE brand and its corresponding "swoosh" are one of the most recognized—and sought after—brands in the world. It is a lesson in simplicity and image congruence with the product behind it. NIKE doesn't sit still with it; rather, they are learning to leverage it into more products outside the traditional athletic wear circuit—golf clubs, golf balls, even a new line of GPS watches and apps. Further, NIKE doesn't just limit the brand appeal to athletes: Slogans like "Just Do It" and "If you have a body, you're an athlete" emphasize the appeal and lifestyle across all segments of the population. We think this is drop-dead smart.

Of course, solid brand and brand reputation lead to category leadership and hence, higher profitability, and NIKE has finished far ahead of the pack in this area too. The brand and "moat" created by the brand seem to have nowhere to go but forward, and improved manufacturing efficiencies, strong channel relationships, and international exposure all keep the company moving faster in the right direction. Despite its size, the company continues to deliver double-digit earnings, cash flow, and dividend growth even as revenues have matured into the high single-digit range. We like the combination of protected profitability through brand excellence, combined with a clean conservative balance sheet, providing a good combination of safety and growth potential.

Reasons for Caution

Two things could put hurdles in NIKE's path. First, the company is continually in the news—and the rumor mill—for "unfair labor practices" and child labor violations in some of its foreign manufacturing plants. The company doesn't actually own or operate these plants, but the rumors can stick nonetheless. A particularly egregious violation could tarnish the brand but there have been none to date. Second, the stock price has run along in lockstep to the good news, so obvious buying opportunities have been hard to find. We also feel the company could return a little more cash to shareholders, although the company has bought back about 8 percent of common "B" shares since 2005.

SECTOR: **Consumer Discretionary**

BETA COEFFICIENT: **0.91**

10-YEAR COMPOUND EARNINGS PER SHARE GROWTH: **15.0%**

10-YEAR COMPOUND DIVIDENDS PER SHARE GROWTH: **15.5%**

		2003	2004	2005	2006	2007	2008	2009	2010
Revenues (Mil)		10,697	12,253	13,740	14,955	16,326	18,627	19,176	19,014
Net Income (Mil)		749	945	1,212	1,392	1458	1,734	1,727	1,907
Earnings per share		1.39	1.76	2.25	2.63	2.86	3.44	3.52	3.86
Dividends per share		0.27	0.37	0.48	0.59	0.71	0.88	0.98	1.06
Cash flow per share		1.9	2.37	2.64	3.2	3.43	4.15	4.25	5.15
Price:	high	34.3	46.2	45.8	50.6	67.9	70.6	66.6	83.4
	low	21.2	32.9	37.6	37.8	47.5	42.7	38.2	60.9

NIKE, Inc.

One Bowerman Drive

Beaverton, OR 97005

(503) 671-6453

Website: *www.nikebiz.com*

Norfolk Southern

Ticker symbol: NSC (NYSE) ◻ S&P Rating: BBB+ ◻ Value Line financial strength rating: B+ ◻ Current yield: 2.6%

Company Profile

Norfolk Southern Corp. was formed in 1982 as a holding company when the Norfolk & Western Railway merged with the Southern Railway. Including lines received in the split takeover (with CSX) of Conrail, the current railroad operates 21,000 route-miles of track in twenty-two eastern and southern states. They serve every major port on the east coast of the United States and have the most extensive intermodal network in the east.

Company business is about 29 percent coal, 19 percent intermodal, 14 percent agricultural and consumer products, 11 percent metals and construction, and 29 percent other. Within those categories, the railroad transports the usual mix of raw materials, intermediate products like parts, and manufactured goods. The company has been an innovator in the intermodal business, that is, combining trucking and rail services—the "Roadrailer," a train of coupled-together highway vans on special wheelsets is an example; at the terminal, a cab simply backs up to the van and drives it off.

The company provides a number of logistics services and has substantial traffic to and from ports and overseas destinations.

Financial Highlights, Fiscal Year 2010

Not too surprisingly, given a railroad's ties to the economy in general and industrial production and import/export activity in particular, Norfolk Southern had a substantially "off" year in 2009, with revenues off almost 25 percent and per share earnings off almost half from the year before. The recovery, and a greater cost consciousness on the part of current and prospective customers, have returned NSC's volumes to a "near normal" level, with freight volumes up 15 percent and quarterly earnings up as much as 50 percent from the prior year. With high fixed costs inherent in the rail business, volumes are exceptionally important to profitability. The company continues to be highly efficient, with an industry-leading operating ratio (variable costs to revenue) of 71.9 percent; maintaining volumes and this level of operating efficiency are key to the company's future. Indeed, FY2011 revenues are expected to grow back toward FY2008 highs, and the effects on profits will be noticeable, as the company is expected to earn $4.75 per share in FY2011. NSC raised the dividend twice in FY2010, a strong sign of management's confidence in the business and in the recovery.

Reasons to Buy

NSC's results for FY2011 should continue the momentum established in FY2011. Volumes are strong, and while cyclical, we think the recession may have led many customers to use more cost-effective transportation methods, particularly intermodal, for the future. NSC's 2009 operating ratio of 71.9 percent (the ratio of variable or operating costs to revenue, down some 3.5 percent from 2009 reflecting volume scale and efficiency, is one still one of the best in the industry and better than the best-ever 76 percent posted by our second favorite rival Union Pacific). This railroad has done an excellent job containing costs and sizing its physical plant for its demand.

NSC has proven over the past thirty years that it can compete effectively for long-haul truck business with its intermodal offerings, and has some of the most competitive service and terminal structures

in the business. It has gained market share from trucks. Additionally, NSC serves some of the more dynamic and up-and-coming manufacturing markets in the United States, namely, Asian and other foreign-owned manufacturing facilities found particularly in the Southeast. The company has created a "Heartland Corridor" time freight and double-stack container routing between Chicago and the East Coast, reducing distance by 250 miles and more importantly, transit times from four to three days. Such innovations will further assert the company's leadership. Additionally, we like the strength and diversity coming from serving the domestic and especially the foreign-owned auto industry—the company serves plants for (in alphabetical order) BMW, Chrysler, Ford, General Motors, Honda, Isuzu, Mazda, Mercedes-Benz, Mitsubishi, Nissan, Subaru, Suzuki, and Toyota. Toyota recently gave NSC its highest award for overall logistics excellence, its seventh such award since 1996.

Reasons for Caution

There are two concerns: first, the strength of the recovery and the overall economy. Recessions hurt this company. Second, much of the growth potential is in the intermodal business (trailers, containers on specialized flat cars); this business tends to be highly competitive and relatively low in margin. Additionally, higher fuel prices can hurt, but this is usually offset somewhat by increased use of rail transport as customers are looking to save on fuel costs, and also on fuel surcharges the company levies on shipments from time to time.

SECTOR: **Transportation**
BETA COEFFICIENT: **1.02**
10-YEAR COMPOUND EARNINGS PER SHARE GROWTH: **15.0%**
10-YEAR COMPOUND DIVIDENDS PER SHARE GROWTH: **5.0%**

		2003	2004	2005	2006	2007	2008	2009	2010
Revenues (Mil)		6,468	7,312	8,527	9,407	9,432	10,661	87,969	9,516
Net Income (Mil)		529	870	1,161	1,481	1,464	1,716	1,034	1,498
Earnings per share		1.35	2.18	2.82	3.58	3.68	4.52	2.76	4.00
Dividends per share		0.3	0.36	0.48	0.68	0.96	1.22	1.36	1.40
Cash flow per share		2.66	3.67	4.72	5.58	5.9	6.88	5.07	6.48
Price:	high	24.6	36.7	45.8	57.7	59.6	75.5	54.8	63.7
	low	17.3	20.4	29.6	39.1	45.4	41.4	26.7	46.2

Norfolk Southern
Three Commercial Place
Norfolk, VA 23510–2191
Phone: (757) 629-2680
Website: *www.nscorp.com*

CONSERVATIVE GROWTH

Northern Trust Corporation

Ticker symbol: NTRS (NASDAQ) ❑ S&P rating: AA– ❑ Value Line financial strength rating: B++ ❑ Current yield: 2.1%

Company Profile

Northern Trust Corporation, founded in 1889, is a multibank holding company headquartered in Chicago that provides personal wealth management and financial services, and corporate and institutional services through the corporation's principal subsidiary, the Northern Trust Company, and other bank subsidiaries. The corporation has seventy-nine offices located in eighteen of the more populous states. As of June 30, 2010, Northern Trust had approximately $50 billion in banking assets, more than $603 billion in assets under management and $3.6 trillion in assets under custody.

Global offices are situated in Amsterdam, Bangalore, Beijing, Dublin, Hong Kong, Limerick, London, Singapore, Tokyo, and Toronto. The corporation also owns two investment management subsidiaries: Northern Trust Investments, N.A.; and Northern Trust Global Advisors, Inc.

Northern Trust Corporation organizes client services around two principal business units: Personal Financial Services (PFS) and Corporate and Institutional Services (C&IS). Northern Trust Global Investments (NTGI) provides investment products and services to clients of both PFS and C&IS.

Personal Financial Services offers personal trust, estate administration, private banking, residential real estate mortgage lending, a securities brokerage, and investment management services to individuals, families, and small businesses. PFS operates through a network of eighty-four offices in the eighteen states where Northern Trust operates. Approximately 25 percent of the wealthiest American families employ NTRS for asset management or administration.

Corporate and Institutional Services is a leading provider of trust, global custody, investment, retirement, commercial banking, and treasury management services worldwide. It provides asset management services to large corporations and institutions such as foundations, public retirement funds, insurance companies, and endowments. Other services include benefit payments, portfolio analysis, and electronic funds transfer.

Northern Trust's institutional clients reside in over forty countries and include corporations, public retirement funds, foundations, endowments, governmental entities, and financial institutions.

Financial Highlights, Fiscal Year 2010

Northern Trust earns about three-quarters of its net income from fees and services, and the other quarter from interest income; that is, net interest income on loans outstanding. Both figures peaked in 2008 and softened with the economic slowdown that followed. Noninterest income, which also includes gains from trading and currency exchange, continues to be somewhat soft as investment management fees and foreign exchange gains have declined slightly. The low interest rate climate has also softened interest income. The company is expected to earn $3.20 per share in 2011 after $2.80 in FY2010 and $3.16 in FY2009.

Reasons to Buy

Due to poor performance, damaged reputations, and ongoing uncertainties, we continue to avoid most financial services companies on our *100 Best* list. But Northern Trust is an exception, based on its solid reputation and relatively strong performance during the downturn. Northern Trust did take $1.6 billion in TARP funds in November 2008 during the financial crisis but was the first institution to repay those funds in February of the following year. The company was also one of very few that did not alter nor suspend its dividend during the crisis.

NTRS's clients concerns, and thus NTRS asset management strategy, is focused on capital preservation. NTRS's investment strategy is very conservative and its leverage is the lowest among all their competitors. The company maintains capital ratios in the mid-13 percent range. These ratios essentially reflect equity capital as a percentage of risk-weighted asset, which in this business, are primarily loans. NTRS's ratios are twice the industry norm, suggesting that the company is well capitalized and on safer footing going forward.

In summary, we like this company's reputation and conservative approach, both of which make it a favorable selection in this industry and a good long-term choice.

Reasons for Caution

It appears that interest rates will remain at historically low levels for the foreseeable future, which will continue to act as a drag on NTRS's treasury-heavy portfolios. We are also concerned about the slight dip in investment fee income; there is a lot of competition chasing a relatively fixed base of trust and investment management accounts; at 58 percent, this is the largest component of the company's revenue and profit. A lot depends on the continued favor of the Northern Trust brand.

SECTOR: **Financials**
BETA COEFFICIENT: **0.80**
10-YEAR COMPOUND EARNINGS PER SHARE GROWTH: **9.0%**
10-YEAR COMPOUND DIVIDENDS PER SHARE GROWTH: **10.5%**

		2003	2004	2005	2006	2007	2008	2009	2010
Assets (Mil)		41,450	45,277	53,414	60,712	67,611	82,054	77,324	83,844
Net Income (Mil)		418	506	584	665	727	782	864	889
Earnings per share		1.95	2.33	2.64	3	3.24	3.47	3.16	2.74
Dividends per share		0.68	0.76	0.84	0.94	1.03	1.12	1.12	1.12
Loans ($Mil)		16,437	16,590	18,649	22,469	25,192	30,526	27,497	27,812
Price:	high	48.8	51.3	55	61.4	83.2	88.9	66.1	59.4
	low	27.6	38.4	41.6	49.1	56.5	33.9	43.3	49.3

Northern Trust Corporation
50 South La Salle Street
Chicago, IL 60675
(312) 444-4281
Website: *www.northerntrust.com*

AGGRESSIVE GROWTH

Nucor Corporation

Ticker symbol: NUE (NYSE) ▢ S&P rating: A ▢ Value Line financial strength rating: A ▢ Current yield: 3.1%

Company Profile

Nucor is the fourth-largest global steel producer (by market cap) and the largest U.S.–based producer. It is also the largest recycler in North America, recycling some 13.4 million tons of scrap steel in 2009. Their production model is unique, based on numerous mini-mills and the exclusive use of scrap material as production input. Nucor operates scrap-based steel mills in twenty-two facilities, producing bar, sheet, structural, and plate steel product. Production in 2009 totaled 14 million tons, after a far more robust 20.4 million tons in 2008.

Nucor's steel mills are considered to be among the most modern and efficient in the United States. Recycled scrap steel and other metals are melted in electric arc furnaces and poured into continuous casting systems. Sophisticated rolling mills convert the various types of raw cast material into rebar and basic shapes such as angles, rounds, channels, flats, sheet, beams, plate, and other products.

The company operates in three primary businesses: Steel Mills, Steel Products, and Raw Materials.

1. The Steel Mills segment produce hot-rolled steel, including angles, rounds, flats, channels, sheet, wide-flange beams, pilings, billets, beam blanks, and plate and cold-rolled products. These products are sold to a variety of heavy manufacturing businesses and some construction.

2. The Steel Products segment produces materials primarily for the commercial construction industry, including steel joists and joist girders, steel deck, fabricated concrete reinforcements, fasteners, metal building systems, and wire and wire mesh.

3. The Raw Materials segment gathers and sells ferrous and non-ferrous metals and provides brokerage, transportation, and other handling services.

Financial Highlights, Fiscal Year 2010

A sharp decline in construction and manufacturing created a deep revenue and profit trough in 2009. During that period, sales fell some 53 percent from 2008, and earnings fell from a record $6.01 per share to a dismal $.94 loss. Not only was there a deep drop in demand, but it came off a couple of years of very tight supply and strong pricing in 2007–08. In FY2010, business recovered to a level respectfully close to FY2007 performance at $15.8 billion (compared to $11.2 billion in 2009 and $23.7 billion in 2009) with earnings still attenuated at $.42 per share; FY2011 looks a little stronger with revenues at about $17.8 billion and earnings in the $2.30 range. Going forward, it appears that the sort of tight markets experienced in 2008 are unlikely to return, and that revenues and earnings in this range are likely to continue. As markets have balanced and pricing has weakened, operating margins have weakened as well into the 7 percent range from a previous high of 22 percent. The numbers show the influence of volume on this high fixed cost business, but pricing is also a key factor. Importantly, cash flows run well ahead of the actual earnings numbers, and the company has been generous with its dividends, albeit with a cut during the downturn.

Reasons to Buy

As bad as things were during 2008–2010, Nucor is in better shape than most of its competitors. It has been very conservative with the business over the past five years of growth

and continues to have low levels of debt.

Nucor is the lowest-cost producer in the world—its gross margin is 40 percent higher than the largest player in the industry. Its capital structure is solid and puts it in better position than any of its competitors to buy up capacity should others fail to recover quickly. Its large, rapid-start capacity positions it well to take advantage of the opportunity as demand turns around, and it is acknowledged to be one of the best-run and most innovative players in the industry.

Additionally, we feel that pent-up construction demand and especially the growing need for infrastructure replacement projects will bode well for Nucor's business. We also like the focus on shareholder returns—the recent dividend track record is excellent—not always found in this sort of industry. Nucor is a "best in class" player in a key industry, and should prosper in any kind of economic recovery or major infrastructure replacement cycle.

Reasons for Caution

The industry is inherently cyclical, and those who fear recessions and slowdowns, or even hints thereof, short-term investors included, should proceed with caution on this company. Nucor (and other domestic producers) still have to compete with what many claim are "dumping" practices from overseas producers, that (it is claimed) sell product in the United States below their cost in order to cripple their competition. Investors should watch operating margins; a protracted period below 10 percent may signal trouble ahead.

SECTOR: Industrials
BETA COEFFICIENT: 1.05
10-YEAR COMPOUND EARNINGS PER SHARE GROWTH: 18%
10-YEAR COMPOUND DIVIDENDS PER SHARE GROWTH: 32.5%

	2003	2004	2005	2006	2007	2008	2009	2010
Revenues (Mil)	6,266	11,377	12,701	14,571	16,593	23,663	11,190	15,845
Net Income (Mil)	63	1,122	1,310	1,758	1,472	1,831	(294)	134.1
Earnings per share	0.2	3.51	4.13	5.73	4.98	6.01	(0.94)	0.42
Dividends per share	0.2	0.24	0.93	2.15	2.44	1.91	1.41	1.44
Cash flow per share	1.36	4.72	5.43	7.05	6.51	7.36	0.60	2.00
Price: high	14.7	27.7	35.1	67.6	69.9	83.6	51.1	50.7
low	8.8	13	22.8	33.2	41.6	25.3	29.8	35.7

Nucor Corporation
1915 Rexford Road
Charlotte, NC 28211
(704) 366-7000
Website: *www.nucor.com*

Oracle Corporation

Ticker symbol: ORCL (NASDAQ) ❑ S&P rating: A ❑ Value Line financial strength rating: A++ ❑ Current yield: 0.7%

Company Profile

Oracle Corporation supplies the world's most widely used information management software, the Oracle database. It is also the world's second largest independent software company. In addition to its namesake database, Oracle also develops, manufactures, markets, distributes, and services middleware and applications software that help its customers manage their businesses. With its 2008 acquisition of Sun Microsystems and 2010 acquisition of former HP CEO Mark Hurd to run its sales and distribution organizations, Oracle has vaulted itself into a strong position as a supplier of hardware and particularly bundled hardware/software solutions targeted to such activities as data warehousing and data mining.

Oracle is organized into five reporting business segments. Sales of new software licenses accounted for 28 percent of FY2010 revenues. License updates and software product support generated 49 percent, while hardware systems generated 5.5 percent and hardware support generated 2.5 percent, and general services including consulting generating the remaining 14 percent.

International sales accounted for 57 percent of revenue in FY2010.

The company's new software licenses segment includes the licensing of database and middleware software, which consists of Oracle Database and Oracle Fusion Middleware, as well as applications software. Oracle's database and middleware software provides a platform for running and managing business applications, once part of the acquired Peoplesoft business, for mid-size businesses and large global enterprises. Designed for enterprise grid computing, the Oracle Database is available in four editions, scaled to the size of the intended application. Oracle Exadata is a family of storage software and hardware products designed to improve data warehouse query performance.

Oracle Consulting assists customers in deploying its applications and technology products. The company's consulting services include business/IT strategy alignment, business process simplification, solution integration, and product implementation, enhancements, and upgrades. The company provides training to customers, partners, and employees. Oracle offers thousands of courses covering all of its product offerings.

Financial Highlights, Fiscal Year 2010 (ended June 24, 2010)

Sales rose 15 percent versus 2009, including an 8 percent contribution from the sales of Sun hardware. Earnings grew only 11 percent, as operating margin fell 130 basis points, reflecting a high level of integration costs. Disciplined cost management led to the generation of over $8 billion in free cash flow from fourth quarter 2009 through the third quarter 2010.

The company completed four notable acquisitions during the year: Relsys International in July 2009, Silver Creek Systems and Sun Microsystems in January 2010, and Phase Forward in April 2010. Relsys and Phase Forward will significantly strengthen Oracle's vertical applications for the pharmaceutical industry. More recently, ORCL acquired Art Technology Group, giving it a sizeable presence in the e-commerce applications space.

During the first part of FY2011, all businesses did well. The Sun/Solaris hardware platforms and the integrated systems they support did well under new management. The first two quarters of FY2011 showed earnings $.12 per share ahead of the prior year, which might not sound like much but with 5 billion shares

outstanding, that adds up, and as a percentage it was up in the 30–40 percent range.

Reasons to Buy

Integration and operational excellence are the names of the game at Oracle, and in addition to strong software license revenues, the company expects to see a far more profitable hardware segment from FY2011 forward. The company emerges from the Sun and Mark Hurd acquisitions with a very strong competitive position, particularly against hardware-centered businesses like HP. New software license revenues were up 13 percent in 3Q2010. New software licenses are a strong indicator of future revenue growth in the maintenance and services business.

Oracle's Exadata product has been selling very well. Exadata is an integrated software/hardware product sold as a unit to run Oracle's database in an online transaction processing (OLTP) environment. It's designed to be easy to deploy and configure, and provide very high levels of performance due to its use of extremely low-latency storage. It's the fastest-growing product in Oracle's history and is turning over $100 million per quarter only a year after being introduced. The product should do wonders for getting Sun's hardware business off to a solid start.

The company continues to generate a lot of cash. Even with recent acquisitions, the cash hoard rose from $18 billion at the end of FY2010 (June 2010) to almost $25 billion in November 2010. It continues to be in an excellent position to build a suite of vertical applications on integrated hardware platforms for customers willing to pay for a preconfigured solution. Research facilities, such as those in the aforementioned pharmaceutical industry, are a perfect example.

The company recently started paying a modest dividend showing a greater orientation toward longer-term shareholder value. It quadrupled the dividend to twenty cents in FY2010. The company also is buying back shares, although fairly conservatively.

Reasons for Caution

The integration of Sun will continue to be a minor question mark for a while, as it always is with the age-old question of whether a software company can really execute in a hardware business. We would also like to see the company do more to reduce the outsized 5 billion share count; with so many shares it takes a rather outsized gain in revenue or profit to even be noticed as we typically measure per share performance today.

SECTOR: **Technology**
BETA COEFFICIENT: **0.9**
10-YEAR COMPOUND EARNINGS PER SHARE GROWTH: **22.0%**
10-YEAR COMPOUND DIVIDENDS PER SHARE GROWTH: **Nil**

	2003	2004	2005	2006	2007	2008	2009	2010
Revenues (Mil)	9,475	10,156	12,119	14,771	18,208	22,609	23,495	27,034
Net Income (Mil)	2,307	2,681	3,541	4,246	5,295	6,799	7,393	8,494
Earnings per share	0.43	0.50	0.68	0.80	1.01	1.30	1.44	1.67
Dividends per share	–	–	–	–	–	–	0.05	.20
Cash flow per share	0.50	0.56	0.73	0.85	1.09	1.37	1.53	1.75
Price: high	14.0	15.5	14.5	19.8	23.3	23.6	25.1	32.3
low	10.6	9.8	11.3	12.1	16.0	15.0	13.8	21.2

Oracle Corporation
500 Oracle Parkway
Redwood City, CA 94065
(650) 506-7000
Website: *www.oracle.com*

GROWTH AND INCOME

Otter Tail Corporation

Ticker symbol: OTTR (NASDAQ) ❑ S&P rating: BBB- ❑ Value Line financial strength rating: B+ ❑ Current yield: 5.3%

Company Profile

Otter Tail Corporation is a holding company and a mini-conglomerate operating primarily in the upper Midwest. The conglomerate is centered on and stabilized by the Otter Tail Power Company, a regulated utility serving about 130,000 customers in rural Minnesota, North Dakota, and South Dakota. The utility accounts for about 30 percent of the total business. Use of wind generation and hydro power, and lower grades of coal available in the region have driven fuel costs down to 11 percent of revenues, a very low figure for the industry. Approximately 12 percent of power generation is from wind or hydro sources.

Beyond the utility, the company operates in five other business segments:

- Wind Energy (18 percent of revenues) produces windmill towers through a subsidiary known as DMI Industries. A specialized flatbed trucking common carrier also resides in this segment.
- The Manufacturing segment (16 percent of revenues) houses three smaller businesses.

BTD Manufacturing is a metal stamping, fabricating, and laser-cutting shop supplying custom parts for agriculture, lawn care, health and fitness, and the RV industry. Shoremaster produces and markets residential and commercial waterfront equipment—boat lifts, docks, marinas. T.O. Plastics supplies packaging and handling products for the horticultural industry.

- The Plastics segment (9 percent of revenues) has two operations supplying commercial and utility grade PVC and other plastic pipe and accessories.
- The Health Services segment (9 percent) has three subsidiaries engaged in the sale of diagnostic medical equipment, patient monitoring equipment and related supplies, maintenance, and shared and staffed diagnostic imaging equipment and supplies.
- The Food Ingredient Processing (7 percent) segment has one business, Idaho Pacific Holdings, a manufacturer of dehydrated potato products

to the snack food, bakery, and foodservice industries.

Overall, the company has 3,652 employees, and most operations are centered in the upper Midwest.

Financial Highlights, Fiscal Year 2010

While the electric utility business was fairly stable, the remainder of the Otter Tail businesses took a hit in FY2009, with a drop of some 20 percent in revenues and 35 percent in earnings for that year. FY2010 saw a partial recovery, with revenues rising 6 percent to $1.1 billion and earnings aside from a couple of non-cash impairment charges, one related to delivery problems in the wind tower segment, remaining relatively flat at $0.66 per share. The company exited Q4 FY2010 on a strong note, with a 19 percent increase in revenue and 29 percent increase in operating income year over year from Q4 FY2009. For FY2011, the company expects earnings in the $1.00–$1.40 per share range on revenues approaching $1.16 billion, a wide range but reflecting other possible costs in the DMI wind tower business. The macroeconomic environment bodes well for recovery in most if not all of Otter Tail's businesses.

Reasons to Buy

If one were to look at the assortment of Otter Tail businesses, without the Otter Tail name attached, one might jump to the conclusion that this was a Berkshire Hathaway portfolio. Aside from the utility, the company operates small niche players in relatively simple, understandable businesses, all well managed with a trusting corporate parent. The utility anchors the portfolio much as Mid-American Energy anchors Berkshire's—but there is no railroad analogous to Burlington Northern Santa Fe, at least as of yet.

We like this combination of safety and income with the other relatively solid businesses—although were a bit surprised about the performance of some of those businesses during the downturn. We generally like the business portfolio, and the yield exceeding 5 percent gives investors plenty of return while awaiting growth in the other businesses. We also like Otter Tail's involvement in—and use—of wind power. The plastics businesses also support another key strategic area in our minds—infrastructure replacement.

One should note that cash flow far and away exceeds earnings as reported. Otter Tail is a good way to participate in several well managed businesses while getting a decent current return, and is the only small cap stock on our *100 Best* list, for those wanting to add a bit of small cap flavor to their portfolios. It is indeed like a "small town" company in contrast to "big city" corporate America.

Reasons for Caution

The dividend isn't presently covered by current earnings, a caution flag in any business, although at least for now is amply covered by cash flow. The utility is stable but not likely to be helped along by population growth. The subsidiary businesses have proven more volatile than expected, and the company is small enough that a glitch in product delivery, as with the wind tower business, can have a large effect on overall performance. Berkshire, by contrast, is more diversified, and has much larger "anchor" businesses.

SECTOR: **Utilities/Industrial**
BETA COEFFICIENT: **1.13**
10-YEAR COMPOUND EARNINGS PER SHARE GROWTH: **-1.0%**
10-YEAR COMPOUND DIVIDENDS PER SHARE GROWTH: **2.0%**

	2003	2004	2005	2006	2007	2008	2009	2010
Revenues (Mil)	753	882	1,046	1,105	1,239	1,311	1,040	1,118
Net Income (Mil)	36.7	40.9	52.9	50.8	54.0	35.1	26.0	13.6
Earnings per share	1.51	1.50	1.78	1.88	1.78	1.09	0.71	0.38
Dividends per share	1.08	1.10	1.12	1.15	1.17	1.19	1.19	1.19
Cash flow per share	3.30	2.88	3.35	3.39	3.55	2.81	2.76	2.82
Price: high	28.9	27.5	32.0	31.9	39.4	46.2	25.4	25.4
low	23.8	23.8	24.0	25.8	29.0	15.0	18.5	18.2

Otter Tail Corporation
P.O. Box 496
Fergus Falls, MN 56538
(866) 410-8780
Website: *www.ottertail.com*

Pall Corporation

Ticker symbol: PLL (NYSE) ❑ S&P rating: BBB ❑ Value Line financial strength rating: A ❑ Current yield: 1.3%

Company Profile

Okay, raise your hand if you're heard of Pall Corporation. Anyone? No? Well, neither had we, until we found this company in 2010 in a search for quality industrial suppliers that were number one or two in their markets.

Pall supplies filtration, separation, and purification technologies for the removal of solid, liquid, and gaseous contaminants from a variety of liquids and gases. Its products are used in thousands of industrial and clinical settings: removal of contaminants from gas reagents in every semiconductor production facility in the world, removal of bacteria and virus spores from water in hospitals and other clinical settings, and detection of bacteria in blood samples. Its products range in scale from simple in-line filters sold 100 to the carton up to entire graywater treatment systems with capacities up to 150,000 gallons/day.

Pall's product and customers fall into two broad categories: Life Sciences (41 percent of the business) and Industrial (59 percent). The Life Sciences category breaks down further into Blood/Medical (16 percent) and Biopharma (25 percent). The company's Life Sciences technologies facilitate the process of drug discovery, development, regulatory validation, and production. They're used in the research laboratory, pharmaceutical, and biotechnology industries, in blood centers and in hospitals at the point of patient care. The company's medical products improve the safety of the use of blood products in patient care and help control the spread of infections in hospitals. Pall's separation systems and disposable filtration and purification technologies are critical to the development and commercialization of chemically synthesized and biologically derived drugs and vaccines. The company provides a range of advanced filtration solutions for each critical stage of drug development through drug production. Its filtration systems and validation services assist drug manufacturers through the regulatory process and onto the market.

Pall provides process technologies throughout the industrial marketplace, including the aerospace, transportation, microelectronics, consumer electronics, municipal and industrial water, fuels, chemicals, energy, and food and beverage markets. Within the Food & Beverage market, filtration solutions are provided to the wine, beer, soft drink, bottled water, and food ingredient markets. The company sells filtration and fluid monitoring equipment to the aerospace industry for use on commercial and military aircraft, ships, and land-based vehicles to help protect critical systems and components. Pall also sells filtration and purification technologies for the semiconductor, data storage, fiber optic, advanced display, and materials markets.

Financial Highlights, Fiscal Year 2010

After a drop in revenues and earnings in FY2009 far more modest than we saw in other industrial suppliers, Pall got its revenue line back on track with a $2.4 billion showing in FY2010, and more importantly, came in with earnings of $2.03 per share, a 24 percent increase over FY2009. Better yet, the company has raised FY2011 guidance to a range of $2.48–$2.63 per share, and raised its dividend 9 percent to an indicated 70 cents per share annually. Strength in the Life Sciences segment helped the company weather the recession, and looks to be the primary growth and margin driver going forward, while a recovery in the industrial segment will also help. The

company has also been executing on share buybacks, reducing share count from 124 million in 2005 to 115 million in 2010.

Reasons to Buy

We like companies with a dominant position in their marketplaces or market niches, and we like industrials with a diversified customer base. The company sells into the medical, biopharma, energy, and water process technologies, and aerospace, and microelectronics spaces, among others. These sectors will continue to show consistency and strength over time. Further, Pall's products are consumables used consistently within the lab and manufacturing processes they sell into; they do not depend greatly on capital spending decisions and are relatively less sensitive to economic cycles. With 68 percent of sales originating overseas, the company has a strong international foothold.

Reasons for Caution

While its presence in the consumables side of the business attenuates the effects of economic cycles somewhat, the company is still sensitive to economic downturns. The recent strength in the business and business model has been noticed by others, too, and has been reflected in the strength of the stock price; new investors should look to buy on dips.

SECTOR: **Industrials**
BETA COEFFICIENT: **1.13**
10-YEAR COMPOUND EARNINGS PER SHARE GROWTH: **8.0%**
10-YEAR COMPOUND DIVIDENDS PER SHARE GROWTH: **-7.9%**

	2003	2004	2005	2006	2007	2008	2009	2010
Revenues (Mil)	1,614	1,771	1,902	2,017	2,250	2,572	2,392	2,402
Net Income (Mil)	144	152	141	146	128	217	196	241
Earnings per share	1.16	1.20	1.12	1.16	1.02	1.76	1.64	2.03
Dividends per share	0.36	0.36	0.40	0.44	0.48	0.51	0.58	0.64
Cash flow per share	1.81	1.90	1.86	1.97	1.81	2.60	2.44	2.90
Price: high	27.0	29.8	31.5	35.6	49.0	43.2	37.3	44.7
low	15.0	22.	25.2	25.3	33.2	21.6	18.2	31.8

Pall Corporation
2200 Northern Boulevard
East Hills, NY 11548
(516) 484-5400
Website: *www.pall.com*

AGGRESSIVE GROWTH

Patterson Companies, Inc.

Ticker symbol: PDCO (NASDAQ) ❑ S&P rating: NA ❑ Value Line financial strength rating: A ❑ Current yield: 123%

Company Profile

Patterson Companies is a value-added distributor operating in three segments—Dental Supply, Veterinary Supply, and Medical Supply. Dental Supply (about 70 percent of sales) provides a complete range of consumable dental products, equipment, and software; turnkey digital solutions; office design and setup; and value-added services to dentists and dental laboratories primarily for the North American market. Veterinary Supply (20 percent of sales) is the nation's second-largest distributor of consumable veterinary supplies, equipment, diagnostic products, vaccines, and pharmaceuticals to companion-pet veterinary clinics. Medical Supply distributes medical supplies and assistive products, primarily for rehabilitation and sports medicine, globally to hospitals, long-term-care facilities, clinics, and dealers.

Patterson has one-third of the Dental Supply market. Their main competitor is HSIC (Henry Schein), which also has about a one-third share, with the remaining third fragmented among a number of smaller players, including Dentsply (XRAY) on our *100 Best* list. As one of the lead dogs, Patterson has the clout to negotiate a number of exclusive distribution deals. It is sole distributor for the industry's most popular line of dental chairs, and also has an exclusive on the CEREC 3D dental restorative system, an increasingly popular alternative to traditional dental crowns. Patterson is also the leading provider of digital radiography systems, which create instant images of dental work, superior to the images generated by traditional x-ray equipment.

Patterson's veterinary business, Webster Veterinary, is the second largest distributor of consumable veterinary supplies to companion-pet veterinary clinics. Its line also includes equipment and software, diagnostic products, and vaccines and pharmaceuticals.

Financial Highlights, Fiscal Year 2010 (ending April 30, 2011)

The soft economy has claimed even dental services as a victim, as many patients deferred procedures and many dentists deferred purchases as a result. The company now projects FY2011 earnings between $1.89 and $1.99 per share, a slight gain from 2010, on low single-digit growth.

In early 2010 the company initiated its first-ever dividend with a $.10 per share quarterly payout, reflecting the company's confidence in its growth prospects and strong current cash flows.

Reasons to Buy

Patterson Dental uses its size market leadership position to offer services that its smaller competitors cannot, such as financing, local service and support, and software services. During the recent business downturn, the company supplied all its customers with its EagleSoft practice management software at no charge and revised its commission structures.

The aforementioned CEREC 3D is an imaging and milling system that allows the dentist to take an image of the area to be restored and in less than thirty minutes produce a crown, inlay, or other device that is then fitted to the patient's existing dental structure. It's a compelling proposition for high-volume offices where patient throughput is at a premium and the equipment can be fully utilized. Sales of this high-ticket item have been very good and generate ongoing supplies revenue. Patterson's exclusive license to this product is a powerful foot in the door for new accounts.

We like the company's moves into the companion-pet veterinary

and rehabilitative markets, both of which are driven by a growing and profitable demographic. Today the company is primarily focused on the North American market, with promised 24–48 hour delivery for most items. They have established an international beachhead with the Patterson Medical group in the United Kingdom and France, and intend to leverage this presence to expand the dental and veterinary businesses; thus far international expansion remains more an opportunity—a good one—than a reality.

The company has been using cash flow to increase shareholder returns, repurchasing about 10 percent of outstanding shares, and starting the aforementioned dividend. This plus the international growth opportunities and relatively recession-proof business are the most compelling reasons to own Patterson.

Reasons for Caution

The company is a bit more dependent on expensive equipment purchases than most of its competitors, and thus may be more vulnerable to economic swings than most. Competition in this arena is strong, and operating and net margins have softened a bit since the middle of the last decade. With only modest growth prospects, this company is more of a steady long-term play than a quick hitter.

SECTOR: **Health Care**
BETA COEFFICIENT: **.86**
10-YEAR COMPOUND EARNINGS PER SHARE GROWTH: **18.0%**
10-YEAR COMPOUND DIVIDENDS PER SHARE GROWTH: **NM**

	2003	2004	2005	2006	2007	2008	2009	2010
Revenues (Mil)	1,416	1,657	1,969	2,421	2,615	2,798	2,998	3,094
Net Income (Mil)	95	116	150	184	198	208	225	200
Earnings per share	0.70	0.85	1.09	1.32	1.43	1.51	1.69	1.69
Dividends per share	0	0	0	0	0	0	0	0.4
Cash flow per share	0.95	1.23	1.53	1.60	1.68	2.05	1.88	2.00
Price: high	27.6	35.8	43.7	53.8	38.3	40.1	37.8	30.9
low	19.1	17.7	29.7	33.4	29.6	28.3	15.8	27.9

Patterson Companies, Inc.
1031 Mendota Heights Road
St. Paul, MN 55120–1419
(651) 686-1775
Website: ***www.pattersondental.com***

AGGRESSIVE GROWTH

Paychex, Inc.

Ticker symbol: PAYX (NASDAQ) □ S&P rating: NA □ Value Line financial strength rating: A □
Current yield: 3.7%

Company Profile

Paychex, Inc., provides payroll, human resource, and benefits outsourcing solutions for small to medium-sized businesses. Founded in 1971, the company has more than 100 offices and serves over 536,000 clients, mostly small to medium-sized businesses with ten to 200 employees in the United States and an additional 1,400 clients in Germany. The company has two sources of revenue: service revenue, paid by clients for services; and interest income on the funds held by Paychex for clients.

Paychex offers a portfolio of services and products, which includes:

- Payroll processing
- Payroll tax administration services
- Employee payment services
- Regulatory compliance services (new-hire reporting and garnishment processing)
- Comprehensive human resource outsourcing services
- Retirement services administration
- Workers' compensation insurance services
- Health and benefits services
- Time and attendance solutions
- Medical deduction, state unemployment, and other HR services and products

The company's products are marketed primarily through its direct sales force, the bulk of which is focused on payroll products. In addition to the direct sales force, the company utilizes its relationships with existing clients, CPAs, and banks for new client referrals. Approximately two-thirds of its new clients come via these referral sources.

The company also sells a Major Market Services product for its larger clients. The MMS product is a license that allows the client to run the Paychex software on the client's own servers and administer the payroll function with its own personnel. They can also have their own HR people manage and control PayChex-hosted payroll processes through the Internet.

In addition to traditional payroll services, Paychex offers complete "full service" HR outsourcing solutions; custom-built solutions including payroll, compliance, HR, and employee benefits sourcing and administration; outsourcing management and even professionally trained onsite HR representatives. The company also manages retirement plans and other benefits, including pretax "cafeteria" plans, and has a subsidiary insurance agency offering property and casualty, workers' comp, health and auto policies to an employer's employee base.

Financial Highlights, Fiscal Year 2010 (ended May 31, 2010)

The Paychex business is directly affected by the number of businesses in the client base, and the number of workers that business employs. Both "bases" went into serious decline during the recession. Paychex experienced its first-ever decline in client base in FY2009, and this decline continued into FY2010. As employment trends slightly lag the recessionary trough itself, and with the Paychex 2010 fiscal calendar ending in May 2010, that year turned out to be the weakest year, with revenues of $2 billion, off about 4 percent from FY2009. 2011 is expected to recover that 4 percent dip. Earnings, in the meantime, are expected to recover to $1.40 per share; again, not stellar but a step in the right direction.

Reasons to Buy

Paychex's primary market is firms with fewer than 100 employees.

This is one of the primary reasons that Paychex has lost clients—many small businesses are undercapitalized and simply went out of business during the recession. On the other hand, as the economy turns around, we expect that smaller firms are the first place that new jobs will appear. Additionally, we believe many larger firms with HR and payroll departments will continue to look into outsourcing these services to cut costs, which should help Paychex.

The company is very conservatively run and is well financed. It carries no debt and will have no difficulty funding the generous dividend, even at its current payout level of 80–90 percent of earnings. Fragmentation in the market and Paychex's extremely strong financial position would allow the company to grow market share through acquisition, should it decide to do so.

Finally, the company handles billions of dollars of "float" every year as it receives payrolls from clients and doles them out to employees, who don't always cash checks right away. This float is as much as $4 billion at any one time. The net interest income from this business dried up to near zero because of low short-term interest rates on safe securities. Any uptick in short-term rates would be an added plus for the company.

Reasons for Caution

This company will always be vulnerable to economic swings. Additionally, the company has many smaller local competitors in most markets, making it hard to raise prices and fees for its services. Finally, while most analysts consider the dividend payout secure, it does account for a substantial fraction of the company's cash flow, and increases may be hard to come by for the immediate future.

SECTOR: **Information Technology**
BETA COEFFICIENT: **0.85**
10-YEAR COMPOUND EARNINGS PER SHARE GROWTH: **18.0%**
10-YEAR COMPOUND DIVIDENDS PER SHARE GROWTH: **26.5%**

		2003	2004	2005	2006	2007	2008	2009	2010
Revenues (Mil)		1,099	1,294	1,445	1,675	1,887	2,066	2,083	2,001
Net Income (Mil)		294	303	369	465	515	576	534	477
Earnings per share		0.78	0.8	0.97	1.22	1.35	1.56	1.48	1.32
Dividends per share		0.44	0.47	0.51	0.61	0.79	1.20	1.24	1.24
Cash flow per share		0.89	0.95	1.14	1.4	1.54	1.82	1.72	1.56
Price:	high	40.5	39.1	43.4	42.4	47.1	37.5	32.9	32.8
	low	23.8	28.8	28.8	33	36.1	23.2	20.3	24.7

Paychex, Inc.
911 Panorama Trail South
Rochester, NY 14625-0397
(585) 383-3406
Website: *www.paychex.com*

CONSERVATIVE GROWTH

PepsiCo, Inc.

Ticker symbol: PEP (NYSE) □ S&P rating: A □ Value Line financial strength rating: A++ □ Current yield: 3.0%

Company Profile

PepsiCo is a global beverage, snack, and food company. It manufactures, markets, and sells a variety of salty, convenient, sweet, and grain-based snacks and foods, carbonated and non-carbonated beverages in approximately 200 countries, with its largest operations in North America (United States and Canada), Mexico, the United Kingdom, and now Russia. You'll recognize most of the major PepsiCo brands which range widely from the familiar Pepsi Cola and are likely to show up in abundance in your refrigerator and kitchen cupboard at any given time.

PepsiCo is organized into three business units and six reportable segments, as follows:

- PepsiCo Americas Foods, which includes Frito-Lay North America (Fritos, Doritos, Lay's, Cheetos, Tostitos, Ruffles, SunChips), Quaker Foods North America (Quaker, Aunt Jemima, Cap'n Crunch, Life, Rice-A-Roni, and Near East), and all of the Latin American food and snack businesses, including the locally branded Sabritas and Gamesa businesses in Mexico
- PepsiCo Americas Beverages, which includes PepsiCo Beverages North America and all of the Latin American beverage businesses, and brings to market Tropicana and Gatorade products, in addition to several familiar soft drink brands
- PepsiCo International, which includes all PepsiCo businesses in the United Kingdom, Europe, Asia, the Middle East, and Africa. The international business accounts for about 43 percent of sales and 29 percent of profits.

Many of PepsiCo's brand names are over 100 years old, but the corporation is relatively young. PepsiCo was founded in 1965 through the merger of Pepsi-Cola and Frito-Lay. PepsiCo now has at least eighteen brands that generate over $1 billion in retail sales. The top two brands are Pepsi-Cola and Mt. Dew, but beverages constitute less than half of Pepsi's sales. It is primarily a snack company, with beverages coming in second. Frito-Lay brands alone account more than half of the U.S. snack chip industry.

PepsiCo began its international snack food operations in 1966. Today, with operations in more than forty countries, it's the leading multinational snack chip company, with more than a 25 percent market share of international retail snack chip sales. Brand Pepsi and other Pepsi-Cola products—including Diet Pepsi, Pepsi-One, Mountain Dew, Slice, Sierra Mist, and Mug brands—account for nearly one-third of total soft drink sales in the United States, a consumer market totaling about $60 billion. Pepsi-Cola also offers a variety of non-carbonated beverages, including Aquafina bottled water, Lipton ready-to-drink tea, and Frappuccino ready-to-drink coffee through a partnership with Starbucks.

PepsiCo acquired Tropicana, including the Dole juice business, in August 1998 and now markets these products in sixty-three countries. Tropicana Pure Premium is the third largest brand of all food products sold in grocery stores in the United States. Gatorade, acquired as part of the Quaker Oats Company merger in 2001, is the world's leading sports drink.

At the beginning of FY2011, the company completed the acquisition of 60 percent of Wimm-Bill-Dan, a major branded food and beverage company in the Russian market for $3.8 billion, giving PepsiCo a 77 percent stake in the company, with plans to purchase all remaining shares eventually.

Financial Highlights, Fiscal Year 2010

Sales through the 2009 recession year were basically flat. In FY2010, the company acquired a substantial portion of its bottling business (a similar strategy to Coke; see that company's analysis) giving a nearly 40 percent boost to the top line. Without this acquisition, top line growth has returned to the mid-single digits, with snack volumes up 2 percent and beverage volumes up 11 percent in late FY2010 quarters compared to the previous year. FY2010 earnings grew 12 percent to $4.13 per share, in line with most estimates, but rising commodity prices dinged Q4 earnings a bit and caused the company to give a cautious outlook for FY2011. Yet, unless commodity prices spike, cost synergies with the bottling business and a change to in-house distribution for Gatorade should bring healthy earnings increases in FY2011: Estimates currently call for $4.60 per share vs. $3.77 in the recession-attenuated 2009. The company raised its dividend to $1.92 per share in early 2011.

Reasons to Buy

PepsiCo continues to offer a compelling combination of earnings, dividend, and cash flow growth potential with a strong measure of safety. Earnings and dividends continue to grow at a faster pace than the business overall, a good sign of increasing productivity and efficiency.

The company is taking an aggressive approach to geographical expansion, with good results so far. Its Russian business is expected to grow at double-digit rates over 2009's $2 billion in revenue, and PepsiCo plans to invest more than $2.5 billion in manufacturing and distribution in China over the next three years.

Reasons for Caution

PepsiCo will need to move quickly to retain the health-conscious market. They have many new and reformulated products in the works that use healthier ingredients and reduced levels of sodium and trans-fats, but the competition for this segment is intense. The company has created a "Global Nutrition Group" to address this challenge. On the plus side, there's no clear leader in this emerging segment, and there's no better distributor for new products than Frito-Lay, but it may require some retooling of this brand image to seriously address the market the company estimates at $30 billion by the year 2020. Also, the company enjoyed a dip in commodity prices in 2010; that cycle is reversing as 2011 progresses and the company will have to deal with higher ingredient costs; the ability to pass them on remains to be seen but has been successful at many of PepsiCo's competitors. In fact, the food business is one of the big differentiators between Pepsi and rival Coca-Cola, and rising commodity prices will hurt Pepsi more than Coke.

SECTOR: **Consumer Staples**
BETA COEFFICIENT: **.54**
10-YEAR COMPOUND EARNINGS PER SHARE GROWTH: **11.0%**
10-YEAR COMPOUND DIVIDENDS PER SHARE GROWTH: **12.5%**

	2003	**2004**	**2005**	**2006**	**2007**	**2008**	**2009**	**2010**
Revenues (Mil)	26,971	29,261	32,562	35,137	39,474	43,251	43,232	57,938
Net Income (Mil)	3,494	4,174	4,078	5,065	5,543	5,142	5,946	6,320
Earnings per share	2.01	2.44	2.39	3.00	3.34	3.21	3.77	3.91
Dividends per share	0.63	0.85	1.01	1.16	1.43	1.60	1.75	1.89
Cash flow per share	2.81	3.14	3.65	3.95	4.38	4.30	4.84	5.47
Price: high	48.9	55.7	60.3	66	79	79.8	64.5	68.1
low	36.2	45.3	51.3	56	61.9	49.7	43.8	58.8

PepsiCo, Inc.
700 Anderson Hill Road
Purchase, NY 10577–1444
(914) 253-3055
Website: *www.pepsico.com*

AGGRESSIVE GROWTH

Perrigo Company

Ticker symbol: PRGO (NASDAQ) □ S&P rating: NA □ Value Line financial strength rating: B++ □
Current yield: 0.4%

Company Profile

Perrigo is the world's largest manufacturer of over-the-counter pharmaceutical products for the store brand market. They also manufacture generic prescription pharmaceuticals, nutritional products, and active pharmaceutical ingredients (APIs).

The company operates in three segments: Consumer Healthcare, Rx, and API. Consumer Healthcare is by far the largest segment, generating about 81 percent of Perrigo's revenue in 2010.

The company's success depends on its ability to manufacture and quickly market generic equivalents to branded products. It employs internal R&D resources to develop product formulations and manufacture in quantity for its customers. It also develops retail packaging specific to the customer's needs.

If you have bought a store-branded over-the-counter medication like ibuprofen or cough medicine in the past year, there's a good chance (a 70 percent chance, in fact) that it was made by Perrigo. The company produces and markets over 2,400 store brand products in 12,000 individual SKUs to approximately 800 customers, including Wal-Mart, CVS, Walgreens, Kroger, Target, Safeway, Dollar General, Costco, and other national and regional drugstores, supermarkets, and mass merchandisers. Wal-Mart is its single largest customer and accounts for 23 percent of Perrigo's net sales. The retail market for the branded equivalents of Perrigo's most widely used products is over $12 billion.

The Rx operations produce generic prescription drugs, obviously benefiting when key patented drugs run past their patent protection. As of April 2010, the company markets approximately 300 generic prescription products, with over 620 SKUs, to approximately 120 customers, accounting for about 10 percent of sales, while the API division markets an assortment of active ingredients to other drug manufacturers, accounting for about 6 percent.

The company's products are manufactured in nine separate facilities around the world. Its major markets are in North America, Mexico, the United Kingdom, and China. About 33 percent of sales are overseas.

Financial Highlights, Fiscal Year 2010

Perrigo's FY2010 finished strong, with record sales of $2.3 billion, a 13 percent gain, and record earnings of $2.83 per share, a 51 percent gain over FY200 (which itself was a record year). In early 2011, the company raised full year FY2011 earnings guidance to between $3.28 and $3.43 per share, an implied growth rate of 24–29 percent.

Gross and operating margin expansion have been a key part of the growth story. The consumer store-branded products market is large and secure but relatively low margin, so the company has been putting more focus on the Rx and API businesses. Operating margins have risen from the low teens in the mid-decade to the mid-teens in 2008 and 2009, 20 percent in 2010 and are projected at 21.2 percent in 2011.

Reasons to Buy

Perrigo is a real success story of solid niche dominance (store-branded medications) with a couple of high-growth, high-margin businesses mixed in. Steady growth in sales combined with a steady growth in margins have a multiplicative effect, and the company has enjoyed well above average profit growth in this industry.

Not only does the company dominate a niche—it is a growing niche. People are becoming more sensitive to their own health care costs and spending in general, and are opting more often for the store brand; after all, 200 mg of ibuprofen is 200 mg of ibuprofen. And this is all affected by the demographic tailwind of the aging population.

Perrigo expects that over the next four years, prescription drugs worth $9 billion in sales will be approved for OTC use. Prescription-to-OTC transitions are one of Perrigo's main revenue drivers. Similarly, Perrigo sees an additional $2.6 billion in sales of branded Rx products with potential for generic equivalent product introductions. With its 70 percent market share of the private-label OTC market, Perrigo is in a position to capture the larger share of those new opportunities.

Perrigo is consolidating its API production and is closing its higher-cost API production facility in Germany. The company has purchased a large stake in an API manufacturing facility in India, which it plans to expand and use as a production center for higher-volume API products as well as Rx and Rx-to-OTC candidates.

Cash flow has improved dramatically over the last three years and the company is well funded for growth through acquisition. The company continues to make acquisitions to increase geographic coverage or expand categories. One was generic drug manufacturer Paddock Laboratories. In early 2010 the company paid $808 million cash for PBM holdings, a $300 million store-brand infant formula manufacturer that did well in FY2010, and expanded its international presence among other things by acquiring a leading OTC pharmaceutical supplier in Australia and New Zealand.

Reasons for Caution

There are some risks in the generic pharmaceutical industry; among them are patent infringement lawsuits and manufacturing problems. The company has had a few lawsuits but fortunately none of the manufacturing problems experienced by rival Johnson & Johnson; a major hiccup could put a dent in the company's business. Also, the stock price has followed the story upward, so new investors should choose buying opportunities carefully.

SECTOR: **Health Care**
BETA COEFFICIENT: **0.81**
10-YEAR COMPOUND EARNINGS PER SHARE GROWTH: **14.5%**
10-YEAR COMPOUND DIVIDENDS PER SHARE GROWTH: **NM**

	2003	2004	2005	2006	2007	2008	2009	2010
Revenues (Mil)	826	898	1,024	1,366	1,447	1,822	2,007	2,269
Net Income (Mil)	51.9	67.5	37.9	74.1	78.6	150	176	263
Earnings per share	0.73	0.93	0.49	0.79	0.84	1.58	1.87	2.83
Dividends per share	0.05	0.13	0.16	0.17	0.18	0.21	0.22	0.25
Cash flow per share	1.11	1.35	0.77	1.41	1.46	2.35	2.67	3.69
Price: high	16.7	25	19.9	18.7	36.9	43.1	61.4	67.5
low	10.5	15.6	12.8	14.4	16.1	27.7	18.5	37.5

Perrigo Company
515 Eastern Avenue
Allegan, MI 49010
(269) 673-8451
Website: *www.perrigo.com*

Praxair, Inc.

Ticker symbol: PX (NYSE) ❑ S&P rating: A ❑ Value Line financial strength rating: A ❑ Current Yield: 2.1%

Company Profile

Praxair, Inc., is the largest producer of industrial gases in North and South America and the second-largest supplier of industrial gases in the world. The company, which was spun off to Union Carbide shareholders in June 1992, supplies atmospheric, process, and specialty gases; high-performance coatings; and related services and technologies.

Praxair's primary products are atmospheric gases—oxygen, nitrogen, argon, and rare gases (produced when atmospheric air is purified, compressed, cooled, distilled, and condensed), and process and specialty gases—carbon dioxide, helium, hydrogen, and acetylene (produced as byproducts of chemical production or recovered from natural gas). Customers include petroleum refiners and makers of primary metals, chemicals, health care products, electronics, glass, pulp and paper, and environmental products.

The gas products are sold into the packaged-gas market and the merchant market. In the packaged-gas market, bulk gases are packaged into high-pressure cylinders and either delivered to the customer or to distributors. In the merchant market, bulk gases are liquefied and transported by truck to the customer's facility.

The company also designs, engineers, and constructs cryogenic and non-cryogenic gas supply systems for customers who choose to produce their own atmospheric gases on-site. This is obviously a capital-intensive delivery solution for Praxair, but results in lower delivered cost to the customer and higher returns for Praxair, as all operational costs are paid by the customer. Contracts for these installations can run to twenty years.

Praxair Surface Technologies is a subsidiary that applies metallic and ceramic coatings and powders to metal surfaces in order to resist wear, high temperatures, and corrosion. Aircraft engine makers are its primary market, but it serves others, including the printing, textile, chemical, and primary metals markets, and provides aircraft engine and airframe component overhaul services.

Financial Highlights, Fiscal Year 2010

Praxair followed most of the industrial world into a soft FY2009, and has followed that world back to a degree of prosperity. As has become a familiar story, Praxair saw a sharp revenue dip in FY2009 but managed to attenuate the drop in earnings with cost-cutting measures. In FY2010, revenues bounced back, and as the cost-cutting and efficiency measures remained in place, the company delivered strong profitability and cash flow. For full year 2010, revenues grew 13 percent to $10.12 billion, while adjusted earnings per share were $4.74, up 19 percent year over year and above management's guidance range of $4.67–$4.72. Most estimates place Praxair's earnings between $5.38 and $6.08, maintaining a steady 13.5 percent growth rate at the midpoint.

Reasons to Buy

Praxair is the largest gas provider in the emerging markets of China, India, Brazil, and Mexico. Praxair China now has fifteen wholly owned subsidiaries and at least ten joint ventures. Asian markets account for 8 percent of Praxair's sales, and these markets are growing steadily.

The petroleum industry is recovering heavier and heavier crude oil sources, such as the tar sands in Alberta. To refine these sources at existing facilities requires the input of greater and greater volumes of hydrogen. The largest of

Praxair's forty-two current major projects are hydrogen production facilities in North America serving refineries, and hydrogen for refining is now Praxair's largest growth market. ExxonMobil's recent purchase of XTO for its oil shale holdings and fracturing technology is a strong indicator of future growth in heavy crude refining.

Praxair is moving quickly on a solution for carbon sequestration at coal-fired facilities (primarily power plants) that may be funded soon by the DOE and, if successful, could generate revenues on the order of $150 million per installation.

Four large players control 75 percent of the world's industrial gas supply. Since the end products are essentially identical, simple transportation costs tend to drive regionalization of the markets. Praxair, with its many plants and pipelines, has created substantial barriers to entry in many of its established and emerging markets.

Reasons for Caution

The company no longer has to deal with the effects of an Air Products-Airgas merger, but consolidation of smaller players by Praxair's competitors may force Praxair to follow suit at some point. As hydrocarbon energy products are feedstock for many of Praxair's products, the company is sensitive to increases in energy prices.

SECTOR: Materials
BETA COEFFICIENT: 0.86
10-YEAR COMPOUND EARNINGS PER SHARE GROWTH: 11.5%
10-YEAR COMPOUND DIVIDENDS PER SHARE GROWTH: 19.0%

	2003	2004	2005	2006	2007	2008	2009	2010
Revenues (Mil)	5,613	6,594	7,656	8,324	9,402	10,796	8,956	10,118
Net Income (Mil)	585	607	726	988	1,177	1,335	1,254	1,195
Earnings per share	1.77	2.10	2.20	3.00	3.62	4.19	4.01	3.84
Dividends per share	0.46	0.6	0.72	1.00	1.20	1.50	1.60	1.80
Cash flow per share	3.36	3.94	4.61	5.25	6.18	8.63	6.85	6.95
Price: high	38.3	46.2	54.3	63.7	92.1	77.6	86.1	96.3
low	25	34.5	41.1	50.4	58	53.3	53.3	72.7

Praxair, Inc.
39 Old Ridgebury Road
Danbury, CT 06810–5113
(203) 837–2354
Website: *www.praxair.com*

The Procter & Gamble Company

Ticker symbol: PG (NYSE) ❑ S&P rating: AA- ❑ Value Line financial strength rating: A++ ❑ Current yield: 3.0%

Company Profile

Procter & Gamble dates back to 1837, when William Procter and James Gamble began making soap and candles in Cincinnati, Ohio. The company's first major product introduction took place in 1879 when it launched Ivory soap. Since then, P&G has continually created a host of blockbuster products and has some of the strongest, most recognizable consumer brands in the world.

P&G is a uniquely diversified consumer products company with a strong global presence. P&G markets its broad line of products to nearly 5 billion consumers in more than 180 countries.

The company is a recognized leader in the development, manufacturing, and marketing of quality laundry, cleaning, paper, personal care, food, beverage, and health care products, including prescription pharmaceuticals. The company operates in three business units: Beauty and Grooming, Health and Well Being, and Household Care. Among the company's nearly 300 brands are Gillette, Tide, Always, Whisper, Pro-V, Oil of Olay, Pringles, Duracell, Ariel, Crest, Pampers, Pantene, Vicks, Bold, Dawn, Head & Shoulders, Cascade, Iams, Zest, Bounty, Braun, Comet, Scope, Old Spice, Charmin, Tampax, Downy, Cheer, and Prell.

Total 2010 sales exceeded $79 billion and the company has nearly 135,000 employees working in more than eighty countries. International sales account for 62 percent of the business.

Financial Highlights, Fiscal Year 2010 (ended June 30, 2010)

P&G's FY2010 revenues and per share earnings remained flat at just under $79 billion and $3.53 respectively. The company issued FY2011 guidance calling for a resumption of single-digit growth, driven primarily by consumer spending and international growth; revenues are expected to grow in the 3–5 percent range. Organic growth is expected in the 4–6 percent range, and the company issued two sets of earnings estimates: $3.89–$3.99 from continuing operations and "core" earnings between $3.91 and $4.01. Translation: The company expects to spin off a few brands, as it did recently with its Zest soap products to a private equity firm, and as it has done several times recently to food products producer J. M. Smucker (a *100 Best Stock*).

Reasons to Buy

Regardless of developments in the world economy, people will continue to shave, bathe, do laundry, and care for their babies, and P&G is the global leader in baby care, feminine care, fabric care, and shaving products. Everyone should consider at least one defensive play in their portfolio, and P&G deserves to be at the top of the list.

P&G is a market leader in consumer health care, a $240 billion market, with just a 5 percent share. Similarly, beauty and grooming is a $300 billion market, and P&G is the market leader with just a 13 percent share. P&G plans to grow their core businesses over the next several years and even small changes in market share in markets this size generate large returns.

P&G is extending its reach to capture share in channels and markets that are currently underserved. Developing markets are a huge opportunity, representing 86 percent of the world's population, and P&G feels it can be a leader in many product categories. Emerging markets already represent 32 percent of their revenue, up from 20 percent in 2002. P&G is also broadening its distribution channels to pursue

opportunities via drug and pharmacy outlets, "convenience" stores, export operations, and even e-commerce. P&G does less than $1 billion in online sales at this time, and the company feels it can increase that substantially.

P&G's recent concentration on the beauty and health care segments has paid benefits, and the company plans to focus on expanding its product offerings in these segments. According to a company spokesperson, "More than 70 percent of the company's growth, or roughly $20 billion in net sales, has come from organic growth and strategic acquisitions in these businesses. Well over half of P&G sales now come from these faster-growing higher-margin businesses."

P&G regards innovation as one of its key differentiators and aggressively pursues new market opportunities, both in the U.S. market and globally. The company has realigned its once-secretive R&D efforts to be more open and collaborative with researchers in the public space, including academic technology research and market research. This should help the company reduce costs and become more nimble in the marketplace.

In a move that should reduce operating and some marketing and advertising costs significantly, the company recently announced a departure from its traditional model of managing brands as wholly separate businesses with brand-specific advertising budgets, products research labs, and so forth. Synergies from combining ads and ad strategies alone should get more bang for the buck and reduce total costs across the company's many portfolios.

Finally, the company offers an excellent combination of brand and marketplace strength, safety and defensiveness (beta = 0.52), current yield, and growth opportunity.

Reasons for Caution

In a slow economy, consumers will be motivated to save wherever possible. Among Procter & Gamble's chief competitors for shelf space are low-cost store brands and generics. A change in consumer preference may dilute market share for P&G, but since it has the number one or number two retail positions in the majority of its key global categories, P&G feels that any shift in purchasing patterns will damage its traditional competitors more than it will P&G. Rising commodity costs can affect P&G, and the expansion into the health and beauty business brings more exposure to often-fickle consumer tastes and shorter brand life than the company may be used to.

SECTOR: **Consumer Staples**
BETA COEFFICIENT: **.52**
10-YEAR COMPOUND EARNINGS PER SHARE GROWTH: **10.0%**
10-YEAR COMPOUND DIVIDENDS PER SHARE GROWTH: **11%**

	2003	2004	2005	2006	2007	2008	2009	2010
Revenues (Mil)	43,377	51,407	56,741	68,222	76,476	83,503	79,029	78,938
Net Income (Mil)	5,186	6,481	7,257	8,684	10,340	12,075	11,293	10,946
Earnings per share	1.85	2.32	2.53	2.64	3.04	3.64	3.58	3.53
Dividends per share	0.82	0.93	1.03	1.15	1.28	1.45	1.64	1.80
Cash flow per share	2.82	3.18	3.51	3.51	4.25	4.97	4.65	4.87
Price: high	50	57.4	59.7	64.2	75.2	73.8	63.5	65.3
low	39.8	48.9	51.2	52.8	60.4	54.9	43.9	39.4

The Procter & Gamble Company
1 Procter & Gamble Plaza
Cincinnati, OH 45202
(513) 983-1100
Website: *www.pg.com*

AGGRESSIVE GROWTH

Ross Stores, Inc.

Ticker symbol: ROST (NASDAQ) ❑ S&P rating: BBB ❑ Value Line financial strength rating: A ❑
Current yield: 1.2%

Company Profile

Ross Stores is the second-largest off-price retailer in the United States. Ross and its subsidiaries operate two chains of apparel and home accessories stores. It ended FY2009 with a total of 1,005 stores, of which 953 were Ross Dress for Less locations in twenty-seven states and Guam and fifty-two were dd's DISCOUNTS stores in four states. Just over half the company's stores are located in three states—California, Florida, and Texas.

Both chains target value-conscious women and men between the ages of eighteen and fifty-four. Ross's target customers are primarily from middle-income households, while the dd's DISCOUNTS target customers are typically from more moderate-income households. Merchandising, purchasing, pricing, and the locations of the stores are all aimed at these customer bases. Ross and dd's DISCOUNTS both offer first-quality, in-season, name-brand and designer apparel, accessories, and footwear for the family at savings of either 20–60 percent off department store prices (at Ross) or 20–70 percent off (at dd's DISCOUNTS). Both stores also offer discounted home fashions and housewares as well.

Ross believes it derives a competitive advantage by offering a wide assortment of products within each of its merchandise categories in well-organized and easy-to-shop store environments. Its strategy is to offer competitive values to target customers by offering a well-managed mix of inventory with a strong percentage of name brands and items of local and seasonal interest at attractive prices.

Financial Highlights, Fiscal Year 2010

Almost overnight, the recession made customers very cost, price, and value conscious, and Ross knocked the ball out of the park in FY2009. That year, sales increased 11 percent to a record $7.2 billion on the strength of a 6 percent rise in comps. Net earnings for the year grew 45 percent to a record $443 million, up from $305 million in 2008. Per share net rose 52 percent to $3.54, on top of a 23 percent gain in 2008.

Even as the economy showed signs of recovery, the strength continued. Earnings grew another 36 percent to $4.83 a share in FY2010, while sales tacked on another 9.5 percent. For FY11, the company sees earnings between $4.90 and $5.10 a share—a nice run from $1.90 in 2007. The company also authorized a $900 million stock repurchase through FY2012, which would retire approximately 12 percent of shares outstanding. The company has already reduced share counts 19 percent in six years, from 146 million in 2004 to about 118 million in 2010. Ross also raised the dividend 38 percent to $0.88 per share.

Reasons to Buy

The recession helped Ross gain mainstream appeal across a wider set of customers. While some of those customers will "defect" back to full-price retail stores as things improve, a greater number will probably continue to shop at the stores. At the same time, the company was successful with operational improvements begun in 2009 to improve merchandising and inventory management, which led to better stocking of a more favorable mix of goods and improved inventory turnover.

These marketplace and operational improvements have led to the financial success one would expect and then some, and the company continues to improve its inventory management and should see greater profitability almost regardless of the economic environment.

We like the combination of brand and operational strength in the business with a bias toward increasing shareholder returns. We also like owning a company that is *helped* by a sudden drop in the Consumer Confidence Index; that's a rare bird these days.

Reasons for Caution

The stock has recently traded at an all-time high, and there are questions about Ross's ability to acquire the same quantity and quality of merchandise as the economy picks up and full-price retailers begin to see higher levels of foot traffic. Such inventory follows a cycle, and if full-price retailers cut back on orders, there is less for everyone— and if the economy picks up, they will sell more, so less to Ross. Upshot: Inventory management improvements at full-price retailers could make things tougher for the company.

SECTOR: Retail
BETA COEFFICIENT: 0.73
10-YEAR COMPOUND EARNINGS PER SHARE GROWTH: 15.5%
10-YEAR COMPOUND DIVIDENDS PER SHARE GROWTH: 23.0%

	2003	2004	2005	2006	2007	2008	2009	2010
Revenues (Mil)	3,921	4,240	4,944	5,570	5,975	6,486	7,184	7,866
Net Income (Mil)	228	180	200	241	261	305	443	1,055
Earnings per share	1.47	1.19	1.36	1.70	1.90	2.33	3.54	4.83
Dividends per share	0.13	0.18	0.22	0.26	0.32	0.40	0.49	0.72
Cash flow per share	2.02	1.87	2.15	2.51	2.85	3.51	4.90	6.06
Price: high	28.1	32.9	31.4	31.8	35.2	41.6	50.5	66.6
low	16.3	21.0	22.3	22.1	24.4	21.2	28.1	42.3

Ross Stores, Inc.
4440 Rosewood Dr.
Building 4
Pleasanton, CA 94588-3050
(925) 965-4400
Website: *www.rossstores.com*

AGGRESSIVE GROWTH
Schlumberger Limited
Ticker symbol: SLB (NYSE) ❑ S&P rating: A+ ❑ Value Line financial strength rating: A+ ❑ Current yield: 1.1%

Company Profile
Schlumberger Limited is the world's leading oilfield services company. It provides technology, information solutions, and integrated project management services with the goal of optimizing reservoir performance for its customers in the oil and gas industry. Founded in 1926, today the company employs more than 77,000 people in eighty countries.

The company operates in two business segments:

Schlumberger Oilfield Services is, at 91 percent of revenues and 93 percent of profits, by far the largest segment, and supplies a wide range of products and services including oilfield services such as formation evaluation, directional drilling, well cementing/stimulation, well completions, and productivity. Consulting services provided include consulting, software, information management, and IT infrastructure services that support core industry operational processes. WesternGeco, which accounted for 9 percent of the company's revenue, provides reservoir imaging, monitoring, and development services to land, marine, and shallow-water well projects.

Schlumberger manages its business through twenty-eight "GeoMarket" regions, which are grouped into four geographic areas: North America; Latin America; Europe, the Commonwealth of Independent States, and Africa; and the Middle East and Asia. The GeoMarket structure provides a single point of contact at the local level for field operations and brings together geographically focused teams to meet local needs and deliver customized solutions.

The company had an event-driven FY2010, with the $11 billion acquisition of oil services giant Smith International, a transaction completed against the backdrop of the BP Gulf disaster, which attenuated offshore drilling at least temporarily. The Smith acquisition adds a line of supplies, including fluids and drill bits, in addition to traditional oilfield services and supply chain offerings to round out, expand, and leverage the existing Schlumberger business.

Financial Highlights, Fiscal Year 2010
Schlumberger's 2010 results reflect the fortunes of the oil exploration and production industry, which in

turn reflect the fortunes of petroleum products demand and prices. Revenues rose from $22.7 billion in 2009 to $27 billion, but this largely reflects the Smith acquisition, which will add approximately $8.5 billion to the top line ongoing. The bottom line remained at a somewhat soft $2.70 per share for the year, but improved oil demand and prices have improved capacity utilization, and together with the Smith integration, earnings are expected back to $3.70 per share range in FY2011.

Reasons to Buy

The first page of Schlumberger's 2009 annual report begins with: "The age of easy oil is over." Written many months before the explosion of BP's deepwater platform in the Gulf of Mexico and the ensuing spill, the sentence seems prescient and is perhaps the most succinct statement of Schlumberger's advantages in the E&P business. Its expertise is most valuable in the most technically challenging projects, such as the several recent sub-salt offshore finds in Brazil, West Africa, and the Gulf of Mexico.

Unlike a lot of players in the oil business, it has been prudent with its money. Income from the boom years has been used to fund selected acquisitions of companies that operate only in its core business segment. It has also plowed money back into the company in the form of increased spending on R&D; Schlumberger invests more each year in R&D than all other oilfield services companies combined. The company has also started to return some cash to shareholders in the form of dividends and share buybacks. The dividend was raised 19 percent in early 2011, and we'll see how fast it retires the 176 million shares issued for the Smith acquisition.

Reasons for Caution

Naturally, Schlumberger is vulnerable to the ups and downs of the oil and gas industry, and the BP disaster highlights an additional risk factor for offshore drilling projects, in addition to the geopolitical risks the company is already exposed to. The company paid a pretty stiff price for the Smith acquisition and the success of that acquisition will depend on how much operating leverage the company can achieve. And, if already-soft natural gas prices take another dip, abandonments and postponements of drilling projects could hurt. Finally, the share price has already taken a strengthening energy market into account, so new investors will have to watch closely for worthwhile entry points.

SECTOR: Energy
BETA COEFFICIENT: 1.25
10-YEAR COMPOUND EARNINGS PER SHARE GROWTH: 14.5%
10-YEAR COMPOUND DIVIDENDS PER SHARE GROWTH: 7.5%

	2003	2004	2005	2006	2007	2008	2009	2010
Revenues (Mil)	13,893	11,480	14,309	19,230	23,277	27,163	22,702	27,447
Net Income (Mil)	911	1,236	2,022	3,747	5,177	5,397	3,142	3,408
Earnings per share	0.78	1.03	1.67	3.04	4.18	4.42	2.61	2.70
Dividends per share	0.38	0.38	0.41	0.48	0.7	0.81	0.84	0.84
Cash flow per share	2.12	2.16	2.86	4.51	5.94	6.42	4.70	4.55
Price: high	28.1	34.9	51.5	74.8	114.8	112	71.1	84.1
low	17.8	26.3	31.6	47.9	56.3	37.1	35.1	54.7

Schlumberger Limited
5599 San Felipe, 17th Floor
Houston, TX 77056
(713) 375-3535
Website: *www.slb.com*

Sigma-Aldrich Corporation

Ticker symbol: SIAL (NASDAQ) ❏ S&P rating: A ❏ Value Line financial strength rating: A ❏ Current yield: 1.2%

Company Profile

Sigma-Aldrich is a manufacturer and reseller of high value-add chemicals, biochemicals, laboratory equipment, and consumables used in research and large-scale manufacturing activities. The company sells over 130,000 chemicals, over one-third of which it manufactures internally. It also stocks over 40,000 laboratory equipment items. Most of the company's 92,000 customer accounts are research institutions that use basic laboratory essentials like solvents, reagents, and other supplies. The company also sells chemicals in large quantities to pharmaceutical companies, but no single account provided more than 2 percent of Sigma-Aldrich's total sales in 2009. Sigma-Aldrich's business model is to provide its generic and specialized products with expedited (in most cases, next day) delivery. The company sells in 165 countries and obtains about 64 percent of its sales internationally.

Sigma-Aldrich operates four business units, each catering to a separate class of customer and product. Research Essentials sells common lab chemicals and supplies such as biological buffers, cell culture reagents, biochemicals, solvents, reagents, and other lab kits to customers in all sectors. Research Specialties sells organic chemicals, biochemicals, analytical reagents, chromatography consumables, reference materials, and high-purity products. Research Biotech provides "first to market products" to high-end biotech labs, selling immunochemical, molecular biology, cell signaling, genomic, and neuroscience biochemicals. Fine Chemicals fills large-scale orders of organic chemicals and biochemicals used for production in the pharmaceutical, biotechnology, and high-tech electronics industry.

The company's biochemical and organic chemical products and kits are used in scientific and genomic research, biotechnology, pharmaceutical development, the diagnosis of disease, and as key components in pharmaceutical and other high technology manufacturing. Sigma-Aldrich has customers in life science companies, university and government institutions, hospitals, and industry.

Financial Highlights, Fiscal Year 2010

Despite a slight softening in Q4, Sigma's FY2010 revenues came in at $2.3 billion, a 7 percent improvement from a soft but not disastrous FY2009. Earnings improved from $2.80 to $3.12 per share, a little shy of the $3.20 some were expecting. For FY2011 the company sees mid-single-digit top line growth with earnings, boosted by gradual operating margin improvements, rising to $3.45 to $3.60 per share. The company continues to post strong financials, with a healthy $569 million in cash and only $300 million in long-term debt, less than 13 percent of total capital. Many feel the company will add some synergistic acquisitions, especially in key international markets. The company continues to grow its e-commerce capability and (via acquisition of a software company) now has the industry's largest searchable database of over 60 million different chemical compounds.

Reasons to Buy

Sigma has been a very steady performer in a high value-add segment of the chemical and health care business. The company is big enough and broad enough to maintain its top-dog position in this lucrative niche, and has a good brand and sterling reputation both in domestic and international markets. For investors, it is a safe, steady grower in a solid business in a solid industry.

Reasons for Caution

The company's growth is tied to the state of research in the chemical and bio/pharmaceutical industries, and, while steady, economic and political factors can create doubts from time to time. Rapid growth in existing businesses isn't likely; when a company depends on acquisitions to grow, that brings some risks with it. While dividends have grown, a company in this industry with such a steady business and cash flow could pay out a little more to shareholders.

SECTOR: **Industrials**

BETA COEFFICIENT: .87

10-YEAR COMPOUND EARNINGS PER SHARE GROWTH: **12.5%**

10-YEAR COMPOUND DIVIDENDS PER SHARE GROWTH: **14%**

	2003	**2004**	**2005**	**2006**	**2007**	**2008**	**2009**	**2010**
Revenues (Mil)	1,298	1,409	1,667	1,798	2,039	2,201	2,148	2,271
Net Income (Mil)	193	233	258	276	311	342	347	384
Earnings per share	1.34	1.67	1.88	2.05	2.34	2.65	2.80	3.12
Dividends per share	0.21	0.26	0.38	0.42	0.46	0.52	0.58	0.64
Cash flow per share	1.84	2.23	2.55	2.74	3.09	3.6	3.61	3.95
Price: high	29	30.8	33.6	39.7	56.6	63	56.3	67.8
low	20.5	26.6	27.7	31.3	37.4	34.3	31.5	46.5

Sigma-Aldrich Corporation

3050 Spruce Street

St. Louis, MO 63103

(314) 771-5765

Website: *www.Sigma-Aldrich.com*

J. M. Smucker Company

Ticker symbol: SJM (NYSE) ❏ S&P rating: NA ❏ Value Line financial strength rating: A+ ❏ Current yield: 2.6%

Company Profile

If you happened to think of a nice jar of refreshing purple grape jam when you heard the name "Smucker" you were on the right track. This eastern Ohio–based firm has been a leading manufacturer of jams, jellies, and other processed foods for years, and thanks in large part to divestitures from the Procter & Gamble food division and other companies, has grown itself into a premier player in the packaged food industry.

Smucker manufactures and markets products under its own name, as well as under a number of other household names like Crisco, Folgers, Jif, Laura Scudder's, Hungry Jack, Eagle, and Pillsbury, among others. The company also produces and distributes Dunkin' Donuts coffee and produces an assortment of cooking oils, toppings, juices, and baking ingredients. The company has had good success in revitalizing such brands as Folgers and Jif through improved marketing, channel relationships, and better overall focus on the success of these brands. Overall, the company aims to sell the number one brand in the various markets it serves. Operations are centered in the United States, Canada, and Europe.

Even as a $4.6-billion-a-year enterprise, the company still retains the feel of a family business, with brothers Tim and Richard Smucker sharing the CEO responsibilities as chairman and president respectively.

Financial Highlights, Fiscal Year 2009 (ended April 30, 2010)

In June 2010, the company announced better-than-expected results for the fiscal year ended April 30, a surprise to many investors who were expecting a relatively tough year with competition and increased prices for certain commodities. That trend continued into the first quarters of FY2011. Led by improved sales in the U.S. retail coffee business, top line revenues actually grew, while many analysts had expected a modest decline as consumers had pulled back from buying premium brands. Performance in the relatively new coffee businesses exceeded expectations, and lower prices for certain commodities actually helped. The company was able to increase cash flow in FY2010 and increase the dividend some 14 percent. Expectations for FY2011 are for more of the same.

Reasons to Buy

In fact, Smucker has raised dividends every year since 2002, and seems on track to continue that trend. This is a very well-managed company with an excellent reputation in its markets. In recent years, it has a proven track record in buying and revitalizing key brands, the most prominent being former Procter & Gamble food brands and International Multifoods brands. We expect this trend to continue. Additionally, the company is trying out new initiatives for packaging and delivering foods, including "jar-free" peanut butter and healthier fare in certain categories, which should add to its competitive lead and to margins. Finally, the company is in a very steady and safe business, and will continue to enjoy a dominant marketing position and opportunities to improve margins in most of its businesses.

Reasons for Caution

In the food business, one must always keep an eye on raw commodity costs, as we learned with regard to corn, wheat, and other commodities in 2008. It appears that we may be headed for another such cycle, although perhaps not to the same degree. While the brands are strong, companies like Smucker must always worry about generic competition and the increased buying power of mega-channel players like Wal-Mart. Future earnings could be attenuated somewhat by advertising spending and other costs.

SECTOR: **Consumer Staples**
BETA COEFFICIENT: **0.60**
10-YEAR COMPOUND EARNINGS PER SHARE GROWTH: **11.5%**
10-YEAR COMPOUND DIVIDENDS PER SHARE GROWTH: **9.0%**

	2003	**2004**	**2005**	**2006**	**2007**	**2008**	**2009**	**2010**
Revenues (Mil)	1,417.0	2,043.9	2,154.7	2,148.0	2,524.8	3,757.9	4,605	4,600
Net Income (Mil)	120.9	150.1	155.1	164.6	178.9	321.4	494	560
Earnings per share	2.40	2.60	2.65	2.89	3.15	3.77	4.15	4.70
Dividends per share	.92	1.02	1.08	1.14	1.22	1.31	1.40	1.64
Cash flow per share	3.20	3.52	3.97	3.94	4.42	3.73	5.60	6.50
Price: high	46.8	53.5	51.7	50.0	64.3	56.7	62.7	66.3
low	33.0	40.8	43.6	37.2	46.6	37.2	34.1	53.3

The J. M. Smucker Company
One Strawberry Lane
Orrville, OH, 44667
(330) 682-3000
Website: *www.smuckers.com*

Southern Company

Ticker symbol: SO (NYSE) □ S&P rating: A □ Value Line financial strength rating: A □ Current yield: 4.8%

Company Profile

Through its four primary operating subsidiaries—Georgia Power, Alabama Power, Mississippi Power, and Gulf Power—Southern Company serves some 4.4 million customers in a large area of Georgia, Alabama, Mississippi, northern Florida, and parts of the Carolinas. The company also wholesales power to other utilities in a wider area.

The revenue mix is balanced: 36 percent residential, 32 percent commercial, 19 percent industrial, and 13 percent other. The service area includes the Atlanta metropolitan area and a large base of modern manufacturing facilities like the many Asian-owned manufacturing facilities, including large auto plants, in the region. The fuel mix is more diverse and less vulnerable to price fluctuations than some, with 55 percent coal, 22 percent oil and gas, 15 percent nuclear, 4 percent hydroelectric, and 4 percent purchased. That said, with its high percentage of coal-fired plants, SO must work to stay up with environmental regulations and pay close attention to transportation costs. Additionally, the company plans to deploy two of fifteen new Westinghouse AP1000 nuclear reactors for its massive Vogtle power station in Georgia, purchased with an $8.3 billion loan guarantee from the U.S. Department of Energy.

The company also has engaged in telecommunications services, operating as a regional wireless carrier in Alabama, Georgia, southeastern Mississippi, and northwest Florida and operating some fiber optic networks collocated on company rights of way. The company also provides consulting services to other utilities.

Financial Highlights, Fiscal Year 2010

A return to prosperity in the manufacturing-intensive service area, plus a hot summer and relatively cool winter propelled SO back to top-line prosperity after an 8 percent dip in 2009. Earnings were attenuated a bit by deliberate spending on plant and right-of-way maintenance, and came in at $2.36, a little below initial forecasts but quite sufficient to maintain the $1.82 per share dividend. The company offered FY2011 EPS guidance in the $2.48–$2.52 per share range. Additionally, Georgia Power, the largest subsidiary, was granted a 10 percent rate hike in late December 2010.

Reasons to Buy

The recovery hoped for in 2010 appears to be underway and should continue going forward, as first quarter results are very encouraging. The appeal of this stock lies almost entirely in its dividend, which has been raised slowly but steadily for years. The percent plus or minus return won't put you into a yacht, but if you've already got one it will certainly help you keep it. The solid history and relationship with local regulatory bodies makes the dividend and its annual raises look secure for the future. The stock price, too, has been very stable over time with one of our lowest beta coefficients of 0.35.

Southern serves a growing, diverse, and economically stable customer base. This is not Detroit Edison; they aren't dependent on any one dominant industry and rate requests are generally treated favorably due to the low overall tax rate in the area. Finally, the company is in the intermediate stages of being licensed to build new nuclear power facilities; in today's environment, while that does add some risk, we feel this is a good economic move for the future.

Reasons for Caution

Electric utilities are always subject to rate and other forms of regulation, and one never knows what will happen in that arena. Additionally, utilities are always vulnerable to capital costs and the attractiveness of alternative fixed income investments, and are sensitive to rising interest rates, especially if rates rise quickly. SO is more exposed to coal prices and rail freight rates for its transport than most, and these have fluctuated a bit more in recent years. Finally, all electric utilities are exposed to new environmental regulations and the need to replace aging infrastructure.

SECTOR: **Utilities**
BETA COEFFICIENT: **0.35**
10-YEAR COMPOUND EARNINGS PER SHARE GROWTH: **3.0%**
10-YEAR COMPOUND DIVIDENDS PER SHARE GROWTH: **2.0%**

	2003	2004	2005	2006	2007	2008	2009	2010
Revenues (Mil)	11,251	11,902	13,554	14,356	15,353	17,127	15,743	17,456
Net Income (Mil)	1,602	1,589	1,621	1,608	1,782	1,807	1,912	2,040
Earnings per share	1.97	2.06	2.13	2.1	2.28	2.25	2.32	2.37
Dividends per share	1.39	1.42	1.48	1.54	1.6	1.66	1.73	1.80
Cash flow per share	3.53	3.65	4.03	4.01	4.22	4.43	4.25	4.30
Price: high	32	34	36.5	37.4	39.3	40.6	33.8	38.6
low	27	27.4	31.1	30.5	33.2	29.8	30.8	30.8

Southern Company
30 Ivan Allen Jr. Boulevard NW
Atlanta, GA 30308
Phone: (404) 506-5000
Website: *www.southernco.com*

Southwest Airlines, Inc.

Ticker symbol: LUV (NYSE) ❑ S&P rating: BBB ❑ Value Line financial strength rating: B+ ❑ Current yield: 0.1%

Company Profile

Southwest Airlines provides passenger air transport, operating almost exclusively in the United States. At the end of FY2010, the company served sixty-nine cities in thirty-five states with point-to-point, rather than hub-and-spoke, service. The company serves these markets almost exclusively with 548 Boeing 737 aircraft.

The company is one of the largest in the United States and is the world's largest by number of passengers flown, which should give an idea of their business model—low cost, shorter flights, and maximum passenger loads. Indeed, the average trip is 885 miles and the average fare is $130.27, one of the lowest in the industry. The business model is one of simplicity—no-frills aircraft, no first-class passenger cabin, limited interchange with other carriers, no on-board meals, simple boarding and seat assignment practices, direct sales over the Internet (84 percent of revenues are booked this way), no baggage fees—all designed to provide steady and reliable transportation, with one of the best on-time performances in the industry, and to maximize asset utilization with

minimal downtime, crew disruptions, and other upward influences on operating costs. The company has long used secondary airports—like Providence, Rhode Island, and Manchester, New Hampshire, to serve Boston and the New England area; Allentown, Pennsylvania, and East Islip, New York, to serve the New York/New Jersey area; and Chicago Midway to reduce delays and costs. This strategy has worked well, although the company, especially with the recent ATA acquisition, is serving more mainstream airports, too.

The simple, straightforward value proposition has been a customer favorite for years. Recently Southwest has embarked on a few initiatives to squeeze out some extra revenue without alienating the core passenger group, mostly targeted to business travelers. One is Business Select, which offers priority boarding, priority security, bonus frequent flyer credit, and a free beverage for an upgrade fee. The company also sells "one-off" early boarding for a small fee. Although the company has avoided the cost and complexities of offering international flights, they are expanding partnerships and experimenting with through flights, now to Mexico, and likely soon to other destinations.

Financial Highlights, Fiscal Year 2010

Southwest, like most carriers, has hit turbulence in the past three years, first with escalating fuel prices, then with the economic downturn. The company experienced a 6 percent revenue falloff in FY2009, and saw per share earnings nosedive from $.61 in 2007 to $.19 in 2009, even with the benefits of well-known fuel price hedging that separated Southwest from its peers during the worst of the fuel crunch.

The solid business model held steady and allowed Southwest to prosper in the economic recovery; the company pulled through with a record $12.1 billion revenue performance in FY2010 and per share earnings of $.73. The ATA acquisition and a resumed capacity expansion is expected to bring in the range of $13.5 billion in revenues and $.85 per share in earnings for FY2011, and many forecast earnings exceeding $1.00 a share in FY2012.

Reasons to Buy

Those who have read *100 Best Stocks* for the past two years have heard us say we'd never put an airline on the list. Why? Because airlines are extremely competitive with little to no control over prices, and with the major cost components of fuel, airport fees, and union labor, have little to no control over their costs. In other words, the exact opposite of what you'd want to see in a business you own.

However, Southwest has continually proven to be the exception. The value proposition is the envy of the industry, and we're frankly surprised that no one else has been able to emulate it (United and Delta, among others, have tried). The airline realizes that what customers want is no-hassle transportation at best-possible prices, and has been able to do that better than anyone else for years. It may be true that competitive pressures make it difficult to control prices, but Southwest nonetheless *sets* the price in most of its markets, and can set it low because of its operating efficiencies. So not being able to control price is more of a problem for the competition than it is for Southwest.

We've continually feared that some other carrier would "get it" and take Southwest's turf—or that Southwest would try to get too big for its britches and start flying 747s from Dallas, San Francisco, New York, and Miami to major world destinations like everyone else. None of these things has happened—the company continues to lead its niche, and at present seems satisfied to stay there. The economic upturn will only make things better as time goes on and other airlines continue to flounder.

Reasons for Caution

The acquisition of ATA and a modest de-simplification of the "Rapid Rewards" frequent flyer program to provide international rewards and sell points to third parties gave us some pause, but the core business model seems intact and should prove successful over time. The company is less hedged against fuel prices than it was in 2008, so a prolonged fuel and commodity spike could hurt, as could a double-dip recession. Investors should watch for any sign that Southwest is straying from its successful, industry-leading business model.

SECTOR: **Transportation**
BETA COEFFICIENT: **1.08**
10-YEAR COMPOUND EARNINGS PER SHARE GROWTH: **-2.5%**
10-YEAR COMPOUND DIVIDENDS PER SHARE GROWTH: **4.5%**

	2003	2004	2005	2006	2007	2008	2009	2010
Revenues (Mil)	5,937	6,530	7,584	9,086	9,861	11,023	10,350	12,104
Net Income (Mil)	296	313	469	592	471	294	140	550
Earnings per share	0.36	0.38	0.57	0.72	0.81	0.40	0.19	0.73
Dividends per share	0.02	0.02	0.02	0.02	0.02	0.02	0.02	0.021
Cash flow per share	0.86	0.95	1.18	1.41	1.40	1.41	1.21	1.02
Price: high	19.7	17.1	17.0	18.2	17.0	16.8	11.8	14.3
low	11.7	12.9	13.0	14.6	12.1	7.1	4.0	10.4

Southwest Airlines, Inc.
P.O. Box 36661
2702 Love Field Drive
Dallas, TX 75235
(214) 904-4000
Website: *www.southwest.com*

St. Jude Medical, Inc.

Ticker symbol: STJ (NYSE) ❏ S&P rating: A ❏ Value Line financial strength rating: A ❏ Current yield: Nil

Company Profile

St. Jude Medical, Inc., designs, manufactures, and distributes cardiovascular medical devices for cardiology and cardiovascular surgery including pacemakers, implantable cardioverter defibrillators (ICDs), vascular closure devices, catheters, and heart valves. The company has four main business segments:

The Cardiac Rhythm Management portfolio (responsible for about 60 percent of St. Jude's FY2009 revenue) includes products for treating heart rhythm disorders as well as heart failure. Its products include ICDs, pacemaker systems, and a variety of diagnostic and therapeutic electrophysiology catheters. The company also develops catheter technologies for the Cardiology/Vascular Access therapy area. Those products include hemostasis introducers, catheters, and a market-leading vascular closure device. Many products in this portfolio use RF (radio frequency) and other leading technologies for rhythm management, ablation, and other advanced cardiovascular problems.

The Cardiovascular segment (20 percent of sales) has been the leader in mechanical heart valve

technology for more than twenty-five years. St. Jude Medical also develops a line of tissue valves, vascular closures, and valve-repair products. The company entered the pericardial stented tissue valve and coronary guide wire markets with new product introductions in the second half of 2010.

The company's Neuromodulation segment (7 percent) produces neurostimulation products, which are implantable devices for use primarily in chronic pain management and in treatment for certain symptoms of Parkinson's disease and epilepsy.

The Atrial Fibrillation business (13 percent) produces a 3D heart mapping system. This tool is used by cardiologists to diagnose and treat irregular heart rhythms, among other uses. The AF unit also produces specialized catheters and other devices used in the treatment of atrial fibrillation.

St. Jude Medical products are sold in more than 100 countries. The company has twenty principal operations and manufacturing facilities around the world. In 2010, the company purchased AGA Medical Holdings, a $200 million producer of devices to treat heart defects and abnormalities with a promising product pipeline.

Financial Highlights, Fiscal Year 2010

By nature, cardiac care is fairly recession proof, and revenue and earnings continued to grow, although at a slightly moderated rate, through the 2009–2010 period. The company had a strong FY2010 and fourth quarter, with revenues reaching the top of guidance at about $1.35 billion, for an annual total near $5.2 billion, about 15 percent ahead of FY2009 and well on the company's traditional growth track. Earnings for FY2010, net of one-time acquisition costs, came in at a solid $3.01 per share, and the company has projected $3.25 per share in FY2011. That figure may depend on share buybacks, as the company has also announced its intentions to retire $900 million in stock covering the 13 million shares expected to be issued in the AGA acquisition and then some. The company has already retired about 10 percent of its outstanding shares since 2004.

Reasons to Buy

Both the Neuromodulation and Atrial Fibrillation segments have grown rapidly and seem well positioned for growth in at least the 15 percent range. The techniques employed in neuromodulation are growing quickly in the field as a preferred treatment for long-term pain management. St. Jude (and others) see this as a disruptive technology, potentially replacing drug and physical therapy regimens and offering improved lifestyle at a reduced cost. These two businesses serve as solid growth "kickers," complementing an already-solid growth businesses.

Medical equipment shares are out of favor at the moment due to the inclusion in the most recent health care legislation of a 2.3 percent excise tax on gross sales of medical devices, due to take effect in 2013. We're not sure why this should have any effect at all on the bottom line of companies like St. Jude Medical, as nearly all of its devices are paid for by insurers, giving device makers a fair amount of price flexibility. Further, the tax is a write-down against earnings. We'd be surprised at any significant impact to earnings in the year following the initiation of the tax.

Finally, the company has a consistent track record of steady growth and relative earnings and share price stability. The company easily scores a triple play with double-digit ten-year compounded growth in sales, earnings, and cash flows, and we expect this to continue. The company could continue to pick up market share in the wake of Boston Scientific's FY2010 recall, and the new technologies and applications are promising, as is the company's rich investment in R&D at 12 percent in sales.

Reasons for Caution

While much of St. Jude's growth is driven by market fundamentals and organic innovation, some of it is also delivered through acquisition, and some of the recent acquisitions have been expensive. The company could also be slowed by a general belt tightening and further legislative action and uncertainty in the medical field. Finally, as Boston Scientific showed us, errors can be very costly in this business.

SECTOR: **Health Care**
BETA COEFFICIENT: **.64**
10-YEAR COMPOUND EARNINGS PER SHARE GROWTH: **20.0%**
10-YEAR COMPOUND DIVIDENDS PER SHARE GROWTH: **NM**

	2003	2004	2005	2006	2007	2008	2009	2010
Revenues (Mil)	1,932	2,294	2,915	3,302	3,779	4,363	4,681	5,185
Net Income (Mil)	339	410	394	548	652	807	838	995
Earnings per share	0.92	1.1	1.04	1.47	1.85	2.31	2.43	4.01
Dividends per share	–	–	–	–	–	–	–	–
Cash flow per share	1.2	1.38	1.42	2.05	2.48	2.92	3.24	3.70
Price: high	32	42.9	52.8	54.8	48.1	48.5	42	43.0
low	19.4	29.9	34.5	31.2	34.9	25	28.9	34.0

St. Jude Medical, Inc.
One Lillehei Plaza
St. Paul, MN 55117
(651) 766–3029
Website: *www.sjm.com*

Staples, Inc.

Ticker symbol: SPLS (NASDAQ) ❏ S&P rating: BBB ❏ Value Line financial strength rating: A+ ❏ Current yield: 1.6%

Company Profile

Staples, Inc., launched the office supplies superstore industry with the opening of its first store in Brighton (near Boston), Massachusetts, in May 1986. Its goal was to provide small business owners the same prices on office supplies previously available only to large corporations. Staples is now a $24 billion retailer of office supplies, business services, furniture, and technology to consumers and businesses in twenty-seven countries throughout North and South America, Europe, Asia, and Australia. Staples is the largest operator of office products superstores in the world, with 2,243 stores of all types.

The company operates three business segments: North American Retail, North American Delivery, and International Operations. The company's North American Retail segment consists of the company's U.S. and Canadian business units that sell office products, supplies, and services.

The North American Delivery segment consists of the company's U.S. and Canadian contract, catalog, and Internet business units that sell and deliver office products, supplies, and services directly to customers. Included in this segment is Corporate Express, the large, delivery-oriented office products distributor acquired in 2008.

International Operations has more than 300 retail stores in seven countries, but reaches further with catalog and delivery options into seventeen countries, some through joint ventures. The company has a foothold in China, Brazil, Argentina, and Taiwan among others. Finally, the company has been developing its own brand and set of branded products for years, and is gaining traction on that brand, selling through Safeway stores and other chains.

Financial Highlights, Fiscal Year 2010

Cost-cutting measures on the part of Staples' customers, large and small, took its toll in FY2009, especially on the newly acquired Corporate Express business. Although FY2010 brought lingering cost-cutting effects on the business, for the most part the year was a different story. The Delivery division, which includes Corporate Express, picked up and was delivering low single-digit gains by the end of the year. Although the timing of the Corporate Express acquisition, which added about $5 billion annually to the top line, could have been better, the integration went well and was considered to be less expensive than originally projected.

The company reported $24.5 billion in sales for FY2010 with earnings of $1.21 per share, both modest gains from the FY2009 pullback. The company is guiding for $25.5 billion in FY2011, delivering earnings in the $1.50–$1.60 range, a healthy gain based on improved economic conditions, success with Staples-branded products, rollout of Tech Services at some stores, lower interest costs and tax rates, and a modest improvement in gross margins.

Reasons to Buy

In our view, Staples is still the best brand in this business, and the company has been doing a lot of the right things to leverage that brand, including the clever "That Was Easy" advertising campaign.

The Corporate Express acquisition, while untimely, gives the company broader access to key markets and key countries, leverages supply chain and purchasing power advantages, and at least at present, offers broader service than its competitors. The company also has stronger financials than its competition. Finally, we like the international expansion opportunities; the company has capitalized well so far but has a long and likely successful road in front of it.

Reasons for Caution

Consumer (and corporate) spending will likely remain soft for some time. Saturation in North America is also a risk, as many existing cities and suburbs have all the office supply superstore coverage they need. This is especially true in a soft market with competition from the likes of Wal-Mart and warehouse club stores. Finally, we've seen active pursuit of acquisitions in the past, and are wary of overdependence on acquisitions going forward.

SECTOR: **Retail**
BETA COEFFICIENT: **0.85**
10-YEAR COMPOUND EARNINGS PER SHARE GROWTH: **13.5%**
10-YEAR COMPOUND DIVIDENDS PER SHARE GROWTH: **NM**

	2003	2004	2005	2006	2007	2008	2009	2010
Revenues (Mil)	13,181	14,448	16,079	18,161	19,373	23,084	24,275	24,545
Net Income (Mil)	552	708	834	974	996	924	794	882
Earnings per share	0.75	0.93	1.04	1.32	1.38	1.29	1.10	1.21
Dividends per share	–	–	0.13	0.17	0.29	0.33	0.33	0.36
Cash flow per share	1.11	1.33	1.56	1.79	1.98	2.06	1.85	1.91
Price: high	18.6	22.5	24.1	28	27.7	26.6	25.1	26.0
low	10.5	15.8	18.6	21.1	19.7	13.6	14.4	17.5

Staples, Inc.
500 Staples Drive
Framingham, MA 01702
(800) 468-7751
Website: *www.staples.com*

AGGRESSIVE GROWTH

Starbucks Corporation

Ticker symbol: SBUX (NASDAQ) ❑ **S&P rating: BBB+** ❑ **Value Line financial strength rating: A** ❑
Current yield: 1.6%

Company Profile

Starbucks Corporation, formed in 1985, is the leading retailer, roaster, and brand of specialty coffee in the world. The company sells whole bean coffees through its retailers, its specialty sales group, and supermarkets. The company has 6,706 company-owned stores in the United States and 2,184 in international markets, in addition to 88,139 licensed stores worldwide. Retail sales constitute the bulk of its revenue. Note that the company-owned store count is actually down, as the company went through a modest downsizing to close 600 low-performing stores, a gutsy move in the retail sector. Note also that the company does not franchise its stores—all are either company owned or operated by licensees in special venues like airports, college campuses, and other places where access is restricted.

Starbucks also has joint ventures with Pepsi-Cola and Dreyer's to develop bottled coffee drinks and coffee-flavored ice creams. All channels outside the company-operated retail stores are collectively known as specialty operations.

The company's retail goal is to become the leading retailer and brand of coffee in each of its target markets through product quality and by providing a unique Starbucks experience, which the company defines as a third place beyond home and work. The "experience" is built upon superior customer service and a clean, well-maintained retail store that reflects the personality of the community in which it operates, thereby building a high degree of customer loyalty.

The company's specialty operations strive to develop the Starbucks brand outside the company-operated retail store environment through a number of channels, with a strategy to reach customers where they work, travel, shop, and dine. The strategy employs various models, including licensing arrangements, foodservice accounts, and other initiatives related to the company's core businesses.

In its licensed retail store operations, the company leverages the expertise of its local partners, and shares Starbucks operating and store development experience. As part of these arrangements, Starbucks receives license fees and royalties and sells coffee, tea, and related products for resale in licensed locations.

The company just ended a long-term arrangement with Kraft Foods for distribution of its products into grocery chains and similar. Most likely the company plans to approach the grocery retail market more aggressively and with more products inside and outside the coffee space, including single-serving products and other coffee and non-coffee based beverages.

Financial Highlights, Fiscal Year 2010

Macroeconomic factors combined with a bloated costs structure to bring a pretty dreary 2009 financial and stock price performance; at one point the stock had dropped 80 percent from its highs set just three years prior. This turned out to be a classic buying opportunity, as revenues were off only 6 percent and earnings 15 percent from previous years. Was the "trendy" Starbucks star finally fading? Was a substantial base of clients about to defect to McDonalds to sip coffee on plastic chairs with vanloads of screaming kids in the background? We never really thought so, and we were right.

We were actually surprised that the recession cut into the business as much as it did, for we've thought Starbucks to be one of those little luxuries people could afford no matter what. That wasn't entirely the case, as same-store comps were dropping 5 or 6 percent during the height of the downturn. Since then, comps have come roaring back, and the company reported FY2010 revenues some $1 billion ahead of the previous year, with earnings of $1.28 well ahead of the previous year's $0.80. Modest price hikes, strategic product and store expansion, and a return to macroeconomic tailwinds are expected to bring earnings back to $1.42–$1.47 per share in the company's view; they frequently deliver something better than that view. We also applaud the company's decision to start paying a meaningful dividend during FY2010.

Reasons to Buy

With founder Howard Shultz back at the helm, the company seems to be hitting on all cylinders again. We never thought the downturn to be permanent; the company's stores continue to be more than coffee shops and really that "third place" where professionals, students, moms, and other prosperous people will meet and dole out a few bucks for quality drinks. Beyond the business itself, the concept and the brand are huge assets that have kept most of the competition to small niches and probably will continue to do so. The company has a steadily (and profitably) growing presence in Europe, Japan, and China. The company plans to target the majority of its near-term growth outside the U.S. market, which may be approaching saturation. The company's financials are solid, and it just sent a strong signal of attention to shareholder returns with the dividend and the willingness to "ungrow" for a couple of years to get its house in order.

Reasons for Caution

It's not completely clear that consumer tastes have not been permanently affected by the recent recession. It may well be that coffee drinkers have learned to get along without the $5 latte and are now just $1.50 drippers. Spending per visit is a stat that will bear watching as the economy continues to turn around—revenues may have a lid on them now. There is some risk that the company won't take root quite as well on the international front, but things seem to be going okay so far.

SECTOR: **Restaurant**
BETA COEFFICIENT: **1.25**
10-YEAR COMPOUND EARNINGS PER SHARE GROWTH: **21.5%**
10-YEAR COMPOUND DIVIDENDS PER SHARE GROWTH: **NM**

	2003	2004	2005	2006	2007	2008	2009	2010
Revenues (Mil)	4,076	5,294	6,369	7,787	9,412	10,383	9,774	10,707
Net Income (Mil)	268	392	495	519	673	525	598	982.5
Earnings per share	0.34	0.48	0.61	0.73	0.87	0.71	0.8	1.28
Dividends per share	0	0	0	0	0	0	0	0.52
Cash flow per share	0.64	0.85	1.09	1.28	1.54	1.46	1.53	2.00
Price: high	16.7	32.1	32.5	40	36.6	21	24.5	31.3
low	9.8	16.5	22.3	28.7	19.9	7.1	21.3	21.3

Starbucks Corporation
2401 Utah Avenue South
Seattle, WA 98134
(206) 447-1575
Website: *www.starbucks.com*

AGGRESSIVE GROWTH

Stryker Corporation

Ticker symbol: SYK (NYSE) ❑ S&P rating: A+ ❑ Value Line financial strength rating: A++ ❑ Current yield: 1.2%

Company Profile

Stryker Corporation was founded in 1941 by Dr. Homer H. Stryker, a leading orthopedic surgeon and the inventor of several orthopedic products. The company now ranks as a dominant player in a $12 billion global orthopedics industry. The Orthopaedic Products segment, comprising about 61 percent of sales, has a significant market share in such "spare parts" as artificial hips, prosthetic knees, craniomaxillofacial implants, and trauma products.

The MediSurg unit, about 39 percent of sales, develops, manufactures, and markets worldwide products such as orthopedic implants, trauma systems, powered surgical instruments, endoscopic systems, and patient care and handling equipment.

Stryker's revenue is split roughly 60/40 among implants and equipment and 64/36 domestic and international. The company has been recently active in acquisitions, and in late 2010 announced the acquisition of Boston Scientific's Neurovascular Division for about $1.5 billion in cash. The company also announced the acquisition of the Porex Surgical business, makers of porous polyethylene products for implants.

Financial Highlights, Fiscal Year 2010

The company reported FY2010 sales of $7.32 billion, a healthy increase over FY2009's $6.7 billion. Earnings came in at the top of previous guidance at $3.30 per share. The company also announced a 20 percent dividend increase and a $500 million share repurchase program, which would reduce share counts about 2.5 percent at current prices. For FY2011, the company sees currency-adjusted sales growth in the 11–13 percent range, including the new Neurovascular business, or 5–7 percent without currency and the acquisitions, for a revenue base just across the $8 billion line. Earnings are projected in the $3.65–$3.70 range.

Reasons to Buy

Stryker's top-line is driven largely by elective surgeries, and 2009 turned out to be the year for delaying whatever medical procedures could be delayed. Many consumers decided to wait and see how the medical care legislation would turn out, and some were simply deciding to hold on to their cash until economic conditions improved. The good news for Stryker is twofold: Medical care reform did not significantly increase the cost to consumers of implant surgeries; and those dodgy hips aren't getting any better and eventually will need to be replaced. In fact, joint-replacement surgeries started to rebound in late 2009 and have continued the pace in FY2010 and early FY2011.

Hospitals and other institutions were under many of the same economic pressures as consumers and simply delayed many of the big-ticket purchases that had been planned for 2009. Stryker's Medical/Surgical equipment sales were off 5 percent in 2009, but came back well in 2010.

Stryker is the number one player in the orthopedic niche, and we like niche dominance as a guiding principle in selecting companies. The niche is important especially in an aging demographic, and aging demographics in overseas markets should bode well for the company's future. Financials are solid, and there were many buying opportunities along the way in 2009 and 2010, which could easily be repeated.

Reasons for Caution

Ongoing scrutiny of health care costs and continued reliance on acquisitions to fuel growth bring risks to the company, but we don't think the risks are excessive.

SECTOR: **Health Care**
BETA COEFFICIENT: **.91**
10-YEAR COMPOUND EARNINGS PER SHARE GROWTH: **22.0%**
10-YEAR COMPOUND DIVIDENDS PER SHARE GROWTH: **27.0%**

	2003	2004	2005	2006	2007	2008	2009	2010
Revenues (Mil)	3,625	4,262	4,872	5,406	6,001	6,718	6,723	7,320
Net Income (Mil)	454	586	644	778	1,017	1,148	1,107	1,330
Earnings per share	1.12	1.43	1.57	1.89	2.44	2.78	2.77	3.33
Dividends per share	0.07	0.09	0.11	0.11	0.22	0.33	0.50	0.60
Cash flow per share	1.71	2.08	2.49	2.85	3.33	3.87	3.75	4.40
Price: high	42.7	57.7	56.3	55.9	76.9	74.9	52.7	59.7
low	29.9	40.3	39.7	39.8	54.9	35.4	30.8	42.7

Stryker Corporation
P. O. Box 4085
Kalamazoo, MI 49003–4085
(616) 385-2600
Website: *www.strykercorp.com*

INCOME

Suburban Propane Partners, L.P.

Ticker symbol: SPH (NYSE) ❑ S&P rating: BB ❑ Value Line financial strength rating: B+ ❑ Current yield: 6.0%

Company Profile

You probably know this company best for its propane distribution business and the white sausage-shaped tanks dotting the landscape, especially in rural areas, and for the trucks serving them. Suburban Propane Partners, L.P., through its subsidiaries, engages in the retail marketing and distribution of propane, fuel oil, and refined fuels, and to a lesser extent, in the marketing of natural gas and electricity in the United States.

The Propane segment is the largest segment, and engages in the retail distribution of propane to residential, commercial, industrial, and agricultural customers, as well as wholesale distribution to large industrial end users. The Fuel Oil and Refined Fuels segment engages in the retail distribution of fuel oil, diesel, kerosene, and gasoline to residential and commercial customers for use primarily as a source of heat in homes and buildings, primarily in the East, while the Natural Gas and Electricity segment markets those commodities to residential and commercial customers in the deregulated energy markets of New York and Pennsylvania.

Suburban Propane Partners, L.P., is also involved in selling and servicing heating, ventilation, and air conditioning (HVAC) units that consume its fuels. As of September 2010, the company served approximately 800,000 residential, commercial, industrial, and agricultural customers through approximately 300 locations in thirty states, concentrated in the East and West Coast regions of the United States, including Alaska.

Financial Highlights, Fiscal Year 2010

Despite the visibility of the white tanks in the residential segment, Suburban's business is more concentrated in non-residential customers, accounting for some 63 percent of its customer base, and these customers have been hurt by the recession. The recession brought a decline both in volumes and in selling prices, with propane gallonage dropping some 7.6 percent through FY2010 from the year before. At the same time, input costs began to rise with energy prices in general in FY2010, putting a pretty tight squeeze on profits. The company booked $1.14

billion in sales in FY2010, comparable to FY2009, but off almost 28 percent from the demand and price-cycle highs in 2008. Earnings came in at $3.26, reflecting a steady modest decline in place for three years, excepting 2008.

This may all seem like bad news, and it is to a degree, but the company had the advantage of strong financials behind its back. Cost-cutting efforts and a relatively strong cash position and cash flow position covered the generous payout with no real concerns, and the company was able to raise the payout, albeit slightly, for the nineteenth consecutive year in early 2011. As 2011 unfolds, colder than normal weather and a stabilizing macroeconomic environment have brought cautious optimism.

Reasons to Buy

The main draw with companies like Suburban Propane is the high, steady, and growing dividend. SPH pays out between 70 and 95 percent of its earnings each year as dividends, although the payout ratio slightly exceeded 100 percent of earnings, but still only about 80 percent of cash flow. In such an arrangement, shareholders are treated like true owners.

Customers who use propane are likely to continue doing so, and propane commodity prices appear to be relatively steady and predictable. Suburban Propane and many of its peers appeal to investors who want the relative safety and security of a utility dividend, but don't want to be exposed to such things as regulatory agencies, nuclear power, high power plant development costs, environmental issues, and other complexities inherent in running a big utility company

Reasons for Caution

As previously mentioned, the recession has hit small businesses hard, and many of these users may be gone for good. There don't appear to be any substantial growth drivers in the form of new propane users on the horizon, although the company has made a few "bolt on" acquisitions in key markets to leverage its operating platform. Additionally, low natural gas prices may motivate some customers, especially in urban fringe areas, to switch away from propane. Suburban should be looked at as a utility, with a relatively steady customer base and a high payout from earnings. This issue should be bought for income, not for price appreciation.

SECTOR: **Utilities**
BETA COEFFICIENT: **0.45**
10-YEAR COMPOUND EARNINGS PER SHARE GROWTH: **16.5%**
10-YEAR COMPOUND DIVIDENDS PER SHARE GROWTH: **7.0%**

		2003	2004	2005	2006	2007	2008	2009	2010
Revenues (Mil)		771.7	1,307.3	1,620.2	1,661.6	1,439.6	1,574.2	1,143.2	1,136.7
Net Income (Mil)		46.2	28.9	(9.1)	90.7	123.3	111.2	165.2	115.2
Earnings per share		1.76	.96	(.29)	2.84	3.79	3.39	4.99	3.26
Dividends per share		2.33	2.41	2.45	2.50	2.69	3.14	3.28	3.37
Cash flow per share		3.70	2.17	.92	4.09	4.66	4.26	5.55	4.13
Price:	high	32.5	35.7	37.4	39.2	49.6	42.6	47.7	57.2
	Low	26.9	27.6	23.5	26.0	35.1	20.4	31.0	39.2

Suburban Propane Partners, L.P.
240 Route 10 West
Whippany, NJ 07981
(973) 887-5300
Website: *www.suburbanpropane.com*

CONSERVATIVE GROWTH

Sysco Corporation

Ticker symbol: SYY (NYSE) ❑ S&P rating: A+ ❑ Value Line financial strength rating: A++ ❑
Current yield: 3.7%

Company Profile

Sysco is the leading marketer and distributor of food, food products, and related equipment and supplies to the foodservice industry. The company distributes fresh and frozen meats, prepared entrées, vegetables, canned and dried foods, dairy products, beverages, and produce, as well as paper products, restaurant equipment and supplies, and cleaning supplies. The company might be familiar for its "institutional" number ten-sized cans of food found in many high-volume kitchens, but the product line and customer base is much larger, including many specialty and chain restaurants, lodges, hotels, hospitals, schools, and other distribution centers across the country. If you eat out at all, you've most likely consumed Sysco-distributed products.

Sysco was founded in 1969 with the goal of becoming a national foodservice network. By 1977, the company had become the largest foodservice supplier in North America, a position they have retained for more than thirty years. They conduct business in over 100 countries.

Sysco operates 186 distribution facilities across the United States, Canada, and Ireland. Their ninety-nine Broadline facilities supply independent and chain restaurants and other food preparation facilities with a wide variety of food and non-food products. They have seventeen hotel supply locations, sixteen specialty produce facilities, twenty SYGMA distribution centers (specialized, high-volume centers supplying to chain restaurants), twelve custom-cutting meat locations, and two distributors specializing in the niche Asian foodservice market.

The company also supplies the hotel industry with guest amenities, equipment, housekeeping supplies, room accessories, and textiles.

Most people are unaware of just how many times during the day they cross paths with Sysco's products and services. Sysco's distribution facilities provide over 400,000 different food and related products (including 40,000 with Sysco brands) to over 400,000 restaurants, hotels, schools, hospitals, retirement homes, hotels, and other locations where food is prepared.

Sysco is by far the largest company in the foodservice distribution industry. The company estimates that they serve about 16 percent of a

$231 billion annual market. Sysco's sales dwarfs those of its two chief competitors, US Foodservice and Performance Food Group.

Financial Highlights, Fiscal Year 2010 (ended June 2010)

The recession hit the restaurant industry hard, and FY2009 sales dropped 1.8 percent from the prior year, not too bad considering the large number of restaurants that disappeared from the landscape. The restaurant business, and particularly some of the larger chains, continued to cut back in 2010, but Sysco managed to recover about half the business lost during the previous year.

Cost-cutting measures and moderating commodity prices gave the company a bit of an earnings tailwind; combined with share buybacks (2 percent of float), per share earnings rose from $1.77 to $1.99. The company took the opportunity to raise the dividend to $1.04 per share per year, a nice gesture to shareholders. The company's shares, however, got "cooked" in February 2011 with an announcement of projected margin pressures due to rising commodity prices; in particular, double-digit cost increases in meat, dairy, and seafood prices were in clear contrast to slight deflation seen the year before. FY2011 Q2 earnings came in slightly below expectations at $.44 versus an expectation of $.47. The stock lost 6 percent of its value over the announcement, but the company did not announce any guidance other than to say things would be a bit more "choppy."

Reasons to Buy

Sysco continues to be a dominant player in a niche that won't go away anytime soon. While near-term commodity prices may add some cost pressure, the value of the franchise and near-term sales should remain unchanged; we think the worst is over for the recession and that any such recurrence in the future should only temporarily slow the business.

Sysco keeps margins high by selling products under its own label, a strategy it began a year after its founding. Its private-label business carries an estimated 24 percent gross margin, or 10 percent more than it earns on national brands. This is a very healthy figure in the food industry.

Sysco's recent investments in technology continue to bear fruit. Improvements in routing and inventory management have allowed the company to increase its shipment frequency by 10 percent with 4 percent fewer people, all while using 10 percent less fuel. Shipments per man-hour are up 15 percent, cases per trip are up 2 percent and errors are down 3 percent, according to the company.

The foodservice business is highly fragmented. Sysco is the largest player with approximately 17 percent market share, and over half the market is split among companies holding less than 1 percent each. This would be a good time to grow market share through acquisition, and Sysco's balance sheet is solid. Of interest is the fact that in the past two years Sysco's two largest competitors were bought and taken private by equity firms.

In sum, this is a steady and safe company with a healthy payout to customers, and has experienced some price dips giving good buying opportunities.

Reasons for Caution

Although the trend is slowing, the recession got many folks away from the habit of eating out, and restaurants and hotels are buying less food and fewer supplies and equipment. Many restaurants disappeared altogether, although we expect that better times will bring most back in some form. Investors seeking rapid growth might want to look somewhere outside of this steady and rather unsexy business.

SECTOR: **Consumer Staples**
BETA COEFFICIENT: **.73**
10-YEAR COMPOUND EARNINGS PER SHARE GROWTH: **12.5%**
10-YEAR COMPOUND DIVIDENDS PER SHARE GROWTH: **17.0%**

	2003	2004	2005	2006	2007	2008	2009	2010
Revenues (Mil)	26,140	29,335	30,282	32,628	35,042	37,522	36,853	37,243
Net Income (Mil)	778	907	961	855	1,001	1,106	1,056	1,181
Earnings per share	1.18	1.37	1.47	1.35	1.6	1.81	1.77	1.99
Dividends per share	0.4	0.48	0.58	0.66	0.72	0.82	0.93	0.99
Cash flow per share	1.63	1.87	2.03	1.92	2.23	2.46	2.44	2.67
Price: high	37.6	41.3	38.4	37	36.7	35	29.5	32.6
low	22.9	29.5	30	26.5	29.9	20.7	19.4	27.0

Sysco Corporation
1390 Enclave Parkway
Houston, TX 77077–2099
(281) 584-1458
Website: *www.sysco.com*

Target Corporation

Ticker symbol: TGT (NYSE) ❑ S&P rating: A+ ❑ Value Line financial strength rating: A ❑ Current yield: 1.9 percent

Company Profile

Target is the nation's second-largest general merchandise retailer, and specializes in general merchandise at a discount in a large store format. The company now operates nearly 1,740 stores in forty-nine states, including 251 "Super Targets," which also carry a broad line of groceries. The greatest concentration of Target stores is in California, Texas, and Florida, with a combined total of about 30 percent of the stores. There is another concentration in the upper Midwest. With the sale of Marshall Field and Mervyn's in 2004, the company has focused completely on discount retail in store locations and on the Internet. In 2000, the company formed "target.direct," the direct merchandising and electronic retailing organization. The business combines the e-commerce team of Target with its direct merchandising unit into one integrated organization. The target. direct organization operates seven websites, which support the store and catalog brands in an online environment and produces six retail catalogs.

Target positions itself against its main competitor, Wal-Mart, as a more upscale and trend-conscious "cheap chic" alternative. The typical Target customer has a higher level of disposable income, which the company courts by offering brand name merchandise in addition to a series of largely successful house brands like Michael Graves and Archer Farms. The company's revenues come from retail sales and credit card operations. Target is one of the few retailers that still finance its in-house credit operations, although in-house credit operations have given the company some problems in tougher times. The company has been looking to sell the receivables and financing operations while still maintaining operational control of the in-house credit name.

Financial Highlights, Fiscal Year 2010 (ended January 31, 2011)

Target took some lumps during the recession, but the strong value proposition of quality for less resonated well with most customers. Although comparable same-store sales were off slightly, store openings kept revenues growing at a modest, low single-digits clip between FY2007 and FY2010. In the second half of FY2010, comparable same-store sales began to improve into the 2–4 percent range on the way to an overall 4 percent revenue increase. While margins have remained steady, a reduction in bad debt losses and some new creative merchandising initiatives brought substantial earnings improvement to $3.88 per share in FY2010, an 18 percent rise. Cash flow has been strong, at almost $7.00 per share in FY2010, and the company has been very aggressive with share repurchases, buying back 25 million shares in FY2010 and some 230 million shares since 2003 to get to an estimated 690 million share count by the end of 2011. The company also reduced long-term debt by $300 million during the year.

Reasons to Buy

Although 2010 started out slow, the fourth quarter numbers were impressive and should provide some momentum for TGT. The company recovered very quickly from the downturn. Moreover, Target has some of the highest customer satisfaction numbers in the industry. The company continues to take share away from specialty retailers in home lines, clothing, children's items, and other areas. People like the Target brand and associate it with quality and good taste at a reasonable price, and more recently have come to make regular and frequent visits to the store because of the grocery department.

Target is also introducing a new store format called PFresh, which is very much like their Super Target in terms of items, but in a smaller format. They will carry 90 percent of the grocery items that a Super Target carries, but the space devoted to the grocery area will be about 40 percent smaller. Grocery traffic may not require the amount of space that has been allocated in the Super Targets, and a "deli" atmosphere may in fact be more conducive to impulse sales.

Improved economic conditions should improve Target's market share. Trend data indicates that Target performs better than its competitors during periods of economic growth. As consumer confidence improves through 2011, we expect Target to get the larger share of consumer spending growth. The company has guided fairly conservatively for 2011, but the company has delivered steady and solid results for so long that we believe the near-term news will continue to be good. Of course, we find the share repurchase activity combined with a reasonable dividend payout for a retailer to be quite an attractive combination.

Reasons for Caution

Target is up against some very tough competitors in Wal-Mart,

Costco, and others. Also, these two competitors are growing their international presence, while Target, other than Canada, has none and has no plans for growth outside the United States. Target is tied more closely to the domestic consumer market, consumer confidence, and access to credit than either of its major competitors. We also see some risk in the grocery business, as groceries are very low margin and the company hasn't really figured out how to make the grocery offering complete with meats and fresh produce. Also, the credit card business is still a bit of a question mark.

SECTOR: Retail
BETA COEFFICIENT: 0.96
10-YEAR COMPOUND EARNINGS PER SHARE GROWTH: 12.0%
10-YEAR COMPOUND DIVIDENDS PER SHARE GROWTH: 12.5%

		2003	2004	2005	2006	2007	2008	2009	2010
Revenues (Mil)		48,163	46,839	52,620	59,490	63,367	64,948	63,435	67,390
Net Income (Mil)		1,841	1,885	2,408	2,787	2,849	2,214	2,488	2,830
Earnings per share		2.01	2.07	2.71	3.21	3.33	2.86	3.3	3.88
Dividends per share		0.26	0.3	0.38	0.42	0.56	0.6	0.66	0.74
Cash flow per share		3.47	3.53	4.37	4.98	5.51	5.37	5.9	6.98
Price:	high	41.8	54.1	60	60.3	70.8	59.6	51.8	60.7
	low	25.6	36.6	45.6	44.7	48.8	25.6	25	46.2

Target Corporation
1000 Nicollet Mall
Minneapolis, MN 55403
(612) 370-6735
Website: *www.target.com*

Teva Pharmaceutical Industries, Ltd.

Ticker symbol: TEVA (NASDAQ) ❑ S&P rating: A- ❑ Value Line financial strength rating: A ❑ Current yield: 1.5%

Company Profile

Teva was founded in Jerusalem in 1901 as Salomon, Levin and Elstein, Ltd., a small wholesale drug business that imported medicines, loaded them onto the backs of camels and donkeys, and distributed them to customers throughout the area. Teva is now among the top fifteen pharmaceutical companies in the world and is the largest generic pharmaceutical company.

The company develops, manufactures, and markets generic and proprietary pharmaceuticals and active pharmaceutical ingredients.

Teva's generic portfolio is extensive—in the United States. Teva USA markets nearly 400 generic pharmaceuticals in 1,300 dosage levels. Its innovative drug line is far smaller, but includes some widely prescribed and very profitable medications, including Copaxone (for the treatment of multiple sclerosis) and Azilect (for early and late-stage Parkinson's disease). The company also makes and markets a line of respiratory products for asthma, allergic rhinitis, and chronic obstructive pulmonary disease, and another line of women's health products including traditional and emergency oral contraceptives. Finally, the company also makes biopharmaceutical products including white blood cell stimulating factors for oncology and human growth hormone for children with growth hormone deficiency, among others.

The company has over sixty manufacturing and marketing facilities worldwide, with the bulk of its operations located in Europe, the United States, and Israel. Over 56 percent of Teva's sales are in North America and 85 percent in North America and Western Europe combined. The company is headquartered in Israel and shares trade as American Depository Receipts in the United States.

Financial Highlights, Fiscal Year 2010

Teva turned in yet another record year in FY2010, with sales up almost 16 percent to $16.1 billion, after a 25 percent gain in FY2009. Earnings rose to $4.55 per share, a gain of 35 percent over the previous year. The year was nothing if not successful. Almost $3.3 billion of sales were from Copaxone alone. Sales were up significantly across all product lines and geographies.

For FY2011, the company projects net sales between $18.5 billion and $19 billion with earnings in the range of $4.90 to $5.25, a bit lower than analyst estimates. One factor appears to be a new competitor for the Copaxone drug. On the other hand, the company has some 206 products, mostly generics, awaiting FDA approval. The branded product equivalents had $121 billion in sales in total. Some 134 of these applications are "Paragraph IV" patent challenges to branded products; if the company wins the cases, the revenue opportunities are large.

Reasons to Buy

Teva is the largest player in the volume-driven generic drug industry. Teva estimates that it supplies 16 percent of all prescriptions written in the United States, nearly twice as many as its next closest competitor (Mylan Labs). As previously mentioned, the pipeline of new product applications awaiting approval is large and lucrative. Strategically, the company intends to expand distribution of the generics worldwide, to start offering biogenerics, and to enrich its portfolio of proprietary medications.

The U.S. medical care reform bill included at least two provisions that should keep Teva shareholders happy. First was the decision not to allow imported prescription drugs into the United States. This will assure drug marketers of continued high margins for U.S.-based sales, and the United States accounts for the majority of Teva's sales. The second was a provision that left intact the negotiation process whereby pharmaceutical patent holders could pay generic manufacturers not to develop competing products for a set period of time. We'd like to get in on that—we tried not growing corn but we failed.

Over the past five years, the company's sales have grown 17 percent compounded, and earnings, cash flow, and dividends have all delivered compounded growth rates exceeding 20 percent. We see no real reason why this won't continue for a while. The company is in outstanding financial shape, with ample cash flow and credit for future acquisitions and funding of internal R&D.

Reasons for Caution

Teva's success is greatly affected by their ability to prevail in so-called "Paragraph IV" patent challenges— challenges to the exclusivity rights granted to the patent holder by the FDA. As of early 2011, 134 of Teva's nearly 206 product applications to the FDA were Paragraph IV applications. These applications tend to have a slow and uncertain outcome. The company has also relied heavily on Copaxone; many think the dominance of that drug in the MS market may be on the wane as Novartis rolls out its orally administered Gilenia drug. Recently, this risk has held the stock price back somewhat, but patient investors should focus on the big picture and regard such slowdowns as a buying opportunity. Also, in contrast to most of the companies on our *100 Best* list, Teva has been adding to share counts to make acquisitions, a practice that is not among our favorites for long-term performance. We would like to see the company use its cash flow to buy back some of those shares.

SECTOR: **Health Care**
BETA COEFFICIENT: **.21**
5-YEAR COMPOUND EARNINGS PER SHARE GROWTH: **22.0%**
5-YEAR COMPOUND DIVIDENDS PER SHARE GROWTH: **26.5%**

	2003	**2004**	**2005**	**2006**	**2007**	**2008**	**2009**	**2010**
Revenues (Mil)	3,276	4,799	5,250	8,400	9,408	11,085	13,899	16,121
Net Income (Mil)	691	965	1,072	1,867	1,952	2,374	3,029	4,134
Earnings per share	1.04	1.42	1.59	2.3	2.38	2.86	3.37	4.54
Dividends per share	0.14	0.16	0.27	0.3	0.39	0.49	0.60	0.74
Cash flow per share	1.36	1.94	2.13	3.03	3.22	3.37	4.45	5.70
Price: high	31.2	34.7	45.9	44.7	47.1	50	56.9	64.9
low	17.3	22.8	26.8	29.2	30.8	35.9	41.1	47.0

Teva Pharmaceutical Industries, Ltd.
·5 Basel Street
P.O. Box 3190
Petach Tikva
Israel 49131
(215) 591-8912
Website: *www.tevapharm.com*

Total S.A. (ADRs)

Ticker symbol: TOT (NYSE) □ S&P rating: AA □ Value Line financial strength rating: A++ □ Current yield: 5.3 percent

Company Profile

Total S.A. (S.A. is short for "Société Anonyme," which is the French equivalent of "incorporated") is the fifth-largest publicly traded oil and gas company in the world. Headquartered in France and primarily traded on the French CAC stock exchange, the company has operations in more than 130 countries. Total is vertically integrated with upstream operations engaged in oil and gas exploration and downstream operations engaged in refining and distribution of petroleum products; the company also has a chemicals subsidiary.

Upstream activities are geographically well diversified, with exploration occurring in forty countries and production occurring in thirty of them. Many of the E&P projects are done through partnerships to spread risk. The largest production regions are (in production volume sequence) in the North Sea, North Africa, and the Middle East, with smaller operations in Southeast Asia and North and South America. Liquids account for about 61 percent of production, while natural gas is 39 percent. The company is a leader in the emerging liquefied natural gas (LNG) market for export. The company has had good results in the exploration and production side, somewhat better than the industry, with production up 6 percent, led by an 18 percent increase in gas output.

Downstream operations are also worldwide and centered in Europe. Operations include twenty-five refineries worldwide, with eleven refineries and 85 percent of the company's total refining capacity in Europe. Total also operates 16,425 service stations, again weighted toward Europe and North Africa. The downstream presence is also growing in Asia Pacific (including China), Latin America, and the Caribbean. The company is currently building a new major refinery in Saudi Arabia to come on-line in 2013.

Financial Highlights, Fiscal Year 2010

The decline in energy prices and worldwide demand led to an "off" year in FY2009, with revenues slumping to a five-year low of $157 billion and earnings to $5.31 a share. FY2010 revenues recovered to the 2007 level preceding the

2008 oil price spike, with earnings of $6.25 per share and cash flows of about $10.65 per share. Total pays dividends in euros, so following dollar denominated dividends from year to year can be tricky, but weeding out this anomaly, dividend growth has been a healthy 19.5 percent over the past ten years and looks to continue at a healthy pace.

Reasons to Buy

Total S.A. is a solid energy sector play with many of the features that make "big energy" attractive—namely strong cash flows and high dividend yields and demand that isn't going away anytime soon. Companies with a price-to-cash-flow ratio under 5, implying a 20 percent annual cash return, aren't easy to find. In addition, Total provides a stronger international play than other energy picks on our list. The company has a dominant position in Europe, which albeit isn't growing but is a steady market, producing plenty of cash flow while allowing the company to dabble in more promising markets like China and others in Asia Pacific and Latin America. Energy prices, at least at this writing, are on the rise, and Total is well positioned to take advantage of higher prices for their production as well as recent strength in the refining business. Finally, those believing that the dollar will weaken longer term, particularly against the euro, will like the fact that the dividend is paid in euros, which would translate favorably to ever-cheaper dollars.

Reasons for Caution

The European economy may still have some speed bumps ahead of it. We also remain cautious on investing in foreign companies because of differences in management style and accounting rules; they aren't necessarily bad but are difficult to understand and follow. Typically, we prefer U.S. companies that do a lot of business overseas. We feel the strengths of Total overcome these concerns.

SECTOR: Energy
BETA COEFFICIENT: 0.90
10-YEAR COMPOUND EARNINGS PER SHARE GROWTH: 19.0%
10-YEAR COMPOUND DIVIDENDS PER SHARE GROWTH: 19.5%

		2003	2004	2005	2006	2007	2008	2009	2010
Revenues (Mil)		107,837	153,375	144,689	167,188	167,149	236,087	157,014	186,131
Net Income (Mil)		7,624	11,118	14,302	15,463	16,718	18,205	11,626	14,006
Earnings per share		3.11	4.49	6.41	6.82	7.35	8.55	5.31	6.24
Dividends per share		1.17	2.19	1.83	2.10	2.81	3.10	3.28	2.93
Cash flow per share		5.79	7.42	9.72	9.60	10.73	12.42	9.49	11.25
Price:	high	46.7	55.3	69.0	73.8	87.3	91.3	66.0	67.5
	low	30.5	43.8	51.9	58.1	63.9	42.6	42.9	43.1

TOTAL, S.A.
2, Place de la Coupole
La Defense 6 92400 Courbevole, France
(713) 483-5070 (U.S.)
Website: *www.total.com*

AGGRESSIVE GROWTH

Tractor Supply Company

Ticker symbol: TSCO (NASDAQ) ❑ S&P rating: not rated ❑ Value Line financial strength rating: A+
❑ Current yield: 1.0%

Company Profile

Tractor Supply Company is the largest operator of retail farm and ranch stores in the United States. Their focus is on the needs of recreational farmers and ranchers and those who enjoy the rural lifestyle, as well as tradesmen and small businesses. They operate retail stores, many in a "big-box" format, under the names Tractor Supply Company and Del's Farm Supply. Their stores are located in towns outside major metropolitan markets and in rural communities. Representative merchandise includes supplies for horses, pets, and other farm animals, equipment maintenance products, hardware and tools, lawn and garden equipment, and work and recreational clothing and footwear.

Tractor Supply stores typically range in size from 15,500 square feet to 18,500 square feet of inside selling space and additional outside selling space. As of December 2010, they operated just over 1,000 retail farm and ranch stores in forty-four states. Del's Farm Supply operates twenty-seven stores, primarily in the Pacific Northwest, offering a wide selection of products (primarily in the horse, pet, and animal category)

targeted at those who enjoy the rural lifestyle. The company does not plan to grow Del's significantly beyond its current size.

For FY2010, sales were divided between the following segments: livestock and pet products (39 percent); seasonal products like mowers and snow blowers (23 percent); tool, truck, and towing products (18 percent); clothing and footwear (10 percent); and agriculture (8 percent). Tractor Supply Company also sells a subset of its store goods online.

Financial Highlights, Fiscal Year 2010

Tractor Supply continued on its post-recession recovery, with a 13.4 percent sales increase in sales to $3.6 billion anchored by a same-store sales growth rate exceeding 4.5 percent. Driven in part by sales of branded feed lines and other consumables, operating margins improved from 7.8 percent to 9.2 percent on a gross margin increase from 32.3 to 33.1 percent, both sizeable figures and sizeable increases in the big-box retail world. The company expects further gross and operating margin improvements through better inventory management, private-label brands, and other initiatives, and expects a FY2011 earnings per share increase in the 16 percent neighborhood on top of FY2010's 42 percent. The company has bought back about 10 percent of its shares since 2006 and plans modest buybacks going forward. Additionally, it paid its first cash dividend—$.28—in FY2010.

Reasons to Buy

TSCO serves a growing, specialized niche in geographies often ignored by other retailers. They carry a specialized mix of merchandise that occupies a broad space—part big-box hardware, part garden shop, and part feed store. Their unique target market nonetheless has broad geographic distribution, giving TSCO room for growth, and they plan to grow more than 10 percent a year, with a target of 1,800 units.

TSCO's financials are rock solid, with practically zero debt. They have learned how to fund growth organically, and have put 450 stores on the ground in the past seven years without incurring debt, and have amassed $273 million in cash besides, again an unusual feat in the mass retail world. The company has scored high double-digit growth in sales, profits, and cash flow, and the dividend initiation rounds out this success story.

TSCO carries a higher percentage of house brands than you would find at a typical hardware retailer. They earn higher gross margins on these products and build rebuy loyalty in the process.

Reasons for Caution

There's not a lot holding them back at this point. TSCO's growth is bound to attract competition. The sooner they can build out to their target size, the better they will be able to protect margins. The stock has performed very well in the past three years, so investors may want to choose their entry points carefully.

SECTOR: **Retail**
BETA COEFFICIENT: **0.95**
10-YEAR COMPOUND EARNINGS PER SHARE GROWTH: **21.5%**
10-YEAR COMPOUND DIVIDENDS PER SHARE GROWTH: **NM**

	2003	2004	2005	2006	2007	2008	2009	2010
Revenues (Mil)	1,473	1,739	2,068	2,370	2,703	3,008	3,207	3,638
Net Income (Mil)	58.4	64.1	85.7	91	96.2	81.9	115.5	168
Earnings per share	0.73	0.79	1.05	1.11	1.20	1.10	1.58	2.25
Dividends per share	–	–	–	–	–	–	–	0.28
Cash flow per share	1.05	1.19	1.52	1.65	1.97	1.99	2.52	3.27
Price: high	44.9	45.8	58.6	67.6	57.7	47.5	54.5	73.1
low	14.7	30.2	33.2	38.8	35.1	26.7	27.8	33.0

Tractor Supply Company
200 Powell Place
Brentwood, TN 37027
(615) 440-4000
Website: *www.tractorsupply.com*

CONSERVATIVE GROWTH

Union Pacific Corporation

Ticker symbol: UNP (NYSE) ◻ S&P rating: BBB+ ◻ Value Line financial strength rating: A ◻ Current yield: 1.6%

Company Profile

Union Pacific has been a familiar name and logo in the railroad business since its inception during the Civil War. With about 32,000 miles of track covering twenty-three states in the western two-thirds of the United States, today's Union Pacific Railroad, the primary subsidiary of the Union Pacific Corporation, describes itself as "America's Premier Railroad Franchise."

With 25,000 customers, a large number in today's era of trainload-sized shipments, UP has a more diversified customer and revenue mix than the other rail companies, including the other three of the "big four" railroads: BNSF, Norfolk Southern, and CSX. Energy (mostly coal from the Powder River Basin area of Wyoming) accounts for 22 percent of revenues; Intermodal (trucks and containers on flatcars), 20 percent; Agricultural, 19 percent; Industrial, 16 percent; Chemicals, 15 percent; and Automotive, 8 percent.

The company has long been an innovator in railroad technology, including motive power, communications and technology automation, physical plant, community relations, and marketing. The company operates with one of the lowest operating ratios in the industry, 70.6 percent, meaning that operating costs account for 70.6 percent of total costs, allowing a good contribution to the substantial fixed costs of owning and running a railroad. This success has translated to a spike in operating margins discussed below.

The company also invests a lot in marketing and community relations. One example is the steam powered excursion train program, where the company operates excursions on selected track segments for the benefit of lineside communities and members of the shipping community. It recently employed Facebook and Twitter to collect 179,000 inputs on where to run the next excursion, a great buzz builder. It also lends support to historic events involving the company, such as the 2009 "With Malice Toward None: The Abraham Lincoln Bicentennial Celebration" exhibition at the Library of Congress. These may seem like fairly ordinary efforts conducted by a major U.S. corporation in the interest of branding and public relations, but for the railroad industry, these activities stretch the envelope, hence the highlighting here.

Railroads have quietly been learning to use technology to improve operations and deliver better customer service. New tools can track shipments door to door, and the railroad will accept shipments and manage them door to door, even over other railroads or with other kinds of carriers. Customers can check rates and routes, and track shipments online. These services, combined with high fuel prices, has led to a migration from trucks back to rail and intermodal rail services.

Financial Highlights, Fiscal Year 2010

Not surprisingly, car loadings sagged in FY2009, with revenues taking about a 21 percent dip from the banner year of 2008 and earnings taking a similar hit. Although some components of the traffic base, like coal for electric utilities, are relatively stable in bad times, the railroad as previously mentioned serves a diverse industrial and commodity base, and with its service to Pacific Rim ports, is also more sensitive than most to changes in international trade.

An increase in economic activity increases volume and car loadings, which helps not only to generate revenue but also absorb fixed costs more effectively, and at

the same time, strengthens pricing. Railroads must not only compete with each other, but also with trucks, and when capacity is fully utilized, base rates can go up, and the railroad on top of that can use fuel surcharges as a device to at least, if not more than, recover costs. Such was the case in FY2010 and continuing on into FY2011. Revenues were up 20 percent in FY2010 and are projected up another 11 percent in FY2011; earnings were up 53 percent in FY2010 and another 18 percent, to $6.50 per share, in FY2011. A key earnings driver was the increase in operating margins from the high 20s since 2000 to the high 30s in the past two years, which is of course related to cost reductions, the pricing environment, and volume.

The company has been aggressive in repurchasing shares, and recently authorized the repurchase of 40 million shares through 2014, about 8 percent of outstanding stock. They have already repurchased about 60 million since 2005.

Reasons to Buy

It's hard not to like a company that grows earnings 16.5 percent and dividends 10.5 percent on a mere 3.5 percent compounded increase in revenue over the past ten years. UP has managed its business well to become more efficient and at the same time more "user friendly" to its customers and to the general public. As fuel prices increase and new short- and long-distance intermodal services move higher-valued goods more quickly and cost effectively than trucks, we see a steady shift toward this business. The company has a good brand and reputation in the industry.

Reasons for Caution

Railroads are and will always be economically sensitive. They are also vulnerable to negative publicity. A single event like a derailment or spill can put them in a bad public light, or worse, tangle them up in regulation and unplanned costs. One example is the "positive train control" requirement emanating from a 2008 Southern California accident where an engineer ran a red signal while texting, resulting in twenty-five deaths and a $13 billion congressional mandate for all railroads to install the devices. The breadth of this requirement has since been attenuated somewhat but still serves as a reminder of what can happen. Finally, railroads are and always will be extremely capital intensive, meaning high fixed costs for physical plant and equipment. A decline in volumes or even a shift to other transportation requirements can be costly and hard to recover from.

SECTOR: **Transportation**
BETA COEFFICIENT: **1.11**
10-YEAR COMPOUND EARNINGS PER SHARE GROWTH: **15.5%**
10-YEAR COMPOUND DIVIDENDS PER SHARE GROWTH: **10.5%**

		2003	2004	2005	2006	2007	2008	2009	2010
Revenues (Mil)		11,551	12,215	13,578	15,578	16,283	17,970	14,143	16,965
Net Income (Mil)		1,056	758	809	1,606	1,856	2,338	1,826	2,780
Earnings per share		2.04	1.45	1.70	2.96	3.46	4.54	3.61	5.53
Dividends per share		0.46	0.60	0.60	0.60	0.68	0.93	1.08	1.31
Cash flow per share		4.11	3.39	3.78	5.15	6.09	7.40	6.47	8.68
Price:	high	34.8	34.8	40.6	48.7	68.8	85.8	66.7	95.8
	low	25.5	27.4	29.1	38.8	44.8	41.8	33.3	60.4

Union Pacific Corporation
1416 Dodge St.
Omaha, NE 68179
(402) 271-5777
Website: *www.up.com*

UnitedHealth Group

Ticker symbol: UNH (NYSE) ❑ S&P rating: A- ❑ Value Line financial strength rating: A+ ❑ Current yield: 1.2%

Company Profile

UnitedHealth Group is the parent company of a number of health insurers and service organizations. They are the second-largest publicly traded health insurance company in the United States, with over $94 billion in revenue reported in 2010.

The company operates in four business units: The first, and largest, business unit is Health Benefits, which includes United-Healthcare, Uniprise, Ovations, and AmeriChoice.

UnitedHealthcare sells health insurance plans to companies and individuals, Ovations provides Medicare benefits and benefits targeted to individuals aged fifty and over, and AmeriChoice provides benefits to Medicaid clients. The company, mainly through this unit, has been an active acquirer of other familiar health care and insurance brands, including Oxford Health in 2004, PacifiCare in 2005, Sierra Health Plans and Unison Health Plans in 2008, and AIM Healthcare Services in 2009. Taken together, these operations generated approximately 92 percent of UNH's overall revenue in 2009. As of January 1, 2010, UNH provided services to over 24,000 employer-sponsored health care plans.

The remainder of the company's revenue comes from its health services businesses, which consists of OptumHealth, Ingenix, and Prescription Solutions. OptumHealth is a comprehensive care management and services company targeted at end consumers. Ingenix provides clinical health care data, analytics, research, and consulting services to other health care providers. Prescription Solutions is a pharmacy benefit management program.

Together, the four business units serve about 70 million individuals in the United States.

Financial Highlights, Fiscal Year 2010

UNH's revenues grew 8 percent year over year to $94.1 billion, a growth rate of 7.6 percent, with earnings of $3.90 per share, representing a 20 percent growth rate. The earnings per share figures reflect the integration of acquisitions and a gradual improvement in operating margins due to benefits of scale and overhead synergies from acquisitions, also an ongoing active share repurchase program, which took about 30 million, or 3 percent of the float, out of circulation, These factors are likely to continue into 2011, and the company is guiding for between $99 billion and $100 billion in revenues. However, the company is guiding earnings a bit lower at $3.67 due to public sector employment reductions and lower Medicare/Medicaid reimbursements. Also, the company expects insured members to use the health care system a bit more as recessionary pressures ease, upping costs a bit.

Reasons to Buy

The company is one of the most solid enterprises in the health insurance industry. The year 2011 got off to a good start with a much better than expected earnings report from rival Aetna. We think many of the fears of reform and other changes will not come to affect UNH or other carriers as much as expected, so recent share prices of between ten and twelve times earnings seem to be a bargain. Of course, it also looks unlikely that demand for the core product—health care and health insurance—isn't going away anytime soon.

The scale of UNH's operation gives it tremendous leverage when negotiating for the services of health care providers. Hospitals are strongly motivated to join UNH's network, as doing so will provide assurance of steady referrals.

The national unemployment rate appears to be turning to the good. After more than a year in the neighborhood of 10 percent, mid-2010 unemployment rates are in the low 9 percent range. As more people return to work, more employer-based insurance programs will require servicing.

The company recently raised the dividend from $.03 to $.48 and is changing from a yearly to a quarterly dividend cycle. This represents a large shift in approach to shareholder value, as the previous dividend was little more than ceremonial. The high level of share repurchases amplifies this shareholder return signal.

Reasons for Caution

Since 2007, the company has paid over $3 billion in fines, legal costs, and settlements pertaining to legal actions brought against them by various private and public agencies. The company is still legally exposed as a result of some actions taken by previous management with regard to Medicare payment rates. Current management appears to be serious about cleaning up the messes left behind, but the investor should be aware of this risk of additional litigation.

In addition, public sector sentiment toward the health insurance industry is hardly favorable these days; additional regulation beyond that already built into the recent health care legislation seems likely, and some insurers have been asked to roll back or delay rate increases by state insurance commissioners in response to angry constituents. These companies will have to be on their best behavior to prosper. Finally, we worry a bit about the potential effects of fiscal pressures on the public sector, and could see both employment and benefit reductions there.

SECTOR: Health Care
BETA COEFFICIENT: 0.95
10-YEAR COMPOUND EARNINGS PER SHARE GROWTH: 25.5%
10-YEAR COMPOUND DIVIDENDS PER SHARE GROWTH: 23.0%

	2003	2004	2005	2006	2007	2008	2009	2010
Revenues (Mil)	28,823	37,218	45,365	71,542	75,431	81,186	87,138	94,155
Net Income (Mil)	1,825	2,587	3,300	4,159	4,654	3,660	3,822	4,633
Earnings per share	1.48	1.97	2.48	2.97	3.42	2.95	3.24	4.10
Dividends per share	0.01	0.02	0.03	0.03	0.03	0.03	0.03	0.38
Cash flow per share	1.82	2.30	2.76	3.59	4.35	3.86	4.20	5.25
Price: high	29.3	44.4	64.6	62.9	59.5	57.9	33.3	38.1
low	19.6	27.7	42.6	41.4	45.8	14.5	16.2	27.1

UnitedHealth Group
9900 Bren Street
Minnetonka, MN 55343
(952) 936-1300
Website: *www.unitedhealthgroup.com*

United Technologies Corporation

Ticker symbol: UTX (NYSE) □ S&P rating: A □ Value Line financial strength rating A++ □ Current yield: 2.0%

Company Profile

United Technologies provides high-technology products to the aerospace and building systems industries throughout the world. Its subsidiary companies are industry leaders and include:

- **Pratt & Whitney**—Large and small commercial and military jet engines, spare parts and product support, specialized engine maintenance and overhaul and repair services for airlines, air forces, and corporate fleets; rocket engines and space propulsion systems; and industrial gas turbines.

- **UTC Fire and Security**—Security and fire protection systems; integration, installation, and servicing of intruder alarms, access control, and video surveillance; monitoring, response, and security personnel services; installation and servicing of fire detection and suppression systems.

- **Hamilton Sundstrand**—Aircraft electrical power generation and distribution systems; engine and flight controls; propulsion systems; environmental controls for aircraft, spacecraft, and submarines; auxiliary power units; product support, maintenance, and repair services; space life support systems; industrial products including mechanical power transmissions, compressors, metering devices, and fluid handling equipment.

- **Sikorsky**—Design and manufacture of military and commercial helicopters; fixed-wing reconnaissance aircraft; spare parts and maintenance services for helicopters and fixed-wing aircraft; and civil helicopter operations.

- **UTC Power**—Combined heat, cooling, and power systems for commercial and industrial applications and fuel cell systems made by UTC Fuel Cells for commercial, transportation, and space applications, including the U.S. space shuttle program. This unit made headlines in early 2011 for a successful installation of a fuel cell unit to power a Stop & Shop store in Massachusetts, paid for with a state grant but able to generate 90 percent of the store's energy in house.

- **Carrier**—Heating, ventilating, and air conditioning (HVAC) equipment for commercial, industrial, and residential buildings; HVAC replacement parts and services; building controls; commercial, industrial, and transport refrigeration equipment.

- **Otis**—Design and manufacture of elevators, escalators, moving walks, and shuttle systems, and related installation, maintenance, and repair services; modernization products and service for elevators and escalators.

Pratt &Whitney, Otis, and Carrier together accounted for almost 70 percent of revenues. Despite UTC's strong presence in the national defense industry, about 46 percent of UTC's revenue came from international customers, while U.S. government contracts accounted for 17 percent of revenues.

Financial Highlights, Fiscal Year 2010

After a 10 percent revenue drop and a 16 percent earnings drop in FY2009, the company bounced back nicely in FY2010. Sales came in at $54.3 billion, just under 5 percent ahead of FY2009. The real story was earnings—an upturn in

some of the more profitable and economically sensitive businesses like Pratt & Whitney, Otis, and Carrier improved margins and leverage, raising earnings to $4.74 a share, 10 percent ahead of FY2009. The recovery in the more sensitive businesses should continue, and the company has put out an FY2011 forecast of $56–$57 billion in revenues and $5.05–$5.35 per share in earnings, roughly the same growth rates experienced in FY2010.

The company returned 75 percent of free cash flow to shareholders in the form of $2.2 billion in share buybacks, reducing share count approximately 3 percent, and is likely to continue to reduce share count to around 925 million from a peak of 1,028 million in 2003.

Reasons to Buy

UTC is a classic conglomerate play. The separate and loosely related or unrelated businesses buffer each other in line with what's happening in the economy. During the recession, the defense and aerospace technology segments performed while business fell off in more economically sensitive businesses and products like jet engines and elevators; as the economy picks up, the sensitive businesses carry the load. That's the way this sort of company works, and in the case of UTC, it has worked well. Unlike many of its competitors, United Technologies maintains a global presence, and UTX will be ready wherever the construction market begins to turn around first. The company's brands, particularly Otis, are well known and very well supported worldwide. And like Honeywell, UTX has a broad portfolio of products geared toward improving energy efficiency, which will be a significant growth market for several years to come.

The company continues to deliver shareholder return through share buybacks and healthy dividend increases.

Reasons for Caution

The stability of the public sector portion of the business may become less so as Congress wrestles with the budget deficit. How many F-35 fighters or Sikorsky helicopters the company supplies or supplies parts to will get greater scrutiny. The rest of the business is still sensitive to construction, and construction may not be out of the woods yet. Finally, like all conglomerates, UTC is a very complex business to manage, and a slipup in one division, as with the problems on the A380 Airbus engines, can be damaging.

SECTOR: Industrials
BETA COEFFICIENT: 1.00
10-YEAR COMPOUND EARNINGS PER SHARE GROWTH: 15.5%
10-YEAR COMPOUND DIVIDENDS PER SHARE GROWTH: 14.5%

	2003	2004	2005	2006	2007	2008	2009	2010
Revenues (Mil)	31,034	37,445	42,725	47,740	54,759	58,681	52,920	54,326
Net Income (Mil)	2,361	2,788	3,069	3,732	4,224	4,689	3,829	4,373
Earnings per share	2.35	2.76	3.03	3.71	4.27	4.9	4.12	4.74
Dividends per share	0.57	0.7	0.88	1.02	1.28	1.55	1.54	1.70
Cash flow per share	3.07	3.68	4.09	4.79	5.5	6.38	5.43	6.22
Price: high	48.4	53	58.9	67.5	82.5	77.1	70.9	79.7
low	26.8	40.4	48.4	54.2	61.8	41.8	37.4	62.9

United Technologies Corporation
One Financial Plaza
Hartford, CT 06103
(860) 728-7912
Website: www.utc.com

Valmont Industries

Ticker symbol: VMI (NYSE) ❑ S&P rating: BBB- ❑ Value Line financial strength rating: B++ ❑ Current yield: 0.7%

Company Profile

Valmont Industries was founded in 1946 as a supplier of irrigation products and became one of the classic post-war industrial success stories, growing along with the need for increased farm output. They were early pioneers of the center-pivot irrigation systems, which enabled much of that growth and which now dominates the high-yield agricultural business. These machines remain a mainstay of its product line. But the company has expanded to make such familiar infrastructure items as light poles, cell phone towers, and those familiar high-tension electric towers that crisscross the landscape. Valmont products and product lines now include:

- **Engineered Support Structures**—Poles, towers, and other metal structures used in lighting, communications, traffic management, wireless phone carriers, and other utilities. Products are available as standard designs and engineered for custom applications as needed for industrial, commercial, and residential applications. If you've ever sat at a stop light and wondered how a single cantilevered arm could support four 400-lb. traffic signals, these are the folks to ask.

- **Utility Support Structures**—This segment produces the very large concrete and steel substations and electric transmission support towers used by electric utilities. This has been Valmont's most profitable operation over the last few years, due mainly to increased volumes in a period of declining costs.

- **Irrigation**—Valmont produces a wide range of equipment, including gravity and drip products, as well as its center-pivot designs, which can service up to 500 acres from a single machine. Valmont also sells its irrigation controllers to other manufacturers.

- **Coatings**—Developed as an adjunct to its other metals product businesses, the coatings business now provides services such as galvanizing, electroplating, powder coating, and anodizing to industrial customers throughout the company's operating areas.

In 2010, Valmont completed a $420 million acquisition of Delta plc, a maker of infrastructure products closely matching the Engineered Support Structures product line in the United Kingdom. The company has operations in Australia, New Zealand, the United States, China, South Africa, and throughout Southeast Asia. The clear strategy is to expand outside the United States.

Financial Highlights, Fiscal Year 2010

FY2010 turned out to be a surprisingly weak year for the company after a healthy FY2009. Valmont products tend to have long lead times, and in 2009, Valmont was working off backlog, especially in the utility segment. As FY2010 arrived, that backlog started to disappear, and reduced government spending after a bump related to the Obama administration stimulus program reduced demand and caused more competitive bidding and softer prices on the supply side. Costs related to the Delta plc acquisition hurt further. After earning $5.73 on $1.79 billion in sales in FY2009, FY2010 brought earnings of $4.00 on revenues of $1.85 billion. Guidance for FY2011 calls for a gradual recovery to $5.10 per share on $2.3 billion in revenues.

Reasons to Buy

Despite the relative turmoil in FY2010, we are sticking with this pick as a key infrastructure play. America's infrastructure needs to be replaced, as does infrastructure in much of the developed world. And as for the less developed world, that infrastructure is needed in the first place. We think, long term, that Valmont is in the right place to capture a decent share of this replacement business, including electric utility infrastructure. The original irrigation business should also do well as agriculture and farm commodity prices strengthen. Valmont has retained market share and remains the leader among the four dominant U.S.–based players in the large-scale irrigation market. The company's continued emphasis on growth into new geographies should pay dividends as India and China begin to build infrastructure and adopt more modern agricultural methods. So far, Valmont has had very little penetration in those two countries.

Reasons for Caution

Many Valmont products are purchased by public sector and government agencies, and these agencies will be scrutinizing purchases to a greater degree than in the past. Escalating raw materials costs may also hurt, especially in a reduced demand, softer pricing environment that might ensue from contracting government purchases. Finally, we would like to see a little more shareholder return; dividends are small and share buybacks haven't happened on a large scale; however, it should be noted that the company only has 26.4 million shares outstanding to begin with.

SECTOR: **Industrials**
BETA COEFFICIENT: **1.55**
10-YEAR COMPOUND EARNINGS PER SHARE GROWTH: **15.5%**
10-YEAR COMPOUND DIVIDENDS PER SHARE GROWTH: **7.5%**

	2003	2004	2005	2006	2007	2008	2009	2010
Revenues (Mil)	837	1,031	1,108	1,281	1,500	1,907	1,787	1,975
Net Income (Mil)	25.9	26.9	40.2	61.5	94.7	132.4	155	109.7
Earnings per share	1.06	1.10	1.58	2.38	3.63	5.04	5.70	4.15
Dividends per share	0.31	0.32	0.34	0.37	0.41	0.50	0.58	0.65
Price: high	24.3	28.0	35.3	61.2	99.0	120.5	89.3	90.3
low	17.7	19.3	21.3	32.8	50.9	37.5	37.5	65.3

Valmont Industries
1 Valmont Plaza
Omaha, NE 68154
(402) 963-1000
Website: *www.valmont.com*

Verizon Communications, Inc.

Ticker symbol: VZ (NYSE) ❑ S&P rating: A- ❑ Value Line financial strength rating: A+ ❑ Current yield: 5.3%

Company Profile

Verizon operates two telecommunications businesses: Domestic Wireless, which provides wireless voice and data services, and Wireline, which provides voice, broadband data and video, Internet access, long-distance, and other services, and which owns and operates a large global Internet Protocol network. The wireless business represents about 57 percent of the total; wireline is about 43 percent of the total by revenues.

The Wireline segment also supplies Verizon's Fiber-to-the-Home (FiOS) broadband data infrastructure. One of Verizon's largest investments, FiOS provides a very high bandwidth link to the Internet, easily surpassing DSL and even cable. Over this network, Verizon can provide hundreds of HD video stream, high-speed data, and voice all simultaneously. This service competes head to head with AT&T's (a *100 Best Stock*) U-verse and Comcast's xfinity services among others.

The Domestic Wireless segment is served by Verizon Wireless, which is a joint venture between Verizon Communications, Inc., and Vodafone. Verizon

Communications owns a 55 percent share in the business, and Vodafone 45 percent. Verizon wireless is now the largest wireless carrier in the United States. The wireless side of the business has been rolling out the new LTE Mobile Broadband network, a leading-edge 4G network designed to be ten times faster than the standard 3G network. Shortly after this December 2010 introduction, Verizon also began marketing Apple iPhone and iPad products and services for the first time in February 2010. Both rollouts have long been anticipated and are thought to be going well, although there were initial reports of disappointment with the Apple rollout. Both introductions are very strategic for the company in its quest for technology leadership and its competition with rival AT&T and others. Adding hardware products and wireless capacity hasn't been the only growth strategy employed at Verizon. The company is actively seeking to become a player in the "cloud" computing phenomenon with a $1.4 billion acquisition of IT and cloud services provider Terremark Worldwide, and a small but interesting partnership with a company called eMeter, which markets devices to automatically read and transmit energy usage for utilities using Verizon's wireless network. The company has also been making numerous smaller acquisitions in the traditional wireless segment to build its base.

Financial Highlights, Fiscal Year 2010

Verizon's revenues grew 10.7 percent to $107.8 billion in FY2009, primarily due to the acquisition of Alltel and the inclusion of its revenues in the Wireless segment. FY2010 saw a slight revenue decline due to macroeconomic factors, competition in the wireless space, and a slow decline in traditional wireline business, with revenues of $106.6 billion. The slightly soft revenues and increased costs and capital spending for the FiOS rollout caused a slight softening in earnings, too, to $2.21 per share from $2.40 in the previous year. For FY2011, a mostly completed FiOS rollout and some cost-cutting measures including layoffs, and a new set of data plans tied to the 4G rollout are expected to create more upside, with the company calling for 4–8 percent top line growth and analysts estimating revenues at the $108.8 billion range and earnings holding steady at about $2.21. It should be noted that cash flows are much stronger than reported earnings figures—while the company earned $2.25 in 2010, it reported cash flow of $7.60 per share. In part due to the strong cash flow, the dividend was increased slightly and the company recently approved a 100 million share buyback program—about 3 percent of total common shares outstanding.

Reasons to Buy

Verizon offers a nice combination of stability and income with a play in the growth of the "new economy" and supporting technology. Although recent price strength has dropped the effective yield to 5.3 percent, this still represents a solid income base for investors looking for steady to slightly growing income streams with a growth kicker. With the high dividend and share buybacks, the company seems to keep shareholder interests in mind. The brand is strong and its reputation hasn't suffered some of the hits for poor quality service that archrival AT&T has experienced. Recent advertising campaigns pushing LTE and the Apple line have been effective, and aside from the Apple rollout, the company hasn't taken its foot off the pedal with other technologies primarily based on the Android platform. Finally, we like the eMeter and other initiatives to maximize use of the network.

Reasons for Caution

The telecommunications business is very capital intensive, and Verizon, like others, is faced with larger and more frequent new technology rollouts like LTE and FiOS, and must spend heavily just to keep up with technology and competition. While current cash flows are strong, this scenario doesn't combine well with a business where competition has cut into margins slightly and where dividend payouts have risen from 50 percent to 80 percent of earnings since 2002. Getting a solid return on new capital investments is thus critical, and one slipup could be costly for shareholders. The business environment is extremely competitive, and Verizon's sheer size may hamper its flexibility to compete. Also, one should consider that Verizon shares ownership of the wireless business with Vodafone; the shared ownership could cause problems or result in an expensive buyout for Verizon.

SECTOR: **Telecommunications Services**
BETA COEFFICIENT: **0.65**
10-YEAR COMPOUND EARNINGS PER SHARE GROWTH: **-1.0%**
10-YEAR COMPOUND DIVIDENDS PER SHARE GROWTH: **1.5%**

	2003	2004	2005	2006	2007	2008	2009	2010
Revenues (Mil)	67,752	71,283	74,910	88,144	93,469	97,354	107,808	106,585
Net Income (Mil)	7,282	7,261	7,151	6,021	6,854	7,235	6,930	7,668
Earnings per share	2.62	2.59	2.56	2.54	2.36	2.54	2.4	2.21
Dividends per share	1.54	1.54	1.62	1.62	1.65	1.78	1.87	1.93
Cash flow per share	7.55	7.64	7.24	7.07	7.4	7.65	7.7	7.60
Price: high	44.3	42.3	41.1	38.9	46.2	44.3	34.8	36.0
low	31.1	34.1	29.1	30	35.6	23.1	26.1	26.0

Verizon Communications, Inc.
140 West Street
New York, NY 10007
(212) 395-1000
Website: *www.verizon.com*

Visa Inc.

Ticker symbol: V (NYSE) ❑ S&P rating: A+ ❑ Value Line financial strength rating: A ❑ Current yield: 0.8%

Company Profile

If we wrote about a company with a steady 37 percent *net* profit margin and a global brand that was in the business of collecting small fees on every one of billions of transactions worldwide, a company that required almost no capital expenditures, plant, and equipment, nor inventory, a company that brought in more than a million dollars per employee in revenue and $436,000 per employee in net profit, a company with a time-tested business model and practically no debt—would you believe that it existed?

It does, and the company, formed in a 2007 reorganization and taken public in 2008, is Visa. Yes, the same Visa whose emblem has traditionally appeared on a majority of the world's credit cards—and now debit cards. The company operates the world's largest retail electronic payment network, providing processing services, payment platforms, and fraud detection services for credit, debit, and commercial payments. The company also operates one of the largest global ATM networks with its PLUS and Interlink brands.

For years, Visa has been synonymous with credit and credit cards, but in recent years has become more of a digital currency company, stitching together consumers, retailers, banks, and other businesses in a giant global network; really, Visa is a global payments technology business that not only develops and supplies the technology but also collects fees upon its use.

The shift from traditional cash and check forms of payment to debit cards and other digital forms is growing at about a 14 percent annual rate, driven by the security and convenience of these transactions as well as a shift away from consumer debt more to "paid for today" debit transactions. Put away your checkbooks—debit payments are projected to increase 15–20 percent in FY2011 and will account for more than half the company's overall business volume.

More than its rivals, Visa derives a significant percentage of transaction volume, about 35 percent, overseas. International volumes are growing faster than in the United States.

Financial Highlights, Fiscal Year 2010

With only three years of operating performance in the books, it is a bit harder to gauge the operating performance and potential for Visa. In its first three years, revenues have grown sharply from $6.26 billion in 2008 to a reported $8.06 billion in 2010, and are projected at about $9.2 billion for FY2011, ending September 2011. Per share earnings have grown from $2.25 to $3.91 over the same period, and are projected at about $4.70 per share. Because the company is for the most part a cash business without much capital equipment, earnings come closer to matching cash flow than in most companies—sad because one gets used to seeing cash flows higher than earnings, but good because earnings accurately reflect the true earning power of the business. The balance sheet is strong: Visa exited FY2010 with only $29 million in long-term debt—effectively zero against a market capitalization of $62 billion. The dividend today is small but growing, and we think patient investors will be rewarded with growing cash returns.

Reasons to Buy

Simply, it would be hard to come up with a better business model—a company that develops and sells the network, and collects fees every time it's used? It would be like Microsoft collecting fees every time a file is created and saved, or a relatively unique e-mail platform that charges fees for every message. Visa is in a great position to not only capitalize on overall world economic growth, as most companies should be, but also to capitalize on a shift in this growth toward electronic payments. Indeed, the "mobile wallet" concept, where consumers can pay for things with a mobile device that reads a bar code-like QR (quick response), is very promising. With cellular providers recently abandoning a competitive platform under development, Visa stands in exactly the right place to benefit from this evolution. Overall, while Visa isn't a monopoly (MasterCard, American Express, and Discover are competitors), it has the strongest franchise, technology leadership, and pricing power at its back.

Reasons for Caution

The somewhat monopolistic power and pricing practices of credit card processors has come under public fire and government scrutiny, and mandates to limit transaction fees may hurt growth somewhat. Also, transaction processors are vulnerable to economic cycles, and a double dip or protracted recession would hurt revenues. Finally, although Visa and others have driven payment technology for years, it is still possible that the mobile wallet opportunity may be capitalized on elsewhere in the industry, leaving credit card providers out of the loop. However, that doesn't look likely right now.

SECTOR: **Financial**
BETA COEFFICIENT: **1.05**
10-YEAR COMPOUND EARNINGS PER SHARE GROWTH: **NM**
10-YEAR COMPOUND DIVIDENDS PER SHARE GROWTH: **NM**

	2003	2004	2005	2006	2007	2008	2009	2010
Revenues (Mil)	–	–	–	–	–	6,263	6,911	8,065
Net Income (Mil)	–	–	–	–	–	1,700	2,213	2,966
Earnings per share	–	–	–	–	–	2.25	2.92	3.91
Dividends per share	–	–	–	–	–	0.21	0.44	0.53
Cash flow per share	–	–	–	–	–	2.50	3.22	3.86
Price: high	–	–	–	–	–	89.6	89.7	97.2
low	–	–	–	–	–	43.5	41.8	64.9

Visa, Inc.
P.O. Box 8999
San Francisco, CA 94128
(415) 932-2100
Website: *www.visa.com*

Wells Fargo & Company

Ticker symbol: WFC (NYSE) ◻ S&P rating: AA- ◻ Value Line financial strength rating: A ◻ Current yield: 0.6%

Company Profile

Wells Fargo & Company is a diversified financial services company, providing banking, insurance, investments, mortgages, and consumer finance from more than 11,000 offices and other distribution channels across North America.

The business is divided into three segments. First and largest is Community Banking, which provides services for consumers and small businesses in thirty-nine states and mortgage services in all fifty states through a combination of branches, ATMs, and online services. Wholesale Banking provides commercial banking, capital markets, leasing, and other financing services to larger corporations. Wealth, Brokerage and Retirement provides financial advisory and investment management services to individuals.

As of late 2010, Wells Fargo had $1.2 trillion in assets, loans of $730 billion, deposits of $814 billion, and a market cap of $149 billion. Based on assets, they are the fourth largest bank holding company in the United States. They have 267,000 employees, or "team members," as they prefer to call them.

With the addition of Wachovia, WFC's profile in the industry has changed considerably. Here are some of the revised industry rankings for Wells Fargo as of December 31, 2009:

- #1 in banking stores
- #1 in small business lending
- #1 in residential mortgage lending
- #1 in retail banking deposits
- #1 in used car lending
- #1 in preferred stock underwriting
- #1 in SBA 7(a) lending in dollars
- #1 in lending for small businesses
- #2 in annuity distribution
- #2 in debit cards
- #2 in U.S. deposits
- #2 in mortgage servicing

Financial Highlights, Fiscal Year 2010

The rebound started in FY2009 after the company completed one of the worst quarters in its history in Q4 FY2008, with an $.84 per share loss for that quarter and a paltry $0.70 per share in income for that year. FY2009 saw a rebound to a per share net of $1.75, still not up to pre-bust levels, but not so bad. FY2010 saw that rebound continue, with a reported $2.21 in earnings per share. Revenues were down slightly, reflecting a deliberate contraction in loans outstanding, and mandated and voluntary reductions in certain fees being charged. The company also reduced loan loss reserves to $16 billion from $21.7 billion in 2009, still about seven times levels retained in 2007.

Reasons to Buy

Last year we recognized Wells for their (relatively) conservative positions and cautious behaviors during the mortgage free-for-all. They had less exposure overall than most and were able to spot trouble earlier than many others. As a result, we're looking at a bank that today is in far better shape than many of its peers. Is it perfect? Certainly not. Wells, especially through its Wachovia foray, still has considerable exposure to real estate and bad mortgages, and there are few times this will abate soon. Based on what's happened in the past four years, it's hard to put *any* bank or financial services firm on the *100 Best Stocks* list, but we'll go with this one as the obvious (to us, anyway) best of the bunch. That said, the company has proven itself to be able to manage through such adversity and still keep a solid public image. The company has a solid brand reputation

and value (number two worldwide according to a BrandFinance study). The company is usually quick to recognize and deal with bad loans and bad decisions. Especially as the macroeconomic environment improves, we think WFC is well positioned to take advantage.

As recently as 2008, the company paid a healthy $1.30 dividend, which would have been about 60 percent of earnings. The financial crisis, TARP fund utilization, and other factors caused Wells to reduce the payout to $.20 per share, which is only about 9 percent of current earnings. The company wants to boost the payout but must clear the action with the Federal Reserve; a boost to prerecession levels would obviously be good for shareholders.

Reasons for Caution

"Headline risk" continues to abound in the banking industry. Any sign of trouble on the mortgage front will obviously hurt. Wells has been at the center of a legal battle over the validity of foreclosures and supporting documents. The company has been profiting from the difference between retail and wholesale interest rates, but if wholesale interest rates, i.e., Fed funds and commercial paper, start to rise, the profit recovery could be jeopardized. The company issued about 500 million shares to build equity, and this and other moves have grown share counts from 3.3 billion to 5.2 billion in three years, jeopardizing dividend increases and potentially reducing shareholder value. While Wells is the best of a bad bunch, there are other companies in other industries that will foster better sleep at night.

SECTOR: Financials
BETA COEFFICIENT: 1.35
10-YEAR COMPOUND EARNINGS PER SHARE GROWTH: 5.5%
10-YEAR COMPOUND DIVIDENDS PER SHARE GROWTH: 11.0%

		2003	2004	2005	2006	2007	2008	2009	2010
Loans (Bil)		249.2	269.6	296.1	306.9	344.8	843.8	758	734
Net Income (Mil)		6,202	7,014	7,670	8,480	8,060	2,655	12,275	12,362
Earnings per share		1.83	2.05	2.25	2.49	2.38	0.7	1.75	2.21
Dividends per share		0.75	0.93	1	1.12	1.18	1.3	0.49	0.20
Price:	high	29.6	32	32.4	37	38	44.7	31.5	34.3
	low	21.7	27.2	28.8	30.3	29.3	19.9	7.8	23.0

Wells Fargo & Company
420 Montgomery Street
San Francisco, CA 94163
(415) 396-0523
Website: *www.wellsfargo.com*

ONE YEAR GAIN/LOSS, APRIL 1, 2010–APRIL 1, 2011

Company	Symbol	Price 4/1/2010	Price 4/1/2011	% change	Dollar gain/loss, $1,000 invested
3M	MMM	$83.85	$93.19	11.1%	$111.29
Abbott	ABT	$52.28	$49.37	-5.6%	($55.66)
Air Products	APD	$73.87	$90.48	22.5%	$224.85
Alexander & Baldwin	ALEX	$32.75	$54.47	66.3%	$663.21
Apache	APA	$103.87	$129.98	25.1%	$251.37
Apple	APPL	$235.97	$348.45	47.7%	$476.67
Archer Daniels Midland	ADM	$29.11	$36.48	25.3%	$253.18
AT&T	T	$26.11	$30.62	17.3%	$172.73
C. R. Bard	BCR	$84.46	$100.88	19.4%	$194.41
Baxter	BAX	$58.23	$53.91	-7.4%	($74.19)
Becton Dickinson	BDX	$78.96	$80.57	2.0%	$20.39
Bed Bath and Beyond	BBBY	$44.18	$48.71	10.3%	$102.54
Best Buy	BBY	$42.57	$28.64	-32.7%	($327.23)
Boeing	BA	$72.99	$74.01	1.4%	$13.97
Bunge Ltd.	BG	$61.85	$73.80	19.3%	$193.21
Campbell Soup	CPB	$35.56	$33.22	-6.6%	($65.80)
CarMax	KMX	$26.08	$32.53	24.7%	$247.32
Caterpillar	CAT	$63.99	$113.12	76.8%	$767.78
Chevron	CVX	$76.69	$108.32	41.2%	$412.44
Chipotle Mexican Grill	CMG	$114.48	$274.00	139.3%	$1,393.43
Church & Dwight	CHD	$67.72	$79.87	17.9%	$179.42
Cincinnati Financial	CINF	$29.08	$32.99	13.4%	$134.46
Clorox	CL	$85.81	$80.52	-6.2%	($61.65)
Coca-Cola	KO	$55.30	$67.22	21.6%	$215.55
Colgate-Palmolive	CLX	$64.28	$70.86	10.2%	$102.36
ConocoPhillips	COP	$52.02	$79.68	53.2%	$531.72
Costco Wholesale	COST	$60.14	$74.25	23.5%	$234.62
CVS/Caremark	CVS	$36.23	$34.96	-3.5%	($35.05)

▼ **Appendix A: Performance Analysis:** *100 Best Stocks You Can Buy 2011* (con't)

ONE YEAR GAIN/LOSS, APRIL 1, 2010–APRIL 1, 2011

Company	Symbol	Price 4/1/2010	Price 4/1/2011	% change	Dollar gain/loss, $1,000 invested
Deere	DE	$59.74	$98.60	65.0%	$650.49
Dentsply	XRAY	$34.48	$36.99	7.3%	$72.80
Dominion Resources	D	$41.83	$44.70	6.9%	$68.61
Dover	DOV	$47.00	$67.24	43.1%	$430.64
Duke Energy	DUK	$16.41	$18.42	12.2%	$122.49
DuPont	DD	$37.91	$55.19	45.6%	$455.82
Ecolab	ECL	$44.43	$51.57	16.1%	$160.70
Entergy	ETR	$82.32	$67.64	-17.8%	($178.33)
ExxonMobil	XOM	$67.61	$84.68	25.2%	$252.48
Fair Isaac	FICO	$25.48	$31.30	22.8%	$228.41
FedEx	FDX	$92.17	$95.00	3.1%	$30.70
Fluor	FLR	$47.60	$72.92	53.2%	$531.93
FMC	FMC	$61.16	$86.12	40.8%	$408.11
General Mills	GIS	$35.69	$36.39	2.0%	$19.61
Google	GOOG	$568.80	$591.80	4.0%	$40.44
W.W. Grainger	GWW	$109.53	$143.17	30.7%	$307.13
Harris	HRS	$47.84	$50.05	4.6%	$46.20
Heinz	HNZ	$45.85	$48.97	6.8%	$68.05
Hewlett-Packard	HPQ	$53.24	$40.98	-23.0%	($230.28)
Honeywell	HON	$45.03	$59.26	31.6%	$316.01
Hormel	HRL	$21.08	$28.23	33.9%	$339.18
IBM	IBM	$128.25	$164.27	28.1%	$280.86
International Paper	IP	$25.24	$30.42	20.5%	$205.23
Iron Mountain	IRM	$27.45	$31.53	14.9%	$148.63
Johnson & Johnson	JNJ	$65.77	$59.49	-9.5%	($95.48)
Johnson Controls	JCI	$33.38	$42.08	26.1%	$260.64
Kellogg	K	$53.61	$54.00	0.7%	$7.27
Kimberly-Clark	KMB	$62.50	$65.38	4.6%	$46.08

▼ **Appendix A: Performance Analysis:** *100 Best Stocks You Can Buy 2011* (con't)

ONE YEAR GAIN/LOSS, APRIL 1, 2010–APRIL 1, 2011

Company	Symbol	Price 4/1/2010	Price 4/1/2011	% change	Dollar gain/loss, $1,000 invested
Kraft Foods	KFT	$30.34	$31.61	4.2%	$41.86
Lubrizol	LZ	$93.14	$133.80	43.7%	$436.55
Marathon Oil	MRO	$32.09	$53.55	66.9%	$668.74
McCormick	MKC	$38.58	$47.91	24.2%	$241.84
McDonald's	MCD	$67.58	$75.99	12.4%	$124.45
Medtronic	MDT	$45.67	$39.50	-13.5%	($135.10)
Monsanto	MON	$70.83	$73.17	3.3%	$33.04
NetApp	NTAP	$34.26	$48.20	40.7%	$406.89
NextEra Energy	NEE	$50.19	$55.93	11.4%	$114.37
NIKE	NKE	$74.01	$76.53	3.4%	$34.05
Norfolk Southern	NSC	$56.99	$69.32	21.6%	$216.35
Northern Trust	NTRS	$56.64	$51.69	-8.7%	($87.39)
Nucor	NUE	$45.95	$46.20	0.5%	$5.44
Oracle	ORCL	$25.46	$34.02	33.6%	$336.21
Pall Corporation	PLL	$40.39	$57.98	43.6%	$435.50
Panera	PNRA	$76.38	$127.87	67.4%	$674.13
Patterson	PDCO	$30.75	$32.85	6.8%	$68.29
Paychex	PAYX	$30.72	$31.83	3.6%	$36.13
Peet's	PEET	$37.64	$47.93	27.3%	$273.38
Pepsi	PEP	$66.68	$65.22	-2.2%	($21.90)
Perrigo	PRGO	$59.08	$79.90	35.2%	$352.40
Praxair	PX	$83.82	$101.98	21.7%	$216.65
Procter & Gamble	PG	$63.36	$62.08	-2.0%	($20.20)
Ross Stores	ROST	$53.42	$71.55	33.9%	$339.39
Schlumberger	SLB	$64.57	$93.70	45.1%	$451.14
Sigma-Aldrich	SIAL	$54.58	$63.94	17.1%	$171.49
J. M. Smucker	SJM	$60.33	$72.44	20.1%	$200.73
Southern Co.	SO	$33.42	$38.31	14.6%	$146.32

▼ **Appendix A: Performance Analysis:** *100 Best Stocks You Can Buy 2011* (con't)

ONE YEAR GAIN/LOSS, APRIL 1, 2010–APRIL 1, 2011

Company	Symbol	Price 4/1/2010	Price 4/1/2011	% change	Dollar gain/loss, $1,000 invested
St. Jude Medical	STJ	$41.50	$52.19	25.8%	$257.59
Staples	SPLS	$23.70	$20.06	-15.4%	($153.59)
Starbucks	SBUX	$24.24	$37.25	53.7%	$536.72
Stryker	SYK	$57.65	$60.90	5.6%	$56.37
Suburban Propane	SPH	$47.47	$56.43	18.9%	$188.75
Sysco	SYY	$29.60	$27.88	-5.8%	($58.11)
Target	TGT	$53.13	$50.36	-5.2%	($52.14)
Teva Pharmaceuticals	TEVA	$63.75	$50.54	-20.7%	($207.22)
TJX	TJX	$42.71	$49.50	15.9%	$158.98
Tractor Supply	TSCO	$29.70	$61.06	105.6%	$1,055.89
United Health Corp	UNH	$32.99	$45.61	38.3%	$382.54
United Technologies	UTX	$74.13	$85.32	15.1%	$150.95
Valmont	VMI	$84.33	$106.89	26.8%	$267.52
Verizon	VZ	$31.28	$38.47	23.0%	$229.86
Walgreen	WAG	$37.75	$40.94	8.5%	$84.50
Wells Fargo	WFC	$31.37	$32.06	2.2%	$22.00

▼ Appendix B: Dividend and Yield, 2011–2012, Sorted by Company

Company	Symbol	2011 Dividend	2011 Yield %	2012 Dividend	2012 Yield %
3M Company	MMM	$2.10	2.8%	$2.10	2.8%
Abbott Laboratories	ABT	$1.76	3.8%	$1.92	3.9%
Aetna	AET			$0.60	1.6%
Air Products	APD	$1.96	2.9%	$2.32	2.6%
Alexander & Baldwin	ALEX	$1.26	4.2%	$1.24	2.3%
Allergan	AGN			$0.20	0.3%
Amgen	AMGN				
Apache Corp	APA	$0.60	0.7%	$0.60	0.5%
Apple	AAPL				
Archer Daniels Midland	ADM	$0.60	2.4%	$0.64	1.8%
AT&T	T	$1.68	7.0%	$1.72	5.6%
Automatic Data Processing	ADP			$1.44	2.8%
C.R. Bard	BCR	$0.68	0.9%	$0.72	0.7%
Baxter International	BAX	$1.16	2.8%	$1.24	2.3%
Becton, Dickinson	BDX	$1.48	2.1%	$1.64	2.0%
Bed Bath & Beyond	BBBY				
Best Buy	BBY	$0.56	1.4%	$0.60	2.1%
Campbell Soup	CPB	$1.10	3.1%	$1.16	3.5%
CarMax	KMX				
Caterpillar	CAT	$1.68	2.9%	$1.76	1.6%
Chevron	CVX	$2.88	4.0%	$2.88	2.7%
Church & Dwight	CHD	$0.56	0.9%	$1.36	1.7%
Cincinnati Financial	CINF	$1.58	6.0%	$1.60	4.8%
Clorox	CLX	$2.20	3.5%	$2.20	3.1%
Coca-Cola	KO	$1.76	3.4%	$1.88	2.8%
Colgate-Palmolive	CL	$2.12	2.7%	$2.32	2.9%
Comcast	CMCSA			$0.44	1.7%
ConocoPhillips	COP	$2.20	4.4%	$2.64	3.3%

▼ **Appendix B: Dividend and Yield, 2011–2012, Sorted by Company** (con't)

Company	Symbol	2011 Dividend	2011 Yield %	2012 Dividend	2012 Yield %
Costco	COST	$0.82	1.5%	$0.80	1.1%
CVS/Caremark	CVS	$0.35	1.0%	$0.48	1.4%
Deere & Co	DE	$1.20	2.1%	$1.40	1.4%
Dentsply	XRAY	$0.20	0.6%	$0.20	0.5%
Dominion Energy	D	$1.83	4.7%	$1.96	4.4%
Duke Energy	DUK	$0.96	6.1%	$1.00	5.4%
DuPont	DD	$1.64	4.8%	$1.64	3.0%
Ecolab	ECL	$0.62	1.3%	$0.68	1.3%
ExxonMobil	XOM	$1.76	3.0%	$1.76	2.1%
Fair Isaac	FICO	$0.08	0.4%	$0.08	0.3%
FedEx	FDX	$0.44	0.6%	$0.48	0.5%
Fluor Corp	FLR	$0.50	1.1%	$0.48	0.7%
FMC Corp	FMC	$0.50	0.9%	$0.60	0.7%
General Mills	GIS	$1.96	5.4%	$1.12	3.1%
Google	GOOG				
W. W. Grainger	GWW	$2.16	2.2%	$2.16	1.5%
Harris	HRS	$0.88	1.9%	$1.00	2.0%
Heinz	HNZ	$1.80	4.1%	$1.80	3.7%
Hewlett-Packard	HPQ	$0.32	0.7%	$0.48	1.2%
Honeywell	HON	$1.21	2.9%	$1.32	2.2%
IBM	IBM	$2.60	2.1%	$2.60	1.6%
Illinois Tool Works	ITW			$1.36	2.5%
International Paper	IP	$0.50	2.3%	$1.04	3.4%
Iron Mountain	IRM	$0.25	1.1%	$0.76	2.4%
Johnson & Johnson	JNJ	$2.16	3.7%	$2.16	3.6%
Johnson Controls	JCI	$0.52	1.9%	$0.64	1.5%
Kellogg	K	$1.50	2.8%	$1.64	3.0%
Kimberly-Clark	KMB	$2.64	4.4%	$2.80	4.3%
Lubrizol	LZ	$1.44	1.7%	$1.44	1.1%

▼ **Appendix B: Dividend and Yield, 2011–2012, Sorted by Company (con't)**

Company	Symbol	2011 Dividend	2011 Yield %	2012 Dividend	2012 Yield %
Marathon Oil	MRO	$1.00	3.3%	$1.00	1.9%
McCormick	MKC	$1.04	2.7%	$1.12	2.3%
McDonald's	MCD	$2.20	3.3%	$2.44	3.2%
McKesson	MCK			$0.72	0.9%
Medtronic	MDT	$0.82	2.2%	$0.88	2.2%
Monsanto	MON	$1.06	2.2%	$1.12	1.5%
NextEra Energy	NEE	$2.00	4.1%	$2.10	3.8%
NIKE	NKE	$1.08	1.5%	$1.24	1.6%
Norfolk Southern	NSC	$1.36	2.5%	$1.60	2.3%
Northern Trust	NTRS	$1.12	2.3%	$1.12	2.2%
Nucor Corp	NUE	$1.44	3.5%	$1.44	3.1%
Oracle	ORCL	$0.20	0.9%	$0.24	0.7%
Otter Tail Corp	OTTR			$1.20	5.2%
Pall Corp	PLL	$0.64	1.9%	$0.68	1.2%
Patterson	PDCO	$0.40	1.4%	$0.48	1.5%
Paychex	PAYX	$1.24	4.4%	$1.24	3.9%
PepsiCo	PEP	$1.92	3.1%	$1.92	2.9%
Perrigo	PRGO	$0.25	0.4%	$0.28	0.4%
Praxair	PX	$1.80	2.4%	$2.00	2.0%
Procter & Gamble	PG	$1.92	3.2%	$1.92	3.1%
Ross	ROST	$0.64	1.2%	$0.88	1.2%
Schlumberger	SLB	$0.84	1.5%	$1.00	1.1%
Sigma Aldrich	SIAL	$0.64	1.3%	$0.72	1.1%
J. M. Smucker	SJM	$1.60	2.9%	$1.76	2.4%
Southern Company	SO	$1.82	5.7%	$1.84	4.8%
Southwest Air	LUV			$0.02	0.2%
St. Jude Medical	STJ			$0.84	
Staples	SPLS	$0.36	1.7%	$0.40	2.0%
Starbucks	SBUX	$0.40	1.5%	$0.52	1.4%

▼ Appendix B: Dividend and Yield, 2011–2012, Sorted by Company (con't)

Company	Symbol	2011 Dividend	2011 Yield %	2012 Dividend	2012 Yield %
Stryker Corp	SYK	$0.60	1.2%	$0.72	1.2%
Suburban Propane	SPH	$3.36	7.3%	$3.40	6.0%
Sysco	SYY	$1.00	3.4%	$1.04	3.7%
Target Corp	TGT	$0.68	1.3%	$1.00	2.0%
Teva Pharmaceuticals	TEVA	$0.65	1.2%	$0.88	1.7%
Total S.A.	TOT			$3.16	5.1%
Union Pacific	UNP			$1.52	1.5%
United Healthcare	UNH	$0.50	1.6%	$0.48	1.1%
Valmont	VMI	$0.66	0.9%	$0.68	0.6%
Verizon	VZ	$1.90	7.0%	$1.96	5.1%
Visa	V			$0.60	0.8%
Wells Fargo	WFC	$0.20	0.7%	$0.28	0.9%

▼ Appendix C: Dividend and Yield, 2011–2012, Sorted by Yield

Company	Symbol	Dividend	Yield
Suburban Propane	SPH	$3.40	6.0%
AT&T	T	$1.72	5.6%
Duke Energy	DUK	$1.00	5.4%
Otter Tail Corporation	OTTR	$1.20	5.2%
Total S.A.	TOT	$3.16	5.1%
Verizon	VZ	$1.96	5.1%
Cincinnati Financial	CINF	$1.60	4.8%
Southern Co.	SO	$1.84	4.8%
Dominion Energy	D	$1.96	4.4%
Kimberly-Clark	KMB	$2.80	4.3%
Paychex	PAYX	$1.24	3.9%
Abbott Laboratories	ABT	$1.92	3.9%
NextEra Energy	NEE	$2.10	3.8%
Sysco	SYY	$1.04	3.7%
Heinz	HNZ	$1.80	3.7%
Johnson & Johnson	JNJ	$2.16	3.6%
Campbell Soup	CPB	$1.16	3.5%
International Paper	IP	$1.04	3.4%
ConocoPhillips	COP	$2.64	3.3%
McDonald's	MCD	$2.44	3.2%
Nucor	NUE	$1.44	3.1%
Clorox	CLX	$2.20	3.1%
Procter & Gamble	PG	$1.92	3.1%
General Mills	GIS	$1.12	3.1%

▼ Appendix C: Dividend and Yield, 2011–2012, Sorted by Yield (con't)

Company	Symbol	Dividend	Yield
Kellogg	K	$1.64	3.0%
DuPont	DD	$1.64	3.0%
PepsiCo	PEP	$1.92	2.9%
Colgate-Palmolive	CL	$2.32	2.9%
Automatic Data Processing	ADP	$1.44	2.8%
Chevron	CVX	$2.88	2.7%
Air Products	APD	$2.32	2.6%
Illinois Tool Works	ITW	$1.36	2.5%
J. M. Smucker	SJM	$1.76	2.4%
Iron Mountain	IRM	$0.76	2.4%
McCormick	MKC	$1.12	2.3%
Norfolk Southern	NSC	$1.60	2.3%
Baxter International	BAX	$1.24	2.3%
Alexander & Baldwin	ALEX	$1.24	2.3%
3M Company	MMM	$2.10	2.3%
Medtronic	MDT	$0.88	2.2%
Honeywell	HON	$1.32	2.2%
Northern Trust	NTRS	$1.12	2.2%
UTX	UTX	$1.82	2.1%
Best Buy	BBY	$0.60	2.1%
ExxonMobil	XOM	$1.76	2.1%
Becton, Dickinson	BDX	$1.64	2.0%
Harris	HRS	$1.00	2.0%
Staples	SPLS	$0.40	2.0%

▼ **Appendix C: Dividend and Yield, 2011–2012, Sorted by Yield** (con't)

Company	Symbol	Dividend	Yield
Target	TGT	$1.00	2.0%
Praxair	PX	$2.00	2.0%
Marathon Oil	MRO	$1.00	1.9%
Archer Daniels Midland	ADM	$.064	1.8%
Teva Pharmaceuticals	TEVA	$.088	1.7%
Comcast	CMCSA	$0.44	1.7%
Church & Dwight	CHD	$1.36	1.7%
NIKE	NKE	$1.24	1.6%
St. Jude Medical	STJ	$0.84	1.6%
Aetna	AET	$0.60	1.6%
IBM	IBM	$2.60	1.6%
Caterpillar	CAT	$1.76	1.6%
Union Pacific	UNP	$1.52	1.5%
W. W. Grainger	GWW	$2.16	1.5%
Monsanto	MON	$1.12	1.5%
Johnson Controls	JCI	$40.64	1.5%
Patterson	PDCO	$0.48	1.5%
Deere & Co.	DE	$1.40	1.4%
Starbucks	SBUX	$0.52	1.4%
CVS/Caremark	CVS	$0.48	1.4%
Ecolab	ECL	$0.68	1.3%
Ross	ROST	$0.88	1.2%
Stryker	SYK	$0.72	1.2%
Pall Corp	PLL	$0.68	1.2%

▼ **Appendix C: Dividend and Yield, 2011–2012, Sorted by Yield** (con't)

Company	Symbol	Dividend	Yield
Hewlett-Packard	HPQ	$0.48	1.2%
Sigma Aldrich	SIAL	$0.72	1.1%
Costco	COST	$0.80	1.1%
Lubrizol	LZ	$1.44	1.1%
Schlumberger	SLB	$1.00	1.1%
United Healthcare	UNH	$0.48	1.1%
McKesson	MCK	$0.72	0.9%
Wells Fargo	WFC	$0.28	0.9%
Visa	V	$0.60	0.8%
C. R. Bard	BCR	$0.72	0.7%
Oracle	ORCL	$0.24	0.7%
FMC Corp	FMC	$0.60	0.7%
Fluor	FLR	$0.48	0.7%
Valmont	VMI	$0.68	0.6%
Dentsply	XRAY	$0.20	0.5%
FedEx	FDX	$0.48	0.5%
Apache Corp	APA	$0.60	0.5%
Tractor Supply Company	TSCO	$0.28	0.5%
Perrigo	PRGO	$0.28	0.4%
Allergan	AGN	$0.20	0.30%
Fair Isaac	FICO	$0.08	0.3%
Southwest Air	LUV	$0.02	0.02%
Amgen	AMGN		

▼ **Appendix C: Dividend and Yield, 2011–2012, Sorted by Yield (con't)**

Company	Symbol	Dividend	Yield
Apple	AAPL		
Bed Bath & Beyond	BBBY		
CarMax	KMX		
Google	GOOG		

About the Authors

Peter Sander (Granite Bay, CA) is an author, researcher, and consultant in the fields of personal finance, business, and location reference. He has written twenty seven books, including *Value Investing for Dummies*, *The 100 Best Aggressive Stocks You Can Buy 2012*, *What to Do When the Economy Sucks*, *101 Things Every American Should Know about Economics*, and *Cities Ranked & Rated*. He is also the author of numerous articles and columns on investment strategies. He has an MBA from Indiana University and has completed Certified Financial Planner (CFP) education and examination requirements.

Scott Bobo (San Jose, CA) has a BS from Miami University in Electrical Engineering Technology. After beginning his career in the defense electronics industry and teaching at the University of Cincinnati, he moved on to the computer and semiconductor industries in California, specializing in audio and applications engineering in a twenty-plus year career. Scott continues to teach, write, and consult on technology issues for private and corporate clients.